SYNDICALISM AND THE TRANSITION TO COMMUNISM

Syndicalism and the Transition to Communism

An International Comparative Analysis

RALPH DARLINGTON
University of Salford, UK

ASHGATE

Published by
Ashgate Publishing Limited
Gower House
Croft Road
Aldershot
Hampshire GU11 3HR
England

Ashgate Publishing Company
Suite 420
101 Cherry Street
Burlington, VT 05401-4405
USA

Ashgate website: http://www.ashgate.com

British Library Cataloguing in Publication Data
Darlington, Ralph, 1954–
Syndicalism and the transition to communism : an international comparative analysis. – (Studies in labour history)
1. Syndicalism – History 2. Labor unions and communism – History
3. International labor activities – History
I. Title
331.8'86

Library of Congress Cataloging-in-Publication Data
Darlington, Ralph, 1954–
Syndicalism and the transition to communism : an international comparative analysis / by Ralph Darlington.
p. cm. – (Studies in labour history)
Includes bibliographical references.
ISBN 978-0-7546-3617-5 (alk. paper)
1. Syndicalism. 2. Labor unions and communism.
3. International labor activities. I. Title.

HD6477.D37 2007
331.88'6–dc22

2007023679

ISBN 978-0-7546-3617-5

Printed and bound in Great Britain by MPG Books Ltd, Bodmin, Cornwall.

Contents

Studies in Labour History General Editor's Preface

This series of books provides reassessments of broad themes in labour history, along with more detailed studies arising from the latest research in the field. Most books are single-authored but there are also volumes of essays, centred on key themes and issues, usually emerging from major conferences organized by the British Society for the Study of Labour History. Every author approaches their task with the needs of both specialist and non-specialist readerships in mind, for labour history is a fertile area of historical scholarship, stimulating wide-ranging interest, debate and further research, within both social and political history and beyond.

When this series was first launched (with Chris Wrigley as its general editor) in 1998, labour history was emerging, reinvigorated, from a period of considerable introspection and external criticism. The assumptions and ideologies underpinning much labour history had been challenged by postmodernist, anti-Marxist and, especially, feminist thinking. There was also a strong feeling that often it had emphasized institutional histories of organized labour, at the expense of histories of work generally, and of workers' social relations beyond their workplaces – especially gender and wider familial relationships. The Society for the Study of Labour History was concerned to consolidate and build upon this process of review and renewal through the publication of more substantial works than its journal Labour History Review could accommodate, and also to emphasize that though it was a British body, its focus and remit extended to international, transnational and comparative perspectives.

Arguably, the extent to which labour history was narrowly institutionalized has been exaggerated. This series therefore includes studies of labour organizations, including international ones, where there is a need for modern reassessment. However, it is also its objective to maintain the breadth of labour history's gaze beyond conventionally organized workers, sometimes to workplace experiences in general, sometimes to industrial relations, and naturally to workers' lives beyond the immediate realm of work.

Malcolm Chase
Society for the Study of Labour History
University of Leeds

Acknowledgements

I am extremely grateful for the assistance I received locating a wide source of material from staff at the Working Class Library in Salford (notably Alain Kahan), National Museum of Labour History in Manchester, British Library Newspaper Library in London, Walther P. Reuther Library in Detroit, and the International Institute of Social History in Amsterdam. The study was financially assisted by small grants from the Lipman-Milliband Trust and British Academy (SG-34667) which enabled overseas archival research trips and a good deal of material to be translated into English. I would also like to extend my thanks to a number of individuals who read various drafts of conference papers, individual book chapters or the whole manuscript, and offered their insightful comments, including Dave Beale, Ian Birchall, John Dobson, Rick Halpern, Helge Hoel, Steve Jefferys, John Kelly, Dave Lyddon, Al Rainnie, Martin Smith and Martin Upchurch. The book could not have been written without the unstinting support of my partner Carol McFarlane and is dedicated to my daughter Saskia.

List of Abbreviations and Acronyms

General

CI	Communist International
Comintern	Communist International
CP	Communist Party
ECCI	Executive Committee of the Communist International
GEB	General Executive Board
IFTU	International Federation of Trade Unions (Amsterdam or 'Yellow' International)
ISNTUC	International Secretariat of National Trade Union Centres
IWMA	International Working Men's Association
KPD	Communist Workers Party of Germany
Profintern	Red International of Labour Unions
RILU	Red International of Labour Unions

America

AFL	American Federation of Labor
ALU	American Labor Union
ARU	American Railway Union
AWO 400	Agricultural Workers' Organization 400 of the IWW
CIO	Congress of Industrial Organizations
CLP	Communist Labor Party
CPA	Communist Party of America
GEB	General Executive Board of the IWW
ITUEL	International Trade Union Educational League
IWW	Industrial Workers of the World
LWIU	Lumber Workers' Industrial Union
MTW	Marine Transport Workers
NEC	National Executive Committee
OBU	One Big Union
RILU	Red International of Labour Unions
SLNA	Syndicalist League of North America
SLP	Socialist Labor Party
SPA	Socialist Party of America
ST&LA	Socialist Trade and Labor Alliance
TUEL	Trade Union Educational League
UMW	United Mineworkers of America
WFM	Western Federation of Miners
WIIU	Workers' International Industrial Union
WLU	Western Labor Union

Britain

ASE	Amalgamated Society of Engineers
BAIU	British Advocates of Industrial Unionism
BSP	British Socialist Party
CLC	Central Labour College
CPGB	Communist Party of Great Britain
IDL	Industrial Democracy League
ILP	Independent Labour Party
ISEL	Industrial Syndicalist Education League
IWGB	Industrial Workers of Great Britain
MFGB	Miners' Federation of Great Britain
MP	Member of Parliament
NAC	National Administrative Council
NMM	National Minority Movement
NUR	National Union of Railwaymen
SDF	Social Democratic Federation
SLP	Socialist Labour Party
SS&WCM	Shop Stewards' and Workers' Committee Movement
SWMF	South Wales Miners' Federation
TUC	Trades Union Congress
URC	Unofficial Reform Committee

France

CCN	Comité confédéral national (Confederation National Committee)
CDS	Comité de Défense Syndicaliste (Syndicalist Defence Committee)
CFTC	Confédération française des travailleurs chrétiens (French Confederation of Christian Workers)
CGT	Confédération Générale du Travail (Confederation of Labour)
CGTSR	Confédération Générale du Travail Syndicalist-Révolutionnaire (Revolutionary Syndicalist General Confederation of Labour).
CGTU	Confédération Générale du Travail Unitaire (or CGT *Unitaire*) (United General Confederation of Labour)
CSR	Comités Syndicalistes Révolutionnaire (Revolutionary Labour Committee)
FBT	Fédération des Bourses du Travail (Federation of Labour Exchanges)
FM	Fédération des Métaux (Metal Workers Federation)
FNC	Fédération Nationale des Cheminots (Federation of Railway Workers)
FNS	Fédération Nationale des Syndicats (National Federation of Syndicats)
FR	Fédération du Bâtiment (Construction Workers Federation)
PCF	Parti Communiste français (Communist Party of France)
SFIO	Parti Socialiste Unifié - Section Française de L'Internationale Ouvrièr (Socialist Party - French Section of the Workers' International)

Ireland

IRA	Irish Republican Army
IRB	Irish Republican Brotherhood
IRSP	Irish Socialist Republican Party
ITGWU	Irish Transport and General Workers' Union
ITUC	Irish Trades Unions Congress
IWWU	Irish Women Workers' Union
NUDL	National Union of Dock Labourers
WUI	Workers' Union of Ireland

Italy

CGL	Confederazione Generale del Lavoro (General Confederation of Labour)
FIOM	Federazione Impiegati Operai Metallurgici (Federation of Metal Workers and Employees
PCI	*Partito communista italiano* (Communist Party of Italy)
PSI	Partito Socialista Italiano (Italian Socialist Party)
UAI	Unione Anarchista Italiana (Italian Anarchist Union)
UIL	Unione Italiana del Lavoro (Italian Union of Labour)
USI	Unione Sindacale Italiana (Italian Syndicalist Union)

Spain

CNT	Confederación Nacional del Trabajo (National Confederation of Labour)
CRT	Catalonian Regional Confederation
FAI	Federación Anarquista Ibérica (Iberian Anarchist Federation)
FNAE	Federación Nacional de Agricultores Españoles (National Agricultural Federation of Spain)
PCE	Partido Communista Español (Communist Party of Spain)
POUM	Partido Obrero de Unificación Marxista (Labour Party of Marxist Unity)
PSOE	Partido Socialista Obrero Español (Spanish Socialist Workers Party)
SO	Solidaridad Obrera (Worker Solidarity) Sindicatos de Oposición (Oppositionist Unions)
UGT	Unión General de Trabajadores (General Union of Workers)

Introduction

During the first two decades of the twentieth century, amidst an extraordinary international upsurge in strike action, the ideas of revolutionary syndicalism connected with, and helped to produce, mass workers' movements in a number of different countries across the world. An increasing number of syndicalist unions, committed to destroying capitalism through revolutionary trade union struggle, were to emerge as either existing unions were won over to syndicalist principles or new alternative revolutionary unions and organisations were formed by dissidents who broke away from their mainstream reformist adversaries. This international movement experienced its greatest vitality in the period immediately preceding and following the First World War, from about 1910 until the early 1920s (although the movement in Spain crested later).

Amongst the largest and most famous unions influenced by syndicalist ideas and practice were the *Confédération Générale du Travail* (CGT) in France, the *Confederación Nacional de Trabajo* (CNT) in Spain and the *Unione Sindacale Italiana* (USI) in Italy. In France (as well as Spain during the early 1930s) syndicalism became, for a period of time at least, the majority tendency inside the trade union movement, as it did in Ireland with the Irish Transport and General Workers' Union (ITGWU). Elsewhere, syndicalism became the rallying point for a significant minority of union activists, as in America with the Industrial Workers of the World (IWW) or 'Wobblies' as colloquially they became known. In Britain, where syndicalism was represented within the pre-war Industrial Syndicalist Education League (ISEL) as well as (in a more diffuse form) the leadership of the wartime engineering Shop Stewards' and Workers' Committee Movement, they continued to operate inside the existing unions but encouraged unofficial rank-and-file reform movements. Within these various syndicalist-influenced bodies and movements a number of prominent industrial militants achieved national and sometimes international reputation. These included Fernand Pelloutier, Victor Griffuelhes, and Emile Pouget in France; Armando Borghi and Alceste DeAmbris in Italy; Angel Pestaña and Salvador Segui in Spain; 'Big Bill' Haywood, Vincent St. John and Elizabeth Gurly Flynn in America; Jim Larkin and James Connolly in Ireland; and Tom Mann and J.T. Murphy in Britain. Other notable syndicalist unions and movements existed elsewhere in Europe, Scandinavia, and Latin America, as well as in Australia, New Zealand, South Africa and Russia.

The emergence of revolutionary syndicalism in the years leading up to and immediately after the First World War was only one, albeit conspicuous, dimension of a wider workers' radicalism inside the international labour movement. It reflected growing levels of discontent with the failure of social democratic parties and mainstream trade unions to deliver real improvements in social and political conditions, with new groups of activists (including militant trade unionists, left-wing socialists, revolutionary Marxists as well as syndicalists), organising along different lines to those of the established labour movement leaders.

To those who were attracted to the syndicalist project, parliamentary democracy and working for reforms through the state were rejected as dead ends. Instead of the statist conception of socialism introduced *from above*, syndicalists insisted that society's revolutionary transformation necessarily had to come *from below*, to be the work of the majority, the product of workers' own self-activity and self-organisation at the point of production. This active, voluntarist conception of revolutionary strategy and the subjective character of self-emancipation was underlined by the way in which the opening words of the Provisional Rules of the First International, originally penned by Marx in 1866 – 'the emancipation of the working classes must be conquered by the working classes themselves'[1] – were rediscovered to become the syndicalists' watchword.

Hostility to the conservatism, bureaucracy and corruption of the socialist party and trade union bureaucracies, encouraged an emphasis on the collective 'direct action' of workers on the *economic* terrain – with the subordination of all political action to the industrial struggle and the complete independence of syndicalist bodies from all political parties. It followed that the traditional function of reformist trade unionism – struggling to improve wages and working conditions within capitalism through collective bargaining with employers – was regarded as inadequate. Instead, syndicalists campaigned in favour of reconstructed and class-based trade unions that would become militant organisations dedicated to the destruction of capitalism and the state. They believed the road to the liberation of the working class lay through an intensification of the industrial struggle (involving boycotts, sabotage, strikes and solidarity action) eventually culminating in a revolutionary general strike that would lead to the overthrow of the capitalist system and its replacement by workers' control of industry and society. Unions would have a double function – as an organ of struggle against the employers on the frontline of the class struggle under the capitalist system and as an organ of economic and industrial administration after its overthrow. Even though individual syndicalist movements adopted varying strategies and organisational forms in different countries they everywhere incorporated 'a vision of the revolutionary power and creative efficacy of self-reliant workers, an insistence on their right to collective self-management, and a faith in their capacity to administer their own affairs'.[2]

Of course the syndicalists were not the only ones advocating a distinct revolutionary approach at the time. Between 1870 and 1914 social democracy in the form of parliamentary reformist socialist parties attached to the Second International had emerged as a significant force in Europe and America, but other more radical varieties of socialism had a longer ideological pedigree. These included Blanquism (with its ideas of insurrection by a select and secret group) and Anarchism (with its libertarian viewpoint), the latter of which was to be influential in varying degrees within the syndicalist movement. But even though initially relatively marginalised on the left, it was to be revolutionary Marxism, amidst the upsurge in militant working class activity of the time, which was to make one of the most important

---

1 K. Marx, *The First International and After* (Harmondsworth, 1974), p. 82.

2 M. van der Linden and W. Thorpe, 'The Rise and Fall of Revolutionary Syndicalism (1890–1940)', in M. van der Linden and W. Thorpe (eds), *Revolutionary Syndicalism: An International Perspective*, (Aldershot, 1990), p. 1.

contributions. For example, Rosa Luxemburg's rebuttal of the 'revisionist' thesis of 'evolutionary socialism', advocated by the German Social Democratic Party leader Eduard Bernstein, and her theory of the 'Mass Strike' developed in 1905, not only took account of the conservatism of the party and union bureaucracies and their readiness to hold back working class insurgency, but also celebrated the spontaneity and revolutionary potential of workers' economic and political struggles. Similarly Trotsky's theory of 'permanent revolution' and Lenin's notion of the vanguard party were to lay the basis for an alternative that placed workers' self-activity at the centre of revolutionary Marxist politics. And Gramsci's sophisticated analysis of the experience of the factory council movement in Italy, viewed as the model for a future proletarian state, also contributed to the debate about revolutionary communist alternatives.

It is true that compared with revolutionary Marxism the syndicalist tradition's influence on the socialist movement in the early 1900s was profound. As Eric Hobsbawm has commented:

> ... in 1905–1914, the Marxist left had in most countries been on the fringes of the revolutionary movement, the main body of Marxists had been identified with a *de facto* non-revolutionary social democracy, while the bulk of the revolutionary left was anarcho-syndicalist, or at least much closer to the ideas and the mood of anarcho-syndicalism than to that of classical Marxism ...[3]

Yet such alternative Marxist politics inevitably acquired a radical new significance and influence internationally after the experience of the October 1917 Russian Revolution. Indeed, the heyday of syndicalism was maintained for only a brief period of 20 or so years. Its existence as a powerful and influential current inside the international trade union movement effectively came to an end with the ebb of the revolutionary workers' struggles that had shaken many countries in the immediate aftermath of the First World War, which was followed by employers' and state directed counter-mobilisation and repression. But it was the seizure of state power by Russian workers under the leadership of the Bolshevik Party, and the subsequent formation of the Communist International (Comintern) and its trade union arm the Red International of Labour Unions (RILU), which was to prove a decisive ideological and political challenge to the revolutionary syndicalist movement. Afterwards, although it remained a residual force in Europe until World War Two, syndicalism only survived as a pale shadow of its former self, being displaced partly by a rejuvenated social democracy (which succeeded in containing workers' discontent within established channels) and partly by the new revolutionary Communist parties that were subsequently established and which were to rapidly supersede syndicalist organisations in most countries. There was only one important exception: a mass following was retained by anarcho-syndicalism in Spain during the Civil War of 1936–1939. As Joseph White has commented (with reference to Britain but relevant more broadly), it is difficult to think of any other distinct tendency inside the labour movement during the twentieth century 'whose historical "moment" was as short as

---

[3] E. Hobsbawm, 'Bolshevism and the Anarchists', *Revolutionaries* (London, 1993), pp. 72–3.

syndicalism's and whose working assumptions were so completely displaced and subsumed by events and fresh doctrines'.[4]

But even if revolutionary syndicalism was short-lived and ultimately unsuccessful in achieving its overall aims – particularly when compared to the architects of the Russian revolution – it nonetheless made a significant contribution to the explosive wave of working class struggle that swept many countries during the early twentieth century. It expressed workers' rising level of organisation, confidence and political consciousness. It came to represent an influential set of policy prescriptions and strategies for labour at a time when all politics was in flux and such matters as the nature of political authority and accountability were open to wide-ranging debate.[5] Emmett O'Connor has suggested that in the 'lacuna between pioneering Marxism and the triumph of Leninist realism in 1917' the syndicalist challenge that was mounted to jaded orthodoxies was both distinctive and far-reaching.[6] Certainly in its uncompromising critique of capitalism, syndicalism raised central questions about the supposed neutrality of the state and the extent to which the social democratic policy of nationalisation without workers' control could change society; and in its celebration of workers' militant direct action it challenged the existing industrial and political order as well as the authority structures of the mainstream labour movement. Even though syndicalist-inspired voices were not the only one raising doubts about the drift of labour politics at the time, nor were the syndicalists the only revolutionary current, they nonetheless made a powerful and distinctive ideological and political contribution to a variety of debates about how society could be fundamentally transformed.

Defining 'Syndicalism'

There is often a great deal of misunderstanding about the meaning of the term 'syndicalism' – a term which is related to its French origins, with *Syndicat ouvrier* meaning a (usually local) trade union and *Le Syndicalisme* literally meaning labour unionism in general. To begin with, it should be noted that whilst in the English language 'syndicalism' is often used as shorthand to describe the syndicalist movement, the French CGT actually described their movement as *syndicalisme revolutionnaire*. This means there is the possibility of some confusion arising when 'syndicalism' is used to refer to practices that are more *reformist* in character – that is practices that concentrate on militant, sectional and non-political union activity but with no specifically *revolutionary* intent. Paradoxically, despite formal revolutionary declarations by the CGT during the first decade of the century, a minority of union members (organised in some of the larger unions and federations) were undoubtedly reformist in outlook. Moreover, after 1910 the union leadership *as a whole* moved a considerable way towards accommodating to capitalist society, tempering their

---

4 J. White, *Tom Mann* (Manchester, 1991), p. 170.

5 R. Price, 'Contextualising British Syndicalism c.1907–c.1920', *Labour History Review*, 63:3 (1998), pp. 261–76; D. Howell, 'Taking Syndicalism Seriously', *Socialist History*, 16 (2000). pp. 27–48.

6 E. O'Connor, *Syndicalism in Ireland* (Cork, 1988), p. 1.

previous ideas with a considerable amount of reformist activity and collaboration with the war effort, although there remained a sizeable revolutionary wing inside the Confédération. Nonetheless, despite such internal tensions and variations in emphasis over time within specific movements (in France as in other countries), the term 'syndicalism' will generally be used in this book to refer to movements, organisations and/or or minority groups that were committed to *revolutionary* objectives, unless specifically qualified otherwise.[7]

On this basis it is possible to define syndicalism in its broadest sense to simply mean: 'revolutionary trade unionism'. Such a definition would, of course, not embrace *all* unions that have in the past been committed to revolutionary politics, given this would also be true at times of communist and other left-wing dominated unions. But what it does underline is the equal importance of *revolution* and *unionism* – the fact that the essence of syndicalism was revolutionary action by unions aimed at establishing a society based upon unions.[8] As we have seen this conception differed from both socialist and communist counterparts in viewing the decisive agency of the revolutionary transformation of society to be unions, as opposed to political parties or the state and of a collectivised worker-managed socio-economic order to be run by unions, as opposed to political parties or the state.

Perhaps more problematic is the fact that 'syndicalism' is necessarily only a very broad term for a number of related but rather *different* revolutionary union movements that flourished in a variety of forms across the world. Larry Peterson has argued the use of this term has the danger of blurring the distinctions between the movements according to a single exclusive model, when in fact syndicalism was merely one of several factions within a more general movement in favour of revolutionary industrial unionism.[9] Certainly it is important to bear in mind different movements were sometimes known by varying terms in their respective countries, including: 'revolutionary syndicalism' (France and Britain), 'industrial unionism' (America), 'anarcho-syndicalism' (Spain and Italy), and 'Larkinism' (Ireland). And although an *international* phenomenon that grew out of similar economic, social and political conditions, syndicalism undoubtedly manifested itself concretely in direct relation to *national* conditions and traditions, with each country producing its own specific version or versions of the movement which were far from uniform.

Nonetheless, arguably the colloquial description of such different movements as 'syndicalist' is both useful and justified because it draws attention to basic fundamental similarities between them, despite some strategic, tactical and organisational differences and variety of labels they used to describe themselves. For example, few of the leaders of the IWW in America called themselves 'syndicalists';

---

7 'Reformist syndicalism' comes close to being a contradiction in terms, although a trade unionism committed to non-revolutionary but tactically militant sectionalism and avoidance of politics has a long history.

8 F.F. Ridley, *Revolutionary Syndicalism in France: The Direct Action of Its Time* (Cambridge, 1970), p. 1.

9 L. Peterson, 'The One Big Union in International Perspective: Revolutionary Industrial Unionism 1900–1925', in J.E. Cronin and C. Sirianni (eds), *Work, Community and Power: The Experience of Labour in Europe and America 1900–1925* (Philadelphia, 1983), pp. 64–6.

most, in fact, preferred the term 'industrial unionist'. Joseph Conlin has attacked those historians who persist in using the term – as 'A Name that Leads to Confusion' – on the basis that the IWW diverged in important aspects of strategic orientation and organisational form from those in Europe (and America) who consciously adopted the term for themselves.[10] But as Melvyn Dubofsky has persuasively argued, an examination of the language used in newspapers, pamphlets, books and speeches of the IWW, reveals ideas, concepts and theories (although not all tactics) that are almost indistinguishable from those espoused by European union militants who described themselves as syndicalists.[11] Indeed, the IWW paper *Solidarity* frequently headed its reports of news of the French syndicalist movement with the statement: 'Le Syndicalisme in France is Industrialism in America. Its principles are substantially those of the IWW in America'.[12] And in the words of the American socialist theoretician Robert Rives LaMonte, writing in 1913: 'In spite of superficial differences this living spirit of revolutionary purpose unifies French and British Syndicalism and American industrial unionism. To forget or even make light of this underlying identity can but substitute muddle-headed confusion for clear thinking'.[13] Similar arguments apply to the Irish 'syndicalism' of the ITGWU (or at least the orientation to a greater or lesser degree of many of its national leaders).[14] In other words the specific strategic approach and organisational forms adopted by individual syndicalist movements and the terms which they used to describe themselves, or have subsequently had pinned on them, are of less importance than the essential underlying nature of the movements that they had in common.

We should also note that any one of the supposedly more nationally-specific terms are themselves problematic given the changes in leadership that tended to occur over time within individual movements. For example, although the term 'anarcho-syndicalist' is often used to describe the Spanish CNT, in reality a 'pure syndicalist' period under the leadership of Salavador Seguí extended from the foundation of the CNT's parent organisation *Solidaridad Obrera* in 1907 to its 1919 national congress; it was only then that the anarcho-syndicalists finally, but briefly, took over. After the CNT's banning in 1924, the union leadership then fell into the hands of more moderate syndicalists; it was with the formation of their own internal minority grouping in 1927 that the anarchists were to eventually come back to the fore with the advent of the Second Republic and the subsequent Civil War. In other words, any attempt to substitute the broad term 'syndicalism' with a more defined term, by no means necessarily clarifies our understanding (outside of context) and can, in fact, sometimes be misleading.

---

10 J.R. Conlin, *Bread and Roses Too: Studies of the Wobblies* (Westport, Connecticut, 1969).

11 M. Dubofsky, 'The Rise and Fall of Revolutionary Syndicalism in the United States', in van der Linden and Thorpe, *Revolutionary Syndicalism,* pp. 207–10. A number of other historians have also used the term 'syndicalism' to describe the IWW, including John Graham Brooks, Paul F. Brissendon, David J. Saposs and Patrick Renshaw.

12 Cited in P.S. Foner, *History of the Labor Movement in the United States, Vol. 4, The Industrial Workers of the World, 1905–1917,* (|New York, 1965), p. 158.

13 R.R. LaMonte, 'Industrial Unionism and Syndicalism', *New Review*, 1 May, 1913, p. 527.

14 O'Connor, p. xvii.

Finally, the use of the broad generic term can also be justified on the basis that syndicalism needs to be understood not only in terms of *ideological* doctrine, but as a mode of action, a *practical* social movement engaged in working class struggle. Frederick Ridley has suggested it was: 'the sum of *ideas* expressed by the movement and the sum of its *activities*; the outlook shared by members and the form their action took'.[15] Marcel van der Linden's inclination is to regard the ideological criteria of syndicalism as the least important compared with what the movement did in practice at both the organisational and shopfloor levels.[16] From this perspective it is justifiable to view not only the movement of the CGT in France as revolutionary syndicalist, but also the generally more anarchist-influenced CNT in Spain, the industrial unionist-influenced IWW in the United States and the 'Larkinite' ITGWU in Ireland.

However, whilst the broad term 'syndicalism' will be used in this book to refer to all these different movements, there will also be an attempt to remain sensitive to the considerable *variations* that existed between (and within) individual movements at any one time, so as not to diminish their distinctive features and trajectories. Similar considerations apply in relation to its more diffuse expression outside of formal organisational boundaries, notably within the leadership of the wartime British shop stewards' movement where most of the attributes of the pre-war syndicalist tradition were carried over and displayed.

Rethinking Syndicalism

Whilst there is a good deal of general literature available on revolutionary syndicalist movements, it suffers from some crucial limitations. First, virtually all of it is confined to *single country* explorations, which although immensely informative in their own right tend to overstate distinctiveness, make little attempt to draw comparisons with the experience of other countries and tend to obscure the general international nature of the syndicalist movement and the similar factors that gave rise to its origin, development, dynamics and trajectory. Although there have been one or two recent attempts to begin to rectify this deficiency,[17] they have been very explorative and leave many questions unanswered or even not discussed. Yet arguably, an international perspective is needed, not only because this allows us to compare and contrast, but also because there were a number of shared themes and common impulses between the syndicalist movements in different countries.

Second, there still remains a surprising amount of confusion in the way syndicalist movements are assessed in individual countries, involving a number of unresolved debates, controversies and conflicting interpretations offered by different historians on central questions such as: What specific objective and subjective conditions gave rise

---

[15] Ridley, p. 1 [emphasis added].

[16] M. van der Linden, 'Second Thoughts on Revolutionary Syndicalism', *Labour History Review,* 63:2 (1998), p. 183.

[17] Peterson, 'The One Big Union'; W. Thorpe, *'The Workers Themselves': Revolutionary Syndicalism and International Labour, 1913–1923,* (Dordrecht, 1989); van der Linden and Thorpe, 'The Rise and Fall of Revolutionary Syndicalism'; van der Linden, 'Second Thoughts', pp. 182–96; Howell, pp. 27–48.

to syndicalist movements? Did the residual strength of syndicalism lie with artisans, agricultural workers, casual labourers and other groups of economically marginalised, often unskilled and unorganised workers? Or was it able to sink genuine roots amongst the rapidly expanding industrial proletariat? Is it the case that, compared with the relative emphasis placed on industrial unionism in America and Britain, syndicalists elsewhere generally regarded unionism as synonymous with organisation on craft lines? To what degree did they reject central leadership in favour of decentralisation and local autonomy? How much influence did syndicalism have? Was it a 'cause without rebels', essentially a failure either as an instructor or stimulant to labour militancy, marginalised on the fringes of the movement except for episodic periods? Or (even if syndicalist activists were relatively few in number) did there exist a far broader 'proto-syndicalist mentality' inside the working class movement arising from the mass strikes and anti-parliamentary ferment of the period? Was the rejection of Bolshevism by syndicalist bodies as a whole a reflection of the antagonistic and irreconcilable gulf between the two traditions? Or was there a new synthesis of politics and economics between syndicalism and communism that grew out of both the successes and the failures of the revolutionary workers' struggles of the period?

In the light of the above considerations, this book attempts to add to our understanding by offering a distinctive comparative historiography of the dynamics and trajectory of the syndicalist movement on an international scale. It does so by providing a rigorous and critical analysis of the existing literature, foregrounding hitherto neglected aspects of the subject, deploying new archival findings, revealing fresh insights, and offering a substantively original interpretation and assessment. In particular, there is an attempt (in the second half of the book) to make the first ever systematic examination of the relationship between syndicalism and communism, focusing on the ideological and political conversion to communism undertaken by some of the syndicalist movements' leading figures across the world. The book explores the response of syndicalist movements to the Russian Revolution, Communist International and Red International of Labour Unions, and to the explicit attempt made by the Bolsheviks to woo syndicalists into the new revolutionary communist parties that were established. It explores the limitations in syndicalist strategy and tactics that contributed to the transition to communism and the degree of synthesis between the two traditions within the new communist parties that emerged. The overall strengths, as well as notable weaknesses, of the alternative Bolshevik and communist tradition are also assessed.

In the process there is a thorough review of a number of crucial dilemmas that were confronted by the syndicalist (and communist) tradition(s), including questions such as: Could the trade unions be turned into instruments of revolutionary struggle? Or did their in-built pressures towards reformism ultimately undermine such potential? How far would their conservative impulses carry the leaders of the social democratic parties and trade unions towards accommodation with the existing order? Would they merely blur the contradictions between capital and labour, or actually change sides? Should revolutionaries organise entirely separately from the reformist bodies, whether in newly founded militant unions or specifically revolutionary parties? What kind of leadership role within the working class movement should be provided by the 'militant minority'? What was the relationship between industrial agitation and socialist politics? Could the revolutionary overthrow of capitalism be achieved by a general strike, or did it require an insurrection?

The book explores such questions by examining the different conceptions of capitalism, revolution, and socialism held by the syndicalist and communist traditions, and the way in which an entire theoretical and organisational heritage was remade on the road from syndicalism to communism. There is a focus on the relationship (and tensions) between trade unionism and capitalism, militancy and accommodation, rank-and-file members and the union bureaucracy, economics and politics, industrial struggle and political organisation, spontaneity and leadership, centralisation and decentralisation and party and class. In examining such issues, questions and themes, the book attempts to provide an overall re-conceptualisation and re-theorisation of the nature of anti-capitalist and revolutionary unionism. In this sense it offers not only a contribution to labour history, but also a contribution to the sociology and politics of trade unionism with contemporary relevance.

It needs to be stated from the outset that the analysis and assessment of syndicalism that is provided derives from a revolutionary Marxist approach (within the tradition of Marx, Engels, Lenin, Trotsky, Luxemburg, Gramsci, and the early congresses of the Communist International). Such a theoretical and analytical framework inevitably means it is sympathetic to the revolutionary aspirations and militant activities of the syndicalists. But it also necessarily means a critical scrutiny of their policies and actions. Naturally the readers of the book are not obliged to share the political assumptions underpinning the study, although they do have the right to demand that it should not simply be the defence of a political position, but rather an internally well-grounded portrayal of the actual underlying social processes of the syndicalist movement. It will be up to the reader to judge how far this criterion has been met.

The study focuses attention on syndicalist movements in six different countries - namely, France (CGT), Spain (CNT), Italy (USI), America (IWW), Britain (ISEL and SS&WCM) and Ireland (ITGWU). These particular geographical locations have been chosen for the contrast between less and more advanced contexts of industrial and political development, the relatively large size or evident influence of their respective syndicalist movements, and for some examples of where syndicalist unions and organisations were decisive in developing and sustaining the impetus of the movement internationally. In addition, such a choice of countries has enabled consideration of a variety of syndicalist organisational forms (including unions, union confederations and propaganda organisations, as well as syndicalist-influenced leadership within broader movements) and strategic approaches (including the construction of separate revolutionary unions or operating within existing reformist-led bodies). Finally, it has also allowed a synchronic comparison between movements which had their origins, developed, reached their high point and subsequently declined during a roughly similar period at the beginning of the twentieth century (albeit with considerable variation in the exact timing of such individual phases). The exception to this is Spain, with the role of the CNT also explored in the later Civil War period.[18]

[18] Germany has not been included essentially because there was no real effective syndicalist movement until after the First World War and the fall of the Kaiser with the 1918 revolution. See H.M. Bock, 'Anarchosyndicalism in the German Labour Movement:

There is no attempt to narrate detailed chronological histories of each of these respective movements; many such accounts can be found elsewhere. Instead, there is an international comparative analysis of the essential dynamics of the movements, concentrating attention on their philosophy, origins, organisational features, influence and demise. Given such a wide-ranging perspective, the study has inevitably primarily drawn from the extensive range of existing secondary literature, including single-country studies on individual syndicalist organisations and the broader labour movements in which they flourished, as well as (where available) comparative overviews on some of the countries concerned. But in addition to providing a synthesis of other historians' work from such a wide range of sources, and often engaging in a critical engagement with the perspectives that have previously been presented, the study is also based on archival research. This includes the writings of syndicalists (and other contemporary commentators) contained in numerous newspapers, pamphlets and books, as well as other material, such as congress declarations and proceedings. In both cases a good deal of foreign language material has been translated into English.

Methodology

There are a number of methodological assumptions on which such a wide-ranging study has been pivoted. First, it attempts to be sensitive to the fact that syndicalist trade unions, like all trade unions generally, were *contested* organisations that had conflicting views about underlying purpose, appropriate forms of action and desirable patterns of internal relations. Second, such organisations are not viewed as *fixed entities* but, on the contrary, fluid in character, dynamic by nature and, therefore, complex and (sometimes contradictory) in practice. Third, whilst focused principally on the dynamics of *syndicalist movements* (their organisation, leadership, ideas and activity), there is an attempt to provide (within the inevitable limits of any comparative project) contextualisation in terms of the broader national *working class movements and struggles* from which they arose and developed. Fourth, there is some consideration of the strategies of those actors who were the principal *antagonists* of syndicalism – notably employers, the state, and reformist labour bodies. Fifth, (following from what has already been indicated above) there is an overarching effort to examine the interplay between structure and agency: to integrate the *objective context* (the overall material social, economic and political environmental and the historical contingencies that shaped and contained what could be achieved) with the *subjective experience* of the syndicalist movements themselves (their constructive engagement as actors in the processes of collective mobilisation and strategic choices that were involved). Although such aspirations for a 'total history' may seem like an

A Rediscovered Minority Tradition', in van der Linden and Thorpe, *Revolutionary Syndicalism*, pp. 59–79 and D.H. Muller, 'Syndicalism and Localism in the German Trade Union Movement', in W.J. Mommsen and H-G. Husung, *The Development of Trade Unionism in Great Britain and Germany, 1880–1914* (London, 1985), pp. 239–49.

impossibly tall order, this study makes every effort to take such multidimensional factors into account so far as this is feasible.[19]

It has long been pointed out that many general histories of trade union and labour organisations have tended to concentrate attention purely on intellectual and ideological debates, the lives of the great political 'leaders', or on 'institutional' developments which appear to be mechanically motivated and controlled by ideology and central-policy making administration.[20] As a result, the lives and work experience of those who actually formed the rank-and-file membership of such bodies are effectively ignored, with members only appearing as 'aggregate numbers' attesting to the significance or insignificance of an institution or the effectiveness of a strike.[21] This study attempts, in so far as it is possible, to avoid such pitfalls. In particular it devotes some attention to the role of activist leadership in mobilising support for syndicalism and to the problematic relationship that sometimes existed between national leaders and sections of the rank-and-file membership. However, the sheer breadth of coverage involved in such an international comparative project, as well as the paucity of empirical evidence available, has necessarily precluded any *detailed* attention to the lives, organisation or activities of the ordinary men and (to a much lesser extent) women supporters of syndicalism on the ground (although it draws, where possible, on existing work).

The *comparative* dimension of this study also has its dilemmas.[22] As Jûrgen Kocka has explained, because comparison of two objects of study can only be done effectively when *specific* aspects are compared, rather than each object as a whole, comparative history is even more influenced by the researcher's standpoint – that is dependent on theory, abstraction, generalisation and selection – than is historical research in general.[23] But this easily conflicts with the demand for contextualisation, something which historians on the whole prefer to avoid. As a consequence, most comparisons tend to deal with two or at most three cases. Yet even then there is the danger that far from broadening our understanding, national comparisons may simply serve to reinforce well-worn stereotypes, not least because of the artificial image that 'national aggregates' can suggest with the potential distortion of local realities (for example, in countries like Spain and Italy where conditions can vary greatly in different geographical regions of the country).[24] In addition, as James Cronin has argued, there is the danger of applying overarching theories about developments,

---

19 A. Callinicos, 'Marxism and the Crisis in Social History', in J. Rees (ed.), *Essays on Historical Materialism* (London, 1998), pp. 36–7.

20 D. Geary, *European Labour Politics from 1910 to the Depression* (London, 1991), pp. 4–5.

21 J.R. Conlin (ed.), 'Introduction', in *At the Point of Production: The Local History of the IWW* (Westport, Connecticut, 1981), pp. 5–6.

22 For one significant contribution to the attributes and dilemmas of comparative, cross-national labour history see M. van der Linden, *Transnational Labour History: Explorations* (Aldershot, 2003).

23 J. Kocka, 'Comparative Historical Research: German Examples', *International Review of Social History*, 38: 3 (1993), pp. 369–79.

24 J.A. Davies, 'Socialism and the Working Classes in Italy Before 1914', in D. Geary (ed.), *Labour and Socialist Movements in Europe Before 1914* (Oxford, 1989), p. 219.

assuming a common set of social and economic processes interacting to produce broadly similar outcomes across countries.[25] Such universalising assumptions can sometimes neglect entirely certain aspects of the diverse trajectories of national labour movements. But arguably, despite all these formidable dilemmas, the task of cross-national comparison is all the more necessary if we are to attempt to understand the full dimensions and significance of syndicalism as an international phenomenon. All a researcher can do is to recognise the difficulties and dangers involved and attempt to navigate around them as best as possible.

On the one hand the assumption that syndicalist movements in all the countries surveyed were moulded by the impact of capitalist restructuring combined with the inadequacies of existing reformist labour movement organisations forms the basis for the selected conceptual framework, and the attempt to highlight the similarities and general patterns of social protest. On the other hand, the book also looks at the unique national features and variations into which the common base was transformed in relation to the trajectories of the syndicalist movements in different countries. In other words, both concerns – international *similarities* and national *differences* (as well as *internal divisions* within individual countries) – are regarded as complimentary.

Finally the question arises, given that syndicalism was a world-wide phenomenon with movements as far apart as South America, Scandinavia and Australia, how far is it possible to generalise from the distinctive experiences of the six syndicalist movements that are featured in this study? Obviously there are important specificities that it would be mistaken to ignore, notably in terms of various material and ideological contextual factors, which inevitably qualify any general picture on such a broader geographical canvas. Nonetheless, arguably this does not preclude a level of *analytical* generalisation being made about the general contours of syndicalist movements beyond this study. In this respect perhaps the six different movements examined here can serve as an exemplar of some important common dilemmas that were confronted by movements everywhere. In this respect, the overall themes are likely to be of much wider relevance, even if specific national conditions need to be constantly borne in mind.[26]

---

[25] J. Cronin, 'Neither Exceptional nor Peculiar: Towards the Comparative Study of Labor in Advanced Society', *International Review of Social History,* 38:1 (1993), pp. 59–75.

[26] By way of example of such common themes in countries not covered in this study, see E. Olssen, *The Red Feds: Revolutionary Industrial Unionism and the New Zealand Federation of Labour 1908–1913* (Auckland, 1988), V. Burgmann, *Revolutionary Industrial Unionism: The Industrial Workers of the World in Australia* (Cambridge, 1995), and L. van der Walt, '"The Industrial Union is the Embryo of the Socialist Commonwealth", The International Socialist League and Revolutionary Syndicalism in South Africa, 1915–1919', *Comparative Studies of South Asia, Africa and the Middle East*, 15: 1 (1999), pp. 5–30. See also van der Linden and Thorpe, *Revolutionary Syndicalism* for syndicalist movements in the Netherlands, Sweden, Portugal, Argentina, Mexico and Canada.

Book Structure

Part One examines the dynamics of the different syndicalist movements, notably, its philosophy of action; the distinctive economic, social and political context in which such movements emerged; their social composition and organisational structure; the extent to which this form of trade union-based anti-capitalist revolt was influential and the reasons for its subsequent demise. Part Two examines the transition from syndicalism to communism made by some of the movement's most prominent figures. It does so in thematic fashion, exploring five specific, although interrelated, areas of tension between the two movements: namely, trade unionism under capitalism; the problem of the trade union bureaucracy; the relationship between economics and politics; the state and revolution; and the role of leadership and the revolutionary party. The final chapter explores the Syndicalist-Communist fusion within the new Communist parties of the early 1920s.

PART 1
Dynamics of the Syndicalist Movement

Chapter 1

Philosophy and Practice

It is not easy to give a precise theoretical statement of revolutionary syndicalism as an ideology because most syndicalist activists openly rejected the formulation of theoretical schema, such as they found among pre-1914 exponents of Marxist, socialist or anarchist philosophy. They did not pretend to develop an integrated philosophy of history or economic analysis of capitalist development. Of course, syndicalists thought about such matters, but they never aimed at producing a really unified body of thought, a systematic theory of the Marxist variety. As Frederick Ridley explained with reference to the French syndicalists:

> The CGT [theorists] ... wrote for the worker rather than the social philosopher. They dealt with issues of the moment. Their ideas were scattered in newspapers, pamphlets and speeches. Nowhere did they attempt to bring these ideas together within the cover of a single book. It would have been difficult to do so. Their views changed; they did not always agree ... certainly no definitive philosophy, was produced by the syndicalists themselves.[1]

In fact, syndicalism was not the creation of one particular writer or even a group of writers. Despite the 'ism' that lends it so a theoretical air, syndicalism was originally the name given to a *movement* rather than any sort of preconceived theory of society.[2] Thus, French syndicalist leaders such as Victor Griffuelhes (secretary of the CGT), Emile Pouget (editor of the union's newspaper *La Voix du peuple*), and Georges Yvetot (head of the *Bourses du Travail* section of the CGT) were more concerned with 'giving expression to the practice of syndicalism as it evolved' in the everyday struggle to improve workers' lives 'rather than building a theoretical framework to which it should conform'.[3] In this respect, it was argued, syndicalism was not an artificial set of doctrines imposed on the working class, but rather an open theory in constant development, the formation of which came about as a result of the experience of the struggle itself. As the Spanish syndicalist E.G. Solano explained in 1919:

> Syndicalism is not only a doctrine, it is a living organisation ... It came into being without a programme, or, rather, its programme does not exist ... today, the same men that direct the syndicalist movement, far from adapting themselves to a thesis formulated *a priori* act, and it is that carried-out action itself that serves as a thesis *a posteriori*, for them; so the action virtually always precedes the idea.[4]

---

1 F.F. Ridley, *Revolutionary Syndicalism in France: The Direct Action of its Time* (Cambridge, 1970), p. 170.

2 Ibid., p. 1.

3 W. Thorpe, *'The Workers Themselves': Revolutionary Syndicalism and International Labour, 1913–1923* (Dordrecht, 1989), p. 15.

4 E.G. Solano, *El sindicalismo en la teoría y en la práctica* (Barcelona, 1919), p. 11.

Indeed syndicalist leaders in most countries considered one of the distinguishing features of the movement to be its non-theoretical character, with abstract theorising regarded as 'at worst inimical to syndicalism, at best irrelevant'.[5] As Pouget stressed: 'What sets syndicalism apart from the various schools of socialism – and makes it superior – is its doctrinal sobriety. Inside the unions, there is little philosophising. They do better than that: they act!'[6] Pierre Monatte, who edited the CGT paper *La Vie ouvrière* (1909–1914), made a similar comment: 'Revolutionary syndicalism, unlike the socialism and anarchism which preceded it, has asserted itself less in theory than in action, and it is in action rather than in books that we should look for it'.[7] In America the most widely circulated IWW pamphlets were *Sabotage, Direct Action, Why Strikes Are Lost! How to Win!* and *Tactics or Methods*, a copy of the last being given to every member of the organisation. As their names indicate, these pamphlets dealt primarily with tactics in the class struggle, and while they did not neglect theory entirely, they were essentially calls to action.[8] Similarly in Britain, the tenor of the syndicalist movement's thinking was organisational and its innovations lay in the field of industrial tactics, not of political strategy as such. As Branko Pribicevic explained:

> They were generally much more concerned with the burning questions of the day than with the distant future, much more with the methods and tactics of the class struggle than with its ultimate aims. Everybody who was willing to take part in the class struggle, regardless of his organisation or his political views, was welcome in the [Industrial] Syndicalist [Education] League. They maintained that it would be idle to insist on theoretical distinctions at a time when the main body of the workers were engaged in practical class struggles.[9]

If syndicalism was 'a practice in search of a theory' rather than the coherent product of a single thinker,[10] its ideas were undoubtedly put on the map by its self-appointed intellectual apostle, the French social philosopher Georges Sorel who wrote *Reflections on Violence* in 1908. However, it is widely acknowledged that Sorel speculated on the movement primarily from the outside, and his connection with syndicalist trade union practice was not influential.[11] Indeed, in many countries, syndicalists displayed a marked distrust of bourgeois liberal intellectuals, who they feared would both exercise a restraining influence on the movement and exploit the working class in search of a position of political power. In short, intellectuals could play a useful role if, as supporters of the working class, they remained external to the movement. Such distrust meant syndicalists struggled throughout their history to keep control of the

---

5 Thorpe, p. 15.

6 E. Pouget, 'Le Parti du Travail', *Librairie du Travail* (Paris 1922).

7 P. Monatte, *Anarcho-syndicalisme et syndicalisme révolutionnaire*, http://en.internationalism.org/ir/120_cgt.html.

8 P.S. Foner, *History of the Labor Movement in the United States: Vol. 4: Industrial Workers of the World 1905-1917* (New York, 1965), pp. 150–51.

9 B. Pribicevic, *The Shop Stewards' Movement and Workers' Control* (Oxford, 1959), p. 17.

10 J.A. Scumpter, cited in R. Wohl, *French Communism in the Making, 1914–1924* (Stanford, Calif., 1966), p. 27.

11 Ridley, p. 5.

movement *with* the working class, for which they were fairly successful since the majority of syndicalist leaders came from essentially working class backgrounds.[12]

Therefore, although syndicalism subsequently acquired a wider ideological significance, perhaps it is best described as a *movement* or as a 'philosophy of action'.[13] It was a general trend within the trade unions that placed much emphasis on the liberating experience of spontaneous revolutionary action as the means to overthrow capitalism, rather than being concerned to develop a coherently formulated set of ideas or a unified body of doctrine.

In some respects syndicalism was a reaction to the deterministic conception of Marxism that dominated most of the labour parties of the Second International, which saw history as governed by iron economic laws and excluded any genuine role for human consciousness and activity in shaping society. Whereas this old approach was a recipe for passivity, the syndicalists' emphasis on the revolutionary potential of working class self-activity was a call to arms. They believed that workers learnt primarily through *action*. 'I am a fanatic of action, of revolution', the Spanish leader Andreu Nin confided to the December 1919 CNT congress. 'I believe in actions more than in remote ideologies and abstract questions'.[14] He called for constant direct action in order to develop the will (*volantá*) to revolution among the workers. Given that the revolution was primarily to be the result of an act of will on the part of the workers themselves, it was assumed there was little need to do more than expose the injustices of the system.[15]

One historian of British syndicalism, Bob Holton, has expressed disapproval of this allegedly 'composite stereotype of syndicalism...as atheoretical' for being a 'particularly striking case of misconception ... that bears little relation to the actual nature of the revolutionary industrial movement'.[16] He insists the apparent anti-theoretical stance of many syndicalists should not be interpreted as unsystematic union militancy, but instead a manifestation of *ouvriérisme* – that is, workers' control of the class struggle and rejection of 'outside experts' and middle class intellectuals. As one IWW member put it: 'It is not the Sorels ... and such figures who count the most – it is the obscure Bill Jones on the firing line, with stink in his clothes, rebellion in his brain, hope in his heart, determination in his eye, and direct action in his gnarled fist'.[17]

It is certainly true the movement was a product of various intellectual and ideological influences, and even if they did not produce any profound analytical texts syndicalists presented coherent and well-argued cases in many of their pamphlets, leaflets and speeches. Newspapers such as the IWW's *Industrial Worker* in America, the USI's *L'Internazionale* in Italy, and the ISEL's *Industrial Syndicalist*

---

[12] C. Bertrand, 'Revolutionary Syndicalism in Italy, 1912–1922', PhD, University of Wisconsin (1970), p. 10.

[13] J.A. Estey, *Revolutionary Syndicalism: An Exposition and a Criticism* (London, 1913), p. 119; Ridley, p. 6.

[14] Cited in G.H. Meaker, *The Revolutionary Left in Spain, 1914–1923* (Stanford, Calif., 1974), p. 388.

[15] J. Jennings, *Syndicalism in France: A Study of Ideas* (Oxford, 1990), p. 30.

[16] B. Holton, *British Syndicalism 1900–1914* (London, 1976), p. 21.

[17] *Industrial Worker*, 8 May 1913.

in Britain served as crucially important propaganda outlets and organisers of the movement. Moreover, whilst most syndicalists were industrial militants necessarily concerned with day-to-day problems of the shopfloor, the horizons of the movement were by no means limited to immediate economic issues. In fact, many syndicalist leaders, despite having little formal education, were what might be termed 'worker intellectuals', not only gifted in their line of political involvement and union work but also intellectually engaged and familiar with anarchist and Marxist theory. Working class education was important for at least a minority of committed syndicalist activists – for example, organised within the local *bourses du travail* (local trade union centres) in France, within IWW halls in the United States, and through bodies like the Plebs League/Labour College Movement in Britain, as well as through a host of more informal discussion circles. Such groups and organisations made genuine attempts to analyse various processes in capitalist development as a social system.[18] Thus, even if it *was* 'a practice in search of a theory', rather than the product of a preconceived and comprehensive body of ideas,[19] syndicalism did add up to a theory, as opposed to a miscellany of more or less loosely constructed propositions on strategies, tactics and ideology.

Nonetheless, it remains the case that theory for most syndicalists merely reflected the day-to-day experience of the mass of workers at the point of production. Ideas were only really used to shine a light on the immediate struggles that workers found themselves engaged in. In *Les Bases du Syndicalisme* Pouget described it as the 'interprétation clairvoyant' of the experience of the labour movement.[20] An 'experiential ideology' which celebrated spontaneity, syndicalism was less dependent on theoretical foundations than rival tendencies in the socialist movement.[21] Unlike Marxism, the syndicalist movement made little attempt to synthesise theory and practice; to relate the analytical tools of a body of general theoretical ideas with the generalised practical experience of the advanced sections of the international working class. It offered no sweeping explanations of social change, no fundamental theory of revolution. And they produced no great revolutionary theorists to rival those produced by Marxism (notably Marx, Engels, Lenin, Trotsky, Luxemburg and Gramsci).

Ironically, that syndicalists were able to establish a major influence during the explosions of working class discontent that occurred in different parts of the world during the early years of the twentieth century was probably due, in part at least, to the vagueness of their ideas. In the short-term it enabled them to gain adherents from diverse elements inside the working class, appealing equally to anarchists and socialists disillusioned with parliamentary politics, to trade unionists eager for more

---

[18] Holton, pp. 19–20; S. Macintyre, *A Proletarian Science: Marxism in Britain 1917–1933* (London, 1986).

[19] K.E. Amdur, *Syndicalist Legacy: Trade Unions and Politics in Two French Cities in the Era of World War 1* (Urbana, 1986), p. 9.

[20] E. Pouget, *Les bases du syndicalisme* (Paris, 1906).

[21] E. O'Connor, *Syndicalism in Ireland* (Cork, 1988), p. 1.

militant policies, and to the discontented without ideological attachments.[22] But this lack of theoretical clarity ultimately proved to be a fatal weakness when such militancy subsided in the 1920s, with the syndicalist movement disintegrating in most countries almost as quickly as it had initially arisen.

Despite the diversified forms that revolutionary syndicalist ideas and movements assumed in various countries there is sufficient unity of aim and method to warrant a picture of the whole body of their philosophy as a description of syndicalism in general. Of course, these elements were not all held to the same extent by every movement, nor were they always expressed unambiguously and coherently. But notwithstanding the danger of over-simplification, there was a central core, both theoretically and practically, which all varieties of syndicalism had in common. We can explore eight of these key elements: Class-Warfare and Revolutionary Objectives; Rejection of Parliamentary Democracy and the Capitalist State; Autonomy from Political Parties; Trade Unions as Instruments of Revolution; Direct Action; The General Strike; Workers' Control; and Anti-Militarism and Internationalism.

Class-Warfare and Revolutionary Objectives

Syndicalism pictured capitalism as a society composed of two great social classes, the proletariat and the bourgeoisie, whose interests were diametrically opposed. In the words of 'Big Bill' Haywood, one of the founders and best-known leaders of the IWW: 'We deny that any identity of interest can exist between the exploiter and the exploited'.[23] Because capitalist society was based on the exploitation of labour such class warfare was inescapable.

> Syndicalism ... bases its activity on the CLASS STRUGGLE. The working class and the employing class have nothing in common ... Such is the nature of the present social system that the only method open to the workers of preserving their existence is by continuous struggle on the economic field with the capitalists and open revolt with the sordid conditions of life which the capitalist system compels them to put up with.[24]

As the leading British syndicalist figure Tom Mann noted: 'The object of the unions is to wage the Class War and take every opportunity of scoring against the enemy'.[25] In the process of battling to improve their immediate conditions of labour workers would realise that the power of the capitalist class rested on its ownership and control of the means of production. Thus, the conflict would be seen as wider than that between any one set of employers and their workers, as a conflict between the two main contending classes, capital and labour. But although important day-to-day concessions could be obtained through the waging of such class struggle this would

[22] R. Hyman, 'Introduction', in T. Mann, *What a Compulsory 8-Hour Working Day Means to the Workers* (London, 1972), p. 12; R. Hyman, 'Foreword', in C.L.G. Goodrich, *Frontier of Control*, (London, 1975), p. x.

[23] Cited in M. Dubofsky, *Hard Work: The Making of Labor History* (Urbana, 2000), p. 91.

[24] H.L.E. Howarth, *The Syndicalist*, November 1912.

[25] *Industrial Syndicalist*, Sept 1910.

not, in itself, free the workers from the relentless process of capitalist exploitation. As Pouget explained:

> It is evident that partial victories (no matter how important we consider them and even when they remove privileges) do not modify economic relationships ... the subordination of the worker by capital and by the state persists ... it follows that ... no matter how short the working day becomes, how high the level of pay and how comfortable and hygienic the factory becomes, etc. ... there will always be two classes as long as these relationships between the employees and employers, the government and the citizens continue to exist. Thus there will inevitably be confrontations between the two classes, one fighting against the other.[26]

Only the complete revolutionary overthrow of the existing capitalist social, economic and political system could bring the final emancipation of the working class, with the establishment of a society based on common ownership and control of the means of production. Haywood told the 1905 founding convention of the IWW:

> We are here to confederate the workers of this country into a working class movement that shall have for its purpose the emancipation of the working class from the slave bondage of capitalism ... The aims and objects of this organisation should be to put the working class in possession of the economic power, the means of life, in control of the machinery of production and distribution, without regard to capitalist masters ... this organisation will be formed, based and founded on the class struggle, having in view no compromise and no surrender, and but one object and one purpose and that is to bring the workers of this country into the possession of the full value of the product of their toil.[27]

Instead of the traditional conservative British trade union motto 'a fair day's wage for a fair day's work', Tom Mann argued syndicalism would be 'revolutionary in aim, because it will be out for the abolition of the wages system, for securing for the workers the full fruits of their labour, thereby seeking to change the system of society from Capitalist to Socialist'.[28]

Rejection of Parliamentary Democracy and the Capitalist State

Syndicalists rejected parliamentary democracy and the path of seeking to obtain legislative reforms through the capitalist state in favour of revolutionary industrial struggle. They argued there was an intimate connection between the economic and political systems of society under capitalism, with the form of the state apparatus being determined by the economic order. Instead of being an independent neutral agent that could be used as a vehicle to transform society for the benefit of workers, as parliamentary socialists assumed, syndicalists agreed with Marx that the state was an instrument of capitalist domination, an 'executive committee of the ruling class'. The centralised and bureaucratic state machine – with its police, army, militia and

---

[26] E. Pouget, *L'Action directe* (Paris, 1907), pp. 14–15.

[27] *Proceedings of the First Annual Convention of the Industrial Workers of the World* (New York, 1905), p.1.

[28] *The Industrial Syndicalist*, July 1910.

judiciary – inevitably allied itself with the capitalist class against the workers; and the maintenance of such a centralised political power was viewed as being incompatible with the syndicalists' goal of workers' control and democracy.[29]

Similarly, they viewed parliament as a bourgeois assembly that merely perpetuated the powers of capitalism. It was a façade that hid the real nature of social conflict; its ideology – universal franchise and equality before the law – distracted from the real economic inequality that it protected. As Tom Mann explained:

> The workers today must learn to hold the ruling class in contempt and to treat the agency through which they keep alive the glamour, viz, parliament, in the manner it deserves. They must realise that it belongs to their enemies and see it as an institution than can never be used effectively by the workers. They must view it as belonging to the capitalist regime.[30]

It was on this basis that the failure of parliamentary socialists could be understood. Either their efforts to ameliorate the lot of workers and enact social reforms were made harmless through capitalist manipulation of parliament and the state, or the bourgeois atmosphere of parliament seduced them into apologists for the system. Either way social reforms did not alter fundamental property relations and conceded nothing of real importance. As Father Thomas Hagerty, a leading figure in the early years of the IWW, sardonically told its founding convention: 'The ballot box is simply a capitalist concession. Dropping pieces of paper into a hole in a box never did achieve emancipation for the working class, and to my thinking it will never achieve it'.[31] If workers were to derive any benefits whatever from parliamentary legislation, it would only be because of the pressure exerted on the capitalists outside through the direct action of the workers. As the ISEL's paper declared:

> Parliamentary Action is secondary in importance to Industrial Action; it is Industrial Action alone that makes Political Action effective; but, with or without Parliamentary Action, industrial solidarity will ensure economic freedom, and therefore the abolition of capitalism and all its accompanying poverty and misery.[32]

Syndicalists completely rejected the notion held by parliamentary socialists that a new social order could only be established after the capture of political power and achieved by political and not industrial action. On the contrary, they insisted *real* power within society was economic, and only by gaining control of industries through direct action at the point of production could workers change society in their interests. Political action alone would never abolish the capitalist economic system. One IWW member posed the issue thus:

---

29 F. Pelloutier, *Historie des bourses du travail* (Paris, 1902), p. 54.

30 *The Syndicalist and Amalgamation News*, March–April 1913.

31 *First IWW Convention*, pp. 244–6.

32 *Industrial Syndicalist*, Feb 1911.

> Shall we follow the road that science clearly indicates to us, to deal strictly with causes and effects – exploitation and economic conditions; or shall we bend our knee to the obtuse teachings of metaphysics and deal with a reflex of economic conditions – politics?[33]

From this perspective *political power*, in terms of the government and the state, was dependent on and secondary to *economic power*, to the class struggle. Therefore to destroy capitalism, overthrow the state and seize control of the means of production, the working class had to concentrate on industrial organisation and struggle through the economic organisation of the trade unions. The parliamentary game was but a means of diverting the energy of the working class into wasted channels.

It should be noted that some individual leading figures within the syndicalist movement did not entirely discount the potential value of 'political action' via parliamentary channels. In America this was true of Eugene Debs, one of the founding figures of the IWW who was a member of the Socialist Party and its presidential candidate in 1900 and 1904 (breaking with the IWW in 1908); Daniel de Leon, leader of the Socialist Labor Party and his supporters inside the IWW (until their expulsion in 1908); and even Bill Haywood, who was a left-wing member of the Socialist Party between 1906–1913. Likewise political action was not discounted by Arturo Labriola, the principal theoretician of Italian syndicalism, who stood for parliament in 1904; Jim Larkin, the leader of the ITGWU in Ireland, who was a candidate for the Dublin Labour Party in municipal elections in 1912; and J.T. Murphy, the British shop stewards' leader who stood as the Socialist Labour Party parliamentary candidate in the general election of 1918. Nonetheless, all leading figures within the syndicalist movement internationally saw the unions as the main arena of struggle, with political action as essentially a propaganda weapon that was not to be corrupted by reformism and parliamentarism. Industrial action remained paramount; politics was no more than the 'echo' of industrial warfare. Syndicalists interpreted Marx's formula that the emancipation of the working class must be the act of the working class itself to mean it could not be achieved by political means (conceived of as electoral and parliamentary in form) but only by the workers *themselves*, through their own efforts in the industrial struggle.

As a consequence, they were completely opposed to state ownership of the means of production, even when proposed by more resolute and left-wing socialists and Marxists, because it was seen as 'the highest form of capitalist centralisation and organisation. In its relationship with the employees [the state] is likely to be as unscrupulous an exploiter as is the private corporation'.[34] Instead of the nationalisation of industry, syndicalists envisaged the workers undertaking 'the entire control and management of them in the common interest by themselves'.[35]

---

33 *Industrial Worker*, 25 January 1912.

34 C. Watkins, *Industrial Syndicalist*, May 1911.

35 T. Mann, *Industrial Syndicalist*, May 1911.

Autonomy from Political Parties

Syndicalism displayed an aversion to all labour and socialist political parties – involving the principle of political neutrality and absolute independence. In France, the CGT followed a consistent policy of disassociation from the competing socialist parties that claimed to speak on behalf of the workers and who finally agreed to fuse into a single party in 1905. The following year the CGT congress adopted the famous *Charte d'Amiens* (Charter of Amiens) which explicitly disapproved of involvement with all political parties. Similarly, in Spain the CNT rejected all organic or ideological links with any party or political group. And in America, although the 1905 Preamble to the constitution of the IWW contained a specific, if contradictory, reference to political action, the purged and purified organisation of 1908 eliminated all mention of politics, resolving instead to spurn any alliances with political parties.

In contrast to the 'political socialists' of both reformist socialist or revolutionary Marxist hue, syndicalists denied that the class war could properly be prosecuted by political parties. As Léon Jouhaux, who was elected secretary of the CGT in 1909, retorted at an international conference of mainstream trade unions:

> Perhaps for you the political organisation is a great ship and the economic organisation is a little boat in its tow. For us, the great ship is the union organisation; it is necessary to subordinate political action to trade union action.[36]

In every country there was active hostility between syndicalist organisations and the socialist parties, compounded not just by ideological differences but also by the attempts made to subordinate unions to political control by the parties.

In France political neutrality had two aspects. First, the CGT and its affiliated bodies were formally bound to remain neutral *vis-à-vis* political parties. This meant no labour organisation was to give official support to either a party or a politician and the '*syndicats*' were not allowed political affiliation or even participation in a political congress. Second, the CGT and its affiliated bodies were themselves to remain on neutral ground. No political discussion, controversy or propaganda from outside the unions was to take place within the CGT; the unions were to limit themselves solely to the economic struggle. Although individual workers were free to engage in political activities outside their union (including voting for or even joining political parties), they were forbidden from using the name of the CGT in connection with any political activities in which they became involved.[37] Similar rules of political neutrality were applied, in varying degrees, in other countries. For example, in Spain although any wage-earner, whatever their political or religious notions, could belong to the CNT, no one could represent the Confederación who had appeared as a candidate in any local or parliamentary elections, or who had accepted political undertakings.

---

[36] Cited in M. van der Linden and W. Thorpe (eds), 'The Rise and Fall of Revolutionary Syndicalism', in M. van der Linden and W. Thorpe (eds), *Revolutionary Syndicalism: An International Perspective* (Aldershot, 1990), p. 3.

[37] Ridley, pp. 88–94.

A number of arguments were used by syndicalists to justify their stance. To begin with, political parties grouped their members according to their belief in certain specific ideological and political conceptions, irrespective of members' class origins. This meant not only workers, but also professionals and intellectuals (doctors, lawyers, professors, journalists and students), landlords and even capitalists could be members. Even those socialist parties that claimed to speak on behalf of 'labour' united people from various classes and were led, by and large, by people who did not belong to the working class itself. Thus parties 'were an incoherent mish-mash of men whose interests were in opposition';[38] therefore, at best they could only possess a fragile unity which was easily broken when a conflict of economic interests arose.[39] By contrast, syndicalists explained, the unions grouped people according to their *class* interests, irrespective of beliefs. All of its members were workers, experienced the common condition of exploitation and entered a collective relationship with fellow workers forced on them by the class struggle itself. If the political party was an association of *choice*, the union was an association of *necessity*.[40] For this reason, unlike parties which inevitably represented a compromise of some kind between classes, only the unions could be relied upon to defend the authentic interests of workers; only unions could override political differences between workers and bind them together as a united fighting force in the struggle for their emancipation.

It followed that different political conceptions (even if they were proclaimed to be class or socialist ideologies) should not be introduced into the unions. This was seen to be necessary since, to be effective in their role of bringing pressure to bear on employers over wages and working conditions, the unions needed to organise as many workers as possible on the basis of their common non-controversial economic interests, irrespective of their political views. They had to be composed of *all* workers of *all* views, which meant that to introduce political views would be to risk division, thereby hindering mass action and weakening the union in the face of the employers. Pouget explained:

> The CGT embraces – outside of all the schools of politics – all workers cognisant of the struggle to be waged for the elimination of wage-slavery and the employer class ... There, on the no man's land of economic terrain, personnel who join, imbued with the teachings of some (philosophical, political, religious, etc) school of thought or another, have their rough edges knocked off until they are left only with principles to which they all subscribe: the yearning for improvement and comprehensive emancipation. Which is why – without erecting any doctrinal barriers, and without formulating any credo – syndicalism looms as the quintessential practice of the various social doctrines.[41]

In addition, the quest for electoral and parliamentary success by political parties, the syndicalists explained, inevitably meant the watering down of principled class-conscious policies, collaboration with bourgeois parties and compromise with the capitalist state, culminating in a betrayal of the interests of the working class.

[38] E. Pouget, *Le parti du travail* (Paris, 1905), p. 3.

[39] E. Pouget, *La Voix du Peuple*, 2 June 1901.

[40] Ridley, p. 173.

[41] *Le parti du travail.*

Parliamentary politics corrupted even the best intentioned of political representatives, and given their goal of the conquest of the political state, political parties were fertile ground for bourgeois opportunists. Often the full-time, relatively well-paid, and bureaucratic functionaries who headed them tended to see the preservation of their organisation, and their personal status within it, of more importance than any rhetorical concern they might express about the need for social transformation.

Yet despite the fact syndicalist movement leaders might denounce socialist politicians, it seems unlikely many individual rank-and-file members voted other than socialist in parliamentary elections. And political autonomy did not necessarily preclude informal links with socialist parties on matters of common interest. For example, in France in 1912 the CGT and Socialist Party worked closely together in a campaign against the Three-Year Draft Law which proposed to extend military service from two to three years. Moreover, whilst many syndicalists dismissed 'political action' they were (by adopting a narrow definition of political action) basically rejecting or minimising what they saw as the dead-end of electoral and parliamentary politics advocated by the dominant wing of labour and socialist parties. This did not mean collaboration was necessarily ruled out between syndicalists and *revolutionary Marxist* parties or radical left-wing elements operating inside the reformist socialist parties who themselves rejected the emphasis on parliamentarism at the expense of the direct action of the workers. Thus, in pre-war Britain ISEL supporters worked alongside members of both the Socialist Labour Party (SLP) and Social Democratic Federation (SDF) in building up radical reform movements inside the unions. And a number of the syndicalist-influenced leaders of the wartime Shop Stewards' and Workers' Committee Movement (notably Arthur MacManus, Tom Bell, William Paul, Willie Gallacher and J.T. Murphy), despite arguing for the primacy of industrial struggle, defined some role for political action and a revolutionary socialist party as members of either the SLP or British Socialist Party (BSP).[42]

Similarly, as we have seen in America some of the most prominent IWW figures were members of socialist parties. Even after the convention split of 1908, at which the Wobblies modified their constitution to ban any acknowledgment of political action, left-wing members of the reformist-led Socialist Party continued to play a central role within its organisation, including Haywood who was elected to the national executive of the Socialist Party in 1910 (before being expelled from the party in 1913).

Even more significantly, in Italy there was a unique situation in which the pioneer syndicalists, who had emerged from amongst revolutionary elements inside the Socialist Party, were prepared to remain inside the party for a few years (where they influenced mainstream socialist political debate via their oppositional propaganda and activity), even though they insisted (until their wholesale expulsion in 1908) that industrial struggle was the primary method of achieving revolutionary change. And in Spain, despite the CNT's advocacy of absolute autonomy from political parties or groups, this did not preclude strong ideological and organisational connections with the *Federación Anarquista Ibérica* (Iberian Anarchist Federation) during the Second Republic and Civil War of the 1930s. The FAI aimed to unite the various

[42] The Social Democratic Federation changed its name to the British Socialist Party (BSP) in 1912.

disparate anarchist groups throughout the peninsular in order to strengthen libertarian influences, particularly within the CNT. It was founded largely with the intention of countering reformist trends among the syndicalists, and its importance was to be its role as the movement's vanguard, or in reality its 'political' wing.

It should also be noted that, despite their own protestations to be 'non-political', and the claims made by some critics that they were 'anti-political', syndicalists were practically involved in a variety of directly political issues. For example, in America the IWW's 'free speech' campaign aimed at defending the right to engage in soap-box oratory on street corners so as to publicise the revolutionary union message, inevitably involved the Wobblies in challenging local state laws and political authorities in the courts. In France the CGT campaigned against the extension of military conscription. In Spain the CNT were absolutely central to the fight against Franco's fascism. And in every country syndicalists opposed the First World War.

Nonetheless, syndicalists generally tended to assume that political questions were something that could be resolved by industrial organisation and direct action in the workplace. It was through militant industrial struggle, as opposed to divisive political organisation, that workers' unity and class consciousness could be developed and that workers could encroach gradually on managerial prerogative to build up the framework of a future industrial republic. Thus, political issues were viewed as *subordinate* to industrial organisation and trade union struggle, and it was the unions, and not party organisations, that were viewed as the salvation of the working class.

Trade Unions as Instruments of Revolution

Syndicalists regarded trade unions as the crucial vehicles of struggle both for immediate and long-term goals. On the one hand, they believed the *raison d'être* of the union was the organisation of workers against employers, standing at the very point where the class struggle arises, organising workers directly against the class enemy.[43] That meant seeking every opportunity to defend and improve workers' wages, hours and conditions of work in their everyday struggle against specific employers. On the other hand, they believed the unions could be transformed into militant organisations dedicated to fighting for the entire working class with the overall objective of overthrowing capitalism and establishing a new society. This dual conception of the unions as both an *organ of struggle* and an *instrument of revolution* was reflected in Victor Griffuelhes's speech at the CGT's 1906 Amiens congress:

> In its day-to-day demands, syndicalism seeks the co-ordination of workers' efforts, the increase of workers' well-being by the achievement of immediate improvements, such as the reduction of working hours, the increase of wages, etc.
>
> But this task is only one aspect of the work of syndicalism; it prepares for complete emancipation, which can be realised only by expropriating the capitalist class ... it maintains that the trade union, today an organisation of resistance, will in the future be

---

[43] Ridley, p. 173. See also E. Pouget, 'What is the Trade Union', in D. Guerin (ed.), *No Gods, No Masters: An Anthology of Anarchism* (Edinburgh, 2005), pp. 432–3.

> the organisation of production and distribution, the basis of social reorganisation. The Congress declares that this double task, the day-to-day and the future task, derives from the position of wage earners, which weighs upon the working class and which charges all workers, whatever their political and philosophical opinions and inclinations, with the duty to belong to the essential organisation, the trade union.[44]

Similarly the CNT's paper *Solidaridad Obrera* published an editorial entitled 'Generalidades sobre la organisación sindicalista' in January 1917 which stressed the two essential objectives of Spanish syndicalism:

> The reduction of the working day, the increase in wages, etc is merely reformism; the emancipation of the proletariat through the abolition of capital and of the wage earner is revolutionism. All syndicalist movements, that are pure class movements, possess these two aspects.[45]

Capitalist society was seen as carrying within itself the means by which it could be overthrown as well as the skeleton of the new order that would replace it. As a paragraph added to the IWW's Preamble at the 1908 convention stated:

> It is the historic mission of the working class to do away with capitalism. The army of production must be organised, not only for the every-day struggle with capitalists, but also to carry on production when capitalism shall have been overthrown. By organising industrially we are forming the structure of the new society within the shell of the old.[46]

But syndicalists also recognised that the unions could constitute instruments of revolution only if they fostered and developed the collective power and militant spirit of the workers, 'the vigour displayed in the battle and the penetration of the revolutionary ideal among the workers'.[47] Success in this endeavour depended not on the negotiating skills of the centralised, bureaucratic and asset-conscious officials who dominated existing reformist trade unions, who contented themselves with wringing short-term concessions for workers and 'whose sole purpose in life seems to be apologising for and defending the capitalist system of exploitation'.[48] Syndicalists condemned the increasing incorporation of trade union officials within formalised collective bargaining mechanisms that encouraged a process of accommodation with employers to take precedence over the pursuit of radical shopfloor grievances. As William Z. Foster, an ex-IWW syndicalist figure, noted:

> Even the most cursory examination of labour history will show that … these [union leaders], either through the innate conservatism of officialdom, fear of jeopardising the rich funds in their care, or downright treachery, ordinarily use their great powers to prevent strikes or to drive their unions' members back to work after they have struck in

---

44 Cited in G.D.H. Cole, *The World of Labour: A Discussion of the Present and Future of Trade Unionism* (London, 1920), pp. 77–8.

45 *Solidaridad Obrera*, 15 January 1917.

46 Cited in J.L. Kornbluh (ed.), *Rebel Voices: An IWW Anthology* (Chicago, 1998), p. 13.

47 E. Pouget, *Le Mouvement socialiste*, 192, 1 December 1907.

48 J. Larkin, *International Socialist Review*, 16, December 1915, pp. 330–331. See also *Daily Herald*, 22 November 1913.

> concert with other workers ... Syndicalists have noted this universal baneful influence of centralised power in labour unions and have learned that if the workers are ever to strike together they must first conquer the right to strike from their labour union officials.[49]

It was for this reason that syndicalists attempted to resist the development of bureaucratic and reformist tendencies inside the unions which they feared would undermine the fighting spirit of the workers (see Chapter 8). One important manifestation of this was the refusal to sign collective bargaining agreements or 'contracts' with employers, especially those that involved a restriction of the right to strike for the lifespan of an agreement. Ironically, at a time when many American Federation of Labor (AFL) unions were fighting tenaciously for contracts on the basis that without them workers could not protect themselves adequately, since employers would repudiate every concession made in a strike unless they were bound by written agreements, the IWW rejected the whole concept of a labour-management contract. 'No contracts, no agreements, no compacts', 'Haywood declared. 'These are unholy alliances, and must be damned as treason when entered into with the capitalist class.'[50]

In the eyes of the Wobblies, employers paid no attention to union contracts unless the union was strong enough to enforce them, 'and when the union is strong enough to force concessions it doesn't need to enter into time agreements'.[51] Such agreements gave the employer the time to prepare in advance for a strike when they expired, rather than allowing workers to take advantage of business conditions to hit the employers when they were most vulnerable.[52] In addition, by restricting the calling of sympathy strikes they provided employers with the opportunity to play one group of workers off against another and encourage 'union scabbing'. No agreements could be allowed to impinge upon the IWW's governing principle: 'An injury to one is the concern of all.' Contracts also bred the feeling that once a strike was over, the class struggle on the job was ended. But as Vincent St. John remarked: 'No terms with an employer are final. All peace so long as the wage system lasts is but an armed truce. If only temporary "truces" could be effected on the "battlefield of capital and labour"' that meant: 'There is but one bargain that the Industrial Workers of the World will make with the employing class – complete surrender of the means of production.'[53]

Similarly in Ireland the ITGWU committed itself to pursue the class war above any other consideration. There was no automatic respect for contracts – working class solidarity came first. James Connolly, the revolutionary socialist who became highly influenced by syndicalist ideas after spending time in America as an IWW organiser before returning to Ireland, summed up the strategy of the ITGWU as follows:

---

49 E.C. Ford and W.Z. Foster, *Syndicalism* (Chicago, 1912), p. 38. Foster is generally credited with having written this pamphlet.

50 W.D. Haywood, *The Industrial Syndicalist*, vol. 1, October 1910.

51 *Solidarity*, 28 September 1912.

52 V. St. John, *The IWW: Its History, Structure and Method* (Chicago: IWW Publishing Bureau, n.d.), p. 17.

53 Ibid., p. 12.

> No consideration of a contract with a section of the working class absolved any section of us from the duty of taking instant action to protect other sections when said sections were in danger from the capitalist enemy.
>
> Our attitude was always that in the swiftness and unexpectedness of our action lay our chief hopes of temporary victory, and since permanent peace was an illusory hope until permanent victory was secured, temporary victories were all that need concern us.[54]

Syndicalists everywhere refused to build up large strike funds or to provide unemployment, sickness and death benefits for members and their families. On the one hand, this was because they were concerned to avoid the amassing of a large treasury in the hands of a centralised union bureaucracy that might develop its own interests remote from the members and attempt to oppose strikes. On the other hand, it was because they believed that anything which encouraged workers to passively depend for strike success on financial savings, rather than their own activity in maximising a strike's economic impact, had the effect of 'dimming' their understanding that 'unless [they] overthrow the system of capitalist exploitation, [they would] always be a wage slave'.[55]

In looking to mobilise the power of the working class through the trade unions, syndicalists advocated their reconstruction on a class and revolutionary basis. All syndicalists were agreed that the *existing* trade unions were 'too sectional in their structure, too collaborationist in their policy and too oligarchic in their government to act as agencies of revolutionary transition'.[56] But there were fundamental disagreements on the strategy of reconstruction. In France and Britain syndicalists adopted the strategy of 'boring from within', of working within the existing trade union movement with a view to transforming the character and goals of the unions towards a revolutionary position. Thus, the French syndicalist movement which emerged among members of the CGT, instead of seceding from the Confédération, successfully captured it and organised its constituent unions (notwithstanding their relatively local craft basis) along class lines, with the aim of uniting all wage earners across industries and regions into a single revolutionary organisation. In Britain the pre-war ISEL, formed by Tom Mann, limited itself to propaganda activities in the belief that a revolutionary movement could only be effectively built up through the amalgamation and reconstruction of the existing unions on an industrially-organised basis infused with syndicalist ideas. As the ISEL founding conference declared:

> Whereas the sectionalism that characterises the trade union movement of today is utterly incapable of effectively fighting the capitalist class and securing the economic freedom of the workers, this conference declares that the time is now ripe for the industrial organisation of all workers on the basis of class – not trade or craft.[57]

---

[54] 'Old Wine in New Bottles', in O.D. Edwards and B. Ranson (eds), *James Connolly: Selected Political Writings* (London, 1973), p. 313.

[55] *Proceedings of the Second IWW Convention*, (1906), p. 589.

[56] J. Hinton, *Labour and Socialism: A History of the British Labour Movement 1867–1974* (Brighton, 1983), p. 91.

[57] T. Mann, *Industrial Syndicalist*, March 1911.

contrast in America, syndicalists saw no alternative to root-and-branch opposition to the craft-based, 'business unionist' and class collaborationist trade unions grouped under the umbrella of the AFL, which they viewed as bulwarks of capitalism. Thus, they advocated the construction of an entirely new, and competing, revolutionary organisation, a strategy referred to as 'dual unionism'. The IWW was formed in the hope of uniting the entire American working class (including those the AFL had shunned – namely immigrant workers, migratory labourers, and women and black workers) on the basis of industrial unionism, so there would be one union for an entire industry and an individual workplace, extended in theory to a single union for the entire working class, the 'One Big Union'. In Ireland, the ITGWU also emerged as a revolutionary alternative to the existing moderate-led (and British based) dock labourers' union.

A hybrid arrangement existed in Spain and Italy where, after an initial period of operating inside their respective national trade union confederations, the syndicalists broke away to form new confederations to act as an alternative revolutionary pole of attraction to their reformist counterparts. However, in both countries they continued to operate essentially from within existing local unions and other labour movement bodies such as Chambers of Labour, albeit linking these together via local, regional and national syndicalist committee structures into revolutionary forms of union organisation.

Paradoxically, syndicalist disagreements on the tactics of trade union reconstruction were also evident inside some *individual* movements, leading to small splinter groups opposing their main rivals. In America IWW organiser William Z. Foster returned from a European trip convinced that the Wobbly's belief in the efficacy of dual unionism was misguided. In 1912 he formed the Syndicalist League of North America (SLNA), which argued the IWW should be disbanded so that its members could concentrate on attempting to win influence inside the AFL unions in a similar fashion to the French syndicalists. By contrast, the IWW's tradition of constructing an alternative revolutionary industrial union influenced the other British current of syndicalist-inclined opinion grouped around the tiny Socialist Labour Party, who briefly tried to build a new revolutionary union outside and antagonistic to the existing trade unions named the Industrial Workers of Great Britain (IWGB). Yet both of these initiatives were small-scale and their direct industrial influence very limited compared with the syndicalist forms of organisation that predominated in each respective country.

Therefore, while most syndicalists concentrated on propaganda and agitation *within* the existing trade unions, some strove to establish an alternative revolutionary union *outside* them, while others adopted a hybrid position of operating from within the existing unions but building an alternative revolutionary confederation to the reformist bodies to which they could affiliate. Nonetheless, what these different strategic trade union orientations had in common was a view that the main task was to unite the working class as a whole across sectional, gender, ethnic or political divisions by a process of building trade unions into class-based revolutionary organisations.

Direct Action

As we have seen, in many respects the most compelling characteristic of syndicalism and that which set it apart from reformist 'political socialism', was its advocacy of direct action. Not through parliamentary activity and the sheer weight of electoral numbers would the working class realise their emancipation, syndicalists argued. Rather, this liberation could only occur through collective action, 'directly by, for, and of the workers themselves'[58] within the economic realm of the workplace. Such direct action included any step taken by workers at the point of production which improved wages and conditions and reduced hours. It encompassed conventional strikes, intermittent strikes, passive resistance, working to rule, sabotage, and the general strike.

Hubert Lagardelle, the editor of the independent French journal *Le Mouvement socialiste* and advocate of syndicalism, declared that direct action signified the will of the working class 'to rule its own affairs in place of representation, delegations, and mandates of a third party intervening in [the workers'] place'.[59] Two contradictory principles were observed: *indirect* action – involving the principle of democracy and its successor parliamentary socialism; and *direct* action – which eliminated all intermediaries existing between the worker and his objective. Direct action was defined by Pouget as:

> Action by the working class, drawing on its own strength, acting independently and through its own organisation, relying on the help of no intermediary, expecting nothing from men or forces outside itself, creating its own conditions of struggle, its own means of resistance and aggression, bringing into everyday life the formula 'the emancipation of the proletariat is the task of the proletariat itself'.[60]

By far the most spectacular form of direct action engaged in by the IWW in its early years was a massive campaign of civil disobedience in the fight for 'free speech'. Wobbly organisers depended on soap-box speaking on street corners to publicise the extortionist practices of local employment agencies and to recruit migratory workers in towns and cities across the far west of America. When municipal officials, under pressure from employers, passed laws banning public speaking to try and prevent the Wobblies from organising, the union responded in one town after another by issuing a call for IWW members across the country to deluge the town and defy the speaking ban. Hundreds responded by jumping on freight trains and travelling to wherever the battle was raging, whereupon they were promptly arrested and imprisoned. The IWW strategy was to pack the jails and make life so difficult for law-enforcement agencies that they would be forced to back down. While such a strategy of passive resistance was regularly met by brutal violence, the crowded prisons, clogged legal machinery, and high costs of supporting extra police and prisoners invariably led town officials to rescind their bans and release the Wobblies. The 30 largely successful 'Free Speech' campaigns conduced between 1908 and 1916 (of up to six months duration) were a unique direct action tactic viewed as a means of educating workers to the

---

58 J. Ebert, *The IWW in Theory and Practice* (Chicago, n.d. [1920]) pp. 59–60.

59 Cited in B. Mitchell, *The Practical Revolutionaries: A New Interpretation of the French Anarchsyndicalists* (New York, 1987), p. 34.

60 Cited in V. Griffuelhes and L. Jouhaux (eds), *L'Encyclopédie du mouvement syndicaliste* (Paris, 1912).

class struggle and a practical necessity to counter opposition to recruitment to the One Big Union.[61] Nonetheless, it was not a tactic repeated in other countries.

A much more common form of direct action adopted internationally was sabotage. Although not a syndicalist invention as such, sabotage became an integral part of syndicalist tactics in France (and was officially adopted by the CGT in 1897), before then spreading elsewhere. Pouget defined it as certain forms of activity – such as slowing down production, working-to-rule, deteriorating the quality of work and, in certain circumstances, the destruction of machinery – aimed at hitting company profits.[62] The Wobblies often used the wooden shoe symbol as signifying the origin of the word 'sabotage' in the act of a French workman throwing his wooden shoe (*sabot*) into the machinery. But the original meaning of the French word 'sabotage' was to work clumsily, carelessly, slowly or without thought or skill, as if by blows of a wooden shoe. As Elizabeth Gurly Flynn, one of the IWW's leading organisers from 1906 to 1917, explained:

> Sabotage means primarily: the withdrawal of efficiency. Sabotage means either to slacken up and interfere with the quantity, or to botch in your skill and interfere with the quality of capitalist production or to give poor service ... And these three forms of sabotage – to affect the quality, the quantity and the service are aimed at affecting the profit of the employer. Sabotage is a means of striking at the employer's profit for the purpose of forcing him into granting certain conditions, even as workingmen strike for the same purpose of coercing him. It is simply another form of coercion.[63]

The simplest, most frequently recommended, and least dangerous form of sabotage was the slowing down of production – the strike on the job. Thus the use of so-called *greve perlee* (string-of-pearls) strikes by railway workers in France (and Italy) on occasion threw the whole system of national transportation into disorder; by adhering to the strict letter of the existing transport laws they made it impossible for any train to arrive at its destination in time. Bad workmanship, with planned carelessness resulting in spoilt goods or damaged machines, was also utilised. A bulletin issued by the Montpellier *Bourse du Travail* in 1900 achieved some fame by advising workers on how to organise accidents without undue suspicion falling on them: shop-assistants could allow fabrics to soil; garment workers could ignore faults in the material that passed through their hands; and engineers could forget to oil their machines. In 1910 the French railway workers misdirected goods and side-tracked perishable commodities. In addition Parisian barbers, campaigning for shorter hours, announced that any client who had the audacity to keep workers beyond eight o'clock in the evening 'would be scalped'.[64] With the use of such 'benign sabotage' acting as the impetus for legislation providing for Monday closings for barbers, Georges Yvetot, head of the *Bourses* section of the CGT from 1901, concluded the tactic

---

[61] Foner, pp. 172–5; Kornbluh, p. 94; P. Renshaw, *The Wobblies: The Story of Syndicalism in the United States* (London, 1967), pp. 119–20.

[62] E. Pouget. *Le Sabotage* (Paris, 1910), p. 16.

[63] E. Gurley Flynn, *Sabotage: The Conscious Withdrawal of the Workers' Industrial Efficiency* (Cleveland, 1915) p. 5.

[64] *La Voix du peuple*, 14 July 1901.

proved to be more effective than 'four years of beautiful discourse at the tribune of parliament'.[65]

Sabotage was also interpreted by some French syndicalists to mean the actual physical damage of machinery. Not long after the 1900 CGT congress the *Bulletin Bourse du Travail de Montpellier* gave the following suggestions:

> If you are a mechanic, it's very easy for you with two pence worth of ordinary powder, or even just sand, to stop your machine, to bring about a loss of time and a costly repair for your employer. If you are a joiner or a cabinet-maker, what is more easy than to spoil a piece of furniture without the employer knowing it and making him lose customers?[66]

Paul Delesalle, assistant general secretary of the CGT's *Bourses* section in its early years, made a submission to a CGT congress which emphasised pacific forms of sabotage, but both Pouget and Yvetot made little effort to disguise the fact that, in their view, sabotage also entailed acts of physical violence against machines and property (although not persons).[67] Either way this form of sabotage aided the success of strikes, serving to impede 'the desertion of the masses' by making a return to work impossible and bringing strikes to a speedy conclusion.[68] In addition such practices were seen as a protection against the employment of strike-breakers and thus a necessary adjunct to the withdrawal of labour. According to Pouget the existence of two completely irreconcilable economic classes, and therefore of two distinct moral codes, meant that such proletarian acts of sabotage could not be judged by bourgeois values. 'It is necessary that the capitalist recognise that the worker will respect the machine only on the day when for him it has become a friend and not, as it is today, an enemy'.[69] The vindication of the use of acts of sabotage lay solely in its efficacy as a means of resisting exploitation and of fulfilling the goals pursued by the working class. And such practices were utilised widely, partly under syndicalist influence, in the French postal and railway strikes of 1909 and 1910, with the cutting of telegraph and signal wires.[70]

In America there was a question mark over the relationship of sabotage to violence, sparked off by political opponents' claims that the IWW was dedicated primarily to the use of violence to gain its ends. From 1910, sabotage was officially included in a list of IWW tactics to be used as a weapon in the class struggle and propaganda for it began to appear regularly in the Wobbly press. Three pamphlets on the subject were widely distributed by the organisation and emblematic symbols of the wooden shoe and a black cat appeared constantly in IWW song, illustrations, cartoons and stickers. On the one hand, officially the IWW did not equate sabotage with destruction of property, most of the time insisting it meant nothing more than the withdrawal of workers' efficiency; even when it was used to disable machinery it

---

65 *La Voix du peuple*, 4 January 1914.

66 Cited in Pouget, *Le Sabotage*, p. 34.

67 See G. Yvetot, *La Voix du peuple*, 28 September 1913.

68 G. Yvetot, *Le Libertaire*, 18 October 1902.

69 Pouget, *Le Sabotage*, p. 16.

70 P.N. Stearns, *Revolutionary Syndicalism and French Labour: A Cause without Rebels* (New Brunswick, 1971), p. 70.

was 'intended not to destroy it or permanently render it defective, but only to disable it temporarily and to put it out of running condition in order to make impossible the work of scabs and thus to secure the complete and real stoppage of work during a strike'.[71] In any case, sabotage was directed against property and not against people. On the other hand, IWW vocabulary was often purposively ambivalent, with publications not always making clear the distinction between merely temporarily *disabling* and violently *destroying* machinery. Individual Wobbly soapbox orators openly advocated sabotage in a deliberately lurid fashion and some union songs implied there were circumstances where violence could not be ruled out. Some commentators have recently suggested: 'The IWW consciously used the terms "direct action" and "sabotage" somewhat ambiguously, in much the same way as the civil rights activists of the 1960s found it useful to employ the vague but menacing phrase "by any means necessary"'.[72]

Whether or not IWW members actually practised violence is difficult to determine, although from 1909 to 1919 many Americans, especially during World War I and the post-war 'Red Scare', became convinced that the Wobblies were:

> cut-throat … desperadoes who burn harvest-fields, drive iron spikes into fine timber and ruin saw-mills, devise bomb plots, who obstruct the war and sabotage the manufacture of munitions – veritable supermen, with a superhuman power for evil, omnipresent and almost omnipotent.[73]

In fact a number of formal independent investigations concluded press reports failed to separate *rhetoric* from *reality* and frequently exaggerated the 'Wobbly menace'. And although the IWW in California was charged with hundreds of crimes involving sabotage, 'not one single case was proved in the courtroom'.[74] Nonetheless, many members across the country were individually persecuted by federal and state governments and the organisation came under sustained assault for its alleged 'lawlessness'.

What *does* seem apparent is that many Wobblies, like many syndicalists in other countries, understood that it was impossible to expect the class struggle to be free of violence – given that the employers and state would always use force and violence in an attempt to defeat workers' struggles and prevent revolution. Violence instigated by the capitalists had to be met by violence on the part of the working class. As St. John stated: 'I don't mean to say that we advocate violence; but we won't tell our members to allow themselves to be shot down and beaten up like cattle. Violence as a general rule is forced upon us'.[75] Indeed, it was pointed, out where violence, such as riot, assault and physical damage, *did* erupt during strikes it was usually provoked by the employers' use of 'blacklegs' and aggravated by the presence of police and/or troops. Such violent methods used in the conduct of disputes were viewed by most syndicalists everywhere as perfectly legitimate and necessary if victory was

---

71 A. Giovannitti, 'Introduction', in E. Pouget, *Sabotage* (Chicago, 1913).

72 S.D. Bird, D. Georgakas and D. Shaffer, *Solidarity Forever: An Oral History of the Wobblies* (London, 1987), p. 6.

73 L.S. Gannett, *Nation*, 20 October, 1920, p. 448.

74 Foner, p. 163.

75 Ibid., p. 165.

to be achieved. The only way that the employers' determined resistance to union organisation could be broken down was militant action, accompanied, if and when necessary, by demonstrative violence.

However, in Spain during 1919–1923 the sabotage tactic was interpreted by the (at this time) anarchist-influenced CNT to justify much more problematic forms of physical violence. Thus, in the wake of a defeated general strike and employers' lock-out in Barcelona, there followed a bitter armed conflict between the CNT and the employers' organisations. It was a 'black period' marked by a cycle of state terror carried out by the police and army (which resulted in the murder of 21 leading CNT members) met by counter-attacks mounted by professional *pistoleros*, the gunmen of the action groups from various anarchist organisations that were supported and funded by the CNT, who carried out a wave of assassinations of employers that refused to make wage concessions. Whilst by no means all the CNT leaders favoured such violent activity (for example, Salavador Seguí and Ángel Pestaña), it was justified as a labour tactic by more anarchist-influenced figures (such as the celebrated guerrilla leader Buenventura Durruti) on the basis of preventing the employers having a completely free hand during a period of defeats for the working class. As Gerald Meaker has argued, whilst initially the motives of the 'young terrorists' were visionary and altruistic, hoping to bring the revolution closer, the *atentado* became a Spanish vulgarisation of the 'direct action' idea that in France, Italy and elsewhere had always implied *collective* rather than *individual* action – strikes, boycotts, even sabotage – but not the murder of individuals.[76] Moreover, with mass trade union organisations relegated to the sidelines as the initiative passed to small, often isolated, armed groups, the tactic only intensified state repression, the use of agent provocateurs and the jailing of thousands of CNT members.

But such individual acts of violence were generally abandoned in Spain with General Primo de Rivera's military coup in 1923, and were not emulated by syndicalist organisations anywhere else. Moreover, even if violence was not necessarily entirely excluded as a syndicalist method, it was not regarded as the primary method, or even the one that would most surely lead to success. Victory would be gained through the organisation of mass industrial action. As the IWW's Elizabeth Gurley Flynn explained:

> I don't say that violence should *not* be used, but where there is no call for it, there is no reason why we should resort to it ... Mass action is far more up-to-date than personal or physical violence. Mass action means that the workers withdraw their labour power, and paralyse the wealth production of the city, cut off the means of life, the breath of life of the employers. Violence may mean just weakness on the part of those workers ... Physical violence is dramatic. It's especially dramatic when you talk about it and don't resort to it. But actual violence is an old-fashioned method of conducting a strike. And mass action, paralysing all industry, is a new fashioned and much more feared method of conducting a strike.[77]

For this reason it was the industrial weapon of the strike that dominated the direct action strategy of the syndicalist movement. Strikes were seen as the clearest possible

---

[76] Meaker, p. 175.

[77] Cited in Kornbluh, pp. 217–18.

expression, and the most vivid symbol, of the class war.[78] For Griffuelhes the strike was direct economic action *par excellence*, the most effective weapon available to the worker that was 'worth more than all the contents of libraries'.[79]

Strikes served a double function, with both reformist and revolutionary aspects. Crucially, they were a sign that workers had overcome 'their habit of submission and passivity', 'no longer recognis[ed] the authority … of the management' and were ready 'to dare to defend their rights and interests'.[80] Even if intended only to obtain some limited and immediate material concession from employers they bore potential revolutionary implications. If *successful* they represented a blow directed against the capitalist system, a weakening of the power of the bourgeoisie. If *defeated* they were still worthwhile because the experience taught lessons that were 'deposits in the workers' memory bank'.[81] Thus French syndicalists saw all strikes whatever their outcome as 'revolutionary gymnastics', as training for the social revolution which instructed workers in the realities of class struggle, exposed them to the viciousness of the employers, encouraged solidarity, reinforced class consciousness and provided valuable lessons for the greater revolutionary battles yet to come. Only in the process of such strike experience could workers be prepared for the revolution. As Griffuelhes put it:

> How about the following truth as motto: man only becomes a smith by forging! ... the worker will be ready for his revolution at that time when, strengthened by a series of sustained struggles, he has learned how best to fight and act.[82]

Likewise the IWW viewed strike action as part of a guerrilla warfare against the employer – as a tactic to strengthen working class solidarity and a vehicle of agitation against the capitalist system. In the words of Flynn:

> What is a labour victory? I maintain that it is a twofold thing. Workers must gain economic advantage, but they must also gain revolutionary spirit, in order to achieve a complete victory. For workers to gain a few more cents a day, a few minutes less a day, and go back to work with the same psychology, the same attitude towards society is to have achieved a temporary gain and not a lasting victory. For workers to go back with a class-conscious spirit, with an organised and determined attitude toward society means that even if they have made no economic gain they have the possibility of gaining in the future. In other words, a labour victory must be economic and its must be revolutionising. Otherwise it is not complete … So a labour victory must be twofold, but if it can only be one it is better to gain in spirit than to gain economic advantage.[83]

The Wobblies rejected the idea that a strike should be a 'passive siege' in which workers stayed in their homes or hung about street corners until, after a period of weeks or months, the strike was declared either lost or won. Instead they advocated the use of

---

78 Ridley, p. 174; Thorpe, *Workers Themselves*, pp. 20–21.

79 V. Griffuelhes, *Le syndicalisme révolutionnaire* (Paris, 1909), p. 13.

80 Ibid., p. 6, 8. See also G. Yvetot, *L'ABC syndicaliste* (Paris, 1908), p. 51.

81 Cited in R. Magraw, *A History of the French Working Class, Vol. 1: The Age of Artisan Revolution* (Oxford, 1992), p. 109.

82 Griffuelhes, p. 6.

83 Kornbluh, p. 215.

mass picketing, parades and demonstrations. Unless they were given something to do, workers could easily become demoralised, whereas through mass activity 'strikers draw courage from one another, feel their common interest, and realise the necessity of solidarity'.[84] IWW strike tactics were designed to educate the workers, through experience, to the realities of the class struggle. As the *Industrial Worker* put it: 'The [IWW] always has one fundamental aim in view when going out on strike ... raising the standard of consciousness and aggressiveness of the working class'.[85]

Crucial to successful militant union organisation for syndicalists was working class solidarity. For example in Ireland, this was 'the central ethic of the ITGWU, the core around which all else revolved'.[86] The aim was for any group of workers in dispute to be able to rely on the active support of the rest of the union membership, not just in terms of financial assistance but also industrial action. Picket lines were to be scrupulously respected and 'tainted' goods (produced or worked under unfair conditions) were not to be handled. The 'sympathetic strike' was viewed as the crucial instrument for breaking employers' resistance, particularly important in circumstances where employers attempted to break strikes by the wholesale replacement of strikers with strike breakers. In every other country syndicalists also sought to spread strikes from one group of workers to another, and to transform individual strikes by workers against a single employer into a generalised confrontation with the capitalist class as a whole.

It followed that the general strike was seen as the ultimate form of 'direct action' through which a new society could be achieved. From this perspective, all strikes were viewed as: 'a reduced facsimile, an essay, a preparation for the great final upheaval.'[87]

The General Strike

Syndicalists believed that the road to the emancipation of the working class lay through an intensification of the industrial struggle to its logical culmination in a revolutionary general strike that would overthrow the capitalist system and replace it by workers' control of industry and society. Whilst every strike, local and general, aimed to obtain individual reforms and thereby rob the employers of some of their authority and privileges, the revolutionary general strike signified nothing less than labour's intent to finally abolish the wage system through which it was exploited. It involved the forcible expropriation of the capitalists and the emancipation of the proletariat. According to Griffuelhes it would be: 'the curtain drop on a tired old scene of several centuries, and the curtain raising on another which will offer a greater, more fertile field of human activity'.[88]

The general strike was viewed as both a means 'of agitation, of protest, of solidarity' as well as of 'conquest and the revolutionary finality of the syndicalist

---

84 Cited in Foner, p. 135.

85 *Industrial Worker*, 19 September 1913.

86 J. Newsinger, 'Irish Labour in a Time of Revolution', *Socialist History*, 22 (2002), p. 2.

87 Georges Sorel, *Reflections on Violence* (New York, 1912), p. 127.

88 Griffuelhes, p. 10.

movement'.[89] *Negatively*, it meant the total suspension of work and the complete paralysis of the whole of the normal functioning of capitalist society and the state; *positively*, it meant the ushering in of a new society. For IWW leader Bill Haywood the general strike would be the moment when 'labour was organized and self-disciplined [so] it could stop every wheel in the United States … and sweep off your capitalists and State legislatures and politicians into the sea'. When that day came, Haywood prophesied, 'control of industry will pass from the capitalists to the masses and capitalists will vanish from the face of the earth'.[90] As the Italian syndicalist leader Alceste DeAmbros explained:

> The general strike … is for syndicalism the revolutionary conclusion which consecrates in an epic moment the struggle that the working class carries on against the bourgeoisie. The general strike will signal the passage of economic power – and consequently of political and legal power – from the hands of the capitalism to the hands of the proletariat.[91]

Although not a clearly defined concept, and despite differences of opinion amongst its advocates, it was generally agreed that a full-blown general strike would break out at an unpredictable moment in a spontaneous explosion of force, probably emerging from some ordinary strike movement within an individual sector of the economy for some quite non-revolutionary reasons. It would then spread like wildfire to other industries and act as the spark that set the revolution aflame. Its climax would be a revolutionary general strike. The task of syndicalists was to prepare the ground in order to hasten such a day.[92]

Perhaps not surprisingly there was some ambiguity about what impact the general strike would have. For Georges Sorel, the foremost intellectual figure associated with the French syndicalist movement, the importance of the general strike depended less on its feasibility than on the power it had to inspire the workers. He believed it acted as a 'myth', stimulating workers to further efforts in their everyday struggle.[93] But for the syndicalist leaders themselves there were two contrasting perspectives (albeit on occasion expressed by the same individual figures at different times).

On the one hand, it was visualised that the workers would merely down tools and wait with 'folded arms' for the peaceful take over of the means of production. The revolution would involve nothing more than a national agreement to cease work on a particular day. Faced with a paralysis of the economy and the manifest determination of workers not to serve them any longer, the employers would be forced to submit. Neither the capitalist class nor the state would be able to provide basic services and overall authority would pass inexorably into the hands of the only bodies able to do so, the trade unions. Thus, a single gesture – the general strike – and the revolution would be accomplished. This philosophy was eloquently voiced by the anarchist Italian-born IWW organiser Joseph Ettor addressing a meeting of Lawrence textile strikers in 1912:

---

89 *L'Internazionale*, 20 December 1913.

90 Cited in M. Dubofsky, *'Big Bill' Haywood* (Manchester, 1987) pp. 65–6.

91 B. Riguzzi, *Sindacalismo e riformismo nel Parmense* (Bari, 1974), p. 119.

92 Estey, pp. 79–95.

93 Sorel.

> If the workers of the world want to win, all they have to do is to recognise their own solidarity. They have nothing to do but fold their arms and the world will stop. The workers are more powerful with their hands in their pockets than all the property of the capitalists. As long as the workers keep their hands in their pockets, the capitalist cannot put theirs there. With passive resistance, with the workers absolutely refusing to move, lying absolutely silent, they are more powerful than all the weapons and instruments that the other side has for attack.[94]

In the visionary novel *How We Shall Bring About the Revolution*, written by Patuard and Pouget, mounting industrial unrest led to a clash with troops in which several workers were killed, precipitating a general strike, which was then followed by the seizure of land and factories and the dissolution of the government, all achieved with remarkable ease.[95] From this perspective, the old French Blanquist idea of insurrection (a revolution made by a select and secret group) was no longer valid. The lesson of the 1871 Paris Commune was that even a vigorous political confrontation could be suppressed by force. By contrast the attraction of the general strike for Fernarnd Pelloutier, the founding father of the CGT, was that it would circumvent the state, because the latter would find no precise target for suppression and would be overwhelmed by the sheer number of people involved. While the army could be deployed against 30,000 Parisian insurgents, it would be ineffective against a revolution that was both 'everywhere and nowhere', that was diffuse and widespread. The army, quite simply, could not protect every factory or every railway line.[96] Rudolph Rocker, a leading figure in the Sydicalist International established in 1922, underlined the point: 'For the workers the general strike takes the place of the barricades of the political uprising'.[97] In other words, simply taking control of the workplace, by means of the general strike, would be enough to topple the existing order and effect a revolutionary transformation of society.

On the other hand, syndicalists often expressed some acknowledgement that even if strikers were not starved into surrender, the state would intervene to settle any general strike by force. This meant the workers could not expect the factories, mines, railways and fields to fall into their lap as a result of their strike action. They would have to seize control over the means of production rather than await their voluntary surrender by the capitalists. At the same time they would have to engage in a lengthy struggle to overthrow the state, in which the use of force would be at least as important as the cessation of work. Thus, Georges Yvetot was in doubt that that use of violence would be an integral part of any successful general strike. Any attempt by the workers to take possession of the means of production, he argued, would meet an immediate response from a government determined to save the bourgeois social order. Faced by repression and what Yvetot referred to as 'the establishment of terror' the proletariat

---

94 Cited in J. Ebert, *The Trial of a New Society* (Cleveland, 1913) p. 61.

95 E. Paturd and E. Pouget, *How We Shall Bring about the Revolution: Syndicalism and the Co-Operative Commonwealth* (London, 1990, first published 1909).

96 Cited in J. Julliard, *Fernand Pelloutier et les origines du syndicalisme d'action directe* (Paris 1971), p. 325–7.

97 R. Rocker, 'The Methods of Anarcho-Syndicalism', *Anarcho-Syndicalism* (London, 1987), p. 69.

would of necessity need to respond or accept defeat.[98] Likewise Emile Pouget (in non-visionary mood compared with the novel he co-authored), commented that it was certain a general strike would be preceded by 'frictions, blows and contacts of a more or less brusque nature' that required an effective counter-response.[99] In this scenario the concept of the general strike merged gradually with the older concepts of insurrection and revolutionary seizure of power.

Workers' Control

Syndicalists were committed to the revolutionary goal of workers' control of production and society. In Britain the objective of the ISEL was clearly stated in every issue of *The Syndicalist* newspaper as:

> CLASS WAR against capitalism, such war having for its object the CAPTURE OF THE INDUSTRIAL SYSTEM and its management by the Workers themselves for the benefit of the whole community.[100]

In America this system 'in which each worker would have a share in the ownership and voice in the control of industry, and would receive the full product of their labour', was variously labelled by the IWW as the 'Co-operative Commonwealth', the 'Workers' Commonwealth', the 'Industrial Commonwealth' or simply 'Industrial Democracy'.[101] In Spain the ultimate goal of the CNT, as agreed at its 1919 (anarchist-influenced) congress, was defined as 'libertarian communism'.

As we have seen, on the road to achieving such an objective the trade unions were viewed as both the chief agency of class struggle in the *present* and the embryo of the new hoped-for classless society of the *future*. In other words, as well as being an organ of struggle against capitalism, they were anticipated to become an organ of economic and industrial administration in the post-revolution society. As the CGT's *Charte d'Amiens* stated: 'The trade union, which is today a fighting organisation, will in the future be an organisation for production and distribution and the basis for social reorganisation.'[102] In effect, this meant unions as the unitary organisation of the working class had a threefold task: first, the defence of workers' immediate interests; second, the revolutionary overthrow of capitalism; and third, the organisation of the future society.

It should be noted syndicalists in every country consistently and intentionally remained vague about the detailed structure of the future society. Griffuelhes commented:

---

98 Yvetot, *L'ABC syndicaliste*, p. 52.

99 Cited in Jennings, p. 49.

100 *The Syndicalist* was a monthly paper produced by the ISEL (January 1912–December 1912). It had been preceded by the *Industrial Syndicalist* (July 1910–May 1911), and was followed by the *Syndicalist and Amalgamation News* (January 1913–August 1914).

101 Cited in Dubofsky, *'Big Bill'*, pp. 66–7.

102 The *Charte d'Amiens* adopted at the *Congrès national corporatif (IX de la Confédération) et Conférence des Bourses du Travail, tenus á Amiens du 8 au 16 octobre 1906. Compte rendu des travaux*. Amiens, 1906, pp. 169–71.

> Can we indicate the nature of the task which we have today, and how we intend to bring about change? No, any more than could thinkers, writers and philosophers in the eighteenth century start to foresee the actions of the French Revolution whose coming was in the wind; we cannot be prophets of the future ... They could not foresee then the way that the bourgeoisie would rise to take power, and we cannot foresee the exact form of a free society.[103]

But even if there were no detailed blueprints of how this future society would be constructed, some guiding principles were clearly discernible: 'the control by the workers themselves of the productive process, the rational organisation and utilisation of production for the common good, and distribution of resources according to need'.[104] Although the specific features of organisation varied from one country to another – with a relatively more centralised structure envisaged in America and Ireland under their 'One Big Union' plans compared with elsewhere – the main lines were the same in all cases, modelled on the principles of decentralisation and federalism. Thus the guiding and most important principle was that the management of production should occur at the base of society, not at its summit, with decisions flowing upwards from below. That meant vesting all economic and social decisions in the hands of the direct producers – the workers in each specific enterprise, administered through an elected committee. In relation to the CGT:

> The *syndicat* would replace the employer and the workers would organise production in their workshops. The [national trade union] federations would be responsible for technical co-ordination within their industries and would run such national undertakings as the railways or the postal service. The *bourses* [local labour council] would replace the town hall in communal affairs and would at the same time become centres for the distribution and exchange of goods. The confederation, finally, largely in the shape of a statistical bureau, would be the nearest approach to a central administration ... The basic slogan was simple: 'The workshop will replace the government'.[105]

A similar schema such as this was envisaged in Italy and Spain. In Britain, although there was more emphasis on the role of national industrial unions possessing and managing their own industries, there was a common conception of workers' control being exercised from below. *The Miners' Next Step* pamphlet, produced in 1912 by the syndicalist-influenced Unofficial Reform Committee in the South Wales Miners' Federation, outlined how such workers' control was to be co-ordinated across different industries:

> Every industry, thoroughly organised, in the first place, to fight, to gain control of, and then to administer, that industry. The co-ordination of all industries on a Central Production Board, who, with a statistical department to ascertain the needs of the people, will issue demands to the different departments of industry, leaving to the men themselves to determine under what conditions, and how, the work should be done. This would mean

---

[103] Griffuelhes, p. 16.

[104] Jennings, p. 23.

[105] Ridley, p. 168.

> real democracy in real life making for real manhood and womanhood. Any other form of democracy is a snare and a delusion.[106]

In every country syndicalists assumed – under the influence of anarchist ideas – that within this new society, instead of a political state apparatus, the only form of government would be the economic administration of industry exercised directly by workers themselves through the unions. Thus, the syndicalist revolution would bring the overthrow of the capitalist state and all its institutions; government, civil service, judiciary, police and army – all would be swept away. 'There will be no such thing as the State or States', Haywood declared. 'The industries will take the place of what are now existing States'. It was the existence of this kind of state power and authority that had created class divisions and all other kinds of inequality. Therefore, syndicalists denounced and renounced, on principle, *all* manifestations of power and authority, and above all every kind of state power. In the process they rejected the Marxist notion of revolution, which envisaged a working class seizure of state power. 'It is not a question of conquering the state', Lagardelle wrote, 'but of destroying it, of paralysing it and divesting it of its functions and attributes'.[107] In *Syndicalism and Reformism* the Italian figure Arturo Labriola expressed his misgivings about the state socialist vision thus:

> … the substitution of State ownership for private ownership does not abolish the capitalist system of production. This system is distinguished by the separation of owners of the means of production and wage-earners. Instead, Socialism seeks to create an autonomous and work-controlled system of production which eliminates the distinctions between producers and owners of the means of production. With the passage of private industry to the state, the State bureaucracy replaces the capitalist and the workers remain a wage-earner.[108]

Once the state was abolished, workers' organisation in civil society would re-absorb most of the political functions of the central state.[109] As the famous May 1936 Zaragoza CNT congress declared, the future society would abolish 'private property, the state, the principle of authority and, consequently, the class division of men into exploiters and exploited, oppressors and oppressed'.[110]

Finally syndicalists believed such a future society would liberate individuals and restore their freedom and spontaneity of development – not merely as producers of goods but in terms of being able to take full command of their destiny and daily life. Pataud and Pouget's novel pictured a world in which there was the freeing of women of the tedious work previously done in the home, such as cooking and cleaning, to enable them to work or to look after children as they pleased. Public laundries

---

[106] *The Miners' Next Step*, Unofficial Reform Committee (Tonypandy, 1912 [reprinted London, 1973]).

[107] H. Lagardelle, *Le Mouvement socialiste*, 22, 1907.

[108] A. Labriola, *Sindacalismo e riformismo* (Florence, 1905), pp. 15–16.

[109] D. Schecter, *Radical Theories: Paths Beyond Marxism and Social Democracy* (Manchester, 1994), p. 36.

[110] Cited in M. Bookchin, *The Spanish Anarchists: The Heroic Years 1868–1936* (Edinburgh, 1998), p. 269.

and kitchens would exist and children would be brought up in communal care.[111] In America, Haywood described the industrial conditions of an ideal society to an audience of striking silk workers in Paterson, New Jersey:

> It will be utopian. There will be a wonderful dining room where you will enjoy the best food that can be purchased; your digestion will be aided by sweet music which will be wafted to your ears by an unexcelled orchestra. There will be a gymnasium and a great swimming pool and private bathrooms of marble. One floor of this plant will be devoted to masterpieces of art and you will have a collection even superior to that displayed in the Metropolitan Museum in New York. A first-class library will occupy another floor ... the workrooms will be superior to any ever conceived. Your work chairs will be morris chairs, so that when you become fatigued you may relax in comfort.[112]

Anti-Militarism and Internationalism

Syndicalists campaigned against patriotism and militarism and promoted international labour unity. Anti-militarism arose from a deep-seated belief that the main function of the army was to act as an auxiliary of the employers and the state, a belief that was encouraged by a long history of repeated police, and sometimes military, interventions in industrial disputes leading to bloody conflicts, arrests and the death of strikers.

For example, in France the army came to be seen as the principal defender of the capitalist system and of the bourgeois Republic. 'The army', Yvetot wrote, 'is the impassable barrier that must be destroyed'.[113] French syndicalists were haunted by the thought of young workers conscripted into the army being used to quell protests of their former comrades. 'The bourgeoisie', Pouget commented: 'has perfected the system of exploitation. It protects itself by the use of the workers who create its wealth and when the workers in overalls demand a better lot it sends against them workers in red trousers'.[114] Thus the immediate purpose of French syndicalist anti-militarist propaganda was to dissuade soldiers, particularly conscripts of the working class, from siding with the employers against their own comrades in periods of strike and playing the role of strike-breaker. In 1901 *Manuel du soldat* was commissioned for circulation among French soldiers by the CGT, clearly inflammatory in nature in that it countenanced desertion as an acceptable alternative to induction. CGT propaganda repeatedly called upon soldiers to disobey orders if told by their officers to shoot at members of their own class. Likewise British syndicalists distributed an 'Open Letter to British Soldiers' leaflet in July 1911 which encouraged troops not to shoot down strikers during disputes but instead to take up the cause of working class solidarity against capitalism:

> Men! Comrades! Brothers! You are in the Army. So are we. You, in the army of Destruction. We, in the Industrial, or army of Construction ... You are workingmen's Sons. When we

---

111 Paturd and Pouget, pp. 227–31.

112 Cited in Kornbluh, p.197.

113 Cited in Jennings, p. 39.

114 E. Pouget, *La Voix du peuple*, January 1904.

> go on Strike to better our lot, which is the lot of Your Fathers, Mothers, Brothers and Sisters, You are called upon by your officers to Murder Us. Don't do it! ... Don't disgrace Your Parents, Your Class, by being the willing tools any longer of the MASTER CLASS … Help to win back BRITAIN for the BRITISH and the WORLD for the WORKERS.[115]

At the same time, anti-patriotic propaganda was seen as a necessary aspect of such anti-militarism. The bourgeoisie relied upon the patriotic sentiments of workers to distract them from their fundamental economic conflict with capital and to bind them more fully to the defence of bourgeois interests. Therefore, syndicalists encouraged campaigns against patriotism. As the IWW paper *Industrial Worker* declared:

> [Workers] have no country. Love of flag? None floats for them. Love of birthplace? No one loves the slums. Love of the spot where they were reared? Not when it is a mill and necessity cries ever 'move on'. Love of mother tongue? They know but the slave driver's jargon whose every word spells wearisome toil followed by enforced idleness.[116]

Since class membership above all shaped and identified workers, they owed their primary loyalty – a loyalty transcending national boundaries – to their class. In place of national patriotism, syndicalists advocated international working class solidarity. They viewed themselves as:

> … locked into an economic struggle against an internationally organised capitalist order, which only an internationally organised working class could ultimately succeed in breaking. They aimed at a revolution that would transcend national boundaries, and hoped to introduce a new social order in which divisive national boundaries and state governments would play no part.[117]

It followed that syndicalists rejected war, which they saw as purely a conflict of capitalist interests quite unrelated to the interests of the working class. The CGT's 1908 Congress recalled the formula of the First International: 'The workers have no fatherland!'[118] In other words, national barriers did not exist for workers. And everywhere syndicalists lambasted the First World War as an object lesson in capitalist folly in which workers were sent into senseless slaughter to help line the pockets of the owners of industry. The real division was not between nations but between the exploited and the exploiters.

In Spain the CGT professed to see only an equality of war guilt among the belligerents. Finding no justice in the existing social order of Europe, they insisted it was of no concern to the workers which side won and demanded Spain's absolute

---

[115] Written by Fred Bower, a Liverpool syndicalist stonemason, the leaflet was published by Jim Larkin's *Irish Worker* on 29 July, 1911 and reprinted in the ISEL monthly *The Syndicalist* in January 1912.

[116] Cited in Foner, p. 131.

[117] W. Thorpe, 'Syndicalist Internationalism and Moscow, 1919–1922: The Breach', *Canadian Journal of History*, 14: 1 (1979), p. 238.

[118] *XVI Congrès national corporatif (X de la CGT) et 3 Conférence des Bourses du Travail ou Unions des Syndicats, tenus á Marseille du 5 au 12 octobre 1908. Compte rendu sténographique des travaux*. Marseille, 1909.

neutrality in the war. When they discovered a number of their old idols in the international anarchist movement – including Kropotkin, Malato and Grave – had issued a 'Manifesto of the Sixteen' declaring support for the Allied cause, they angrily repudiated them.[119] Jóse Negre, the first secretary of the CNT, even went so far as to declare: 'Let Germany win, let France win, it is all the same to the workers, who will continue to be exploited and tyrannised just as before the war, and probably more than before'.[120]

In America neither the outbreak of the war in Europe nor the subsequent intervention of the United States caused Wobblies to change their approach. A leaflet prepared by one Wobbly summarised their attitude sharply: 'General Sherman said "War is Hell!" Don't go to Hell in order to give the capitalists a bigger slice of heaven'.[121] Wobblies advised American workers to remain at home in order to fight the bosses in the only war worthwhile: the class war. In 1914, when the United States and Mexico had appeared on the verge of hostilities, Haywood told a protest meeting: 'It is better to be a traitor to your country than to your class'. He later wrote: 'Let the bankers, the rentiers and the dividend-takers go to Sherman's Hell'.[122] And the IWW proposed, in the words of the editor of its paper *Solidarity*: 'to get on the job of organising the working class to take over the industries, war or no war, and stop all future capitalist aggression that leads to war and other forms of barbarism'.[123]

Although there was the collapse into patriotism of the CGT in France and an important pro-war 'interventionist' minority inside the USI in Italy (see Chapter 4), syndicalism generally, more than any other ideological persuasion within the organised trade union movement in immediate pre-war and wartime Europe, constituted an authentic movement of opposition to the war, refusing to subordinate class interests to those of the state, to endorse policies of 'defencism', or to abandon the rhetoric of class conflict.[124]

Some Qualifications

One obvious problem when considering syndicalist philosophy is that it is often not clear how far the views of the movement's ideologists and political leaders were shared by rank-and-file supporters. No doubt as with any other social movement there were different levels of engagement, a kind of pyramid structure ranging from members with sophisticated knowledge who were committed to very particular courses of action to those who merely signified their support for the broad objectives of a movement in which they had only a limited understanding.

---

119 Meaker, p. 29.

120 *Solidaridad Obrera*, no. 25, 1914.

121 *Industrial Worker*, 11 May 1914; *Solidarity*, 20 May 1911.

122 *Solidarity*, 25 April 1914; 23 May 1914.

123 Cited in M. Dubofsky, 'The Rise and Fall of Revolutionary Syndicalism in the United States', in van der Linden and Thorpe, *Revolutionary Syndicalism*, p. 215.

124 W. Thorpe, 'The European Syndicalists and War, 1914–1918', *Contemporary European History*, 10:1 (2001), p. 1.

For example, in France syndicalism clearly owed much to a small group of leading figures, notably Griffuelhes, Pouget, Yvetot and Delesalle. These four were the most articulate members of the *revolutionary* syndicalist wing of the CGT – they wrote most of its pamphlets, occupied the leading positions in the Confédération, edited its newspaper, and were the real intellectual driving force behind the organisation. There is an obvious temptation to identify syndicalism merely with what they wrote. But his would be misleading as their ideas were often more radical than those officially adopted by the CGT (a body which anyway, unlike other countries, contained a strong reformist current within its ranks). Moreover, it seems likely some members of the CGT were not attracted to the organisation *primarily* because of syndicalist philosophy as such, as opposed to its readiness to do something about immediate injustices and the practical solutions if offered.[125]

On the other hand, drawing too sharp a distinction between CGT leaders/activists and the bulk of rank-and-file members would also be mistaken given that syndicalism's overall 'philosophy of action' enjoyed popular support precisely because it appeared to fit the needs and aspirations of a significant layer of French workers. The membership would have learnt a great deal of the doctrines of syndicalism once they were in the organisation and, in the main, they appear to have accepted them, even if variations in emphasis and commitment to syndicalist philosophy is something that cannot be ignored. Even in the ITGWU, the least formally ideologically syndicalist-committed of the bodies within this comparative study, the general revolutionary union and direct action philosophy and orientation of Larkin, Connolly, O'Brien and other national leaders would appear to have been absorbed to a greater or lesser degree by most members.

At the same time, it is clear that syndicalist movements in each country were not homogenous politically, but internally differentiated between various groupings whether formally organised or not (see Chapter 4). There were also changes over time within syndicalist organisations in different countries, for example inside the IWW during 1905–1908 in terms of their attitude towards political action, or inside the CGT up to 1910 and afterwards in terms of the commitment to revolutionary objectives. And the emphasis placed on certain aspects of policy by individual syndicalist movements varied somewhat, for example with sabotage much more prominent in France and America than elsewhere. The stress placed on certain policies by individual syndicalist leaders also varied at different times. Finally, given its primary orientation on *action*, we should also bear in mind that syndicalist philosophy generally was inevitably diverse across the different movements, with few 'sacrosanct' principles. Nonetheless, whilst it is necessary to take full account of such variation and differentiation (internally and over time) in any comprehensive appreciation of the dynamics of revolutionary syndicalism, this does not invalidate the general summary of the predominately held philosophy as outlined above.

Having provided a brief sketch of syndicalism's philosophy of action, it is now possible to consider the reasons for its origin and development and the varied forms that syndicalist movements assumed in practice within different countries.

[125] Ridley, pp. 182–3.

Chapter 2

Origins and Growth

How can we explain the origins and growth of, as well as variation between, revolutionary syndicalist movements across the world in the years leading up to and immediately after the First World War? Whilst there are some very insightful explanations of why syndicalism became influential in individual countries, only Marcel van der Linden and Wayne Thorpe have attempted to provide a cross-national set of explanations for the international movement as a whole (albeit in brief form).[1] Although they acknowledge that wherever syndicalism emerged it was ultimately the distinctive and unique expression of a specific set of national factors, they suggest there were a number of long-term developments that converged to encourage the spread of syndicalism in a variety of countries across the world. They pinpoint (a) *the general growth of a radical mood among workers*: with an upsurge in workers' militancy expressed in the rising level of strike action; (b) *the nature and changes of labour processes and labour relations*: with technical and organisational changes intensifying the pressure of work and enhancing managerial control; (c) *rejection of the dominant labour strategy*: with a growing criticism of the perceived inadequacies of the existing labour and socialist parties and trade unions; (d) *the feasibility of general strikes as an alternative strategy*: with the mass strike seen as a viable replacement for electoral politics and reformist unionism; and (e) *spatial and geographical influences*: with a 'radiation effect' whereby syndicalist attitudes and practices were spread from one group of workers to another in both regional and international contexts.

Whilst van der Linden and Thorpe's analysis undoubtedly makes a valuable contribution to identifying a number of factors that converged to encourage the spread of syndicalism, it also suffers from some important limitations. First, they provide a mainly analytical explanation that tends to make broad generalisations from a variety of single-country studies, but with little examination of the way in which the developments they identify actually manifested themselves in different countries. Second, there is no real attempt to assess the degree of interdependency between the different variables, illustrating the ways in which each was directly influenced by the other. Third, there is inadequate consideration of the substantial variations between (and within) countries in the way in which these factors impacted. Fourth, some important additional factors which contributed to the development of an international syndicalist movement, including the role of state and employers' repression and various ideological influences (notably anarchism) on the movement, are ignored.

---

[1] M. van der Linden and W. Thorpe, 'The Rise and Fall of Revolutionary Syndicalism', in M. van der Linden and W. Thorpe (eds), *Revolutionary Syndicalism: An International Perspective* (Aldershot, 1990), pp. 4–17; M. van der Linden, 'Second Thoughts on Revolutionary Syndicalism', *Labour History Review*, 63:2 (1998), pp. 185–6.

However, one of the main problems with van der Linden and Thorpe's pioneering analysis is that they downplay the role of conscious organisational activity and leadership by syndicalists themselves (although this is less the case in Thorpe's complimentary studies on syndicalist internationalism).[2] Clearly, there were various *objective* factors (economic, social and political) that together made an international revolutionary syndicalist movement possible, even likely. However, in the last resort such historical 'causes' are insufficient to explain more than the possibility. Social movements depend on people, activity and leadership, on the *subjective* element; that means consideration of how the syndicalists themselves turned potentiality into actuality. In turn, this is intimately related to the ideological and political role of employers and the state in both stimulating and responding to syndicalist militancy, an internal dynamic with an indeterminate outcome.

What follows is an attempt to build on and considerably expand the initial work of van der Linden and Thorpe, by providing a multifaceted set of explanatory variables for the origin and growth of the syndicalist movements in the six selected countries at the centre of this study. It pivots on: Industrial and Economic Backcloth; Political Context; Trade Union Framework; Anarchism and Other Ideological Influences; Level of Workers' Struggle and Political Radicalisation; Conscious and Organised Syndicalist Intervention; and International Cross-Fertilisation of Syndicalist Movements.

As a means of providing an account which is clear and concise each of these influencing variables is discussed in turn, although attention is drawn to the interconnections between them. Even though these multifaceted factors can be seen to have contributed to the *general* upsurge in workers' militancy that took place during the early twentieth century, they also help to highlight why some of this radicalism was channelled *specifically* into syndicalist movements.

Industrial and Economic Backcloth

Whilst it is commonly assumed that the origins of syndicalism and its distinctive labour movement activity lay in the birth pangs of a locally weak capitalism at the beginning of its industrial development,[3] there are conflicting interpretations of the way in which this impacted and its significance relative to other factors. The common perception that the residual strength of syndicalism lay not with the factory workers of the new large-scale heavy industries of the early twentieth century, but with artisans, agricultural workers, casual labourers and other groups of marginalised, often unskilled and unorganised workers, is assessed in Chapter 3. For now, we can

---

2 See W. Thorpe, 'Towards a Syndicalist International: The 1913 London Congress', *International Review of Social History*, 23 (1978), pp. 33–78; 'The European Syndicalists and War, 1914–18', *Contemporary European History*, 10:1, (2001), pp. 1–24; 'Syndicalist Internationalism and Moscow, 1919–1922: The Breach', *Canadian Journal of History*, 14: 1 (1979), pp. 199–234; *'The Workers Themselves': Revolutionary Syndicalism and International Labour, 1913–1923* (Dordrecht, 1989).

3 For example see E.J. Hobsbawm, *Primitive Rebels, Studies in Archaic Forms of Social Movement in the Nineteenth and Twentieth Centuries* (Manchester, 1972), pp. 74–92.

examine the extent to which the overall level of economic capitalist d
was a decisive contextual influence.

Certainly in France the CGT emerged in a country in which
modernisation had proceeded only slowly and large-scale industrialisation had lagged behind that of Britain, Germany or America. Despite the fact the pace of change quickened from 1871 to 1914, small and medium sized workshops continued to play a prominent role in production and to exist alongside rarer, geographically concentrated, more highly-industrialised enterprises. As late as 1906, workshops employing less than ten workers still employed one third of the industrial labour force; 59 per cent of all industrial workers worked in establishments of fewer than 100 employees, with only 12 per cent employed in plants of more than 1,000.[4]

Bernard Moss has argued that it was this 'exceptional' French economic development which created the conditions under which important sections of the relatively large semi-artisanal skilled workforce, faced with the growing threat of mechanisation, de-skilling and the absorption into the factory system, were encouraged towards distinctive syndicalist forms of 'trade socialism'.[5] The workplace became the conduit by which French workers came to their ideas and consciousness, with a correspondence between skilled workers' values and their position in the production process. Their pride, their quest for autonomy from managerial control and devotion to direct action, reflected their domination over work. The constrictions that capitalism inevitably produced encouraged them to search for ways to end wage labour, to develop a vision of social re-organisation, a form of co-operative socialism. The very way of life of skilled workers militated against great, bureaucratic working class institutions, such as trade unions and socialist parties, in favour of alternative decentralised and locally organised syndicalist forms of organisation. Thorpe has summarised the analysis:

> Industrialised workers frequently remained unorganised ... [and] the dispersal of the working population within a decentralised, craft-oriented economy made the formation of large unions difficult. An extensive series of small local unions characterised French trade union organisation ... Decades of experience in the smaller workshop and the prevalence of small local unions meshed well with the syndicalist vision of a socialised economy based upon decentralisation and producers' control. The relative absence of large powerful unions, moreover, also encouraged the endorsement of methods of direct action. The lack of organised strength to negotiate effectively with employers disposed workers to resort to forms of [militant 'direct action'] ... particularly as they confronted employers ... who tended to be intractable ... The direct action extolled and embraced in French syndicalist doctrine thus reflected constraints of economic development and union organisation.[6]

---

[4] W. Kendall, *The Labour Movement in Europe* (London, 1975), p. 36; R. Magraw, *France 1814–1915: The Bourgeois Century* (Oxford, 1983), p. 233.

[5] B. Moss, *The Origins of the French Labor Movement, 1830–1914: The Socialism of Skilled Workers* (Berkley, Calif., 1976), pp. 25–8.

[6] Thorpe, *Workers Themselves,* p. 24; See also R. Magraw, 'Socialism, Syndicalism and French Labour Before 1914', in D. Geary (ed.), *Labour and Socialist Movements in Europe Before 1914* (Oxford, 1989), pp. 48–100; R. Magraw, *A History of the French Working Class, Vol. 2: Workers and the Bourgeois Republic* (Oxford, 1992).

However, there are a number of studies that counter the view that the origins of French syndicalism lie mainly with the backwardness of capitalist economic development.[7] From this alternative perspective, the primary focus on 'artisanal' direct action on the shopfloor is misplaced given that French industry was not especially small in scale compared with some other European countries such as Spain and Italy. Although marked by uneven development, growth was particularly rapid in the decade after 1905, with the size of the industrial workforce increasing significantly. In practice, it is argued, French workers' predilection for direct action and syndicalism was encouraged less by their work experience or skill level than by their profound distrust of the reactionary bourgeois state and parliamentary democracy of the Third Republic and the existing political organisations. Such distrust occurred within the context of a French revolutionary political tradition, grounded on the experience of the 1789 revolution, 1830 and 1848 revolts, and 1871 Paris Commune, which established a popular culture of change from below. It was as a consequence of this *political* situation that sections of workers (particularly but not exclusively the skilled), who were relatively powerful in the sphere of the relations of production but powerless in the political arena, were encouraged to rely primarily on their relative bargaining power resources on the job and their own informal co-operation as the essential means by which to develop class-based action.

Likewise in Spain, whilst syndicalist (particularly anarcho-syndicalist) ideas and methods of struggle appeared to fit the prevailing backward economic and industrial conditions, they were also encouraged by broader social and political factors. By the turn of the twentieth century Spain was still predominately an agricultural country at the beginning of its capitalist industrial development. For over a hundred years the country had been torn by civil war in the long and unsuccessful struggle to overthrow a semi-feudalist absolutist regime and consolidate a modern capitalist bourgeois state. Centrifugal tendencies were reinforced by the advance of industrial development in the north and north-eastern seaboards, which coincided with a growth of local Basque and Catalan nationalism directed against an agrarian and centralist ruling class in Madrid. Thus, Spain was historically torn between the owners of the vast landed estates of central Castillian Spain who demanded a strong unified state and the industrialists of the Basque and Catalan provinces who demanded regional autonomy and independence in keeping with their separate languages and cultures. The country was effectively saddled with a politically weak commercial and manufacturing bourgeoisie and an absolute monarchy that relied on the twin pillars of the Catholic Church and aristocratic army officers to maintain itself in power. Chronic political instability and fierce employer opposition did not create

[7] See L. Berlanstein, *Big Business and Industrial Conflict in Nineteenth Century France: A Social History of the Parisian Gas Company*, (Berkeley, Calif., 1991) and 'The Distinctiveness of the Nineteenth Century French Labour Movement', *The Journal of Modern History*, 64: 4 (December 1992), pp. 660–85. See also A. Cotterau, 'The Distinctiveness of Working Class Cultures in France, 1848–1900', in I. Katznelson and A. Zolberg (eds), *Working Class Formation: Nineteenth Century Patterns in Western Europe and the United States* (Princeton, N.J., 1986), pp. 111–54 and T. Judt, *The French Labour Movement in the Nineteenth Century, Marxism and the French Left* (Oxford, 1986), pp. 24–114.

suitable conditions for the development of 'normal' trade union practices. Instead, *syndicalist* principles of revolutionary unionism combined with *anarchist* notions (of federalism, anti-clericalism, anti-militarism and a deep hostility to all political parties) fell on fertile soil amongst both the impoverished landless labourers who worked on the absentee-owned estates of Andalusia in the south and the industrial workers of Barcelona and other advanced Catalan towns in the north.[8]

In Italy, another predominately agricultural country, an important underlying explanation for the appeal of syndicalism (and anarchism) appears to have been the profound differences between north and south, between the highly capitalised modern industrial plant with its new factory proletariat in the so-called 'industrial triangle' formed by the northern cities of Milan, Genoa and Turin, on the one hand, and the semi-stagnant peasant and artisan economy in the agricultural south, on the other.[9] The appalling poverty of the south, perhaps the most terribly exploited industrial area in all Europe, involved conditions in which no stable trade union or socialist organisation could possibly exist. Labour revolts tended, to a great extent, to take the form of spontaneous hunger movements, which were more easily captured by anarchists than directed into the channels of organised reformist socialist agitation.[10] This provided the basis for the subsequent development of a revolutionary syndicalist movement which (adopting part of the anarchist tradition, but linking it to a highly localised trade unionism with direct action tactics) was able to pull towards it a wide layer of agricultural labourers and artisan groups, as well as some industrial workers (primarily in the south but also subsequently in the north). But again, as in other countries, such a socio-economic appeal can only be fully understood in combination with widespread alienation from existing political channels for redress.

By contrast, in the more advanced industrialised societies of Britain and America revolutionary syndicalist sentiment appears to have been encouraged more as a means of matching the increasing industrial concentration in the hands of fewer and fewer capitalists and associated co-ordination via employers' associations, which simultaneously exposed the inadequacy of existing local, craft and sectional trade union organisation. For example, although British trade unions were relatively stronger than anywhere else in the world, power was still dissipated across literally hundreds of different trade union organisations. As a result, amalgamation and industrial unionism increasingly came to be seen as an essential means of consolidating labour's strength in the face of the growth of big business and 'federated capital'.[11]

Similarly in America, the appeal of the IWW was related to the growth of corporate power. Between 1870 and 1917 the pace of industrial development was phenomenal, transforming the country into the world's leading industrial nation. The

---

8 See G. Brenan, *The Spanish Labyrinth: An Account of the Social and Political Background of the Spanish Civil War* (Cambridge, 1998); P. Heywood, 'The Labour Movement in Spain Before 1914', in Geary, *Labour and Socialist Movements*, pp. 231–65.

9 See J.A. Davies, 'Socialism and the Working Classes in Italy Before 1914', in Geary, *Labour and Socialist Movements*, pp. 182–230; D.L. Horrowitz, *The Italian Labor Movement* (Cambridge, Mass., 1963).

10 G.D.H. Cole, *A History of Socialist Thought: The Second International, 1889–1914: Part 1* (London:, 1974), pp. 732–3.

11 B. Holton, *British Syndicalism 1900-1914* (London, 1976), p. 275.

spread of the new great industries brought with it the concentration of ownership and wealth into vast industrial corporations.[12] The founders of the IWW sought to meet the challenge of such 'trusts' with integrated industrial unions affiliated to 'One Big Union'. The appeal of the IWW was related to the way the AFL had organised only a small minority of the workforce into highly sectional unions almost exclusively restricted to skilled, male American-born workers. Thus, there was the need for a form of unionism that could organise the mass of unorganised workers ignored by the AFL – namely the unskilled, foreign-born, women and black workers.

Of course, in both Britain and America industrial unionism was by no means equivalent to revolutionary syndicalism, being quite compatible with a more reformist approach. Yet:

> Organisational changes of this kind were increasingly linked with militant policies. This was because the concentration of capitalist power was often associated with aggressive employer policies against organised labour. Where this was so industrial unionism, combined with direct action methods, brought militants much closer to syndicalist affiliation.[13]

However, the contrast between less developed and more advanced societies should not be drawn too far, given that syndicalist sentiment and organisation was encouraged in both by the way in which technical and organisational changes led to an erosion of the security, status and capacity of job control of many skilled workers. In particular, it was managerial attempts to consolidate their control over the work process that helped to radicalise skilled workers, whatever the relative level of industrial development of the specific country. Thus, France experienced what Michael Hanagan has called an 'industrial war' in the quarter-century before the First World War, when syndicalism emerged there:

> In shops and factories throughout the country a tremendous struggle raged over the control of the production process. Everywhere employers strove to seize control on the shop floor and acquire a monopoly of expertise over the manufacturing process; everywhere skilled workers resisted these attempts.[14]

A related process took place in Britain's long established and rapidly developing engineering, railway and building industries. The changes in technology and the organisation of work encouraged skilled workers to look to trade union amalgamation as a means of creating a new bargaining strength. Again whilst industrial unionism did not tend automatically towards syndicalism, it was nonetheless quite often associated with fierce shop-floor resistance to managerial interference within the workshop, which meant the gap between skilled workers' aspirations for 'job control' and the syndicalist emphasis on workers' control of industry was not a large one. Moreover, the appeal of

---

[12] M. Dubofsky, *We Shall Be All: A History of the Industrial Workers of the World* (Chicago, 1969), pp. 48–9.

[13] Holton, p. 29. See also B. Holton, 'Revolutionary Syndicalism and the British Labour Movement', in W.J. Mommsen and H. Husung (eds), *The Development of Trade Unionism in Great Britain and Germany 1880–1914* (London, 1985), pp. 266–82.

[14] M. Hanagan, *The Logic of Solidarity: Artisans and Industrial Workers in Three French Towns, 1871–1914* (Urbana, Illin., 1980), p. 3.

syndicalism to a sizeable layer of radical skilled workers was also encouraged by the revolutionary industrial emphasis on direct action at the point of production.[15]

On a more general level the origin and development of syndicalist organisation was also clearly rooted in the deep hostility often displayed by employers towards any form of independent trade union organisation. In the relatively less developed Spain and Italy, whilst the land-owning classes were prodigiously reactionary and exploited the agricultural workforce, the rising class of industrialists were hardly less determined to vigorously resist any attempt to organise in unions. But the ferocity of employers' resistance to the CNT and USI was more than matched by what happened in the more developed American context where the backdrop to the formation of the IWW was stark class warfare. The industrial workforce (largely unskilled and with a high proportion of immigrant labour) had been attracted from Europe with the promise of a better life, only to be confronted with long and arduous working hours for poor wages, often in industries and workplaces where union organisation was almost non-existent. Workers found they had to fight for the most basic of rights – the right to organise, to strike and to picket. Many who tried to organise were sacked, blacklisted, imprisoned and sometimes killed. For example, in the western states of Montana, Colorado, Idaho and Utah, the industrial and mining companies carried out an aggressive attack against their workforces in an attempt to drive up productivity and profitability. In such circumstances, the appeal of the Western Federation of Miners (one of the original constituent elements of the IWW) under its leader Bill Haywood – who pronounced a willingness to 'fight fire with fire' by mounting direct, often violent, methods of industrial action – proved attractive to a layer of workers who felt they had no other realistic means of attempting to redress their grievances.[16]

The significance of employers' attacks in encouraging syndicalist sentiment was highlighted in sharp relief in Ireland during the Dublin strike and lockout of 1913. Previously most Irish unskilled workers had remained unorganized, primarily as a result of the way that employers had systematically defeated attempts at union organisation by mass strikebreaking and wholesale victimisation. This led a growing section of workers to the view that the methods of respectability and moderation championed by the official union leadership were woefully inadequate. Instead, they increasingly became attracted to the idea propagated by Jim Larkin's ITGWU that the only way the employers' determined resistance to union organisation could be broken down was by militant aggressive action. When such methods began to enjoy considerable success they were met with a determined employers' counter-offensive in Dublin; 400 employers locked out over 25,000 workers for five months, although this had the effect of galvanising support for Larkin's syndicalist methods of class warfare and working class solidarity.[17] Whilst British employers generally were less

---

15 Holton, *British Syndicalism*, p. 30. See also. J. Hinton, *The First Shop Stewards' Movement* (London. 1973).

16 Dubofsky, pp. 36–8.

17 E. Larkin, *James Larkin: Irish Labour Leader, 1876–1947* (London, 1968) pp. 117–43. P. Yeates, *Lockout: Dublin 1913* (Dublin, 2001).

determined, aggressive and violent in relation to trade unionism than other countries, similar processes were at work in certain industries.[18]

A related contextual factor encouraging the growth of syndicalist movements internationally was the fact that the capitalist system across the world in the first few years of the century showed signs of real economic instability. Significantly, the generalised economic crises that Eduard Bernstein (one of the leading intellectuals in the German Social Democratic Party) had claimed was no longer an integral part of capitalism, returned with a vengeance, helping to fuel a wave of industrial unrest in many countries. For example, the increasingly precarious position of British capitalism – amidst the challenge of foreign competition, declining rates of growth and industrial productivity – led to a very rapid deterioration of working class living standards. Between 1900-10 real wages fell by roughly 10 per cent, producing a massive build-up of economic grievances among workers.[19] Likewise in Ireland, between 1905 and 1912 food prices rocketed by 25 per cent, whilst unemployment stood at around 20 per cent.[20] Even if economic problems of this kind did not by itself stimulate support for the direct action methods of syndicalism, it did provide a general sense of material deprivation on which it could build, which was further reinforced by disaffection with orthodox trade unionism and parliamentary socialism to effect reform.[21]

Dick Geary is justified in pointing out that there is not necessarily a *direct* link between degrees of deprivation suffered by workers and political radicalism.[22] Indeed in France skilled workers appear to have been more inclined to syndicalism than the lowest paid; and in Britain the syndicalist-influenced industrial unrest during the First World War was spearheaded by relatively well-paid skilled engineering workers. Yet there is no doubt syndicalist agitation could also be particularly attractive to sections of unskilled workers who faced appalling poverty. Thus, in Ireland, the ITGWU built its strongest base amongst low-paid and unskilled transport workers in the city of Dublin, where a third of the population lived in single-room flats in slum tenements and infant mortality and tuberculosis accounted for a very high death rate.[23] Likewise in America one contemporary journalist noted: 'The IWW's deepest strength lies in the fact that it extends the red hand of fellowship to the lowliest of the workers, that it has made itself the special champion of those who are paid the least and work the hardest.'[24] Syndicalist leaders were able to appeal to workers' bitterness and anger at their impoverished predicament (fuelled by heightened but unfulfilled expectations) and direct it towards revolutionary forms of trade unionism.

---

[18] N. Kirk, *Labour and Society in Britain and the USA: Vol. 2: Challenge and Accommodation, 1850–1939* (Aldershot, 1994), pp. 35–41.

[19] Holton, *British Syndicalism*, p. 274.

[20] C. Bambery, *Ireland's Permanent Revolution* (London, 1986), p. 28.

[21] Holton, *British Syndicalism*, p. 28; H. Pelling, 'The Labour Unrest 1911–1914', *Popular Politics and Society in Late Victorian Britain* (London, 1968), p. 150.

[22] See D. Geary, *European Labour Politics From 1900 to the Depression* (Houndmills, 1991), pp. 15–16.

[23] Larkin, p. 37. See also J. Newsinger, *Rebel City: Larkin, Connolly and the Dublin Labour Movement* (London, 2004).

[24] W. Woehlbe, *Sunset*, September 1917.

Political Context

The origins and growth of the syndicalist movement internationally also have to be set within their political context, reflecting a widespread disaffection with parliamentary politics and reformist socialist parties. As Lenin commented: 'In Western Europe revolutionary syndicalism in many countries was a direct and inevitable result of opportunism, reformism and parliamentary cretinism.'[25] However, this disaffection manifested itself in varying ways in different countries depending on the level of political development.

At one extreme were Italy, Spain and Ireland, where the parliamentary process was generally not viewed as a serious channel for redressing workers' grievances. Thus in Italy, one of the reasons for the attraction of syndicalist (and anarchist) ideas, even in the industrial north, was the narrowness of the franchise. Although the electoral laws were modified from time to time the great majority of Italian workers and agricultural labourers, especially in the south, were completely disenfranchised. Whilst Giolitti's 1913 reforms more than doubled the electorate to nearly a quarter of the population, there was still 'the domination of the parliamentary group by lawyers, professors and journalists [who were] a constant source of suspicion among the class-conscious workers'.[26] And in the south, where the overwhelming mass of the population consisted of landless labourers, electoral reform mean little given the corruption of political affairs, with judiciously administered patronage the standard method by which parliamentary majorities were composed.

In Spain, unlike any other country in Europe, universal male suffrage was instituted from the late nineteenth century. Nonetheless, there was the glaring failure of the very weak parliamentary institutions to function properly in an underdeveloped and basically agrarian society dominated by an absolute monarchy. Where possible the lower classes were deliberately excluded from the political process, with corrupt local political bosses securing the election of the government's preferred candidates in return for favours.[27] Whilst in France and even Italy parliamentary socialist parties had by 1914 achieved real political significance, in Spain by the same date the socialist movement was barely established at a national level. Despite being founded in the late nineteenth century by Marx's son-in-law, Paul Lafargue, the Socialist Party had subsequently developed into a moderate constitutional party, ineffectual in an environment of extreme violence from the state, landowners and employers. Although there was more to Spanish anarcho-syndicalism than mere detestation of bourgeois politics, the electoral issue attracted many landless labourers and industrial workers to the 'anti-political' CNT.[28] Moreover, for a number of years during the late 1920s parliament was abolished under the military dictatorship of General Primo de Rivera. In such circumstances, compounded by the continuing relatively very weak

---

25 *On Trade Unions* (Moscow, 1970) p. 190.

26 Cole, *History of Socialist Thought*, pp. 710–11.

27 A. Smith, 'Spain', in S. Berger and D. Broughton (eds), *The Force of Labour: The Western European Labour Movement and the Working Class in the Twentieth Century* (Oxford, 1995), pp. 174–5.

28 G.H. Meaker, *The Revolutionary Left in Spain, 1914–1923* (Stanford, Calif., 1974), pp. 4–5.

Socialist Party, militant direct action rather than social reform appeared the only way forward. The establishment of the Second Republic in 1931 and reformist and bureaucratic approaches of both newly advancing Socialist and Communist Parties did not diminish the appeal of revolutionary initiatives from below.

In Ireland the ITGWU's emergence has to be set against the backcloth of British colonial domination. Even if by 1911 there was the prospect of Home Rule, it was clear the proposed Irish parliament would be severely limited in powers, with a real danger (in the face of Unionist opposition) of partition of the country between north and south. The Irish Labour Party, which developed in the shadow of Irish nationalism (to which it later capitulated in the 1918 election by not standing candidates against Sinn Fein), ferociously attacked the Home Rulers and Irish Volunteer Force for their betrayal over partition. But national Labour party organisation was viewed as being ineffectual and instead the ITGWU concentrated its efforts within the industrial rather than political arena.

In the economically more advanced America political circumstances were not much more favourable. In those parts of the country where black labour was predominant, procedural harassment and outright intimidation kept most Afro-Americans from voting. Meanwhile, more stringent registration rules eliminated many of the new immigrants and transient citizens from the voting rolls. For example, large sections of workers – seamen, itinerants and lumberjacks – were unable to maintain registration at fixed polling booths. Therefore, placing hopes in the ballot box, in politics, was not seen to be particularly attractive. It appeared to select a field of combat where working class power was at its weakest compared with a concentration on the point of production where its potential economic muscle appeared strongest.

In Britain and France, despite the fact parliamentary government appeared much more relevant to (male) workers, with about 62 per cent of men entitled to vote in the former and almost 91 per cent in the latter (although women were disenfranchised in both), there were similar problems of credibility. In such countries, as elsewhere, parliamentary labour and socialist parties affiliated to the Second International agreed to prosecute the class war by the method of electoral political activity with the aim of capturing the state. They looked forward to the time when, with universal suffrage, a socialist majority would be elected into parliament and would use the government machine to abolish, either gradually or at a single stroke, the capitalist organisation of society and install in its place state ownership over the means of production. The formation of a political party, and the mustering of the working class to the polling booth, was viewed as an important method of action, from which would result fundamental change. As for the trade unions, to them was delegated the daily task of ameliorating workers' wages and conditions of work. The two forms of organisation, the party and the unions, were seen as indispensable, but it was the former that the 'political socialists' (including both parliamentary socialist and mainstream 'Marxist' tendencies within the Second International) looked to for the ultimate work of transformation.

However, by the decade preceding the First World War, many workers had had the opportunity to witness the efforts of such parties on behalf of labour and had found them seriously wanting, even though in some countries they contained strong left-wing elements. For example, in Britain, at least among a sizeable minority of union activists, there was disaffection with parliamentary politics caused by the functioning of the Labour Party in the House of Commons. Although Labour's electoral representation rose from 26 in 1906 to 42 in 1910, the party remained merely a loose federation of trade union officials and small socialist groups with no real national or constituency organisation. Unable to win more than 8 per cent of the popular vote in any pre-war election, it proceeded to act as a mere adjunct of the post 1906 Liberal Party government, failing to set out an alternative to 'welfare capitalism' and frowning upon militant industrial struggle. One syndicalist delegate told the 1912 Trades Union Congress: 'Let us be quite clear as to what Syndicalism really is ... a protest against the inaction of the Labour Party'.[29] And as ISEL leader Tom Mann explained, parliamentary politics tended to corrupt Labour Party representatives:

> Those who have been in close touch with the Movement know that in recent years dissatisfaction has been expressed in various quarters at the results so far achieved by our Parliamentarians. Certainly nothing very striking in the way of constructive work could reasonably be expected from the minorities of Socialists and Labour men hitherto elected ... [In all countries] a proportion of those comrades who, prior to being returned, were unquestionably revolutionary, are no longer so after a few years in Parliament. They are revolutionary neither in their attitude towards existing Society nor in respect of present day institutions. Indeed, it is no exaggeration to say that many seem to have constituted themselves apologists for existing Society, showing a degree of studied respect for bourgeois conditions, and a toleration of bourgeois methods, that destroys the probability of their doing any real work of a revolutionary character.[30]

In France, where there was the emergence of a relatively large socialist movement in the shape of the *Parti Socialiste Unifié – Section Française de L'Internationale Ouvrière*, the quest for electoral success and parliamentary office was much more advanced. The Third Republic was a relatively democratic polity, with an elected government that was open to socialist influence. The party vote (878,000 in 1905) passed one million by 1910 and developed steadily until by June 1914, on the eve of the First World War, it reached 1.4 million, with 100 members elected in its name to the French Chamber of Deputies, making it the second largest party in parliament. Nonetheless, Socialist Party figures entering government were viewed as adopting policies indistinguishable from their bourgeois predecessors, thereby creating a similar process of workers' alienation. Thus, in 1899 the reformist socialist party leader Alexandre Millerand was appointed Minister of Commerce in the Waldeck-Rousseau government in which General Gallifet, who was directly implicated in the suppression of the Paris Commune, was Minister of War. In 1910 Aristide Briand, the Minister of the Interior, and former leading advocate of the general strike, responded to a national railway strike by declaring a state of emergency and arresting the strike leaders to force a return-to-work:

> The conclusion seemed obvious: the parliamentary system was essentially bourgeois: those [labour and socialist party leaders] drawn into its orbit inevitably succumbed to its spell and became bourgeois themselves. Disillusionment with the parliamentary system

29 Trades Union Congress *Report* (1912), p. 274.

30 *Industrial Syndicalist*, July 1910.

> in general, the socialist parties in particular, many workers came to reject both ... The revolutionary class struggle was inevitably emasculated in parliament; it could only be carried on in the unions, where the clarity of conflict between capitalist and proletariat was maintained and from which the bourgeois socialists were rigorously excluded. Socialism having degenerated into mere parliamentarism, its original goals could only be achieved by the direct action of the labour movement.[31]

Thus, syndicalism, in France as elsewhere, represented both a reaction to and a rejection of the politics of gradualism – the belief in piecemeal reform – in favour of militant action through industrial struggle. In the process, in every country syndicalists attracted support on the basis that socialist party politics, particularly as practised in parliamentary circles, violated the principles of the class struggle by subordinating workers' interests to the need to win electoral support and to class collaborationist policies.

Paradoxically in Italy, despite the narrowness of the franchise, syndicalism developed (initially at least) not so much from within the trade unions as inside the *Partito Socialista Italiana* (PSI). It began as a spontaneous revolt by party militants and socialist intellectuals opposed to attempts by elements within the leadership to manoeuvre the PSI into collaboration with Prime Minister Giolitti's liberal cabinets. Arturo Labriola and Enrico Leone launched their attack on reformism at the Socialist Party congress in 1902, criticizing the idea that the actions of parliament could benefit the working class.[32] Riding a wave of labour militancy, the Italian syndicalists subsequently gathered widespread influence inside the Socialist Party, including control of its Milan section, and published *L'Avanguardia socialista* as a vehicle for syndicalist opposition to the party's reformist wing. Unlike in France, Spain and elsewhere where syndicalists were formally completely opposed to any participation with political parties (including socialist parties), the Italian syndicalists, partly because of their relative initial weakness inside the trade unions as well as the existence of a strong 'maximalist' wing inside the PSI, stayed within the Socialist Party until their eventual expulsion in 1908. Nonetheless, their principled vigorous opposition to parliamentary politics and the reformist practice of the Socialist Party leadership, in favour of direct action through revolutionary unionism, eventually led to their organisational as well as political break, with the formation of the USI in 1910.

There was a parallel antipathy towards the Socialist Party in America where, notwithstanding the problems of voter registration, the prospects for a significant socialist presence during 1910–1912 appeared to look encouraging. The Socialist Party's presidential candidate Eugene Debs (one of the IWW's founding figures) spectacularly polled more than 900,000 votes (about 6 per cent) in 1912, and the party had 1,200 candidates elected in 340 municipalities, including 79 mayors in 24 states.[33] At the same time party membership grew to a peak of about 120,000, with hundreds of thousands of readers for its 300-plus English and foreign-language papers. But whilst it rejected the industrial unionism of the IWW (expelling members who supported the Wobblies in 1912–1914), it simultaneously failed to capture the primary bastion of

31 Ridley, p. 61.

32 A. Labriola, *Storia di dieci anni: 1899–1909* (Milan, 1910), p. 138.

33 P. Le Blanc, *A Short History of the U.S. Working Class* (New York, 1999), p. 64.

the American labour movement, the AFL, and after 1913 the socialist electoral tide began to recede. The IWW attracted support from militants opposed to attempts by the party's dominant faction to win votes by trimming their programme to conform to the views of the skill-based and conservative-minded AFL unions.

Meanwhile, in a number of countries the desire to escape from consuming polemical squabbles between different socialist and Marxist groupings tended to reinforce the process whereby sections of workers were attracted to the syndicalist emphasis on trade union autonomy from political parties. For example, in France, at least five different factions had engaged in internecine combat in the late nineteenth century, each vying for trade union support. Personal and political conflicts continued to divide the socialists into the twentieth century, fractured between a moderate wing led by Jean Jaurés and an orthodox Marxist wing led by Jules Guesde. These rivalries brought political socialism into disrepute among many workers and reinforced the tendency of radical trade unionists to repudiate political activity in favour of direct action. Only in 1905 did the French socialists achieve unity in the form of the SFIO, but by then the great majority within the CGT agreed on the need to distance their organisation from all political parties. Thus, the autonomy of the labour movement, as proclaimed by the CGT, was an expression of workers' hostility to politicians, political doctrines and political parties, and narrowly conceived of as 'political action' in general.

The absence or relative weakness of viable alternative revolutionary Marxist parties with an orientation on linking day-to-day economic and industrial struggle in the trade unions with general socialist politics in both parliamentary *and* anti-parliamentary forms (similar to the Bolshevik Party in Russia) was also important to syndicalism's appeal. As we have seen, the syndicalist movement emerged at a time of stagnation in socialist thought, in the gap between pioneering revolutionary Marxist ideas and the triumph of the Leninist concept of the revolutionary party that reached its culmination in the Russian Revolution of 1917. Thus, in France, Italy and Spain, syndicalism represented a reaction against the deterministic conception of Marxism as practiced by most of the parties of the Second International (which combined a theory of the economic inevitability of socialism with reformist and bureaucratic practice).

In Britain, the largest Marxist organisation, the Social Democratic Federation, despite a claimed membership of 10,000, alienated many potential working class supporters with its dismissal of practical trade union activity and militant industrial struggle in favour of sterile, abstract socialist propaganda. On the other hand, although the Socialist Labour Party's (SLP) theories of industrial unionism exerted a powerful ideological influence on a layer of young militants and were taken over and incorporated into the general ISEL philosophy of syndicalism, the SLP's sectarianism towards all other labour movement organisations meant it did not effectively participate in the industrial struggles of the pre-1914 period (although a later change of approach enabled it to win influence amongst some of the leaders of the wartime shop stewards' movement). Therefore, instead of being attracted to a *political* organisation a layer of pre-war class-conscious British workers turned instead towards the ISEL's strategy of investing industrial struggle in the workplace with revolutionary significance.[34]

---

[34] See Kendall, *Revolutionary Movement in Britain*, and R. Challinor, *The Origins of British Bolshevism* (London, 1977).

In addition to such factors syndicalism's attraction for many workers also reflected their antipathy towards the capitalist state. By emphasising the coercive role of the state as an organ of class rule, which instead of being 'neutral' acted in the interests of the employers, syndicalists tapped indigenous traditions of working class hostility to state intervention in industrial disputes. At the one extreme were the authoritarian and repressive political regimes of Spain and Italy, where the frequent deployment of troops against strikes and demonstrations fuelled the syndicalist appeal. In Spain, the brutality of the Civil Guard was notorious, and the CNT came into being as a direct result of the July 1909 Barcelona general strike, when a rapidly escalating full-scale insurrection was crushed by violent government repression. Following what became known as the 'Tragic Week', many activists became convinced of the need for an uncompromising revolutionary syndicalist organisation that would defend workers' interests against both capital and the state. Such sentiments were further encouraged between 1911–1914 and 1923-30 when the CNT was banned and driven underground. Similarly, in Italy the shock of 'Red Week' in June 1914, when the government deployed 100,000 troops to suppress a general strike, involving violent clashes in which 16 people died and 400 were wounded, reinforced the syndicalist message that workers should scorn politics and seek to destroy the state.

In France, in the century following the 1789 revolution workers had been engaged in a long and bitter struggle with the state. The bloody suppression of the June Days of 1848 and the Paris Commune of 1871 (when up to 25,000 workers were killed in battle or executed) were only the most dramatic examples of this. But the French state had also demonstrated its open hostility to the development of a trade union movement by introducing laws that placed limits on workers' right to organise, forcing workers into opposition to the state. Only in 1884 was the legal right to associate granted, and then only under the strictest supervision. Thereafter, the Republican state machine repeatedly intervened in industrial disputes with troops (notably in the coal-mining, building, railway, postal and dock industries), utilising hard-line tactics such as the declaration of martial law, the mass dismissal of strikers, military conscription, and the arrest of CGT leaders for conspiracy, resulting in several bloody clashes in which many workers were shot dead and others wounded. In such circumstances, the syndicalist doctrine that the labour movement must develop outside the state and create its own institutions to replace it, proved attractive.[35]

This picture was repeated in America where, despite a formally more democratic political system, the judiciary, police and military power of both state and federal governments were consistently used to support the employers and prevent workers' attempts to organise. The scale of American state repression was quite remarkable. For example, during the Goldfield, Nevada, 1907 miners' strike, President Roosevelt agreed to the mine operators' appeal for support by flooding the area with federal troops, in the process enabling the employers to smash trade unionism and reduce wages across the region. During the 1909 strike at the Pressed Steel Car Company in McKees Rocks, Pennsylvania, the area became an armed camp with state police evicting families of the strikers from company houses, and engaging in pitched battles with strikers that left 13 killed and 500 wounded. In the Paterson silk workers'

---

[35] Ridley, pp. 20–24.

strike of 1913 4,800 strikers were arrested and 1,300 sent to prison. And during the 1909–1914 'Free Speech' campaigns against local state ordinances specifically directed against IWW meetings, thousands of Wobbly supporters were imprisoned, hundreds badly beaten and some killed. The American state also engaged in the false accusation of murder of IWW leaders such as Haywood and Joseph Ettor, as well as the successful trial, conviction and execution of the celebrated Wobbly songwriter Joe Hill in 1915. Not surprisingly, scarred and embittered by such industrial warfare, many workers turned violently against the existing social order, with daily experience demonstrating the truth of IWW organiser Elizabeth Gurly Flynn's comment that the state was simply 'the slugging agency of the capitalists'. In the process some found both an explanation of and a remedy for their predicament in syndicalism.

In Britain, despite a relatively more liberal parliamentary system of government, the anti-state propaganda of syndicalism also struck a chord inside the working class movement. This was partly because the Board of Trade repeatedly acted as an industrial trouble-shooter during protracted strikes and tried to foist compromise settlements on militant groups of workers, and partly because the Liberal government's 'social welfare' legislation was viewed as a means of state encroachment over independent working class self-initiative that yielded minimal economic benefits.[36] In addition, the government's regular use of the police and military to break strikers' picket lines meant the anti-state attitudes of syndicalists tended to mesh with the actual experiences of many rank-and-file workers. Thus, in 1911 mass strike action on the docks and railways spread to a Liverpool city-wide transport strike, spearheaded by a powerful unofficial strike committee led by Tom Mann. The government was only able to crush the revolt by sending gunboats down the Mersey and flooding troops onto the streets to break up an 80,000-strong demonstration. Later, two strikers were shot dead by the military.[37] In 1912 troops rushed into the mining areas to break a national strike and were met with *Don't Shoot* leaflets that were distributed by syndicalists agitating for soldiers not to gun down fellow members of the working class. Following prosecution of the ISEL newspaper *The Syndicalist*, Tom Mann and Guy Bowman were sentenced to six months imprisonment for 'incitement to mutiny'. Such experiences, as in other countries, reinforced support for the syndicalist message that the state was the tool of the capitalists and parliamentary government was a sham.

Finally, in every country the looming prospect of world war combined with each government's bellicosity towards other nations underlined the relevance of syndicalist agitation that attempted to link capitalism with militarism.

Trade Union Framework

The emergence and subsequent development of the syndicalist movement internationally also reflected a cynical disregard for the existing reformist trade unions, which were condemned for not representing workers' interests more effectively. The largest and strongest trade union movement was to be found in

---

[36] Holton, *British Syndicalism*, pp. 35–6; 278–9.

[37] See E. Taplin, *Near to Revolution: The Liverpool General Transport Strike of 1911* (Liverpool, 1994).

Britain, where in 1910 there were some 2.5 million organised workers, representing about 14.6 per cent of the labour force.[38] The sheer antiquity of the country's pioneer industrialisation allowed a rather primitive, largely decentralised trade unionism, mainly of craft unions, to sink roots within all the main industries such as cotton, mining and engineering.[39] In other European countries (such as France, Italy, Spain and Ireland) the situation was rather different, with effective trade unionism only functioning on the margins of modern and especially large-scale industry – in workshops, on work-sites or in small and medium industries, but largely absent in the large plants of modern industry. Whilst the union organisation that existed might in theory be national, in practice it was often extremely localised and decentralised, for example in countries such as France and Italy there were mainly alliances of small local unions grouped around local labour halls. Total trade union membership was only a tiny fraction of the non-agricultural labour force (even as late as 1911 only 4.9 per cent of eligible workers were in unions in France), with the remainder usually lacking any effective means of protecting their interests in the labour market.

Even in the more advanced United States trade unionism survived essentially in small-scale industry and among the craft unions of the building trades and was largely absent in the new mass production industries. The only exception to this pattern was the miners who, bound together by the solidarity of work and community and by the arduous and danger of their work, showed a marked tendency towards collective organisation and struggle. Total union membership stood at less than 10 per cent, with the AFL embracing only 5 per cent at the time of the IWW's birth in 1905.

Syndicalists accused the established trade unions of subordinating the interests of the wider working class to organised craft or sectional interests; of being too preoccupied with 'bread and butter issues' rather than the transformation of society; of being too closely identified through collective bargaining procedures with the employers and through arbitration and welfare schemes with the state; of being dominated by a highly bureaucratic and administratively and cautiously minded officialdom; and of being too insensitive to dissent and initiatives from the rank-and-file within them and the needs of the unorganised outside them.[40] Syndicalism was able to grow as a movement internationally as a direct result of this critique of the existing trade unions, although (as in other respects) there were variations between countries.

One of the most striking features of the labour militancy that swept Britain immediately before the First World War was its predominately unofficial character and hostility to the existing trade union leadership. Certainly, British syndicalism drew considerable strength from working class disaffection with the increasing incorporation of trade union officials within formalised collective bargaining and conciliation machinery introduced by employers, in part at least, as an important means of defusing industrial militancy. Official union policies it was claimed had tended to become cautious and conservative as the consolidation of the unions' bureaucratic strength took precedence over radical shopfloor grievances. In such circumstances, with its emphasis on 'direct action' that bypassed the orthodox

---

38 R. Hyman, *The Political Economy of Industrial Relations* (London, 1989), p. 231.

39 E. Hobsbawm, *The Age of Empire, 1875–1914* (London, 1987), pp. 121–2.

40 Van der Linden and Thorpe, 'The Rise and Fall', pp.13–14.

bargaining machinery and class collaboration of official leaders, the British syndicalist message fell on fertile ground (notwithstanding fierce union and Labour Party opposition). This pre-war syndicalist tradition was to remain highly influential inside the wartime Shop Stewards' and Workers' Committee movement, as well as during the post-war labour militancy of 1919–1921. The advice offered by the ITGWU leader Jim Larkin to 'Never trust leaders ... trust yourselves' typified the militancy of the period, as rank-and-file dissatisfaction led to an increasing incidence of unofficial strikes and activity.[41]

There was also widespread support for Tom Mann's formula of working within the existing trade unions and campaigning to amalgamate them on a revolutionary basis until the principle of 'one union for one industry' was achieved, with industrial organisation of all workers on the basis of class, not trade or craft. Thus, a number of unofficial Amalgamation Movements, which had developed independent of, and prior to, the establishment of the ISEL (notably within the engineering, transport, railway and building industries), joined with the syndicalists to successfully campaign for changes in trade union structure in specific industries. This contributed to the formation of the National Transport Workers' Federation in 1910, the National Union of Railwaymen in 1913 (which brought all but one of the existing manual workers' unions into a single industrial organisation), and the progress of negotiations during 1913–1914 for a 'Triple Alliance' of the miners, railway and transport workers' unions. Whilst broader forces played a role in shaping such developments, syndicalist ideas and activities were very much to the fore.

The strategy of 'boring from within' the existing trade unions appeared feasible in Britain, in part because the country had a much longer history of industrialisation than elsewhere, which meant the established unions, with their much greater relative size and influence, had begun to organise unskilled workers even before the birth of syndicalism. By contrast in America, which only industrialised after 1870, and where 'industrial concentration, the growth of mass production industries, technological changes and corporate control all developed in largely virgin territory, preceding, superseding or breaking whatever labour union traditions had previously existed', it was felt there was no alternative than to set up a separate revolutionary union in opposition to the existing unions, to adopt a policy of 'dual unionism'.[42] By the 1890s the AFL had become a powerful trade union confederation, but concerned to preserve the position of a minority of skilled workers it refused to make any serious efforts to organise the unskilled and frequently broke strikes by independent unions. In response, William Trautmann, one of the key figures who helped set up the IWW, insisted the AFL 'had long since outgrown its usefulness and had become positively reactionary, a thing that is but an auxiliary of the capitalist class'.[43] Eugene

---

41 Cited in P. Taylor, 'Syndicalism', *Socialist Worker Review*, 77 (1985), p. 24.

42 L. Peterson, 'The One Big Union in International Perspective: Revolutionary Industrial Unionism 1900–1925', in J.E. Cronin and C. Sirianni (eds), *Work, Community and Power: The Experience of Labour in Europe and America 1900–1925* (Philadelphia, 1983), pp. 56–7.

43 *Proceedings of the First Annual Convention of the Industrial Workers of the World* (New York, 1905), p. 118.

Debs concurred: 'There is certainly something wrong with that form of unionism ... whose leaders are the lieutenants of capitalism ... whose sole purpose is to chloroform the working class while the capitalist class go through their pockets.'[44] Debs concluded: 'To talk about reforming these rotten graft infested [AFL] unions, which are dominated absolutely by the labour boss, is as vain and wasteful of time as to spray a cesspool with attar of roses.'[45]

In these circumstances, the attempt by the IWW to set up an alternative class-based industrial union with revolutionary aspirations appealed to a layer of unskilled workers who had been spurned by the AFL. As Howard Kimeldorf has commented:

> ... the Industrial Workers of the World (IWW) self-consciously defined itself as the antithesis of the AFL. Where the AFL broke up the working class into a multitude of tiny craft unions, the IWW envisioned 'One Big Union' consisting of a handful of industrially based affiliates. Where the AFL's membership consisted mostly of native-born, skilled white craftsmen, the IWW was committed to organising almost everyone else, targeting in particular the unskilled, recent immigrants, women, and workers of colour. Where the AFL monopolised employment opportunities for its current members by restricting union access through closed shops, prohibitive initiation fees, and high dues, the IWW offered a true 'communism of opportunity' based on mass recruiting, low initiation fees, and work sharing. And where the AFL advocated an industrial peace based on the sanctity of contracts, the IWW promised unrelenting class war, refusing as a matter of principle to sign labour agreements or any other such 'armistice' until the working class secured its final emancipation from capitalism.[46]

In Ireland, trade unionism had been established in Dublin, Belfast and Cork during the 1870s and 1880s, but was limited largely to small craft societies often British-based. The ITGWU was formed with the explicit aim of modernising this trade unionism through the notion of industrial unionism, and decolonising it by building an Irish union rather than one tied to a British body.[47] Jim Larkin had been taken on by the Liverpool-based National Union of Dock Labourers (NUDL) as a full-time organiser working in the ports of Scotland and Ireland. In 1907 he led a militant Belfast strike of 2,500 workers, comprised of dockers, carters and coal labourers, effectively uniting Catholic and Protest workers. By the end of 1908 branches of the union had been successfully established in every port in Ireland, but Larkin's militant methods brought him into conflict with the moderate union leadership. He urged a general campaign to organise all the unskilled and casually employed workers in Ireland and threatened to launch a breakaway industrial union to accomplish the task. Following his suspension from office the ITGWU was formed, with the great majority of the NUDL's Irish membership switching allegiance.

In France, the establishment of the CGT was encouraged by two developments related to the existing trade unions. On the one hand it emerged from a coalition of

---

44 Ibid., p. 506.

45 Cited in D. Brody, *Workers in Industrial America: Essays on the Twentieth Century Struggle* (Oxford, 1981), p. 35.

46 H. Kimeldorf, *Battling for American Labour: Wobblies, Craft Workers, and the Making of the Union Movement* (Berkeley, Calif., 1999), p. 2.

47 E. O'Connor, *Syndicalism in Ireland* (Cork, 1988), p. xiv.

militant forces opposed to the country's first central trade union body, the *Fédération nationale des syndicats* (FNS). This organisation, created in 1886, had quickly fallen under the control of supporters of the 'Marxist' Jules Guesde and his *Parti Ouvrier Français* (one of the five components that subsequently formed the French Socialist Party). Under its influence, trade union activity was seen as subordinate to the quest for votes and to political control by the party. It was as a corrective to this socialist emphasis on parliamentary elections, that anarchists, socialists and other union militants within the FNS campaigned for direct, economic action through the *syndicat* or trade union, to culminate in a revolutionary general strike, as the most direct method of abolishing the wage system. The rebels eventually managed to unseat the Guesdists and the FNS transformed itself into a new national union confederation aspiring to function as a central organising institution for all unions, championing the replacement of craft unions by industrial unions.

On the other hand, the shift towards syndicalism was also encouraged by the role of a uniquely French labour institution, the *bourse du travail*. The *bourse* was a kind of trades council which co-ordinated the actions of all the different trade unions in a particular area and provided a focal point for the social and cultural life of the working class community. Originally intended to be a sort of labour exchange, the *bourse* supplemented its assistance in job-finding with the creation of mutual aid societies, strike funds, education courses, library facilities and many other services. A national federation of *Bourses* was soon established under the influence of anarchists and other revolutionaries and it was the merger of the national union confederation and the federation of *Bourses* that eventually led to the formation of the united CGT in 1902.

In Italy there were the similar impulses as in France. In part, the USI emerged from a split with the Socialist Party-dominated *Conferazione Generale del Lavoro* (CGL), Italy's first national union confederation, which had been set up in 1906. The CGL concentrated on obtaining piecemeal gains for northern workers to the systematic neglect of the agrarian south and was organised on the basis of a strict subordination of workers' interests to the need to win electoral support for the Socialist Party. The success of the Italian syndicalists stemmed from their willingness to take an intransigent stance against such a reformist approach, and to support workers who were unskilled in non-union industries and trades, as well as agricultural labourers.

In addition, the idea of local autonomy which came to dominate the Italian syndicalist movement developed out of the traditions of the Chambers of Labour (*Camere del Lavoro*), one of the most distinctive features of the Italian labour movement (influenced by the French *bourses*). In many towns and cities the Chambers provided a focus for the activities of the different unions, leagues and associations that existed in the locality, and because of the local character of many disputes often become more effective than official union bodies in providing solidarity and leadership. Although the syndicalists controlled many of the Chambers, Socialist Party members dominated the trade union movement, and the conflict between the two intensified. For a number of years most syndicalists felt the struggle against the reformists could best be waged inside the CGL, although the deadening impact of bureaucratism and parliamentarism meant they made virtually no headway. Finally in 1912, after six years of hesitation and vacillation, the syndicalists, by now driven out of the Socialist Party and CGL structures, made the definitive break and set up a rival confederation (USI), which was to grow rapidly in the years ahead.[48]

In Spain, the CNT was also set up (in 1910) as a result of the perceived inadequate ideology and methods of struggle of the Socialist Party-dominated union confederation, the *Unión General de Trabajadores* (UGT). The UGT for the most part shared the Socialist Party's moderation and did its best to follow peaceable methods of collective bargaining, when it was allowed to by employers. But it had only a very limited following and its influence was confined to only certain geographical areas. Ideologically three traits were to stand out in the new alternative CNT organisation: direct action, which related to the socio-economic situation; 'apoliticism', which was seen as necessary to maintain workers' unity; and federalism, which related to the oldest traditions of the workers' movement in Spain.[49] As in other countries, the CNT received widespread support for its advocacy that labour unions constituted instruments of revolution and the means for working class emancipation.

Anarchism and Other Ideological Influences

If Marxism was a convergence of German philosophy, British political economy and French socialism,[50] the traditional assumption, by contrast, that syndicalism was simply an outgrowth of anarchism would be an over-simplification although the two were certainly directly related (particularly in the less developed countries of Spain and Italy). Historically, the theory and practice of anarchism arose as a radical answer to the question of what had gone wrong in the wake of the 1789 French Revolution. Anarchists argued that the working masses, grasping the chance to end centuries of exploitation and tyranny, had been betrayed by a new class of politicians who had re-established centralised state power and utilised violence and terror to maintain themselves in power. The implication was that the institution of the state was itself the enemy. Pierre-Joseph Proudhon, the French propagandist, was the first person to call himself an 'anarchist', and was widely proclaimed the 'father of anarchism'. He took part in the subsequent 1848 French revolution and became an early disillusioned member of the National Assembly. It was largely under his influence that the famous, ill-fated alliance of European socialists, the International Working Men's Association (later known as the First International) was founded in 1864, the year before his death. There was a subsequent bitter conflict and struggle for control inside the International between Marx and the Russian anarchist Mikhail Bakunin, with the International collapsing after eight years as a result of theoretical and organisational differences, and Bakunin subsequently becoming the founder of a European-wide anarchist movement.[51]

---

[48] See D.L. Horowitz, *The Italian Labor Movement* (Cambridge, Mass, 1963).

[49] A. Durgan, 'Revolutionary Anarchism in Spain: the CNT 1911-1937, *International Socialism* 2:11 (1981), p. 93.

[50] See V.I. Lenin, 'The Three Sources and Three Component Parts of Marxism', *Selected Words, Vol. 1* (Moscow, 1970), pp. 66–7.

[51] See. J. Joll, *The Anarchists* (London, 1964); R. Kedward, *The Anarchists* (London, 1971); D. Guerin, *Anarchism: From Theory to Practice* (New York, 1971); G. Woodcock (ed.),

The two points around which this disagreement turned were whether or not there should be participation in a political struggle for state control, and whether the organisation of the International should be centralised or federal. But these points of tactics concealed deep divergences of aim and conception. Marx was convinced of the paramount necessity of waging a political battle against capitalism through independent and centrally organised workers' parties aiming ultimately at seizing and utilising state power to effect the transition to socialism. He advocated the need for a 'dictatorship of the proletariat', a transitional period between a workers' revolution and the achievement of full communism, during which time the working class would have to arm and organise itself against the threat of counter-revolution through the establishment of a workers' state. It was assumed this workers' state would endure only so long as class antagonisms persisted, before eventually 'withering away'.[52]

By contrast the anarchists were critical of the Marxist belief that the proletariat was the 'revolutionary' class. Believing class exploitation to be merely one form of oppression they highlighted the revolutionary potential of a wide variety of other social groups, including the rural peasantry and the urban underclass. They urged the oppressed and exploited masses to eschew all forms of political action, and to rely exclusively upon their own efforts. They placed their faith in spontaneous uprisings and insurrections in the course of which the state would be abolished. Crucially they insisted that the power of capitalism and the power of the state were largely synonymous and that the masses could not emancipate themselves through the use of state power. *All* governments, whether in representative parliaments or dictatorships, served only the interests of their own elite group and denied the majority of the population their liberty. This would be as true of a workers' state as any bourgeois state. Genuine revolution required the simultaneous destruction of all forms of state power and the capitalist system. It should be accompanied by a federalist system of administration, a direct democracy of autonomous communes, a society without government, in which producers' groups would assume control of all industrial production on behalf of the community.[53]

During the nineteenth century such anarchist ideas had a certain appeal to sections of the French radical petty bourgeoisie, which felt alienated from the development of large-scale capitalism and a centralised state which safeguarded the interests of the rising capitalist class. But it also proved attractive to groups of workers who were still closer in outlook to independent craftsmen than to the industrial proletariat. The existence of a decentralised artisan-based labour movement in small units of organisation encouraged anarchist-influenced hopes of a locally-based and controlled producer society. It was partly on the basis of Proudhon's teachings that new working class organisations in France developed. As we have seen, these took two forms: on the one hand, workers in individual factories formed *syndicats* and, on the other hand, in each town local unions joined together to form *bourses*. The movement spread rapidly and in 1892 the *bourses*, already functioning in many parts of France, were linked into

---

The Anarchist Reader (London, 1977); G. Woodcock; *Anarchism: A History of Libertarian Ideas and Movements* (Harmondsworth, 1979); P. Thomas, *Karl Marx and the Anarchists* (London, 1980); D. Miller, *Anarchism* (London, 1984).

52 K. Marx, *The Civil War in France* (Moscow, 1970).

53 A. Heywood, *Political Ideologies: An Introduction* (Houndmills, 2003), pp. 197–8.

a national federation. In 1895 Fernand Pelloutier, who advocated an anarchist doctrine very similar to Proudhon's, was appointed secretary general of the *Fédération des Bourses du Travail* and it was he who made the movement into a powerful force and inspired it with a particular kind of anarchist idealism. He aimed to make the *Bourses* federation the embryo of a future reorganisation of society based on workers' control of industry, in the process replacing political forms of government. Such ideas laid the foundation stone of the CGT that subsequently emerged.[54]

Such developments were encouraged by the way anarchists increasingly began to look to the trade unions as a potential base for support. In the period following the defeat of the Paris Commune, some French anarchists had adopted the tactic of 'propaganda by the deed' – acts of assassination of political leaders and terrorism of the bourgeoisie – that were intended to encourage popular insurrections. But the failure of an assassination attempt on the French President in 1894 had been followed by a fierce state-directed attempts to repress the anarchist movement, with groups broken up, newspapers suppressed and leaders imprisoned. A period of exile in London had an important effect on the thinking of Emile Pouget, editor of the most famous of the French anarchist papers published in Paris. Having become impressed with the effectiveness of British socialist initiatives in the trade unions and the 'New Unionism' movement of 1889–1890, he called on French anarchists to enter and revolutionise the *syndicats*.

Many French anarchists joined the unions and were quick to see the new possibilities for the spread of their ideas. Pouget later became assistant secretary of the CGT, the main editor of the union's paper *La Voix du peuple* and one of the leading theoreticians of the syndicalist movement. Other anarchists also took leading positions within the Confédération, including Georges Yvetot (secretary of the *Bourses* section from 1901–1918) and Paul Delesalle (*Bourses* assistant secretary from 1898–1908). It was the anarchists who led the attack on the Socialist Party and political action in the CGT, and who were largely responsible for its rejection of parties, elections and parliament in favour of direct action by the unions. They reached the peak of their influence in the years during 1902 to 1908 (although always a minority element in the organisation as a whole), and remained an important minority faction opposed to the moderate leadership of the union until 1925.

Anarchists in other countries also entered the labour movement in increasing numbers with even more success than in France. In Italy anarcho-syndicalism became a potent force after the Russian anarchist Bakunin had arrived in the country in the late 1860s and won support amongst all but two of the 300 branches of the First International.[55] Bakunin's strong following can be explained by his determined attempts to gain support among poor peasants (something that the emerging socialist movement systematically failed to do) and the peasants' willingness to rebel in an almost spontaneous fashion. But anarchist support was concentrated in the towns and countryside of the South and had relatively little following in the northern cities,

[54] See Ridley; B. Mitchell, 'French Syndicalism: An Experiment in Practical Anarchism', in van der Linden and Thorpe (eds), *Revolutionary Syndicalism*, pp. 25–43; J. Jennings, *Syndicalism in France: A Study of Ideas* (London, 1990), pp. 25–43.

[55] Horrowitz, p. 129.

which were then industrialising rapidly (and where socialists gained influence).[56] The acknowledged leader of Italian anarchism was Errico Malatesta, who became an almost legendary figure for his advocacy of revolutionary action by the trade unions to establish a 'society without authority'.[57] Such ideas quickly gained a mass following and when the USI was founded in 1912 by dissident syndicalists who had broken with the socialist CGL confederation, the anarchists agreed to join the new organisation and to seize the opportunity to build a base for the revolution. Following the victory of the anti-war faction inside the USI in 1916, the anarchist Armando Borghi took over the leadership of the *Unione* and anarchists played a leading role as organisers at the base. With its revolutionary commitment to working class unity, the USI succeeded in capturing militant working class opinion (which the socialist movement failed to channel) amongst both landless labourers in the backward agricultural regions of the south, as well as amongst some industrial workers in the northern cities.[58]

But the connection between anarchism and syndicalism was undoubtedly most complete and most successful in Spain, where for a long time the anarchists remained the most numerous and powerful in the world.[59] In 1868 an Italian disciple of Bakunin, Giuseppe Fanelli, had visited Barcelona and Madrid, where he established branches of the Bakuninist wing of the First International. By 1877 there were 60,000 members, organised mainly in working men's associations. Although the anarchist movement was driven underground in 1874, it continued to flourish amongst both factory workers in the Catalan region and landless labourers in the south who became involved in spontaneous, violent and insurrectionary general strikes and rural revolts. Anarchist ideas and methods of struggle fitted many of the traditions of Spanish workers (particularly its federal organisation that demanded regional autonomy and independence) during the key formative years of the trade union movement, in a context where the socialist movement was relatively very weak and where indigenous Marxist theory was undeveloped. As in France, Spanish anarchists recommended their supporters to join trade unions and take a forceful role in their activities and direction: 'It was in this way that the "*trabazõ*", the close connection between the labour union and the "specific anarchist" group – as the leading force of the former – came into being.'[60]

---

56 T. Behan, *The Resistible Rise of Benito Mussolini* (London, 2003), pp. 6–7.

57 See V. Richards (ed.), *Errico Malatesta: His Life and Ideas* (London, 1977).

58 See C. Levy, 'Italian Anarchism, 1870–1926', in D. Goodway (ed.), *For Anarchism: History, Theory and Practice* (London, 1989), pp. 25–78; C.L. Bertrand, 'Revolutionary Syndicalism in Italy', in van der Linden and Thorpe, *Revolutionary Syndicalism*, pp. 139–53; G. Woodcock, *Anarchism: A History of Libertarian Ideas and Movements* (Harmondsworth, 1979).

59 See Meaker; M. Bookchin, *To Remember Spain: The Anarchist and Syndicalist Revolution of 1936* (Edinburgh, 1994); S. Dolgoff (ed.), *Anarchist Collectives: Workers' Self-Management in Spain 1936–9* (Montreal, 1990); Bookchin, *The Spanish Anarchists: The Heroic Years 1868–1936* (Edinburgh, 1998); Durgan, pp. 93–112; A. Bar, 'The CNT: The Glory and Tragedy of Spanish Anarchosyndicalism', in van der Linden and Thorpe, *Revolutionary Syndicalism*, pp. 119–38; R. Alexander, *The Anarchists in the Spanish Civil War: Vols. 1 and 2* (London, 1999).

60 Bar, p. 124.

The CNT's establishment in 1911 combined *syndicalist* principles of revolutionary unionism with the more traditional Spanish *anarchist* principles, of federalism, anti-clericalism, anti-militarism and a deep hostility to all political parties and governments. The result was *anarcho*-syndicalism, and with the formation of the Iberian Anarchist Federation (FAI) in 1927 – which during the Civil War claimed a membership of 30,000 organised into federated affinity groups – anarchists began to exercise hegemony over the union. As David Miller has commented: 'We can see in Spain the unique spectacle of a mass trade union movement being led along the revolutionary path by a minority of conscious anarchists – the original anarcho-syndicalist strategy came to fruition.'[61] The CNT became the only mass syndicalist organisation to survive the First World War and Russian Revolution, and with the fall of the monarchy and advent of the Second Republic in 1931 the more radical anarchist militants from the FAI saw their influence grew rapidly amidst a series of libertarian-communist insurrections against the regime which they inspired. By 1933 the anarcho-syndicalists effectively controlled the CNT and were subsequently to be put to a decisive test during the Civil War. In 1936 they were mainly responsible for the defeat of Franco's military offensive in Barcelona and Valencia, as well as in country areas of Catalonia and Aragon; and for many early months of the Civil War they were in virtual control of eastern Spain, where they regarded the crisis as an opportunity to carry through a social revolution. Factories and railways in Catalonia were taken over by workers' committees and in hundreds of villages in Catalonia, Levante and Andalucia the peasants seized the land and established libertarian communes.

The widely favoured explanation for the success of a distinctive *anarcho*-syndicalist movement in Spain and Italy (and to a lesser extent France) – a logical consequence of the countries' social and economic backwardness – is only accurate in very broad terms given that there were considerable regional variations within each of these countries. For example, with reference to Spain, the CNT gained a mass base both in rural Andalucia with its underclass of landless day labourers working on huge estates, as well as in the more industrially advanced Catalonia with its workforce concentrated in small textile factories. However, as Dick Geary has argued, rural anarchism was not simply the preserve of unskilled labour on the large estates, but was also given support by some small producers and skilled workers in the Cadiz area. By contrast, the CNT did not prove attractive amidst the small-scale industrial production in the Basque province of Guipúzcoa, despite its similar nature to that in Catalonia.[62]

This makes it necessary to look at a number of additional contributory factors within Spanish society, which are often ignored. Paul Heywood has suggested the following: the role of the Spanish federalist state; the brutality of employers and the harshness of labour; the survival of artisanal, familial, concerns; frustration at the failure of democratic reforms; the respective organisational strength of anarchist and socialist movements; and the poverty of indigenous Marxist theory to the development of Spanish socialism generally.[63] Similar specific considerations would need to be involved in any

[61] Miller, p. 137.

[62] Geary, *European Labour Politics*, pp. 22–3.

[63] Heywood, pp. 231–9.

attempt to explore the powerful influence of the anarchist element within the syndicalist movements in other less developed countries such as Italy and France.

By contrast, the anarchist influence was effectively absent in the equally less developed Ireland, and it played a negligible role in the much more economically advanced Britain with its more firmly established and politically conservative labour movement organisations.[64] In America, anarchists succeeded in establishing an important base amongst immigrants in Chicago in the late nineteenth century and contributed to the building of a Central Labour Union which won the support of most of organised labour in the city in a campaign for the eight-hour day. However, after a bomb was thrown at a protest meeting killing seven police officers, fierce repression reduced anarchist influence to the margins. A few dynamic personalities, like the Russian immigrants Emma Goldman and Alexander Berkman, kept anarchist doctrine in the public eye, but after 1905 those anarchists interested in labour organisation tended to join the IWW, including the Italian immigrant Carlo Tresca.

But if the development of revolutionary syndicalism was directly related to anarchist ideas and organisation, it was far from simply being an anarchist invention and it is important not to conflate the one into the other. With reference to France, Yvetot claimed:

> I am reproached with confusing syndicalism and anarchism. It is not my fault if anarchism and syndicalism have the same ends in view. The former pursues the integral emancipation of the individual, the latter the integral emancipation of the working man. I find the whole of syndicalism in anarchism. When we leave the theories of syndicalism to study its methods, we find them identical with those of the anarchists.[65]

Yet anarchists generally were internally split in the extent of their enthusiasm for syndicalist methods. Thus, syndicalism received extensive and lively attention at the 1907 International Anarchist Congress held in Amsterdam, where the young French CGT militant Pierre Monatte took the lead in defending its principles, whilst the Italian anarchist and veteran insurrectionist Errico Malatesta challenged them for not being sufficiently 'revolutionary'.[66] Moreover, the core of syndicalist philosophy was not explicitly anarchist in character despite the fact that anarchists were influential in a number of countries. It is true, as we have seen, that syndicalism revealed a certain affinity with the ideas of anarchism, notably its hostility to political organisation and activity and its principles of federalism and decentralisation. But the connections should not be exaggerated. Proudhon had not been an advocate of class warfare, or indeed a committed supporter of the working class; he had even gone so far as to oppose trade unions. Unlike the classical anarchists, who sought a social basis for the revolutionary movement amongst the peasants, lumpen-proletariat and petty-bourgeois elements, syndicalists looked to mass *working class* collective action at the point of production in the workplace to change society. Syndicalists saw it necessary to transform the trade unions into revolutionary instruments of the proletariat in

---

64 In Britain the one notable leading anarcho-syndicalist figure was Guy Bowman. See A. Meltzer, *First Flight: The Origins of Anarcho-Syndicalism in Britain* (Berkeley, Calif., 2004).

65 Cited in R. Hunter, *Violence and the Labor Movement* (New York, 1914), p. 247.

66 Woodcock, *Anarchism*, pp. 220–25.

its struggle against the bourgeoisie, in the process making the *unions*, rather than communes, the basic units of a future socialist order.

In Italy the anarchists were much less trade union orientated than the syndicalists. They placed the emphasis on the need to prevent the formation of a labour elite, on promoting political strikes (rather than economic ones), and advocating revolutionary insurrectionism. By contrast, the syndicalists wanted a more explicit trade union organisation to enact the social revolution, and believed a viable new social order could only be built through a long, gradual process of industrial development and proletarian maturation, until a spontaneous general strike overthrew the Italian regime.[67]

The influence of the anarchists was also limited and by no means uniform. For example, not all the syndicalist leaders of the CGT in France were anarchists. In the pre-war phase some still favoured a form of trade unionism that concentrated on collective bargaining for immediate gains, whilst others such as Victor Griffuelhes (the CGT's secretary general during 1901–1909) merely believed in direct action for its own sake irrespective of social theories. And after the war there were deep tensions within the revolutionary wing of the by now moderate-led CGT, between 'pure' syndicalists and anarcho-syndicalists.

In Spain, there was also a permanent tension between distinct revolutionary syndicalist and anarcho-syndicalist groups. From the foundation of the CNT's parent organisation, *Solidaridad Obrera,* in 1907 until 1917, there was the adoption of a purportedly self-sufficient revolutionary syndicalist position. But amidst economic and political crisis, the revolutionary wave of struggles in Europe, the impact of the Russian Revolution, and massive industrial unrest at home, the anarcho-syndicalist element successfully took control of the union. After the CNT had been banned in 1924, the union leadership then fell into the hands of more moderate syndicalists. However, following the formation of the Iberian Anarchist Federation (FAI) in 1927, the anarchists were to come back to the fore with the advent of the Second Republic in 1931 and the renewed class struggle that ensued. There then occurred a split between the syndicalists, some of whom were expelled or left the CNT to form Oppositionist Unions and the Liberation Syndicalist Federation in 1932–1933, and the more radical anarcho-syndicalists groups belonging to the FAI who controlled the official CNT apparatus. Finally all the groups re-united with the onset of the Civil War in May 1936, primarily under anarchist influence.

The same sort of division between anarchists and syndicalists was true in Italy: 'even when the USI was dominated by anarchists after 1916, it never became an anarcho-syndicalist organisation'.[68] In America, although anarchist ideas influenced some leading figures, the Wobblies contained too many 'political socialist' elements to be truly 'libertarian', and its central idea of the 'One Big Union' was fundamentally opposed to the anarchists' passionately held ideas of localism and decentralisation.

In reality syndicalism was always an alliance between at least three core ideological elements. First, there was *anarchism*, from which it took anti-state,

---

[67] D.D. Roberts, *The Syndicalist Tradition and Italian Fascism* (Manchester, 1979), p. 74; Bertrand, 'Revolutionary Syndicalism in Italy', p. 145.

[68] C. Levy, 'Currents of Italian Syndicalism Before 1926', *International Review of Social History*, 45 (2000), p. 243.

anti-political action and anti-militarist ideas, as well as the notions of federalism, decentralisation, direct action and sabotage. Second, *Marxism* also influenced it significantly. For example, it is clear that a number of the leading American IWW figures were familiar with and sympathetic to Marxist theory and were themselves members of socialist parties that espoused such ideas. This included Daniel De Leon (Socialist Labor Party), Eugene Debs and Bill Haywood (Socialist Party). Even the 'direct-actionists' Vincent St. John, William Trautmann and Father Thomas Haggerty agreed with Marxist economic theory.[69] In Ireland, this was also true of Jim Larkin and James Connolly, both of whom were involved with various labour and socialist parties, as were many of the syndicalist-influenced British wartime shop stewards' movement leaders. Similarly, the French CGT and the Italian USI were set up through the active participation of revolutionary socialists alongside radical trade unionists.[70]

Thus, in every country a number of syndicalist movement leaders inherited some central components of the Marxist tradition, in however a diffuse form. Apart from its view of the state as an instrument of capitalist rule, this included the Marxist conception of the necessity and desirability of class struggle (of which strikes were the primary expression) as a means of collective resistance to capitalism that could develop the confidence, organisation and class consciousness of workers; the utter primacy of the working class as the sole agency of revolution that could liberate the whole of society; and a conception of socialism arising from the need for workers to take power *themselves* rather than relying on the enlightened actions of parliamentary and trade union leaders who would reform capitalism *on behalf of* workers. Many of the movement's leaders also accepted the economic and materialist analysis of capitalist society provided by Marxism, including its theories of the exploitation of labour based on the extraction of surplus value and of recurrent economic crisis.

Third, syndicalism was influenced by the ideas of *revolutionary trade unionism*, the notion that the unions should go beyond merely attempting to improve workers' terms and conditions of employment within the framework of capitalist society, to become the instrument through which workers could overthrow capitalism and establish a new society. For example, there was the heritage left behind by the Knights of Labor, the first important national labour organisation to appear in industrial America, whose membership in 1886 had grown to over 700,000. The Knights had committed themselves to a form of revolutionary trade unionism which placed little, if any, emphasis on collective bargaining and had been the first union to attempt to build on industrial lines.[71] And it was Daniel De Leon, leader of the Socialist Labor Party, who effectively formulated the theory of industrial unionism (leading to the overthrow of the capitalist state and its substitution by an industrial administration based on industrial unions) that the IWW embraced.

---

[69] J.P. Cannon, *The IWW: The Great Anticipation* (New York, 1956), p. 14; Foner, *IWW*, p. 129; Dubofsky, p. 79.

[70] B. Moss, 'Socialism and the Republic in France', *Socialist History*, 18 (2000) pp. 146–7; Levy, 'Currents of Italian Syndicalism', p. 213.

[71] P.F. Brissendon, *The IWW: The Study of American Syndicalism* (New York, 1919), pp. 30–33; P. Renshaw, *The Wobblies: The Story of Syndicalism in the United States* (London, 1967), pp. 34–6.

In Britain, there was the heritage left by the Grand National Consolidated Trades' Union of the 1830s that aimed to build a massive single union that would represent the whole working class. The utopian socialist Robert Owen promoted the body as the vehicle for the concerted and simultaneous 'Grand National Holiday' (general strike) that would force the capitalists to voluntary abdicate their position as owners and directors of the means of production and usher in a new socialist society. And there was the heritage of the Chartist movement whose extra-parliamentary agitation for universal manhood suffrage briefly fused with militant trade unionism in an unsuccessful attempted general strike in 1842.[72] Similarly, in other countries, there was a long tradition of struggle to establish independent trade unionism which, combined with familiarity with the international use of the general strike, helped to encourage revolutionary trade union aspirations.

In other words, syndicalism represented a synthesis of these three different ideological influences, all overlaid with a singular pattern in each respective country. Moreover, we should note some additional distinct *national* ideological influences on each of the different syndicalist movements. For example there was a rich revolutionary tradition within the French labour movement which exhibited a variety of ideological trends of a revolutionary kind apart from syndicalism, namely Proudhonism, Bakuninism, Blanquisim, Marxism and Allemanism. All of these were reflected in some way amongst the elements that went on to form the CGT.[73] In Ireland, 'Larkinism', as the employers dubbed Jim Larkin's ITGWU, involved a combination of very diverse elements, namely syndicalism, industrial unionism, labourism, socialism, Irish nationalism and Catholicism, 'with the principle of working class solidarity the core around which everything evolved'.[74] Italian syndicalism thrived in a broader libertarian-tinged 'second culture', a 'bundle of cultural practices and organisational activities associated with localism, anti-statism, anti-clericalism, republicanism and *operaismo* (workerism)'.[75] In fact, one of the reasons why anarchism was able to prosper in countries with strong religious traditions, such as Catholic Italy and Spain, was that it helped to articulate already existing anti-clerical sentiments, with the tendency for agrarian radicalism to be directed against the landowners and their protectors, the monarchy and, in particular, the Catholic Church.[76]

So there were a number of ideological influences rooted in national conditions that had their impact on the different syndicalist movements apart from the core elements of anarchism, Marxism and trade unionism. Significantly, most of these ideological influences had a common origin; they belonged to the same family. As David Goodway has pointed out in relation to anarchism and Marxism, such revolutionary ideas were not born purely and simply in the brains of human beings.

---

72 See R.G. Gammage, *The History of the Chartist Movement 1837–1854* (London: Merlin Press, 1969); M. Jenkins, *The General Strike of 1842* (London: Lawrence and Wishart, 1980); J. Charlton, *The Chartists: The First National Workers' Movement* (London: Pluto Press, 1997).

73 See Ridley, pp. 25–52.

74 J. Newsinger, 'Jim Larkin, Syndicalism and the 1913 Dublin Lockout', *International Socialism*, 2:25 (1984), p. 13.

75 Levy, 'Currents of Italian Syndicalism', p. 228.

76 G. Lichtheim, *A Short History of Socialism* (Glasgow), p. 223.

On the contrary, they reflected the experience gained by the working class movement through class struggle. They 'drank from the same proletarian spring' and under the pressure of the newly-born working class they assigned themselves the same final aim, the revolutionary overthrow of society and the entrustment of society's wealth into the hands of the workers themselves.[77] Indeed, the widespread receptivity of syndicalism was rooted in the way it related to broader material factors and their reflection in working class struggle and consciousness. In other words, ideological influences were not the only impetus behind the syndicalist movement as a whole. Undoubtedly, ideology helped to give the movement coherence and the various ideas on strikes, sabotage, the nature of the state, the revolutionary role of unions, and workers' control helped to provide the language. But it was the actual struggles workers engaged in within the context of an attack on their material conditions, which provided the fertile soil and the popular base for these revolutionary ideas to gain a mass hearing.

Level of Workers' Struggle and Political Radicalisation

The upsurge in workers' militancy and the growing political radicalisation that occurred generally during the early years of the twentieth century is another factor that needs to be taken into account. During 1910–1920 there was an extraordinary international upsurge in strike action, with the First World War interrupting the pattern, but only to delay and to reinforce it, and the inspiration of the Russian Revolution acting as a further stimulus. In his study of long-term strike patterns, Ernesto Screpanti sees in this period a seismic upheaval comparable only to the great international strike waves of the period 1869–1875 and 1968–1974.[78] Whilst such strike activity was usually caused by demands for wage increases, shorter hours and union recognition, it increasingly became more political, with demands for workers' control and a changed social order common immediately after the war. New groups of activists began to organise along different lines to those of the established socialist parties (with their parliamentary reformist orientation) and union leaders (with their fixation on negotiating compromise deals with the employers). The question as to what extent this widespread radicalism was directly influenced by the ideas and practical activities of syndicalists themselves is explored in the next section of this chapter. But there is no doubt the industrial and political unrest directly contributed to the emergence, as well as to the subsequent growth, of the international syndicalist movement.

The chronology and rhythm of this international strike wave obviously varied from country to country,[79] but its flavour can be illustrated by looking briefly at each in turn. In Britain between the years 1910–1914 there was a huge upturn in workers'

---

[77] Goodway, p. 119.

[78] See E. Screpanti, 'Long Cycles and Recurring Proletarian Insurgencies', *Review*, 7:2 (1984), pp. 509–48; 'Long Cycles in Strike Activity: An Empirical Investigation', *British Journal of Industrial Relations*, 25:1 (1987), p. 107.

[79] For one general assessment of such variations see C. Tilly, 'Introduction', in L.H. Haimson and C. Tilly (eds), *Strikes, Wars and Revolutions in an International Perspective* (Cambridge, 1989), p. 435.

militancy (known as the 'Labour Unrest'), centred on national strikes by dockers, seamen, and railway workers in 1911, and miners in 1912, but spilling over into many other industries and often involving unskilled, non-unionised workers. In turn, this unprecedented period of industrial unrest led directly to a massive expansion of trade union membership. In 1910 total trade union membership stood at about 2.5 million: by 1914 it was over 4 million. There were frequent outbursts of strike violence, often associated with the interventions of police and troops, with some deaths and many injuries. The most serious challenge to capitalist authority occurred during the 1911 Liverpool transport strike led by Tom Mann, when mass pickets were mounted and a strike committee began to act as an alternative organ of class power through its control over the city's transport system, with the issuing of permits for the movement of essential supplies of milk and bread. Even though the chief causes of the strikes were the rise in the cost of living and the failure of wages to keep pace with prices, many of the strikes had struggles for union recognition at or near the centre, and a considerable number were rank-and-file revolts against agreements signed by national union officials with the employers. Although the First World War saw a lull in strike activity, there was the emergence of the powerful engineering Shop Stewards' and Workers' Committee Movement, and immediately after the war there was a renewed explosion of workers' industrial and political militancy during which demands for nationalisation and workers' control were widely made.

In Ireland, a rising level of industrial struggle, intimately tied to the unrest in Britain, culminated in the 1913 five-month Dublin strike and lockout. Remarkably, despite defeat and subsequent union decline (with the failure of the subsequent 1916 Irish republican Easter Rising and execution of James Connolly by a British firing squad), the ITGWU experienced a dramatic reversal of its fortunes between 1917–1923, amidst a huge wages strike movement in which sympathetic action became widespread. The largest protest occurred in January 1919 when 30,000 Belfast engineering and shipbuilding workers struck unofficially over working hours, with the unrest spreading to other industries. Control of power supplies gave the joint strike committee some authority and (following the establishment of a permit system enforced by pickets) journalists referred to the 'Belfast Soviet'. Also during this period the general strike at a local level emerged as unique trait of the struggle, for example, in Dungarvan in 1919 paralysing local commerce and transferring the control of trade to the ITGWU. The main battle came in 1920 when the British government attempted to remove price restrictions on bacon and butter, leading to workplace seizures, including the occupation of 13 Limerick creameries.[80] Trade unionism exploded from under 100,000 in 1916 to reach 225,000 by 1920.[81]

Between 1909 and 1922 there were some of the most celebrated and bitter labour struggles of American labour history in industries such as mining, steel, textiles, railways, forestry and agriculture.[82] Such militancy, unlike most other countries, continued during the war, with more than one million workers involved in strike action in every year between 1916 and 1922. Between September 1917 and April

---

80 O'Connor, pp. 29–53.

81 E. O'Connor, *A Labour History of Ireland, 1824–1960*, (Dublin, 1992), p. 94.

82 See P.K. Edwardes, *Strikes in the United States, 1881–1974* (Oxford, 1981).

1918 there were five city-wide strikes, and in 1919 more than 4 million workers participated in the greatest number of strikes ever in a single year, an incredible 20 per cent of the labour force. The membership of the trade unions doubled between 1915 and 1920, rising to some 5 million workers, often involving unskilled and immigrant labour whom AFL leaders had considered unorganisable.[83] However, it was not simply the size of the movement that caught the imagination of labour activists, but also its industrial and social breadth. The main causes of the labour militancy were the high cost of living, poor working conditions and lack of union organisation, with many workers after the war inspired by new currents of radical thought which considered labour unions less a bargaining agent within the prevailing capitalist system than a primary instrument for fundamental change.

In France many workers greeted the socialist Millerand's accession to the ministry of commerce in June 1899 with an enormous groundswell of support, viewing his arrival in office as a signal that the government would take steps to 'republicanise' the workplace. During 1898–1900 workers launched the biggest wave of strikes than ever before.[84] During 1906–1910 there was another country-wide strike wave after rapid disillusionment with 'Millerandism' set in. In 1906 there was a 24-hour May Day strike over the eight-hour day, involving over 150,000 workers in open confrontation with the state as the government sent troops into the strike-hit areas and arrested CGT leaders.[85] In the months that followed there were city-wide strikes in Dunkirk, Mazamet, Voiron, Le Havre, and twice in Marseilles, as well as major strikes in the postal and telegraph industry in 1909 and on the railways in 1910.[86] Although many strikes arose from wage disputes, the length of the working day assumed a new importance with the introduction of more rigorous controls over labour in the factory and an increase in the pace of work.[87]

The post-war years witnessed an unprecedented wave of militancy, with strike levels in 1919–20 surpassing the previous high points of 1906 and 1910. The most important included the Parisian metalworkers' strike of May–June 1919, followed by two national railway workers' strikes in February and May 1920 (both led by the CGT).[88] Total trade union membership rose from half a million in 1900 to a new peak of nearly 2 million by mid-1920.[89] As elsewhere what was important was not just the sheer level of strike action, but their prevailing mood. Certainly, the strikes of 1919–1920 went beyond the defence of jobs and purchasing power,

---

83 D. Montgomery, 'New Tendencies in Union Struggles and Strategies in Europe and the United States, 1916–1922', in J.E. Cronin and C. Sirianni (eds), *Work, Community and Power: The Exercise of Labor in Europe and America, 1900–1925* (Philadelphia, 1983), p. 89.

84 B. Vandervort, *Victor Griffuelhes and French Syndicalism, 1895–1922* (Baton Rouge, 1996), pp. 34–5.

85 R. Magraw, 'Socialism, Syndicalism and French Labour', p. 90.

86 P.N. Stearns, *Revolutionary Syndicalism and French Labor: A Cause Without Rebels* (New Brunswick, 1971), p. 30.

87 D. Geary, *European Labour Protest, 1848–1939* (London, 1981), p. 105.

88 See R. Magraw, 'Paris 1917–20: Labour Protest and Popular Politics', and J. Horne, 'The State and the Challenge of Labour in France, 1917–20', in C. Wrigley (ed.), *Challenges of Labour: Central and Western Europe, 1917–1920* (London, 1993), pp. 125–48 and pp. 239–61.

89 Magraw, *History of the French Working Class*, p. 247.

towards revolutionary aspirations of workers' control of industry, a sentiment that was considerably encouraged by the impact of the Bolshevik Revolution.

Finally, in Italy and Spain, apart from comparable high levels of industrial unrest there were also semi-insurrectionary movements. In Italy in 1914 there was a 'Red Week' of violent bloody clashes between workers and the police in Ancona, with a general strike in which one million workers participated in a popular uprising which paralysed almost all the major cities in Italy for at least two days, with the USI centrally involved. Italy's entry into the world war in May 1915 provoked a two-day general strike with prolonged and bloody clashes with the police, and in August 1917 the failure of bread supplies, general discontent over the war, and the inspiration of the February Russian Revolution sparked off a general strike and spontaneous insurrection in Turin. The four day uprising, in which anarchists and syndicalists organised defence of the barricaded working class quarters, was only crushed with machine guns and tanks. Nonetheless, continued economic strain from the war and the success of the October Russian Revolution only intensified the powerful movement of unrest during the years 1919–1920. In what became known as the *Bienno Rosso* ('Two Red Years'), a massive country-wide wave of strikes and land seizures culminated in a revolutionary movement of factory occupations in 1920. Based in the industrial heartlands of Milan and Turn, the revolt spread across the country and involved one million workers, many of them organised into workers' councils similar to the soviets in Bolshevik Russia. Again, the USI played an important role in events.[90]

In Spain there were also semi-insurrectionary protests. In 1902 4,000 landless labourers seized the town of Jerez in Andalusia and in 1909 there was a general strike of industrial and agricultural workers in Barcelona, with an uprising and week-long bout of violence against the Catholic Church. In 1916 and 1917 the CNT joined with the socialist-led UGT union to call two general strikes, the first over price rises and the second with the object of bringing about a fundamental change in regime in the Catalan region. Both protests spread over large parts of Spain. In southern Spain, with their vast estates employing day labourers, the years 1918–1920 were known as the *Trieno Bolchevista* ('The Bolshevik Three Years'). There was a rising wave of strikes and confrontations encouraged by news that the Russian Bolsheviks were dividing estates up among the poorer peasants, with 'Bolshevik-type republics' proclaimed in some towns. During a week-long strike in Valencia workers renamed various streets 'Lenin', 'Soviets' and 'October Revolution', and widespread bread riots in Madrid led to the looting of 200 shops. In 1919 workers occupied the La Canadiense plant, which supplied most of Barcelona's power, paralysing public transport and plunging the city into darkness. Some 70 per cent of the city's textile

90 See P. Spriano, *The Occupation of the Factories: Italy 1920* (London, 1975); G.A. Williams, *Proletarian Order: Antonio Gramsci, Factory Councils and the Origins of Italian Communism in Italy, 1911–1921* (London, 1975); M. Clark, *Antonio Gramsci and the Revolution That Failed* (New Haven, 1977); L. Bordogna, G.P. Cella and G. Provasi, 'Labor Conflicts in Italy Before the Rise of Fascism, 1881–1923: A Quantitative Analysis', in Haimson and Tilly, pp. 217–46.

plants went on strike, as did the gas and water workers, while the printers' union exercised a 'red censorship'.

An employers' counter-offensive in the early 1920s and military coup in 1923 saw a sharp decline in struggle in Spain. But with the advent of the Second Republic in 1931 there was a renewed explosion of class struggle and libertarian-communist insurrections against the regime. In 1934 there was a miners' strike supported by other workers in the northern province of Asturias, in which workers took over the region and mobilised 15,000 'armed' workers. With the election of a Popular Front government in February 1936, there was a massive strike wave accompanied by widespread land occupations leading to a near revolutionary situation in the southern countryside. And following Franco's coup in July 1936, real power in the Republican areas lay in the hands of workers, scattered in a thousand towns and villages among different revolutionary committees in which the CGT often played a crucial role.[91]

Of course, it is true this international explosion of industrial and political militancy was fashioned by a variety of material and social factors which, even if in part associated with syndicalism, did not necessarily signify mass support for the ideology of syndicalism. Nonetheless, according to Marcel van der Linden and Wayne Thorpe whilst 'the spread of syndicalist attitudes and organisations was by no means identical with this upsurge of workers' militancy, which took many forms of expression … it is inexplicable apart from it and is certainly one of its most distinctive manifestations'.[92] At the very least the upsurge in strike action appears to have been of significance in two respects.

First, it provided the radicalising context which (along with other economic, social and political factors) encouraged the *emergence* of the syndicalist movement. American developments can serve to illustrate the process by which this occurred internationally. Thus, in 1913 the labour economist and historian Louis Levine explained the origins of syndicalism as 'born of conditions of life in America'.[93] By this he meant the bitter industrial conflicts of the early years of the century had a profound influence in moulding a section of American workers' attitudes toward employers, society and the state. Even though early IWW members read revolutionary literature, it was primarily their experiences of bloody industrial warfare (often associated with the interventions of government, police and troops on behalf of the employers) that politically radicalised them and encouraged their belief in solidarity, industrial unionism and syndicalism. Out of these violent conflicts, a sizeable layer of workers (particularly from the West) turned violently against the existing social order and found both an explanation and a remedy for their predicament in syndicalist theory, organisation and activity.[94] A similar process occurred in other countries.

Second, the wave of industrial and political struggles subsequently enhanced the *appeal* of syndicalism in each country, providing the mass force to sustain and extend the movement. For example, as Joseph White has commented, if the 'Labour Unrest'

---

91 See F. Morrow, *Revolution and Counter-Revolution in Spain* (New York, 1974).

92 van der Linden and Thorpe, 'The Rise and Fall', p. 7.

93 L. Levine, 'The Development of Syndicalism in America', *Political Science Quarterly*, 28 (September 1913), pp. 451–79.

94 Dubofsky, p. 36; 73–4; 147; 204.

in Britain between 1910–1914, owed more to material conditions than to the spread of syndicalist theories, 'the size and scope of the unrest gave syndicalism a prominence and notoriety that it almost surely would not otherwise have possessed while at the same time providing a context for syndicalist ideas to be broadcast and syndicalists to assume the leadership of major strikes'.[95] In the process, the power of example was important. The success of the strikes clearly led to greater confidence in collective and militant action among previously acquiescent workers. One hostile observer at the time put it: 'The masses of workers in Great Britain are not socialists nor are they syndicalists. But they are being converted to the methods of socialism and syndicalism by the proof that in following those methods they are able to win great concessions'.[96]

Moreover, Europe witnessed a series of general strikes – in Belgium (1893; 1902), Sweden (1902; 1909), Holland (1903), Russia (1905), France (1906), Italy (1904, 1914, 1915, 1920), Spain (1909, 1911, 1916) and Ireland (1918, 1920), as well as numerous city-wide strikes including Liverpool (1911), Dublin (1913–1914), Turin (1917) and Barcelona (1917, 1919) – which helped to fuel the debate on the mass strike inside the labour movement and lend credence to the syndicalist preference for the general strike over parliamentary politics. Syndicalism was not the only beneficiary of workers' radicalism during this period and certainty from 1919 onwards the rise of Bolshevism was ultimately to be a major contributory factor undermining syndicalism's appeal. Nonetheless, such radicalism, particularly during the pre-war years, helped lay the foundations for an international syndicalist movement.

Conscious and Organised Syndicalist Intervention

An additional contributory factor to the rise of an international syndicalist movement was the role of ideological and organisational intervention by syndicalists themselves. E.P. Thompson has remarked: 'Nothing in history happens spontaneously, nothing worthwhile is achieved without expense of intellect and spirit.'[97] But this inevitably raises the important, and yet remarkably hitherto much neglected, question as to what extent syndicalist ideas and activity contributed to the labour militancy and political radicalisation that swept the world during this period?

Syndicalists were often accused of being the direct instigators of strikes and other forms of industrial strife. For example, in Britain Lord Robert Cecil in a speech in Parliament in March 1912 laid the blame for the 'Labour Unrest' entirely on the activities of syndicalist 'agitators'[98] and the government's own leading industrial conciliator, Lord Askwith, stated the employment of active propaganda, notably by syndicalists, appeared to be the most important source of conflict between the

---

95 J. White, 'Syndicalism in a Mature Industrial Setting: The Case of Britain', in van der Linden and Thorpe, *Revolutionary Syndicalism*, p. 104.

96 Cited in G. Brown, 'Introduction', in *The Industrial Syndicalist* (Nottingham, Spokesman Books, 1974), p. 29.

97 E.P. Thompson, 'Homage to Tom Maguire', in A. Briggs and J. Saville (eds) *Essays in Labour History 1886–1923* (London, 1967), p. 314.

98 Cited in Brown, p. 22.

classes.[99] In a long article entitled 'Syndicalism in England: Its Origin and History', *The Times* newspaper stated with considerable confidence: 'The existence of a strong Syndicalist movement in this country can no longer be denied, though attempts have been made up till quite recently to deny it', and put forward the claim that the successful transport workers' strikes in the summer of 1911 had been organised 'under syndicalist influence'.[100] Even historians like Elie Halévy argued that the pre-war strike wave in Britain was primarily a 'Syndicalist Revolt'.[101] In America, so feared were the IWW that newspaper and magazine readers were treated to an unending stream of literature about the 'Wobbly menace' on the shopfloor fomenting strikes. Likewise in pre-war France employers attributed the rise in strikes to the influence of the militant leaders of the CGT who they accused of planning strategy on a national scale, organising conflicts and inciting workers to revolt.[102]

In fact as we have seen, the emergence and subsequent growth of syndicalist organisation was itself a *response* to the growing labour unrest and political radicalisation that occurred, rather than being its *cause*. Invariably workers' militancy derived from factors directly related to economic grievances, work intensification, erosion of job control, and either lack of union recognition or the constraints of existing union organisation, as well as certain contingent circumstances that gave workers the self-confidence to take collective action in the belief that their demands were realisable. Faced with such material grievances and perceived opportunities for redress, it seems possible there would have been an upsurge in strike activity with or without the presence of syndicalists (or any other left-wing political influence). For example, reporting on the relationship between the IWW and strike activity, President Wilson's Labor Commission found that:

> The IWW had exercised its strongest hold in those industries and those communities where employers have most resisted the trade union movement, and where some form of protest against unjust treatment was inevitable ... Sinister influences and extremist doctrines may have availed themselves of these conditions; they certainly have not created them.[103]

In other words, syndicalist agitation would have been unlikely to fall on receptive ears unless there were genuine grievances and justifiable demands to agitate about. To wholly attribute the industrial and political militancy of the period to agitators, syndicalist or otherwise, would be to exaggerate their influence.

Nonetheless, as Robert Magraw has argued with reference to the relationship between French syndicalism and the labour movement, 'a reductionism which explains all workers protest as a pragmatic response to work experience and technological change is unconvincing ... politics and ideology also play a role'.[104] Indeed, there is evidence to suggest that workers' readiness to engage in militant

---

99 G.R. Askwith, *Industrial Problems and Disputes* (London, 1974), p. 294.

100 *The Times*, 16 April 1912.

101 E. Halévy, *A History of the English People, Vol. 2: 1905–1914* (London, 1961), p. 433.

102 P. Gonnot, *La grève dans l'industrie privée* (Paris, 1912), p. 190.

103 Cited in P.S. Foner, *History of the Labor Movement in the United States: Vol 7: Labour and World War 1: 1914–1918* (New York, 1987), p. 293.

104 Magraw, 'Socialism, Syndicalism and French Labour, p. 70.

strike action in France, as in other countries, also often critically depended upon the *subjective* element – the encouragement they received from the minority of organised activists within their own ranks. It was precisely this role that syndicalist activists and leaders (along with other union militants and radical left-wing currents) assumed; in the process stimulating awareness of grievances, spreading a belief in the desirability and feasibility of militant strike action, and convincing individuals to commit resources to the building of revolutionary union movements dedicated to the overthrow of capitalism.[105] Thus, while the 'agitator theory' often propounded at the time fell into the trap of grossly overstating the role of syndicalist activists in strikes, some historians have subsequently effectively fallen into the opposite trap, of ignoring or at least minimising their significance.

Significantly, in every country syndicalist newspapers – such as the IWW's *Industrial Worker*, the USI's *L'Internazionale*, the CGT's *Solidaridad Obrera* and the ISEL's *Industrial Syndicalist* – served as important strike propaganda outlets and organisers. As one historian has commented on the ITGWU's *Irish Worker*:

> Week after week the sordid tales of mischief, misery, jobbery, and injustice poured forth in a plaintive and never-ending painful dirge. Week after week … Larkin attacked with a monumental perseverance the sweating, exploitative employers and the corrupt, cynical politicians, who in his eyes were responsible for the reprehensible social condition of Dublin. He gave no quarter and expected none as he vilified any and all, high or low, who had the misfortune to come under the notice of his pen.[106]

Syndicalist pamphlets – like *Sabotage* produced by the CGT and *The General Strike* produced by the IWW[107] – played a similar propaganda role, identifying capitalism as the enemy, denouncing the employers, providing analysis of state policy and the limitations of official labour leaders and advocating uncompromising militant strike action and revolutionary unionism as the most appropriate response. In addition, syndicalists distributed leaflets, organised meetings and actively intervened in workers' strikes at every opportunity. The central objective of such propagandist, agitational and organisational effort was to foment strike activity and revolutionary workers' struggle. Jim Larkin commented: 'I have got a divine mission – to make men and women discontented'.[108] Thus, when serious industrial unrest smouldered syndicalist activists were often to be found encouraging workers to see their grievances as a part of a wider class struggle against the capitalist system.

Syndicalists were by no means always present during all or even most strikes or insurgent phases of the unrest that swept different countries. But there is no doubt they *were* prominent in a sizeable number of strikes, both local and nation-wide,

---

[105] G. Friedman, *State-Making and Labour Movements: France and the United States, 1876–1914* (New York, 1998), p. 260.

[106] Larkin, *James Larkin*, p. 69.

[107] *The Miners' Next Step,* Unofficial Reform Committee (Tonypandy, 1912 [reprinted London, 1973]); E. Pouget, *Le Sabotage* (Paris, 1910); W.D. Haywood, *The General Strike* (Chicago, n.d.).

[108] Cited in G. Dangerfield, *The Strange Death of Liberal England 1910–1914* (London, 1997), p. 255.

including some of the largest confrontations and general strikes, and in the process were able, at least on occasion, to display considerably influence within them. Even in Britain, where syndicalism was not a particularly deeply-rooted mass movement, their influence was significant. For example, in the pre-war South Wales mining industry, syndicalist activists such as Noah Ablett, Noah Rees, W.H. Mainwaring and W.F. Hay, played an important leadership role in transforming an unofficial Cambrian Combine dispute over local wage payments in 1910–1911 into a national campaign for a minimum wage, which culminated in the first ever national strike in 1912. This was associated with the establishment of the syndicalist-influenced Unofficial Reform Committee which successfully campaigned for the transformation of the policy, structure and ideological orientation of the miners' union, and advanced the cause for workers' control independent of state intervention. It resulted in the writing and publication of the influential pamphlet *The Miners' Next Step* which sold many tens of thousands of copies.[109] Likewise, the 1911 railwaymen's strike and 1914 London building workers' lockout both witnessed a substantial organised syndicalist presence and influence, with rank-and-file activists encouraging powerful unofficial opposition to the union leadership.[110]

Meanwhile, throughout the 'Labour Unrest', the leader of the ISEL, Tom Mann, was at, or near, the centre of many disputes, the most important of which was the Liverpool transport strike of 1911, where he headed the strike committee. Reflecting on Mann's presence at many of the strikes, and his indefatigable oratory and propaganda work throughout the country on behalf of syndicalism, G.D.H. Cole acknowledged:

> Tom Mann did not in any sense cause the strikes or the unrest: he contributed a great deal to the direction they took and to the guiding of the 'unrest' into definite and constructive channels, but he cannot be said to have caused it. He utilised an existing state of affairs with an eye to a wider future as well as to the present ... Tom Mann's success came no doubt largely from his personal qualities, his gift of oratory, and his strong personality, and vivid enthusiasm; but it came much more from the fact that he chose the right moment for his reappearance. The time was ripe, and it was his fortune and privilege to be the spark to set the train alight.[111]

Despite the disintegration of the ISEL over organisational disputes by the outbreak of war, a number of syndicalist-influenced revolutionaries, such as J.T. Murphy, went on to occupy a prominent role within the leadership of the wartime engineering

---

[109] See M.G. Woodhouse, 'Rank and File Movements Amongst the Miners of South Wales 1910–26', D.Phil, University of Oxford, 1970; D. Egan, 'The Unofficial Reform Committee and the Miners' Next Step, *Llafur*, 2:3 (1978), pp. 64–80; Holton, *British Syndicalism*, pp. 84–8; D.K. Davies, 'The Influence of Syndicalism and Industrial Unionism on the South Wales Coalfield 1898–1921: A Study in Ideology and Practice, PhD, University of Wales, 1991.

[110] Holton, *British Syndicalism*, pp. 97–110; 154–63; R.W. Postgate, *The Builders' History* (London, 1923), pp. 385–422.

[111] G.D.H. Cole, *The World of Labour: A Discussion of the Present and Future of Trade Unionism* (London, 1913), p. 40.

shop stewards' movement, organising a number of large-scale strikes, notably by 200,000 workers across England in May 1917.[112]

In other countries syndicalists played an even wider and more influential role. In Ireland Jim Larkin was the undisputed leading figure in the 1913 Dublin strike and lock-out, as was the ITGWU in many of the workplace occupations and 'soviets' that swept the country during the wages movement strike wave of 1919–1920.[113] In Italy syndicalists were centrally involved in the landless labourers' strikes in Parma of 1907–1908, the quasi-insurrectionary 'Red Week' general strike of 1914, the Piedmontese general strike of April 1920 and the nation-wide factory occupations of September 1920.[114] In Spain the CNT was at the centre of the general strikes in Barcelona in 1917 and 1919, as well as the strikes and revolutionary uprisings of the 1931–1936 and subsequent Civil War period.[115] In America IWW activists were acknowledged to have been noticeably active in at least 150 strikes. These included the Goldfield, Nevada miners' strike in 1906–1907; the McKees Rocks, Pennsylvania, steel workers' strike in 1909; the Lawrence, Massachusetts textile workers' strike in 1912; the Louisiana and Arkansas timber workers' strikes in 1912–1913; the Mesabi Range ironworkers' strike of 1916; and the Northwest lumber workers' strike and Montana and Arizona copper miners' strikes of 1917–1918. Again and again the IWW offered strikers' advice, direction and leadership.

The most outstanding example of this occurred in 1912 at Lawrence. After discovering the employers had reduced their wages, thousands of immigrant workers walked out on strike. The IWW, who at best could lay claim to only 300 paid-up union members, was overwhelmed by events. However, they immediately contacted the national organisation for aid, and the Wobblies responded by sending a number of full-time organisers. These included Joseph Ettor and Arturo Giovannitti, specially chosen because of their exceptional ability as speakers and their fluency in Italian, important during a strike in which Italian immigrants formed a large minority. They were soon followed by Bill Haywood, Elizabeth Gurly Flynn and William E. Trautmann, who helped teach the 23,000 strikers how to bridge their ethno-religious differences and how to turn a spontaneous strike into a highly organised campaign for higher wages and better working conditions.

First, the IWW helped organise a 56-strong strike committee composed of representatives of each of the 14 largest different language groups, with sub-committees for relief, finance, publicity, investigation and organisation. Mass meetings, with simultaneous translation for the thousands of workers who did not speak English, were held on a daily basis, and the IWW strove to develop leaders from among the rank-and-file in order to have the leadership vested, so far as possible, in the workers

---

[112] B. Pribicevic, *The Shop Stewards' Movement and Workers' Control* (Oxford: Blackwell, 1959); J. Hinton, *The First Shop Stewards' Movement* (London, 1973).

[113] J. Newsinger, 'Jim Larkin, Syndicalism and the 1913 Dublin Lock-Out', *International Socialism* , 2:25 (1984), pp. 3–36; O'Connor, *Syndicalism in Ireland*, pp. 38–53.

[114] T.R. Sykes, 'Revolutionary Syndicalism in the Italian Labor Movement: The Agrarian Strikes of 1907–8 in the Province of Parma', *International Review of Social History*, 21 (1976), pp. 186–211; A. Borghi, *L'Italia tra due Crispi: cause e conseguenze di una rivoluzione macata* (Paris, n.d. [1924]), pp. 45–56; Spriano; Clark.

[115] Meaker.

themselves. Second, the IWW helped the strikers organise mass picketing, with long queues of pickets moving in an endless chain around the textile mills to discourage strike breakers. Every day there was a demonstration held, with between 3,000 and 10,000 marching through the streets. Third, the IWW used their many publications and contacts with reformers and radicals outside Lawrence to raise desperately needed funds for the nine-week long strike. Fourth, the IWW devised a scheme to increase favourable publicity for the strikers and to lessen the burden of relief, by arranging for strikers' children to be cared for by families outside Lawrence (as had previously been done on occasion in France and Italy). Fifth, and as importantly, the IWW propagandised about the value of solidarity and revolutionary trade unionism, as well as the necessity for the overthrow of capitalism.[116] In stark contrast to most other disputes in which the IWW was involved, the Lawrence strike was victorious, sparking off a wave of militancy among New England textile workers.[117]

In France there were also repeated requests for CGT assistance by workers who had already spontaneously embarked on strike action. For example, in 1903 a textile workers' strike of over 40,000 workers took place in Armentières and Houplines in the Nord region, in which the principal grievance was the diversity of wage scales and the desire of workers to make them more uniform. Griffuelhes, the Confédération's general secretary, was invited to assist the dispute as a representative of the CGT's General Strike Committee. Likewise, during a large agricultural workers' strike over increased wages and union recognition in the Midi in December 1904, Griffuelhes and Louis Niel were called in and proceeded to travel from village to village 'as a sort of peripatetic strike committee, boosting morale, baptising new unions, and helping in negotiations with the winegrowers'.[118]

On other occasions CGT leaders were more explicitly involved in fomenting strikes, even if spontaneity still played a part with workers' pent-up grievances exploding into open rebellion. For example, in the wake of the Confédération's 1904 congress proposal for a nationally co-ordinated direct action campaign for the eight-hour day and six-day week, Paul Delesalle, sponsor of the campaign, saw the issue as a 'pretext for action and agitation', leading toward a universal work stoppage that would put 'the proletariat in a state of war with capitalist society'.[119] For the next 18 months, the CGT circulated brochures, held meetings and organised strikes to fan workers' rage into a 'white heat', and on May Day 1906 150,000 workers in Paris and the provinces responded by taking 24-hour strike action. Although regarded as a material and financial failure by some commentators, the 1906 strike considerably boosted the membership growth of the CGT.[120]

---

[116] For accounts of IWW organization in the Lawrence strike see Foner, *IWW*, pp. 318–349; Renshaw, pp. 133–49; Dubofsky, pp. 234–57; M. Dubofsky, 'Big Bill' Haywood, (Manchester, 1987), pp. 69–72; B. Watson, *Bread and Roses: Mills, Migrants and the Struggle for the American Dream* (New York, 2005).

[117] Brissendon, p. 292; Renshaw, pp. 133–49.

[118] Vandervort, *Victor Griffuelhes and French Syndicalism*, pp. 74–83; 101.

[119] J. Maitron, *Le Mouvement anarchiste en France: De 1914 á nos jours: Vol. 2* (Paris: Maspere, 1975), pp. 294–5.

[120] Vandervort, pp. 117–19; Moss, p. 148.

In America there were also instances where the IWW played a major contributory role in promoting strike activity. For example, unlike other pre-war strikes in which they had been actively involved, the union's highly successful recruitment campaign during the spring and summer of 1917 in the copper mining industry of Montana and Arizona and lumber industry of the Northwest involved strikes by groups of workers who had joined the Wobblies explicitly to present a series of demands to their employers and who then fought effectively through the IWW to redress their grievances.[121] In similar vein Ralph Chaplain, one of the IWW's most prolific songwriters and poets, vividly described how, under Haywood's direction, he and other Wobblies agitated for militant strike action around the steel plants of Chicago:

> The procedure, perfected over a period of years, was simple: First came appraisal of the job to determine immediate complaints; then the trick of magnifying all minor complaints into major grievances. That was called 'sowing the seeds of discontent'. Once the seeds took root, the rest was easy. First, the distribution of propaganda or strike leaflets and posters; then, meetings at the factory gates, followed as soon as possible by a mass meeting to draw up demands, appoint organisation and publicity committees, and prepare to picket the plant and line up new members.[122]

At the same time the IWW used graphics, ranging from posters and handbills to drawings, prints and cartoons to convey its message. Three million self-sticking labels featuring revolutionary symbols and slogans, known as 'silent agitators', were printed in 1917 alone and stuck on walls across America. Probably one of the most effective propaganda mediums were the lyrics which Wobbly folk poets like Ralph Chaplin, T-Bone Slim, Covington Hall, Charles Ashleigh and Joe Hill wrote to popular melodies and gospel hymns, published in the *Little Red Songbook*, which contained the provocative sub-title 'Songs to Fan the Flames of Revolt'. Reprinted in newspapers or on pocket-sized cards distributed to workers, the songs used bitter satire, ridicule and humorous parody to expose the exploitation of workers, the hypocrisy of priests, and the viciousness of employers, police and vigilantes.[123]

All of this conscious ideological and organisational initiative and leadership was of immense importance in understanding how syndicalist movements were built, and how they could be 'simultaneously a contributory cause, a symptom and a beneficiary'[124] of the extraordinary wave of workers' militancy that occurred during the early years of the twentieth century.

International Cross-Fertilisation of Syndicalist Movements

Finally, there was the international cross-fertilisation of the movement, in which national syndicalist organisations both learnt from and influenced each other, contributing to the development of an *international* movement. As Wayne Thorpe

---

[121] Foner, *Labor and World War 1*, p. 248.

[122] R. Chaplain, *Wobbly: The Rough and Tumble of an American Radical* (Chicago, 1948), pp. 176–7.

[123] J.L. Kornbluh (ed.), *Rebel Voices: An IWW Anthology* (Chicago, 1998), p. 65.

[124] Thorpe, *Workers Themselves*, p. 30.

has commented, 'syndicalists conceived of their movement as international just as the working class was international, and therefore hoped to co-ordinate their struggle across national borders against an equally international capitalist system'.[125]

To some extent cross-national contacts were established on a *formal* basis, for example in meetings that accompanied the sessions of the International Anarchist Congress at Amsterdam in 1907, following which a *Bulletin International du Mouvement Syndicaliste* began to appear financed by syndicalists from across Europe. Formal contacts were also established at an International Syndicalist Congress convened in London in September 1913, and attended by delegates from a number of European countries (although not by the CGT or IWW). Significantly, as the only syndicalist organisation that could claim to be the largest union organisation in its country, the CGT was entitled to a seat in the reformist trade union International, the International Secretariat of National Trade Union Centres (ISNTUC), which later metamorphosed into the International Federation of Trade Unions. From the perspective of attempting to revolutionise the ISNTUC from the inside, the CGT opposed the idea of a rival permanent international Syndicalist International as being divisive. This was not only because it could jeopardise the work of the CGT inside the ISNTUC but also because it could encourage schism between syndicalist and reformist trade union organisations in countries where there was none yet.[126]

Nonetheless, the London congress went on to formulate the first international declaration of syndicalist principles. It also founded an International Syndicalist Information Bureau (with headquarters in Amsterdam) to act as a correspondence centre, foster international solidarity, and organise congresses as first tentative steps towards the establishment of a fully-fledged International. However, such efforts remained limited and did not extend beyond informal contacts. The war intervened before the organisation could get properly under way, and by 1918 the syndicalist urge toward international organisation was temporarily diverted by the Russian Revolution.[127]

Apart from these formal contacts, it was the predominately *informal* network of relations which were to prove crucial to the movement's growth and development. In an attempt to explain the international diffusion between different countries on a global scale, Marcel van der Linden has suggested three factors were important:[128] *international migration* (for example, with Argentinian and Brazilian anarcho-syndicalism influenced by the arrival of radical southern European migrants); *international labour processes* (for example, with sailors playing an important role in spreading the IWW model to port cities in Australia, New Zealand, Chile and other countries); and *cross-border activities* (with movements in one country regularly, if not intentionally, having an influence on parts of the labour movement in another country; for example, the impact of the IWW inside Mexico). However, van der Linden provides no specific examples of how this diffusion operated in Europe.

---

125 Ibid., p. 1.

126 See S. Milner, *Dilemmas of Internationalism, French Syndicalism and the International Labour Movement, 1900–1914* (New York, 1991).

127 Thorpe, *Workers Themselves*, pp. 75–7.

128 van der Linden, 'Second Thoughts', p. 186.

In fact, all three factors were of some, albeit limited, significance to the countries surveyed in this book. First, international migration was certainly relevant in America, where a layer of rank-and-file militants attracted to the IWW were immigrants from Italy and Spain with some experience of anarchist organisation in their home countries. Indeed, many of the IWW's leaders and featured writers were of European origin, and one of the organisers at the 1913 Paterson strike, Edmondo Rossini, divided his efforts between the IWW and the Italian USI. Similarly, the forced exile of hundreds of anarchists from France, Italy and Spain during the 1890s facilitated the exchange of ideals, ideologies and models of subsequent anarcho-syndicalist organisation within these European countries.[129] Second, the role of international labour processes was evident in the way some British seamen played an important role in the transmission of syndicalist ideas from America back to British soil, for example with George Hardy, who became an IWW supporter in the United States, even carrying his syndicalist ideas further afield to Canada and Australia.[130] Third, cross-border activity was also relevant. Not surprisingly, as a result of the national importance of the CGT and their early elaboration of syndicalist philosophy, the French syndicalists provided an important inspiration for other countries to follow. Thus, when *Solidaridad Obrera* was launched in Spain in 1907 it closely followed the pattern of the well-known *Charte d'Amiens* of 1906.[131] Likewise Alceste De Ambris, the chief pre-war spokesperson of the USI, maintained close contacts with the French syndicalists;[132] and the philosophical framework of IWW leaders William Trautmann and Father Thomas Hagerty was influenced by the syndicalist ideas they had gathered from their contacts in Europe, particularly France.[133]

But there were also *other* important socially contagious processes through which syndicalist ideas migrated from country to another, notably their transmission in books, pamphlets and newspapers. Thus, in the years 1911–1913 the IWW's *Industrial Worker* and *Solidarity* carried numerous articles on the French syndicalists, particularly on the tactic of sabotage – on which it also propagandised via stickers, posters, illustrations and cartoons. The pioneering 1909 CGT pamphlet *Le sabotage*, written by Emile Pouget, was also translated with an introduction by IWW organiser Arturo Giovannitti in 1913 and widely circulated within the organisation. Likewise Elizabeth Gurly Flynn's pamphlet *Sabotage* (1915) drew widely on the French

---

129 B. Cartosio, 'Gli emigrati italiani e l'Industrial Workers of the World', in B. Bezza, *Gli italiani fuori d'Italia: gli emirate italiani nei movimenti operai dei paesi d'adozione 1880–1940* (Milan, 1983), pp. 359–97; D.R. Gabaccia, 'Worker Internationalism and Italian Labor Migration, 1870–1914', *International Labor and Working Class History*, 45 (1994), p. 70; Levy, 'Italian Anarchism', p. 215.

130 T. Lane, 'A Merseysider in Detroit', *History Workshop Journal*, 11 (1981), pp. 139–40; B. Holton, 'Syndicalism and Labour on Merseyside, 1906–14', in H.I. Hikens (ed.), *Building the Union: Studies on the Growth of the Workers' Movement: Merseyside 1756–1967* (Liverpool, 1973), pp. 121–50; G.H. Hardy, *Those Stormy Years* (London, 1956).

131 Bar, 'The CNT', p. 121.

132 C.L. Bertrand, 'Revolutionary Syndicalism in Italy, 1912–1922' (University of Wisconsin, PhD, 1970), p. 30.

133 Foner, *IWW*, p. 23.

experience.[134] Many of the founders of the CNT also closely followed the writings of French syndicalists and there were Spanish translations of the work of Yvetot, Pataud, Griffuelhes and Pouget.[135] Similarly, there were regular international reports in the ISEL's monthly newspaper *The Syndicalist*, including a book review of the English translation of Patuad and Pouget's *How We Shall Being About the Revolution*, lengthy individual reports from syndicalist movements in America, Italy and France, and a first-hand account of the 1913 International Syndicalist congress.[136] In France, Pierre Monatte's *La Vie ouvrèire* prided itself on its international syndicalist coverage, with Tom Mann a frequent contributor on the British labour movement.[137]

The establishment of personal contacts between key leaders of different national syndicalist bodies also played a role in helping to develop an international movement. This can be illustrated by looking at the inter-relationship between Britain, France, America and Ireland. Thus, the British syndicalists Tom Man and Guy Bowman chose to visit and learn from the experience of leading French CGT syndicalists in Paris before they launched the ISEL in Britain in 1910.[138] E.J.B. Allen, the ISEL's assistant general secretary, translated articles from *La Bataille syndicaliste* for *The Syndicalist* and Jack Tanner, an executive committee member of the ISEL and editor of the wartime shop stewards' movement paper *Solidarity*, regularly corresponded with the French syndicalists around *La Vie ouvrière*. Conversly, Leon Jouhaux, secretary of the CGT from 1909, was present at the ISEL's founding conference.

At the same time, in 1913 Tom Mann visited America on a 22-week speaking tour sponsored by the IWW in 70 towns and cities.[139] Conversely, IWW leader Bill Haywood, made several pre-war visits to Europe where he took the opportunity of making contact with French, British and Irish syndicalist-influenced revolutionaries, including Pierre Monatte, Alfred Rosmer, Tom Mann, Jim Larkin and James Connolly. And in 1910–1911 William Z. Foster also visited Europe, where he stayed in France for six months, learnt the French language, held lengthy discussions with CGT leaders and devoured the writings of Pelloutier, Griffuelhes, Pouget and Sorel, before returning to America to set up the SLNA breakaway from the IWW and writing a regular column reporting on developments in America for *La Vie ouvière*. James Connolly, who spent some time as an organiser with the IWW in America, went on to become a leader of the ITGWU and his ideas subsequently guided the union towards a 'One Big Union' organisational scheme as advanced in his Wobby-influenced pamphlet *The Lines of Progress*. And in the wake of the Dublin lockout, ITGWU leader Jim Larkin spent 8½ years in America where he was in regular contact with the IWW, and spoke alongside Haywood at the funeral of executed Wobbly song-writer Joe Hill, before

---

134 A. Giovannitti, 'Introduction', in E. Pouget, *Sabotage* (Chicago, 1913), E. Gurly Flynn, *Sabotage: The Conscious Withdrawal of the Workers' Industrial Efficiency* (Cleveland, 1915).

135 A. Bar, *Syndicalism and Revolution in Spain: The Ideology and The Syndical Practice of the CNT in the Period 1915–1919* (New York, 1981), p. 106–107; 'The CNT', p. 121.

136 *The Syndicalist*, October 1912; January 1914; January 1913; December 1913.

137 Jennings, p. 147.

138 Brown, pp. 12–13.

139 J. White, *Tom Mann* (Manchester, 1991), p. 185.

returning back to Ireland.[140] Such contacts were obviously important in reinforcing syndicalists in their overall philosophy and objectives, and encouraging a view of themselves as part of an *international* movement aimed at overthrowing capitalism across the world.

Obviously this does not mean that syndicalism in any one country was merely some kind of 'foreign import', as Independent Labour Party leader Ramsey MacDonald, insisted as a way of denigrating its British manifestation under French influence: 'It is a stranger in our language, with no registered abode as yet.'[141] Similarly though it drew some of its ideas and much of its revolutionary vocabulary from European syndicalist writers, the IWW was rooted in American experience and shaped by national events. Nonetheless, American conditions produced a set of ideas and practices in all essentials indistinguishable from those espoused by syndicalists in Europe.[142] In this sense, it would be more appropriate to comprehend the syndicalist experience in Britain, America and other countries as being international in scope because of the *similar* economic and political conditions, combined with the bitter experience of industrial struggle, which gave rise to a *common* desire to organise a new form of revolutionary unionism. Whilst this common syndicalist experience was rooted in distinct *national* conditions, it was undoubtedly considerably deepened by the cross-fertilisation that took place between syndicalist organisations *internationally*. Such international cross-fertilisation was obviously not a unilinear process in the sense of one movement being an absolute imitation of the other, and it clearly varied in intensity, but the syndicalist phenomenon as an international movement can only be understood by taking into account such exogenous influences.

Some Common Elements

That the emergence of revolutionary syndicalism was only part of a wider upsurge in workers' militancy across the world in the years leading up to the First World War needs to be restated. No doubt it was the coalescence of some of the different factors that have been discussed separately above that contributed to heightening workers' radicalism generally. However such a combination of elements also helps to provide an explanation for why some of this radicalism was specifically channelled into a syndicalist direction. It is impossible to assign relative weightings to the range of different influencing factors, to provide a hierarchy of variables. This is because the relative explanatory power of each variable differed over time and from one country to another and anyway the origin and development of the different syndicalist movements was inevitably influenced by a complex interaction between them.

Clearly syndicalist movements were to a large extent an expression of specific *national* economic, social, political and historical circumstances (as well as regional and occupational parameters). One expression of this national distinctiveness was

140 C.D. Greaves, *The Life and Times of James Connolly* (London, 1961), pp. 168–245; Larkin, *James Larkin*, pp. 167–226.

141 R. MacDonald, *Syndicalism: A Critical Examination* (London, 1912), p v.

142 M. Dubofsky, 'The Rise and Fall of Revolutionary Syndicalism in the United States', in van der Linden and Thorpe, *Revolutionary Syndicalism*, pp. 207–10.

their varying dates of origin. Thus, the French CGT and American IWW were the first to emerge in 1895 and 1905 respectively (the former with the merger of the CGT and *Bourses* federation in 1902); although a syndicalist current operated in Italy from about 1900 it was not until 1912 that the USI was formed. In Spain syndicalists grouped together from 1907 but the CNT was not launched until 1910 (and was then banned in 1911 and unable to operate openly until 1916). And the ITGWU and ISEL were not founded in Ireland and Britain until 1908 and 1910 respectively. Such bodies did not spring fully formed from their foundation conferences; it was only through the experience of struggle inside the working class movement and organisational co-existence that each movement grew in influence. Inspired at times by the French example, but shaped and buttressed by distinctive national (and regional) circumstances, the movement as a whole spread internationally.

Yet, as will have become apparent, there were also important common features across the range of different countries, a singular concatenation of circumstances peculiar to the period, which created a propensity for syndicalist action and organisation on an *international* scale. The period between the 1890s and 1930s represented an important epoch of Western capitalist advance, during which rapid industrial concentration and the attempt to secure managerial authority in the workplace – in the face of a working class that was growing in size and organisational strength – facilitated basic collective economic organisation and encouraged militant trade union methods as a means of attempting to resolve the naked antagonism between capital and labour. Crucially during this period there was the weakness of firmly established institutionalised channels or organisational mechanisms that could encourage the attainment of social reform through more gradualist means. Such political mechanisms existed, but often were in embryonic stage and under the impact of profound social change and economic instability were found inadequate to satisfy the growing aspirations of many sections of newly radicalised workers. In other words, a precondition of growth, in all of these countries, was disillusionment with the ability of prevailing approaches to social and political struggle to defend working class living standards. In this sense, syndicalism was 'spawned out of a crisis' of reformist and socialist politics (as well as the inadequacies of the prevailing deterministic Marxist alternative).[143]

Such underlying factors help to explain the emergence of an international syndicalist movement that, despite contrasting organisational forms, was united by a *common* objective: to chart a way forward independently of official channels and in direct confrontation with the existing framework of capitalist society.

[143] O'Connor, *Syndicalism in Ireland*, p. 182.

Chapter 3

Composition and Structure

Compared to many of the labour and socialist parties they recoiled against, the social composition of both the membership and leadership of the syndicalist movements internationally were overwhelmingly working class. It is true that, like their reformist counterparts, they were also primarily male and white dominated, although some distinctive efforts were made to attract female, black and immigrant workers into their membership ranks. And they attempted in some countries to confront the issue of Catholicism in novel fashion. While the organisational dilemma of balancing central direction and leadership with decentralisation and local control was common to mainstream labour movement bodies, the syndicalists' emphasis was again distinctive, as was the nature and style of their leadership personnel. This chapter examines briefly these various features of the syndicalist movement, in each case looking at different countries by way of example.

Occupational Composition

There is a common perception that the residual strength of syndicalism lay not with the industrial working class, but with artisans, agricultural workers, casual labourers and other groups of economically marginalised, often unskilled and unorganised, workers.[1] For example, it is assumed the CGT had only limited support amongst the 'genuine' factory workers of the new large-scale heavy industries that developed in the early twentieth century. Bernard Moss has provided new life to this image with his concept of the 'socialism of skilled workers'.[2] Likewise, there is a widespread belief the IWW recruited almost exclusively among the migratory workers of the West, with only transitory support amongst factory workers in the East; that the USI attracted mainly landless labourers, as opposed to the engineering workers concentrated in the giant plants located in the industrial cities of Milan and Turn; and that the CNT also appealed primarily to rural labourers with only limited support from industrial workers in one or two urban geographical areas of small-scale production and anarchist influence such as Barcelona.

By contrast, it is often assumed it was the mass reformist labour and socialist parties, with their affiliated trade unions, that were able to sink genuine roots amongst the rapidly expanding industrial proletariat. In other words, syndicalist bodies attracted only marginal support on the fringes of the existing labour movement,

[1] For example, see E. O'Connor, 'What Caused the 1913 Lockout? Industrial Relations in Ireland, 1907–13', *Historical Studies in Industrial Relations*, 19 (2005), p. 120.

[2] B. Moss, *The Origins of the French Labor Movement: The Socialism of Skilled Workers, 1830–1914* (Berkeley, Calif., 1976).

were usually reliant on the recruitment of workers neglected by the established trade unions, and were anyway to be rapidly superseded with the development of mass-production industries. Hence syndicalism's apparent 'irrelevance to the maturing corporate system of the twentieth century'.[3]

In reality the situation was nowhere near as clear cut as these simplified images would suggest. The question as to whether structural changes in the composition of the labour force brought on by rapid capitalist industrialisation meant that syndicalism was inevitably subject to extinction is examined in Chapter 5. But for now it is important to note that despite attempt by historians to link various forms of labour politics to different occupational or skill groupings within the working class, syndicalism appealed, in varying degrees, to relatively *diverse* groups of workers – skilled, semi-skilled and unskilled – depending on the context.

According to Marcel van der Linden and Wayne Thorpe, syndicalism was disproportionably influential among two groups of workers.[4] First, seasonal, casual or project workers, such as agricultural day labourers, dockers and building workers who frequently changed jobs, employer and site and rarely had formalised contact with trade unions. Amongst such workers the risks of striking were reduced, as often changing their place of work meant they had less to fear from dismissal than those with a semi-permanent employer. Moreover, when grievances arose workers were forced to act immediately to achieve anything (before a particular harvest, construction project or work assignment was complete). Such structural conditions of work naturally encouraged tactics of immediate direct action against the employer, and hence the appeal of syndicalism. Second, syndicalism could also appeal to those in large, more settled and routinised working populations, such as factory workers, miners and railwaymen, particularly when such workers were faced with a dilution of skills, reorganisation of work processes and labour intensification. The combination of changes in technology and the organisation of work led to a decline in the influence of craft unionism, sometimes prompting artisanal workers to ally with industrial workers, thereby acting as a powerful stimulus for a unionism designed to unite and mobilise all the workers in a particular industry.

In exploring how such workers, as well as others, could be attracted to syndicalism, it is useful to look at each of our chosen countries. At the IWW's 1905 founding convention Bill Haywood expressed his commitment to organising the forgotten unskilled workers, those without votes and without unions. 'I do not care a snap of my fingers whether or not the skilled workers join the industrial movement at this time' Haywood shouted at the meeting. 'We are going down into the gutter to get at the mass of workers and bring them up to a decent plane of living'.[5] And undoubtedly the Wobblies *were* able to successfully implant themselves among workers whom

---

3 R.H. Zieger, Book Review of 'Bread and Roses Too: Studies of the Wobblies', *Labor History*, 11:4 (1970), p. 568.

4 M. van der Linden and W. Thorpe, 'The Rise and Fall of Revolutionary Syndicalism', in M. van der Linden and W. Thorpe (eds), *Revolutionary Syndicalism: An International Perspective* (Aldershot, 1990), pp. 7–12.

5 *Proceedings of the First Annual Convention of the Industrial Workers of the World* (New York, 1905), pp. 575–6.

the AFL-affiliated unions would not and did not reach. Chief among these were migratory or seasonal workers, who formed the majority of the IWW members in the western United States and made up the core and backbone of the organisation.

The IWW's western roots lay in the inexorable intrusion into this region of the corporate capitalism that had tamed older economic sectors in the industrial east. A dispossessed labour force of young, semi-skilled or unskilled migratory workers emerged, a roaming army of several million not attached to any particular locality or special line of industry. A unique product of peculiar western American economic and social conditions, lumberjacks, construction workers, miners and agricultural labourers moved from one job to another travelling across the country in the empty 'side door coaches' of freight trains. Often termed 'bindle-stiffs' because of the small bundle of worldly goods they rolled in a blanket and slung by a cord around their shoulders between jobs, they congregated in labour camps or 'jungles' in which the food and living quarters were desperately poor. They had no families with them, and did not stay long enough in any one town to register and vote. Constantly moving and working in appalling conditions for extremely low pay, many of these vote-less and economically weak workers saw direct action through industrial organisation as their only weapon against the system that oppressed them. According to a Federal Commission report into conditions in the lumber industry at the time, one lumber operator recognised the IWW as 'the cry of the oppressed … it is misery articulate'.[6]

Most importantly, the IWW's militant philosophy gave outlet, meaning and dignity to a group of workers who were despised and exploited by many in society and unwanted by any other labour organisation. An article in *Solidarity* in November 1914 stated:

> The nomadic worker of the West embodies the very spirit of the IWW. His cheerful cynicism, his frank and outspoken contempt for most of the conventions of bourgeois society, including the more stringent conventions which masquerade under the name of morality, make him an admirable exemplar of the iconoclastic doctrine of revolutionary unionism …
>
> Nowhere can a section of the working class be found so admirably fitted to serve as the scouts and advance guards of the labour army. Rather they may become the guerrillas of the revolution – the *franc-tireurs* of the class struggle.[7]

Yet whilst migratory workers formed the core of the IWW, it is important to note the Wobblies also built a base amongst other sections of the American working class movement. One of the key constituent groups that helped to found the organisation was the Western Federation of Miners (WFM), which organised copper, lead, silver and gold miners. Even after the WFM broke away, the Wobblies attracted support from iron and copper miners in Goldfield, Nevada and the Mesabi Iron Range, northern Minnesota. In addition, they won influence amongst longshoremen (Philadelphia, Baltimore and Norfolk), seagoing maritime workers, as well as (albeit on a less stable and permanent basis) amongst factory workers in the textile

---

6 Cited in P. Renshaw, *The Wobblies: The Story of Syndicalism in the United States* (London, 1967), p. 118.

7 *Solidarity*, 21 November 1914.

(Lawrence and Patterson, Massachusetts), auto (Detroit), rubber (Akron, Ohio) and power (Schenectady, New York) industries. Significantly, if the IWW's migratory membership was native-born, in the Lawrence and Patterson textile factories, amongst others, they recruited many newly-arrived southern and Eastern European immigrants (from Italy, Poland, Russia, Hungary, Slovakia, Croatia, Greece and Spain) whose ethnicity, religion, language and customs tended to separate them from the mainstream of American life.

David Montgomery has suggested that one of the reasons why the IWW ultimately failed was the sheer disdain its leaders expressed towards skilled workers in the AFL unions.[8] By condemning the highly skilled as reactionary 'aristocrats of labour' in order to concentrate their energy on organising those workers long beyond the effective reach of the labour movement, the Wobblies effectively dismissed the radical potential of precisely those workers who possessed enormous power in the workplace. However, this disdain was not because the IWW officials were unfamiliar with the traditions of the craftsmen. In fact, the vast majority of IWW officials came from the ranks of the more skilled workers and many had experience as members of craft unions.[9] As Melvyn Dubofsky has argued:

> They chose to organise among the less skilled because their personal experience with craftsmen convinced the Wobbly leaders that such workers in the main preferred the 'bread and butter' business unionism of the AFL to the revolutionary appeal of the IWW. Rightly or wrongly, the Wobblies believed that those workers with the least to lose in the class struggle made the best recruits for a revolutionary labour movement.[10]

In France syndicalism proved to be particularly attractive to skilled craftsmen engaged as wage earners in small-scale capitalist production in Paris and elsewhere. As Bernard Moss has explained, these skilled workers have traditionally been characterised as 'artisans', a term which is vague and misleading, notably because it places independent artisans, master artisans and skilled wage earners on the same footing, thereby obscuring the class distinction based on the ownership of capital. As neither traditional artisans nor industrial workers, skilled wage earners remained of significance despite industrialisation because of the need to supply the expanding markets with consumer and luxury goods, provide housing and public facilities in expanding cities, and outfit and maintain the new industrial machinery. Yet without destroying the crafts, industrialisation eroded the traditional income, security and status of skilled craftsmen and threatened them with unemployment, stagnating wages and intensified labour. Thus, skilled workers experienced industrialisation as a transitional process of proletarianisation that tended to unite them with new elements of the working class, the factory workers. Many concluded that they would never obtain the 'full product' of their labour until they had come into the collective

---

[8] D. Montgomery, *Workers' Control in America* (Cambridge), p. 106.

[9] T. Nomura, 'Who Were the Wobblies? The Defendants of the Chicago IWW Trial of 1919: Collective Biographies', *Journal of the Aichi Prefectual University* (1985), pp. 135–150.

[10] M. Dubofsky, 'The Rise and Fall of Revolutionary Syndicalism in the United States', in van der Linden and Thorpe, *Revolutionary Syndicalism*, p. 213.

possession of capital in a federalist trade association, owning and managing their own workshops.[11]

Nonetheless after 1900 such skilled workers were increasingly joined in the CGT by new sections of skilled, semi-skilled and unskilled workers from a variety of different large-scale industries.[12] These included miners (Pas-de-Calais and Loire Valley), railway workers, notably footplatemen and drivers (nationally); construction workers, notably carpenters and joiners (Paris and elsewhere); dockers and shipyard workers (Nantes Saint Nazaire); metal/engineering workers in small and medium-sized factories (Paris, Saint Etienne and Saint Nazaire); food industry workers, such as pastry cooks, chefs, bakers, waiters, grocery assistants in chain stores, and factory sugar and cake workers (Paris and elsewhere); and school teachers (nationally). In addition, the CGT won support from France's vast pool of agricultural labour, notably vineyard workers in the south of the country (Midi). Kathryn Amdur's study of contrasting patterns of industrial development during and immediately after the war in the cities of Limoges and St. Etienne has convincingly demonstrated that the decline of artisan traditions did not mean the demise of the syndicalist movement, which had 'long since broadened its appeal beyond the mere handful of skilled craftsmen who had reputedly constituted its "active minorities" during the 'heroic years' before World War 1'.[13] Certainly by 1909 the CGT had added nearly half a million new adherents, most of whom were not members of the craft unions that had previously dominated the Confédération.[14]

In Italy the USI was comprised first and foremost of agricultural workers (landless farm labourers) who constituted over one-third of the membership, with construction workers (including masons, carpenters and brick makers) forming the second largest group. Although trade unionism in most European countries was almost exclusively an urban industrial phenomenon, by contrast the Italian labour movement was strongly rooted in both town and country, a development related to the existence of a large group of people displaced by modernisation in agriculture, but who remained in agriculture and were not absorbed by the new industries.[15] Such rural unionism operated in an isolated and extremely hostile environment, with labour disputes demanding combative tactics (as advocated by the USI) if they were to be brought to a successful conclusion, and tending to be violent. Significantly syndicalist membership geographically by the end of 1914 came almost exclusively from northern Italy, with almost a total absence of USI groups in any area south of Tuscany. Strength was concentrated in the Po Valley, in the areas of Emilia-Romagna

---

[11] Moss, pp. 13–19.

[12] A. Kriegal and Jean-Jacques Becker, *1914: La Guerre et le mouvement ouvrier français* (Paris 1964), pp. 280–85.

[13] K.E. Amdur, *Syndicalist Legacy: Trade Unions and Politics in Two French Cities in the Era of World War 1* (Urbana, Illin., 1986), p. 12; 269.

[14] B. Vandervort, *Victor Griffuelhes and French Syndicalism, 1895–1922* (Baton Rouge, 1996), p. 247.

[15] S.J. Surace, *Ideology, Economic Change and the Working Classes: The Case of Italy* (Berkeley, Calif., 1966), p. 68.

and Lombardy.[16] The prominence of Parma as a centre of syndicalist activity reflected the very sharp contrast between tenant farmers and day labourers.[17]

But there has been a long-held common misconception that a disproportionate number of Italian syndicalists were from the *south* of the country where supposedly pre-industrial radical populist traditions remained strong. For example, the revolutionary Marxist Antonio Gramsci viewed syndicalism as a movement linked to the special concerns and revolutionary aspirations of the south and especially the southern peasantry:

> In the ten years 1900–1910 there took place the most radical crisis in the Socialist and workers' movement: the masses reacted spontaneously against the policy of the reformist leaders. Syndicalism was born, which is the instinctive, elementary, primitive but healthy expression of working class reaction against the bloc with the bourgeoisie and in favour of a bloc with the peasants, and in the first place with the peasants of the South. Just so: moreover, in a certain sense, syndicalism is a weak attempt by the southern peasants, presented by the most advanced intellectuals, to lead the proletariat.[18]

In fact, as David Roberts has argued, the USI discerned absolutely no revolutionary or socialist capacity in the southern peasantry. It was, they believed, the industrial classes located in the north of the country – including the landless day labourers in the heavily capitalised agricultural Po Valley along with the factory-based proletariat in Milan and Turin – that could redeem Italy, not the decaying pre-industrial classes of the south. As Angelo Oliviero Olivetti, one of the leading intellectuals within the USI until 1911, made clear:

> The syndicalist mentality can only mature in the factory or in intensive, industrialised agriculture: it supposes, then, large industry and intense vibration of capitalist life, and of necessity must leave behind itself all the grey zone of small industry and small agriculture: the artisans and the petty bureaucracy … that is a whole mass which is specifically proletarian, but incapable by its very structure and economic position to feel the unique revolutionary impulse that is syndicalism pulsating in its veins and stimulating its will.[19]

The extent of the USI's appeal to the industrial working class, more narrowly defined to exclude agricultural labour, should not be underestimated even it represented a minority of the overall membership. To begin with, tens of thousands of workers enrolled in the Unione in 'company towns' in Liguria, Tuscany and Apulia, where economic and political life was dominated by one great anti-union trust or had state industries (such as arsenals and armament factories) where the law restricted strikes,

[16] C.L. Bertrand, 'Revolutionary Syndicalism in Italy, 1912–1922', PhD, University of Wisconsin, 1970, pp. 141–2.

[17] R. DeFelice, *Sindacalismo rivoluzionario e fiumanesimo nel carteggio DeAmbris – D'Annunzio, 1919–1922* (Brescia, 1966), p. 17.

[18] A. Gramsci, 'The Southern Question', *The Modern Prince and Other Writings* (New York, 1957), pp. 37–8.

[19] A.O. Olivetti, 'I sindicalisti e la élite', *Cinque anni di sindicalismo e di lotta proletaria in Italia*, (Naples, 1914), pp. 267–8.

and there were segregated workers' districts with few municipal amenities.[20] Thus during the 1920 factory occupations that swept the country, although the socialist-led metal workers' federation (FIOM) controlled the main industrial cities, the USI controlled Verona, Savona and Spezia, as well as enjoying extensive backing amongst metal-working and shipbuilding workers in Sestri Ponente, Cornigliano and Campi.[21] The USI claimed 30,000 workers in its own metal-workers' federation alone, not quite 10 per cent of the total number of strikers.[22]

It is true that Italian syndicalism never succeeded in capturing a mass following from the large industrial centres of Milan, Turn and Rome. This is to be explained partly by the way the established socialist-led union confederation (CGL) had previously concentrated its organisational activities on workers in these areas; partly by the way the CGL's industrial union structure (as opposed to the syndicalists' local and craft-based structures) proved relatively successful, with the USI's decentralised vision of the future appearing more relevant to workers whose economic livelihood was rooted in small units of production rather in huge modern factories; and partly as a result of the disillusionment that followed the defeat of Turin metalworkers' and Milan automobile workers' strikes in 1912 and 1913 respectively, during which the USI had unsuccessfully demanded unlimited general strikes against the CGL's more moderate stance. In the wake of such strike setbacks, the USI spent the next few years trying to regain some influence in these industrial centres.[23]

But immediately before and during the 1920 factory occupations, amidst a huge increase in membership generally, the syndicalists' *were* able to gain an important foothold among some engineering workers in both cities. Thus, the USI's journal *Guerra di Classe* was transferred from Florence to Milan in early March 1920[24] and there was a tremendous amount of anarchist and USI activity in favour of factory councils and the occupation tactic, with one observer noting: 'anarchism dominates the piazza and Malatesta and Borghi are the bosses' (of the workers' movement).[25] In Turin (where Gramsci's *Ordine Nuovo* group supportive of the city-wide network of workers' councils had established some influence), it was not until July 1920 that a branch of the USI-affiliated metal-workers' federation was set up, although it eventually succeeded in building a credible base.

In Spain the CNT exercised influence amongst agricultural workers in the south (Andalucia), east (the area of the Levant around Valenica), and in north-east Aragon (around Saragossa). Many rural areas were characterised by the widespread use of *latifunda*, absentee-owned massive estates which relied upon the systematic

---

[20] C. Levy, 'Italian Anarchism, 1870–1926', in D. Goodway (ed.), *For Anarchism: History, Theory and Practice* (London, 1989), p. 65.

[21] T. Abse, 'Italy', in S. Berger and D. Broughton (eds), *The Force of Labour: The Western European Labour Movement and the Working Class in the Twentieth Century* (Oxford, 1995), p. 140.

[22] P. Spriano, *The Occupation of the Factories: Italy 1920* (London, 1975), p. 69. See also *Guerra di Classe*, 6 September 1919.

[23] Bertrand, pp. 145–6.

[24] *Guerra di Classe*, 6 March 1920.

[25] Cited in M. Clark, *Antonio Gramsci and the Revolution That Failed* (New Haven, 1977), p. 94.

exploitation of an underclass of landless labourers who were badly-paid, often hired on a daily basis, and liable to lay-offs and victimisation, as well as subject to food shortages and long periods of unemployment. The appalling hardships of their daily existence made Andalucia's peasants in particular receptive to the CNT's seemingly straightforward promise to break the stranglehold of the *latifundistas* through seizure of the land followed by the destruction of state power.[26]

However, Antonio Bar has provided evidence to suggest that contrary to the commonly expressed view, the CNT was from its beginning (and even more so in the 1930s) a labour movement of an industrial character. Thus, it was concentrated in the urban and more or less industrialised areas of the country, such as Barcelona, Valencia, Seville and Saragossa. It won significant influence in such sectors as construction, fisheries, leather and footwear, textiles, printing and a wide variety of other trades. The typical profile of the Confederación member was a manual worker in a workshop of medium to small size. By contrast, the CNT was always conspicuously weak (in terms of formal organisation at least) in the important rural areas of Spain. Even though in Andalucia, Aragon or Castille, anarchist and 'libertarian communist' uprisings were quite significant, the CNT as such never managed to establish an important and stable organic structure in these areas.[27] Whilst it built considerable support in the cities of the south during the early 1930s, especially in Cádiz, Málaga, Córdoba and Seville, as well as in a number of Andalucian villages, ties between the cities and the villages were extremely weak and the Confederación tended to concentrate most of its efforts in the larger cities among industrialised workers.[28]

A particularly important stronghold of the CNT in both the period around the First World War and the 1930s was the industrial and factory workers of Barcelona and other Catalan towns. There is considerable debate among historians as to why anarchists generally and the CNT specifically found such a responsive audience in this north-eastern province.[29] Some have suggested that arising from the stagnation and poverty of the agricultural sector there was a significant change in the composition of the labour force in Barcelona during the First World War, with the arrival of large numbers of rootless peasant migrants from the south (which itself possessed a long history of violent social conflict and anarchist allegiance) who were more susceptible to anarchist appeals than other groups.[30] Indeed by 1930, when migrants from elsewhere in Spain formed 35 per cent of the city's population, workers of non-Catalan origin were even more prominent in the CNT.[31]

---

26 P. Heywood, 'The Labour Movement in Spain Before 1914', in D. Geary (ed.), *Labour and Socialist Movements in Europe Before 1914* (Oxford, 1989), pp. 235–6.

27 A. Bar, 'The CNT: The Glory and Tragedy of Spanish Anarchosyndicalism', in van der Linden and Thorpe, *Revolutionary Syndicalism*, pp. 133–4.

28 M. Bookchin, *The Spanish Anarchists: The Heroic Years, 1868–1936* (Edinburgh, 1998) p. 203.

29 See A. Smith, 'Anarchism, the General Strike and the Barcelona Labour Movement, 1899–1914, *European History Quarterly*, 27: 1 (1997).

30 See G.H. Meaker, *The Revolutionary Left in Spain, 1914–1923* (Stanford, Calif., 1974), pp. 2–9; 147; Bookchin, *The Spanish Anarchists*, pp. 69–71.

31 See C. Earlham, *Class, Culture and Conflict in Barcelona, 1898–1937* (London, 2004).

Other historians have drawn attention to the way in which the concentration of industry in small factories and the survival of artisanal concerns may have favoured anarchist penetration.[32] However it should be noted that Madrid, the epitome of a highly skilled artisanal labour force, was a bastion of the Socialist Party, and in the Basque region where industry was also small-unit based there was a lack of CNT implantation. In addition, in Barcelona the Confederación recruited among a wide variety of industrial workers, including those in the metalworking, construction (bricklayers and their labourers) and woodworking (carpenters) industries, as well as among textile workers, dockers and carters. A different potential factor was the way in which, in the adverse Catalan economic climate, the major employers' federations adopted an intensely anti-union stance which made it impossible for workers to establish stable collective bargaining relations, thereby encouraging them to embrace the CNT's emphasis on combativity and solidarity. Finally, other historians have paid greater attention to the overall context of social and political relations, notably frustration at the failure of democratic reforms, as well as the national, historical and linguistic differences which separated Catalans from Castillians and which made the former highly suspicious of any form of central Spanish state apparatus.[33]

In Ireland the bulk of ITGWU members were recruited in Dublin, although important blocs were also secured outside, notably in Belfast and Sligo. Larkin believed that the key to the port of Dublin was in the hands of the dockers, and they subsequently became the nucleus and backbone of the union. And since Dublin was a city that depended primarily on trade rather than industry, it meant subsidiary employments were also very much at the mercy of the dockside workforce. Thus the ITGWU made successful efforts to pull into the union many unorganised workers in transport, dockside and essential services who operated at the fringes of commercial infrastructure. By 1913 it controlled almost all the unskilled labour in Dublin (albeit with some important exceptions including workers employed by Guinness and the Dublin United Tramway Company). It also made important inroads into organising agricultural labourers, particularly those who worked on the large farms around Dublin and were employed on a permanent basis. After the war the union witnessed a burst of growth among farm workers in the south and the 'land campaign' of 1919 helped to establish the ITGWU's credentials as the One Big Union.[34]

Finally British syndicalism proved to be attractive to long-unionised skilled workers in large metal production and engineering factories threatened with skill-displacing technological change (notably in Glasgow and Sheffield). But it also built influence among a variety of other sections of the industrial working class, including miners (notably in South Wales), construction workers (especially in London) and

---

[32] For example see A. Balcells, *El arraigo del anarquismo en Cataluña: Textos de 1926–1934* (Madrid: Júcar. 1980), p. 18; M. Tuñón de Lara, *El movimiento obrero en la historia de España*: *Vol. 1* (Madrid, 1977), p. 281; 307–308.

[33] For example see Heywood, pp. 231–65; B. Martin, *The Agony of Modernisation: Labour and Industrialisation in Spain* (Ithaca, NY, 1990); A. Smith, 'Spain', in Berger and Broughton, pp. 171–209.

[34] E. Larkin, *James Larkin: Irish Labour Leader, 1876–1947* (London, 1968), pp. 96–106; E. O'Connor, *Syndicalism in Ireland* (Cork, 1988), pp. 20–39.

transport and railway workers (across the country). Significantly, writing about the widespread strikes of 1910 in Britain, most of them carried out in opposition to the trade union leaders, Lord Asquith, head of the Labour Department of the Board of Trade, recorded they were 'largely due to the action of young men'.[35] In many respects, the major changes in industrial organisation and the nature of employers' attacks on established working practices encouraged a section of the younger generation of workers to take up more aggressive methods of organisation, in the process transcending the defensive mentality associated with earlier forms of trade unionism. Beatrice Webb could write contemptuously in 1913:

> Syndicalism has taken the place of the old-fashioned Marxism. The angry youth, with bad complexion, frowning brow and weedy frame is now always a Syndicalist; the glib young workman whose tongue runs away with him today mouths the phrases of French Syndicalism instead of those of German Social Democracy.[36]

As in many other countries where syndicalism won a base, it was young workers, largely free from past ingrained traditions and loyalties that were at the fore of attempts to find alternative forms of trade union organisation to established structures.

To sum up, although it is true the syndicalist movement did not implant itself as deeply and as broadly as the reformist trade unions amongst workers in large industrial factory settings, it nonetheless appealed, in varying degrees and in different contexts, to diverse groups of workers, skilled, semi-skilled and unskilled. And compared to the labour and socialist labour parties, its social composition was virtually exclusively working class.

Gender

On gender issues syndicalism's contribution was fairly mixed, as an examination of the movements in France, Britain and America, by way of example, reveals. A number of commentators have justifiably criticised the syndicalists' preoccupation with workplace issues and struggles – in which their core constituency was narrowly perceived to be unionised or about to be unionised, usually male, workers. The problem is that such a primary focus on workplace struggle ignored the way in which women's oppression cut across home and work and often led to an explicit rejection of wider political issues, notably the franchise for women. 'It confused a healthy cynicism of the existing political system with a disregard for all those who sought to work within it, regardless of their political standpoint'.[37]

---

35 G.R. Askwith, *Industrial Problems and Disputes* (London, 1974; originally published 1920), p. 134.

36 M.I. Cole (ed.), *Beatrice Webb's Diaries 1912–1924* (London, 1952), p. 7.

37 M. Davies, *Comrade or Brother?: The Hidden History of the British Labour Movement, 1789–1951* (London, 1993), p. 101. See also S. Rowbotham, *Hidden From History: 300 Years of Women's Oppression and the Fight Against It* (London, 1973), p. 114.

Jeremy Jennings has highlighted the marked indifference of the French syndicalist movement to the question of votes for women.[38] With the notable exception of Marie Guillot, a school-teacher from Sâone-et-Loire, female enfranchisement had few supporters within the CGT. Guillot's argument was that votes for women would have an educative value: 'How do you arrive at enlightening women if you do not give her the right to concern herself with social and political questions?'[39] But for the most part such arguments were dismissed from the vantage point of the anti-voting stance of syndicalist theory. Alfred Rosmer, a journalist on *La Vie ouvriére*, reflecting without 'the least enthusiasm' upon the possible acquisition of the vote by women in Britain, could see only one possible benefit from this measure: 'When they have ascertained the limited effectiveness of parliamentary action', he wrote, 'women will go much farther, towards the search for other means'.[40] To vote was to participate in a system syndicalists wanted to destroy. From this critical perspective:

> feminism was a bourgeois movement led by middle-class ladies which sought to destroy the solidarity of interests between men and women of the same class only to replace it with a fallacious solidarity based upon membership of the same sex regardless of position within the economic order.[41]

Similarly the IWW considered the vote largely irrelevant and of little importance to working class women. Even Elizabeth Gurly Flynn, the 'rebel girl' of Joe Hill's famous song and outstanding female Wobbly organiser, insisted: 'The vote will not free women.' She advised women to 'find their power at the point of production where they work'. She considered the women's suffrage movement to be dominated by 'rich faddists' and emphasised that 'the queen of the parlour' had no interest in common with 'the maid of the kitchen', the wife of the department store owner showed no sisterly concern for the 17 year-old girl who found prostitution the only door to avoid becoming a $5-a-week clerk.[42] In 1916 the *Industrial Worker*, reflecting on the use of direct action tactics by American suffragists in their fight for the ballot, wondered why 'if the women are to use direct action, they do not use it to get for themselves something of value'.[43]

Although a slightly more sympathetic stance was adopted by the ISEL in Britain, the same underlying dismissive sentiments towards the Women's Social and Political Union were expressed in *The Syndicalist*:

> The suffrage movement is exerting a fine educative influence on our girls and women. It is moulding the stuff of which the revolution will be made. By their militant tactics the Suffragists will assuredly gain their end. But to us it is somewhat ironical that they are by DIRECT ACTION bringing about a state of things under which they will be as impotent

---

[38] J. Jennings, 'The CGT and the Couriau Affair: Syndicalist Responses to Female Labour in France Before 1914', *European History Quarterly*, 21: 3 (1991), pp. 321–37.

[39] M. Gulliot, *L'Ecole émancipée*, 4 February 1911.

[40] A. Rosmer, *La Vie ouvrèire*, 25, 5 October 1910, pp. 415–22.

[41] Jennings, 'The CGT', p. 332.

[42] Cited in P.S. Foner, *Women and the American Labor Movement: From the Trade Unions to the Present* (New York, 1982), p. 197.

[43] *Industrial Worker*, 15 July 1916.

> as the male 'voting cattle' are now! From the day when the women get the vote will date the degeneration of the women's movement.[44]

Such a dismissive stance placed the British syndicalists alongside every other labour and socialist organisation of the day, none of whom made the enfranchisement of women, or women's rights in general, a campaigning priority. In turn, the distaste for industrial action by workers expressed by some Suffragette leaders contributed to driving a wedge between the two movements, such that 'the tragedy of both movements was that they ran side by side without appearing even to notice one another'.[45]

Meanwhile, one crucial issue that had to be confronted by syndicalists everywhere was what attitude to take to the growing presence of women in the labour market? French syndicalists disagreed among themselves on this issue:

> not least because amongst their ranks were to be found divergent general conceptions of the status of women, marriage and the family. When it came to the fundamentals of sexual politics, the syndicalist movement as a whole was not able to articulate a consistent or coherent response.[46]

No doubt some individual syndicalists in France, as elsewhere, shared the conventional prejudices of their time – that women's role was primarily within the home. Such attitudes have to be set in the context of a time when paid women's work was scarce, and most women carried out intensive unpaid labour to service male family members. This marginalised position was even more marked in countries such as Italy and Spain. Only in 1918 did the CNT congress grant women membership for the first time. But in general syndicalists shared the viewpoint of most of their progressive contemporaries, that the exploitation of women could only be ended through class-based action: for working class women that meant entry into the paid workforce, trade union experience and political mobilisation. However, that these supposed instruments of emancipation might themselves be sexually in-egalitarian in their internal practices seems to have been rarely discussed, or even acknowledged. Moreover, there were differences in the way syndicalist movements related to female labour.

In France by 1911 women comprised over 35 per cent of the non-agricultural labour force (a high proportion compared with other countries), yet only just over 8 per cent of unionised workers by 1914 (a quarter of whom were in women-only unions).[47] But it was not just the Socialist Party and mainstream trade unions that paid scant attention to the specific grievances and aspirations of such women workers. From the outset, syndicalist attitudes to the 'woman question' tended to reflect the male chauvinism of skilled workers who viewed women workers as 'capitalism's Trojan horse', frequently introduced into the workshops to undercut wage levels and dilute the skills of male craftsmen. As a counter to the feminisation of industry, some CGT members called for equal pay for equal work 'as a cynical device to persuade

---

44 J. Radcliffe, *The Syndicalist and Amalgamation News*, December 1913.

45 P. Foot, *The Vote: How it was Won and How it was Undermined* (London, 2005), p. 227.

46 Jennings, 'The CGT', p. 321–2.

47 M. Guilbert, *Les femes et l'organisation syndicale avant 1914* (Paris, 1966), p. 14; 29; 38.

employers that it was no longer profitable to employ women'.[48] The use of women blacklegs to break a printing strike at Nancy in 1901 'accentuated stereotypes of women as cheap docile workers'.[49]

Little CGT effort was made to organise working women and all too frequently syndicalist propaganda was directed solely at the male labour force. On those few occasions when this was not the case it usually mirrored the conventional image of a women's domestic duty and fidelity. Gradually though some in the CGT began to reassess their attitude to female workers, influenced by increasing evidence of French women workers' involvement in protest actions, as well as by the direct action militancy of British suffragettes. Delegates to the 1900 CGT congress were urged to put aside their anti-feminism and recruit women workers. And in 1907 there was the establishment of a *Comité d'Action Féministe Syndicaliste*, with local groups meeting in the *bourses*, which were regarded as a more suitable forum for female trade unionists than male-dominated cafés. According to Robert Magraw, 'the tone and content of CGT propaganda at the time suggests that many vestiges of traditional prejudices persisted', for example with posters designed to woo women's support for the campaign for the 'English Week' portraying scenes 'in which dad and son are spending Saturday afternoon fishing whilst mum happily spends her "free" Saturday afternoon on household chores!'.[50]

But an important turning point came with the so-called 'Couriau affair' in 1913, when a local print union not only refused membership to a Lyon woman who took a job as a printing worker, but also expelled her husband for refusing to tell her to give up her job – action that was effectively supported by the union's (reformist) syndicalist leader Auguste Keufer. In the pages of *La Bataille syndicaliste*, Alfred Rosmer published the views of some of those most immediately concerned in the affair. J. Bottinelli, for the typographers, admitted that: 'Yes, we seek the eviction of women from the printing works ... people regard us as egotists: who cares; we are defending our professional interests'.[51] However, other leading CGT members, such as Monatte, sought to distance themselves from the 'antediluvian' male chauvinism of the printers, and Rosmer campaigned for a women's right to work. Gradually female wage labour was accepted as a permanent reality and some efforts were made to unionise women rather than exclude them from the labour market. By 1914 the CGT was beginning to take a fresh interest in women workers, sponsoring enquiries into their specific problems, seeking to 'educate' its own male members and to recruit female cadre.

Despite similar ambiguities inside the IWW there were much greater attempts made to organise women workers. In the main the Wobblies dismissed the argument that women workers were impossible to organise, attributing their distrust for unionism entirely to their bad experience with the AFL. Male workers were urged:

---

[48] R. Magraw, 'Socialism, Syndicalism and French Labour Before 1914', in Geary, *Labour and Socialist Movements in Europe*, p. 61.

[49] R. Magraw, *France 1814–1915: The Bourgeois Century* (Oxford, 1983), p. 288.

[50] R. Magraw, *A History of the French Working Class: Vol. 2: Workers the Bourgeois Republic* (Oxford, 1992), p. 69.

[51] Cited in Jennings, 'The CGT', p. 334.

> Don't fight against woman labor; women find it necessary to work. They do not work because they enjoy making some corporation 'rich beyond the dreams of avarice!' They work, because they have got to make a living.

The advice continued: 'Do not blame the women; blame the system. Educate, agitate and organise for the purpose of improving conditions and changing the system.'[52] Yet as Philip Foner has pointed out, the Wobblies also contradicted themselves on the question of women workers, so that while they thought it justifiable, and even desirable for young, unmarried women to enter the labour market and be organised, the case of the married woman was entirely different. Believing that 'the factory girl of today is the helpful and encouraging wife of the union man of tomorrow', the Wobblies viewed with horror the thought of married women 'leaving her home and children unprotected and uncared for during the working hours' and believed it important they be eliminated from the workforce.[53]

From the outset the IWW aimed to draw women into membership and to encourage their militancy. Shortly after its founding convention the IWW employed women as union organisers (the most notable being Elizabeth Gurly Fynn and Matilda Rabionowitz). Nonetheless, according to some historians: 'The IWW commitment to women's rights c[ould] be characterised as "workerist" rather than feminist, concentrating on the exploitation of women on a class rather than a sexual basis'.[54] While adamant about the principle that women must have full membership and equal rights in the union, the Wobblies could only recruit women who were *wage-earners*, which necessarily deterred women not in the paid workforce.

Like the work settings in which it primarily operated, the IWW was primarily a male organisation. As we have seen, its main base of support lay in the mid-west and far west, among lumberjacks and harvest workers, metal miners, and migratory labourers of all kinds. 'The hobo jungles, lumber camps, and frontier mining towns that spawned and nurtured IWW activism were overwhelmingly male in composition and character. The raw and rather brutal quality of such work environments seemed to validate the IWW's class war language and worldview'.[55] Francis Shor has even suggested IWW culture was characterised by the way in which the rhetoric of struggle in the workplace and on the picket line celebrated male virtues, an oppositional masculinism, and a 'virile syndicalism'.[56] For example, in the West, IWW literature

[52] *One Big Union Monthly*, 1 September 1919.

[53] Cited in Foner, p. 190.

[54] S.D. Bird, D. Georgakas and D. Shaffer, *Solidarity Forever: An Oral History of the Wobblies* (London, 1987), p. 141.

[55] J.R. Barrett, *William Z. Foster and the Tragedy of American Radicalism* (Chicago, 1999), p. 38. See also A. Baron (ed.), *Work Engendered: Towards a New History of American Labor* (Ithaca, NY, 1991), pp. 1–46; A. Schofield, 'Rebel Girls and Union Maids: The Woman Question in the Journals of the AFL and IWW, 1905–1920', *Feminist Studies*, 9 (Summer 1983), pp. 335–58; A. Kessler-Harris, *Out to Work: A History of Wage Earning: Women in the United States* (New York, 1982), pp. 153–9.

[56] F. Shor, '"Virile Syndicalism" in Comparative Perspective: A Gender Analysis of the IWW in the United States and Australia', *International Labor and Working Class History*, 56 (1999), pp. 65–77.

proclaimed that the migratory worker, usually a young, unmarried male, was 'the finest specimen of American manhood ... the leaven of the revolutionary labour movement' around who would be built a militant nucleus for revolutionary industrial unionism.[57]

Perhaps such a culture amongst the migratory workers of the west was not too surprising given that they not only spent enormous amounts of time at work in the company of only other males, but also frequently lived and socialised in virtually all-male environments. Even so a significant aspect of the 1907 Portland lumber workers' strike in the Pacific Northwest was the women's brigade organised by IWW member Nina Wood, and similar brigades were established in the West whenever lumber or mine workers on strike had established families with them. The women involved actively engaged in picketing, often leading to physical confrontations with strike-breakers and law officers.[58]

Moreover, even though *western* IWW members were mainly men (reflecting the fact that most of the industries the Wobblies organised in had few women workers), the organisation was much more successful in attracting women workers in the *east*. The major industry in the east earmarked for organisation by the IWW was textile manufacturing. Approximately half the textile workers were female, a large percentage under the age of 20 with many less than 14. Women played such a pivotal role in textiles that industrial unions without their full participation were inconceivable. In the famous 1912 Lawrence strike IWW female strikers played a central role. Special women's meetings organised by Elizabeth Gurly Flynn and Bill Haywood encouraged them to stand up to their husbands and fellow male workers who disapproved of their participation. And women assumed positions of authority and leadership by participating in all committees, and speaking and picketing in public. Flynn recalled:

> There was considerable male opposition to women going to meetings and marching on the picket line. We resolutely set out to combat these notions. The women wanted to picket. They were strikers as well as wives and were valiant fighters. We knew that to leave them at home, isolated from the strike activity, a prey to worry, affected by the complaints of trades people, landlords, priests and ministers, was dangerous to the strike ...
>
> We talked to the strikers about One Big Union, regardless of skill or lack of it, foreign-born or native-born, colour, religion or sex. We showed how all the differences are used by the bosses to keep workers divided and pitted against each other ... We said firmly: 'You work together for the boss. You can stand together and fight for yourselves!' This was more than a union. It was a crusade for a united people – for 'Bread and Roses'.[59]

Notwithstanding such efforts Flynn insisted male chauvinism generally within the IWW prevented many women from actively participating within the organisation. As a consequence she often emphasised the need for the Wobblies to 'adapt [its] propaganda to the special needs of women' and to develop special kinds of

---

57 *Solidarity*, 17 September 1910.

58 Bird et al., p. 100.

59 E. Gurly Flynn, *The Rebel Girl: An Autobiography: My First Life, 1906–1926* (New York, 1994), p. 132; 133–4.

organisation suited to the conditions of women's lives if it was to have lasting success in organising women workers. 'Some of our male members are prone to underestimate this vital need and assert that the principles of the IWW are alike for all, which we grant with certain reservations'.[60]

After 1913 the IWW was increasingly active in male-dominated industries, although it never abandoned efforts to organise women. It was the first American labour union to discuss the status of housework as a category of labour and the first to organise chambermaids and prostitutes. And it adopted a progressive position on one major issue of sexuality: reproductive rights. Pioneer birth control advocate Margaret Sanger reprinted the famous IWW Preamble in the premier issue of her magazine *The Woman Rebel*, and 100,000 first edition copies of her *Family Limitations* were clandestinely produced by an IWW printer and distributed nation-wide through union outlets and supporters. Female Wobblies such as Georgia Kotsch, Caroline Nelson and Marie Equi were also major disseminators of birth control information.[61]

Yet despite the fact the Wobblies formally proclaimed that women were entitled to 'equal opportunities, duties and privileges even to the holding of executive office', absolute parity between the sexes was rarely achieved, with few women ever achieving positions in the IWW national leadership. Many male members retained conventional views on sexual issues, as was reflected in a number of articles that appeared in the union's western paper *Industrial Worker* defending, without protest, the use of prostitutes by migratory workers.[62] And the IWW's image of a worker's utopia continued to include a family in which the male worker was so well paid that he could return at night to the embrace of his wife and children and a well-cared for home.[63] But the fact remains that in many respects the IWW's approach to, and treatment of, women workers was an enormous positive advance from that of the AFL and Socialist Party, neither of whom made the enfranchisement of women, or women's rights in general, a campaigning priority.

The gender politics of the Italian and Spanish syndicalist movements were no more progressive, particularly in a context in which parliamentary representation and feminist agitation was even less developed. And both movements were likewise primarily male-dominated bodies, although some individual women rose to prominent positions, (for example the anarchist Federica Montseny became CNT Minister of Health in Spain's Popular Front government in 1936). But if the CNT did not explicitly campaign over gender issues during the 1930s it by no means just concerned itself with the workplace, but often intervened directly in the community to play a pivotal role in local protests in which women (waged and non-waged) were involved. For example, during the 1931 Barcelona rent strike, union members reconnected electricity to strikers' flats and participated in avoiding evictions; on other occasions CNT-led strikes involved whole communities in acts of solidarity

---

60 *Solidarity*, 15 July 1915.

61 M. Tax, *The Rising of the Women* (New York, 1980), pp. 125–63; M. Sanger, *An Autobiography*, (New York, 1971); Bird et al., p. 142.

62 A.S. Kraditor, *The Radical Persuasion, 1890–1917: Aspects of the Intellectual History and the Historiography of Three American Radical Organisations* (Baton Rouge, 1981), p. 188.

63 Foner, p. 194.

to provide for strikers' families.[64] By contrast in Ireland, whilst the ITGWU from the outset championed women's rights and was an enthusiastic supporter of the campaign for women's suffrage, it only admitted men to membership in September 1911 when an Irish Women Workers' Union was founded by Larkin's sister Delia, who became general secretary (with Larkin as President).[65] But as elsewhere, the union's confrontations with employers and the state necessitated the winning of support from the wider community, including strikers' families, and some women were attracted to the organisation as a consequence.

Ethnicity and Immigrant Labour

Syndicalists also had to confront potential ethnic divisions inside the working class movement as well as the question of immigrant labour, albeit this was much more of an issue in certain countries than others. In France by 1911 there were 1.16 million immigrants, comprising some 10 per cent of the industrial workforce.[66] Belgian workers, one-third of the textile workforce, presented some complexities in terms of trade union organisation for the Roubaix labour movement; Flemish-speaking and strongly Catholic, they remained culturally distinct from French workers and lived in ghetto areas. At the same time employment agencies recruited Germans who entered the Parisian crafts, and tens of thousands of Italians in the Lorraine iron and steel sectors, as well as a variety of ethnic groups in the fast growing Pas-de-Calais coalfield. According to Robert Magraw, even where immigrants themselves brought with them traditions of radicalism, as with Italians from Romagna or Spaniards from Catalonia, they lacked civil rights and could be intimidated by threats of deportation if they became involved in trade union activities. Their presence during the Great Depression of 1873–1896 helped nurture a wave of working class xenophobia, with trade wars with Italy fuelling anti-Italian sentiments, just as revanchist aspirations encouraged anti-German feeling in eastern France. Moreover, with foreign workers sometimes used as 'blacklegs' in strikes, it further fed the anti-immigrant sentiments of some French workers.[67]

Even though before 1914 the CGT expressed a formal commitment to organising foreign-born workers, it 'often evidenced a real hostility to immigrant workers when they invaded local job markets'. After the First World War, the (by now) reformist-led CGT supported immigration, but called for controls on the numbers entering sensitive labour markets, with the union securing some seats in public placement offices (immigrant employment agencies) in large cities. [68]

By contrast the IWW adopted a much more inclusive stance. America's working class was notable for its ethnic and religious heterogeneity.

---

64 See Earlham.

65 E. O'Connor, *James Larkin* (Cork, 2002), p. 35.

66 G.S. Cross, *Immigrant Workers in Industrial France: The Making of a New Labouring Class* (Temple, Philadelphia, PA, 1983).

67 R. Magraw, *France 1814–1915: The Bourgeois Century*, pp. 298–9.

68 Cross, pp. 144–56.

> Native Americans had nothing but contempt for Irish Catholic immigrants; and Irish workers in turn looked down upon the late-coming Poles, Slavs and Italians. Whites feared [black workers] ... Employers easily played off one group against another and shrewdly mixed their labour forces to weaken group solidarity.[69]

Nonetheless, the IWW did what other American unions refused to do; it opened its doors to all regardless of race, creed or sex. As one West Coast organiser, George Speed, put it: 'One man is as good as another to me. I don't care whether he is black, blue, green or yellow, as long as he acts the man and acts true to his economic interests as a worker'.[70] An IWW leaflet proclaimed there was only *one* labour organisation 'that admits the coloured worker on a footing of absolute equality with the white – the Industrial Workers of the World'.[71] This was a stance substantiated by Mary White Ovington, one of the founders of the National Association for the Advancement of Coloured People: 'There are two organisations in this country', she wrote, 'that have shown they do care [about full rights for the Negroes]. The first is the NAACP ... The second organisation that attacks Negro segregation is the Industrial Workers of the World ... The IWW has stood with the Negro'. [72]

According to Philip Foner the IWW attempted to educate its members to recognise all workers as equal regardless of colour.[73] All IWW journals participated actively in this educational campaign, including *The Voice of the People*, the Southern organ of the IWW published in New Orleans, which constantly reminded members that the organisation of black workers was an 'economic bread and butter issue'. 'Leaving the Negro outside of your union makes him a potential, if not an actual, scab, dangerous to the organised workers, to say nothing of his own interests as a worker'. Such prejudice on the job could have only one result – 'keeping the workers fighting each other, while the boss gets the benefit'. The idea fostered by the capitalists that the white worker was 'superior' was part of the same game.[74] And the IWW practised what it preached with a union rule of total racial integration, especially courageous in an era when racist so-called Jim Crow laws were being strengthened throughout the South and when the Klu Klux Klan still marched in presidential inauguration parades.

In May 1912 Bill Haywood travelled to Louisiana to address the second regional convention of the Brotherhood of Timber Workers (BTW), an independent union of forest and sawmill workers in Louisiana, Arkansas and Texas that was one of the first southern unions to admit black workers (who formed half the membership of the union). In the midst of a large strike against the lumber companies Haywood promised them funds and organisers if they affiliated to the IWW and made a rousing

---

[69] M. Dubofsky, *We Shall Be All: A History of the Industrial Workers of the World* (Chicago, 1969), p. 10.

[70] *Industrial Worker*, 17 June, 1909.

[71] Cited in P.S. Foner, *History of the Labor Movement in the United States: Vol. 4: The Industrial Workers of the World 1905–1917* (New York, 1965), p. 124.

[72] Ibid., p. 124.

[73] Ibid., p. 124.

[74] *Industrial Worker*, 26 December 1912.

call for a bi-racial united front to fight employers.[75] But surprised to find no black workers at the convention (it was illegal to hold interracial meetings in Louisiana), he made a direct appeal:

> You work in the same mills together. Sometimes a black man and a white man chop down the same tree together. You are meeting in convention now to discuss the conditions under which you labour. This can't be done intelligently by passing resolutions here and sending them to another room for the black men to act upon. Why not be sensible about this and call the Negroes into the Convention? If it is against the law, this is one time when the law should be broken.[76]

Black workers were subsequently invited into the convention session which voted three to one for the BTW to affiliate to the IWW, and officially adopted its principles and integrated its committees and meetings. The re-named Southern District of the National Industrial Union of Forest and Lumber Workers set out to organise mill towns one by one, and during a series of strikes in 1912–1913 successfully expanded its membership. But the employers quickly counter-attacked with a lockout which shut down 46 mills and amidst subsequent blacklisting, jailing and mob violence, the union was effectively destroyed by the spring of 1914. Nonetheless, it left behind an impressive tradition of militant struggle and labour solidarity, uniting black and white workers as never before in a southern industry.[77]

Another important base amongst black workers was built on the north east coast of America. The IWW's Local 8 of the Marine Transport Workers (MTW), which constituted one of the largest and most effective IWW units when it was first organised in 1913, was composed primarily but not entirely of black workers. It was led by Ben Fletcher, a prominent African-American who staunchly advocated working class solidarity over ethnic and racial rivalry and had 4,000 members in and around the Philadelphia docks. Fletcher was elected to the General Executive Board of the IWW and was one of the leading Wobbly figures in 1918 imprisoned for 'obstructing' World War One. Other black workers within the IWW who attained national renown as organisers and orators were Rosco T. Sims and Alanzo Richards.[78]

Although no statistics are available which indicate black workers' membership of the IWW on a national level some commentators have claimed it recruited up to 100,000 during its lifespan, although the absence of similar claims by the Wobblies at the time

---

75 S.D. Spero and A.L. Harris, *The Black Worker: The Negro and the Labor Movement* (New York, 1931), p. 331.

76 W.D. Haywood, *Bill Haywood's Book: The Autobiography of William D. Haywood* (New York, 1929), pp. 241–2.

77 See Foner, *IWW*, pp. 245–57; J.F. Fickle, 'Race, Class and Radicalism: The Wobblies in the Southern Lumber Industry, 1900–1916', in J.R. Conlin (ed.), *At the Point of Production: The Local History of the IWW* (Wesport, Conn, 1981), pp. 98–113; H. Kimeldorf, 'Radical Possibilities? The Rise and Fall of Wobbly Unionism on the Philadelphia Docks', in C. Winslow (ed.), *Waterfront Workers: New Perspectives on Race and Class* (Illinois, 1998); L. McGirr, 'Black and White Longshoremen in the IWW: A History of the Philadelphia Marine Transport Workers Industrial Union Local 8', *Labor History*, 36 (1995), pp. 377–402.

78 J.L. Kornbluh (ed.), *Rebel Voices: An IWW Anthology* (Chicago, 1988), p. 439.

might suggest much fewer were attracted.[79] However, it should be noted that whilst the IWW attempted to battle on behalf of black workers and recruit them to their organisation, it also tended to reduce the whole question of discrimination, segregation, deprivation of civil and political rights and racist violence, to the issue of class and workplace struggles. As a result it effectively failed to concern itself and connect with broader racial and political struggles within society, thereby restricting its potential appeal to black workers.

Prejudice against Asian workers ran as high or higher on the American West Coast as prejudice against blacks. Many workers believed there was a 'yellow menace' that would take their jobs or depress their standard of living, and the total exclusion or rigid control of Asian immigration was a constant demand of AFL-affiliated unions. In a sharp departure from this view, the IWW welcomed Chinese, Japanese, Filipino and other Asian workers to its ranks:

> The AFL is fighting against Chinese, Japanese and Southern European races calling them an "undesirable" class of immigrants; and is agitating for laws to bar them from America. The IWW extends a fraternal hand to every wage-worker, no matter what his religion, fatherland or trade.[80]

Japanese and Chinese workers had their own labour organisations that worked with the IWW, although not usually affiliating directly.

At the same time in the Southwest the IWW mine and harvest unions had a very high level of participation by Mexican immigrants, and on the East Coast the Marine Transport Workers also had a substantial Hispanic membership.[81] Foreign-language Wobbly pamphlets, leaflets and papers were also issued (including French, Italian, Spanish, Hungarian and Russian) and foreign-language branches of some local IWW unions were established, such as the Hungarian branch of the Metal and Machinery Workers' Industrial Union, and Mexicans formed their own IWW locals in San Diego and Los Angeles.[82] IWW organisers who could speak foreign languages were constantly sought to work in centres of immigrant workers and the Italian Socialist Federation's paper *Il Proletario* became an official Wobbly organ.

By contrast in the less developed Italy and Spain, where foreign immigration was less prevalent, the main internal division inside the working class movement which syndicalists had to confront was that between workers from different geographical regions of the country, notably between those from the (primarily industrial) north and (primarily agricultural) south. Both the USI and CNT consistently sought to challenge myths and prejudices about the alleged threat from southern migrant labour often stoked by bourgeois political forces. For example, in Barcelona the fact that by 1930 migrants from elsewhere in Spain formed more than a third of the city's

---

[79] For claims of a black IWW membership of up to 100,000 see Spero and Harris, p. 331; J.S. Gambs, *The Decline of the IWW* (New York, 1932), p. 167. For a more sober assessment see D.M. Barnes: 'The Ideology of the Industrial Workers of the World', PhD, Washington State University, 1962, p. 21. See also P.S. Foner, *Organised Labor and the Black Worker, 1619–1973* (New York, 1978), pp. 107–19.

[80] *Industrial Union Bulletin*, 13 July 1907.

[81] Bird et al, pp. 140–41.

[82] P.F. Brisendon, *The IWW: A Study of American Syndicalism* (New York, 1919), p. 160.

population and were prominent in the CNT, both added and simultaneously helped to challenge such prejudice. But the authorities' unsuccessful attempt to organise the repatriation of such 'undesirable elements' was testimony to the Confederación's base of influence and its solidaristic philosophy, to which anarchist affinity groups made an important contribution.[83]

Catholicism

Another issue syndicalists had to confront in some countries was the problem of religion, specifically Catholicism. It was no accident that *anarcho*-influenced syndicalist movements became prominent in Spain and Italy, both of which were Catholic societies in which the great economic transformation from an agrarian to an industrial order had begun (and then got stuck) under the auspices of a weak and ineffective liberal movement. In consequence, there was a tendency for agrarian radicalism to take on an anarchist colouration, a movement directed not only against the landowners but also their protectors, notably the monarchy and the Catholic Church. In this respect, the alleged 'fanatical' anti-clerical sentiments of Italian and Spanish anarchists inside the USI and CGT were rooted on firm ground.[84]

Italian working class politics were bedevilled by the 'religious problem'. According to G.D.H. Cole the USI, along with the entire left 'found itself ranged against the Papacy' and supporting the principle of 'laicity' (or secularism) in political matters. By contrast:

> the more conservative Catholic elements rallied the faithful against the syndicalists, and the Papacy emphatically took the side of the more reactionary Catholic groups, and did its best to suppress those who gave their support to agricultural workers in their struggle against social oppression.[85]

In Spain it was in revenge for the murder of the CNT leader Salvador Seguí by police gunmen in 1921 that the Archbishop of Saragossa was shot by the celebrated CGT guerrilla leader, Buenventura Durutti. And during the Civil War it was groups of anarchists (some of whom were linked to the CNT) who carried out most of the church burnings that became a veritable epidemic in the summer of 1936, and which in the process destroyed many remarkable works of religious art. It was also such groups who carried out many of the summary executions of suspected fascists which took place during the same initial period. Their favourite victims included priests and monks.[86] Gerald Brenan has explained such activity thus:

> The fanatical hatred of the Anarchists for the [Catholic] Church and the extraordinary violence of their attack upon it during the Civil War...can only, I think, be explained as

83 Earlham, p. 152.

84 G. Lichtheim, *A Short History of Socialism* (Glasgow, 1970), p. 223.

85 G.D.H. Cole, *A History of Socialist Thought: The Second International, 1889–1914: Part 1 (*London:, 1974), pp. 730–31.

86 G. Woodcock, *Anarchism: A History of Libertarian Ideas and Movements* (Harmondsworth, 1979), pp. 353–67.

> the hatred of the heretics for the Church from which they have sprung. For in the eyes of Spanish libertarians the Catholic Church occupies the position of Anti-Christ in the Christian world. It is far more to them than a mere obstacle to revolution. They see in it the fountain of all evil, the corrupter of youth with its vile doctrine of original sin ...
>
> The priests and monks left them at a critical moment in their history and went over to the rich.[87]

In France Catholicism remained influential over many women and among workers in Flanders and some Midi towns, but elsewhere Catholic clergy were widely hated for preaching the divine origins of social inequalities and that elite charity was the only remedy for poverty. The French labour movement shared much of the legacy of Enlightenment rationalism, thereby viewing science, education and positivism as inseparable from Republican democracy, an essential component of socialism. It viewed the assault on clerical influence and the secularisation of education as prerequisites for cultural, intellectual and social progress. Yvetot agreed that the Church was the enemy of the people 'but it is not the only enemy'. Getting rid of the clergy would make no difference if the religion of Christ was replaced by the religion of the Republic: 'We do not wish to free ourselves from one only to become dupes of the other.'[88] The real enemies of the people were those who oppressed and enslaved them and this meant not only the removal of the Church but principally the bourgeois state in the guise of the Republic. 'Down with the church', Yvetot proclaimed, 'and all the filthy vermin of the mind who live in it! Down with the state and all those who support and perpetuate it!'.[89] However, relative unimportance was attached to the clerical issue and the activities of the Church by CGT.

In Ireland Jim Larkin and the overwhelming majority of the ITGWU's members were practicing Catholics and the great majority of the working class in Dublin, both men and women, identified with the Church and the Catholic faith. Such attitudes stood in stark contrast with the working class in Italy, Spain and France. But, as John Newsinger has explained, whereas on the continent, the Catholic Church was allied with the great Catholic landowners and Catholic governments, in Ireland the great landowners and the government were Protestant. Whereas on the continent the rising middle class had to fight for power and influence against a feudal-royalist reaction that was allied with the Church and accordingly tended to seek popular support around a programme of anti-clericalism, in Ireland the Church supported the middle class against the Protestant Ascendancy and the British.[90] Thus Larkin himself once famously insisted to a sceptical audience in America:

> There is no antagonism between the cross and socialism. A man can pray to Jesus the Carpenter, and be a better socialist for it. Rightly understood, there is no conflict between

---

[87] G. Brenan, *The Spanish Labyrinth: An Account of the Social and Political Background of the Spanish Civil War* (Cambridge, 1988), p. 189; 191. See also J. Peirats, *Anarchists in the Spanish Revolution* (London, 1990).

[88] Cited in J. Jennings, *Syndicalism in France: A Study in Ideas* (London, 1990), p. 39.

[89] Ibid.

[90] J. Newsinger, *Rebel City: Larkin, Connolly and the Dublin Labour Movement* (London, 2004), pp. 33–4.

> the vision of Marx and the vision of Christ. I stand by the cross and I stand by Karl Marx. Both *Capital* and the *Bible* are to me Holy Books.[91]

But Larkin's Catholicism did not stop Catholic priests using the press to attack the ITGWU, denouncing it for atheism, for supporting divorce and birth control, and for being the work of the 'Anti-Christ'. The degree of clerical hostility that greeted the union reached a crescendo at the time of the 1913 Dublin Lockout, following an attempt to send victimised workers' children to stay for a holiday with sympathisers in Britain. According to Emmet Larkin, the rise of the ITGWU was from the very beginning greeted with 'nonsensical abuse' and 'hysterical anti-Socialism' by the Church.[92]

At the same time, the historical legacy of British imperialism meant that the city of Belfast, with its inter-class linkages within Ulster Protestantism, had a labour movement that was blighted by Orange as well as Catholic sectarianism. Partly for this reason, and partly because of the different structure of the north's economy (much more developed industry compared with the ITGWU's stronghold of Dublin), Irish syndicalism was almost entirely a southern experience. In 1907 Larkin led a strike in Belfast of 2,500 dockers, carters and coal labourers which united Catholic and Protestant workers and helped to undermine political and religious bigotry. More than 100,000 workers marched down the Protestant Shankill Road in a demonstration involving both Orange and nationalist flute bands. However, British troops invaded the Catholic Falls Road and shot dead two workers, and the employers moved quickly to reinforce sectarianism by sponsoring a 'yellow' union, an exclusively Protestant body. As a result, in the long run the ITGWU achieved little of a tangible nature in Belfast.[93]

At the 1914 Irish TUC Congress, at which Larkin was the chairman, he denounced the bigotry and intolerance that was dividing the country north and south. 'The question of religion', he maintained, 'was a matter for each individual's conscience and in a great many cases was the outcome of birth or residence in a certain geographical area'. 'Claiming for ourselves liberty of conscience, liberty to worship', he continued, 'we shall see to it that every other individual enjoys the same right'. 'Intolerance', he noted, 'has been the curse of our country. It is for us to preach the gospel of tolerance and comradeship for all women and men.' 'There must be freedom for all to live, to think, to worship' he added, 'no book, no avenue must be closed.'[94] Nonetheless, Larkin remained a staunch Catholic and on one occasion actually refused to share the platform with a divorcee at a solidarity meeting organised by the British Socialist Party in Grimsby, England.[95] In a country in which the Catholic Church had considerable popular support and great influence even the revolutionary socialist James Connolly, who also played an influential leadership role inside the ITGWU, felt obliged to pose as a Catholic.[96] And Connolly also

91 B. Wolfe, *Strange Communists I Have Known* (London, 1996), p. 55.

92 Cited in Newsinger, p. 32.

93 J. Gray, *James Larkin and the Belfast Dock Strike of 1907* (Belfast, 1985).

94 Cited in Larkin, *James Larkin*, p. 153.

95 C.D. Greaves, *The Life and Times of James Connolly* (London, 1986), p. 331.

96 J. Newsinger, 'Irish Labour in a Time of Revolution, *Socialist History*, 22 (2002), p. 6.

condemned divorce as a product of capitalism, although he combined this position with a strong attack on the Church's attitude towards women.[97]

In America the IWW, while emphasising its membership included workers from all religious faiths, insisted its position was not affected by the religious ideas of its members. The Catholic Church was viewed as a tool of the exploiting class, and although Wobblies occasionally paid tribute to individual clergymen who supported labour's cause, they generally viewed the majority as betrayers of the workers' fight against the capitalists by inculcating slavish acceptance of the status quo. Such sentiments were vividly expressed in Joe Hill's derisive parodies of religious hymns, notably in the 'Preacher and the Slave' (sometimes called 'Pie in the Sky' or 'Long Haired Preachers'). This was printed in the third edition of the IWW songbook and sung to the hymn tune 'Sweet Bye and Bye'.

> Long-haired preachers come out every night,
> Try to tell you what's wrong and what's right;
> But when asked how 'bout something to eat
> They will answer with voices so sweet
>
> *Chorus*
>
> You will eat, bye and bye
> In that glorious land above the sky;
> Work and pray, live on hay,
> You'll get pie in the sky when you die.[98]

After the Lawrence strike of 1912 there was a local general strike to coincide with the opening of the trial of IWW leader Joseph Ettor and fellow Italian-born agitator Arturo Giovannitti. Faced with a mass parade, the City Council, whilst permitting the American flag to be carried, prohibited red flags and bands, and insisted the march was orderly. But several thousand Italians arrived in the city from nearby towns, bringing a band, 90 red flags and a large sign which read 'No God, No Master'. When a cordon of police tried to arrest the anarchist IWW leader of the parade, Carlo Tresca, there was a riot and two policemen were stabbed. The event was seized upon by the press throughout the country for a mammoth offensive against the Wobblies. The Catholic clergy, led by Father James T. O'Reilly, began an all-out drive to convince the foreign-born workers that the parade proved the IWW was opposed to all religion. It subsequently gave the anti-union forces a chance to drive a

---

[97] See J. Connolly, 'Labour, Nationality and Religion' which is reprinted in O.D. Edwards and B. Ransom (eds), *James Connolly: Selected Political Writings* (New York: Grove Press, 1974), pp. 61–162. Significantly, the ITGWU as an organisation did not effectively take up the cause of Irish national independence. It is true that Connolly, in the book *Labour in Irish History* (1910), argued that it was the Irish working class rather than the nationalist leaders who were the key force for revolution, that the struggle for national independence was an inseparable part of the struggle for socialism. However, neither Larkin nor other ITGWU leaders played an independent part in the national struggle, instead restricting it to support for the republican movement Sinn Fein.

[98] Reprinted in Kornbluh, p. 133.

wedge between immigrant Catholic workers, loyal to their God and to their adopted country, and the atheistic and unpatriotic IWW leaders.[99]

Organisational Structure

Displaying a real hostility to bureaucratic forms of organisation, and insisting on the self-emancipation of the working class through its own direct action, the syndicalists' organisational structures differed markedly from the more hierarchical and authoritarian practices in the reformist trade unions and socialist parties. There was a good deal of variety in syndicalist organisational structure between different countries, notably between the relative emphasis placed on industrial unionism by the IWW, ITGWU and ISEL, compared with the craft unionism of the CGT, CNT and USI, although gradually the latter bodies also adopted essentially industrial-based forms of organisation. Related to this was the relatively centralised structure adopted by the IWW compared with the more federalist and decentralised structures of the European syndicalists, although in practice all movements balanced between tendencies towards central control and local autonomy.

The IWW wanted to create a centralised organisation on the national level which could confront the concentrated power of American monopoly. Delegates at the union's 1905 founding convention adopted an elaborate structure for their new organisation based on a detailed illustration (sarcastically labelled 'Father Hagerty's Wheel of Fortune' by Samuel Gompers of the AFL). It was a circular diagram with the general administration (General Executive Board) of the IWW centred at its hub from which spokes emanated to 13 (later reduced to six) constituent industrial departments (such as agriculture, mining, transportation, construction), further subdivided into national industrial unions (such as lumber workers, railroad workers and metal mine workers), and subdivided again into local industrial unions that aimed to embrace everyone in individual workplaces irrespective of craft, skill or tool. In addition, there were to be 'mixed IWW locals' formed of workers living in the same locality and working in those industries where there were no industrial unions.

In practice, few Wobblies knew how to interpret or implement the structure of the 'Wheel' and most ignored its grandiose scheme, instead adopting a simpler plan of industrial unionism. In 1907 the General Executive Board took the decision that if 3,000 members were engaged in the same industry and organised in no less than seven different localities they could constitute a national industrial union. And emphasis was placed on organising workers into a dozen or so big industrial unions, such as the National Industrial Union of Textile Workers, the Marine Transport Workers, and the Agricultural Workers' Organisation. However, except in a few industries, such as mining and lumbering, it proved impossible to recruit sufficient numbers to justify the creation of local industrial unions. As a result, the 'mixed locals' tended to become more and more the standard form of IWW organisation in many areas of the country, all directly connected with the central office. In Goldfield, Nevada, the Local No. 220

[99] Foner, *IWW*, p. 348; Dubofsky, *We Shall Be All*, p. 256; B. Watson, *Bread and Roses: Mills, Migrants and the Struggle for the American Dream* (New York, 2005), pp. 217–40.

of the IWW embraced practically all the workers in the community, including 'miners, engineers, clerks, stenographers, teamsters, dishwashers, and waiters – all sorts of what are called common labourers'.[100] Such mixed locals were particularly relevant in the West, where Wobblies were often migrants whose connection with any particular industry was likely to be a transient one, with a potential variety of jobs in any single year, including logging, construction, agriculture and mining. In such circumstances, the IWW membership was transferred and honoured by locals everywhere.[101]

In Ireland the ITGWU was also founded as a union for all workers with an industrial-wide form of organisation. However, the 'Transport' tag to the ITGWU signalled the primary area of employment on which Jim Larkin concentrated the union' organising efforts, albeit with the aim of branching out from the union's base amongst unskilled dock-related workers to skilled railway workers. No real provision was made for a comprehensive industrial union structure as such. It was James Connolly who was to make a distinctive appeal for the development of industrial unionism, for trade union amalgamations that would unite with the Transport Union in 'One Big Union' with 'one card, one badge, one EC and one front to the common enemy, the capitalist'.[102] After the war Connolly's syndicalist teachings remained a living force within the union, providing it with its whole theoretical basis as the new leaders around William O'Brien endeavoured to formally outline an industrial unionist policy for general consumption along the lines previously outlined by Connolly.[103]

In Britain the ISEL was not intended to be an alternative revolutionary union organisation, but limited itself to propaganda activities in the belief that such a revolutionary movement could only be effectively built up through a campaign for the re-organisation of existing union structures. Specifically this was to be achieved by the amalgamation and reconstruction of the existing unions on an industrial basis infused with revolutionary syndicalist ideas. The ISEL attracted support from trade union branches, trades councils, and unofficial amalgamation committee movements (which campaigned in industries such as engineering, mining and transport), as well as numerous individual union militants. It was essentially a localised movement with neither a formal membership nor branch structure, and only a loose national organisation.

At first glance the organisational structure of French syndicalism appears to have been quite different from America, Ireland or Britain. Thus, many commentators point to the way the CGT generally regarded unionism as synonymous with organisation on craft lines, and envisioned the *syndicats* of the new society to be craft rather than industry-based units and characterised by a highly decentralised system of production and control.[104] In fact, such an interpretation overstates its case, because while the initial structure of the CGT was certainly not industrial as such, its organisation of individual local craft unions was nonetheless integrated

---

[100] *Industrial Union Bulletin*, 30 March 1907.

[101] Foner, *IWW*, pp. 37–8, 133–4; Dubofsky, *'Big Bill' Haywood*, p. 37; *We Shall Be All*, p. 132.

[102] Cited in Greaves, p. 378.

[103] E. O'Connor, *A Labour History of Ireland, 1824–1960* (Dublin, 1992), p. 99.

[104] For example, see Renshaw, p. 68.

into a broader federated movement which increasingly moved towards more explicit industrial forms. The CGT was composed of three types of organisation.

First, the *syndicat* (or local trade branch) was the basic unit of organisation which united workers who were employed in the same trade or industry in a particular town. Such syndicates differed a great deal from the much larger nationally-based British trade unions, in that they were small (with an average of 200 members) and locally-based. The *syndicat* was an autonomous body; it established, directed and controlled its own administrative machinery, and within wide limits could formulate its own policy and choose the line of action to be pursued at any moment. It had its own general assembly of all members, an administrative council responsible for the execution of policy, and a bureau responsible for administration. By 1912 there were 2,837 *syndicates* with 600,000 members.

Second, there were national trade federations (except in rare cases where a union, such as that of the railwaymen, was itself national) which united local *syndicats* within their respective industries on the basis of craft solidarity. Such federations were organised on similar lines to the *syndicates*, each with its own congress, council and bureau. In general each *syndicat* sent one delegate to the federal congress, regardless of size. The principle of federalism ensured that each *syndicat* adhered to its federation as an autonomous unit, casting a single vote equal to all other units. In 1908 there about 66 national federations which, through their national organisation, aimed to secure uniform wages and conditions within the industry across the country.

Third, there was the *bourses du travail*, formed by the union of *syndicats* of different industries situated in the same town or locality, organised on similar lines as above. Fernand Pelloutier, in large measure their creator, saw the functions of the *bourses* under four heads: first: mutual aid (employment bureau, unemployment and sickness benefits); second: education (general culture, economic research, information service); third: propaganda (encouragement to form new *syndicats*); and fourth: resistance (organisation of strikes and strike funds, agitation against laws hostile to the labour interest). On the whole, this plan was followed. The real importance of the *bourses* lay in the sense of solidarity they established in the district, uniting in common action workers of different trades and industries, who might otherwise have remained divided in the various individual *syndicats*. In 1906 there were 1,609 *syndicats* affiliated to the *Bourses* federation.

Each of these three bodies, the individual *syndicats*, the national trade federations, and the federation of *Bourses* were brought under a national umbrella by the *Confédération Générale du Travail*. But they allied together on the basis that *syndicats* could not affiliate directly to the CGT (with the exception of a few national *syndicats*) but must belong both to a national trade federation and to its local *bourse*, although this dual membership was never full achieved. However, at the biennial congresses of the CGT (at which general policy was set) after 1904, all *syndicats*, regardless of size, were represented directly, and entitled to the same vote as federations or *bourses*. This became a common source of conflict given the small individual unions' voting preponderance, and there were periodic demands for proportional representation based upon membership. The rules adopted by the CGT reflected its confederal character. The council of the CGT consisted of delegates from the two equal sections of the union, the federations and *Bourses*, although because of its numerical superiority, the more revolutionary *Bourses* had a greater voice than the federations and often pursued policies contrary to those adopted by the Confédération as a whole.[105]

Significantly, as Steve Jefferys has documented, by the early 1900s it increasingly became apparent to CGT leaders that this organisational structure was too dominated by craft interests.[106] The CGT's general secretary Victor Griffuelhes argued it could only aspire to mobilise workers around its key general strike demand if its trade-based local *syndicats* merged into national industrial federations which grouped several trades within broadly defined industries. From 1906 the CGT only admitted industrial federations, and both Griffuelhes and his successor from 1909, Léon Jouhaux, campaigned for all the skilled trades to combine into single-industry unions. This led to the organisation in 1907 of a single building trades affiliate (*Fédération du Bâtiment*) and in 1909 of a single metal trade union (*Fédération des Métaux*). Other industry-wide unions included those for agricultural workers (*Fédération des Travailleurs Agricole du Midi*) and food workers (*Fédération de l'Alimentation*). 'Before growing capitalist concentration', Jouhaux declared to the 1909 unity congress of the metal trades federation '[our] conclusion must be to realise the concentration of the workers' forces'.[107] Thus, the CGT explicitly rejected craft unionism and sought to encourage the emergence of industrial unions. By 1914, virtually all the remaining trade-based unions had completed industrial mergers, with the federations of miners, textile and railway workers dwarfing the craft federations in membership. In the same year it was agreed that the *bourses* should be replaced by area committees of union branches from the same industry.[108]

In Spain, although the CNT changed its organisational structure several times in its history its basic features remained throughout based on the principles of localism and federalism.[109] Initially the basic cell of the organisation was the local craft union, which brought together the workers of all crafts in one factory or possibly one town. Thus, the union and the locality tended to be identified, in accordance with the traditional anarchist stress on the commune, as the basic social unit. Organised on a local basis there were no national craft unions; instead the CNT was highly decentralised, and had very little by way of a bureaucracy. Outside Catalonia, where the Catalonian Regional Confederation provided an intermediate level, adherence to the CNT came through isolated *sindicatos*; and since there were perhaps 350 of these, it was hard for the National Committee to maintain communications and co-ordination across the country.

---

[105] J.A. Estey, *Revolutionary Syndicalism: An Exposition and A Criticism* (London, 1913), pp. 32–48; F.F. Ridley, *Revolutionary Syndicalism in France: The Direct Action of Its Time* (Cambridge, 1970), pp. 72–7.

[106] S. Jefferys, 'Review Essay: The Exceptional Centenary of the Confederation generale du travail, 1895–1995', *Historical Studies in Industrial Relations*, 3 (1997), p. 132.

[107] L. Jouhaux in 'Fédération des ouvriers des métaux', *Congrès unitaire 1909* (Paris, 1909), p. 9.

[108] M. Dreyfus, *Histoire de la CGT* (Brussels, 1995), pp. 69–70.

[109] See A. Bar, p. 133; M. Bookchin, *To Remember Spain: The Anarchist and Syndicalist Revolution of 1936* (Edinburgh, 1994), p. 19, 20, 33, and *The Spanish Anarchists*, pp. 145–65.

But, amidst a rapid rise in union membership (notably of unskilled workers), the Catalan CNT 1918 congress agreed a significant change regarding structural organisation. The old craft unions were now replaced by local unions of industry – *sindicato único* (single union) – which aimed to unite all workers in any given industry (skilled and unskilled alike) within the same union.[110] Thus, for example, the metals industry of Barcelona was organised as a single *sindicato* with subordinate sections for welders, braziers, machinists and so on. Each *sindicato* was headed by a 'junta general' composed of representatives of all its sections; and when this body approved a strike proposed by any one section, all sections were obliged to render assistance, either by joining the strike or by offering financial aid. Meanwhile, the diverse local unions were grouped into local federations, which in turn became a loose collection of regional labour committees of the CNT. After the declaration of the republic in 1931 the CNT was re-organised once more with the establishment of national industrial federations to co-ordinate the local unions of the same industry (although this proposal came up against the opposition of the most radical anarchist elements who saw it as engendering their control of the organisation and significantly the CNT never really developed the full panoply of *national* industrial unions).[111]

In Italy the USI was also organised on the basis of local autonomy via the *Camere del Lavoro* and local craft unions, albeit with aspirations towards more industrially-structured and national forms. As we have seen, local autonomy partly developed out of the traditions of the *Camere,* and in many Italian towns and cities it was the Chambers that came to provide a focus for the activities of the different unions, leagues and associations, stimulating a spirit of co-operation among workers in different occupations. In addition, local autonomy was encouraged by the Italian syndicalists' belief that large centralised organisations inevitably led to bureaucracy and reformism. By contrast, local autonomy, it was thought, would help to control leaders and prevent stagnation of the movement with regard to action and to ideology. As a result, the USI voted to limit the powers of its Central Committee based in Palma to general agitation and technical and statistical tasks, with the preparation and carrying out of strikes the responsibility of the local syndicalist groups.

While the USI aimed to build national union organisations there were not enough individual members or *Camere* in its early days to make this effective. Instead, their organisation was essentially based on horizontal links between local unions from the different sectors in particular communities and via an alliance of the different Chambers of Labour across the country. In the key city of Milan the *Unione Sindacale Milanese* became a bulwark of the syndicalist movement throughout northern Italy, linking with the USI and from 1914 publishing a special edition of *Internazionale* in the city. The USI agreed to set up some National Syndicates, panels of experts from various industries or agricultural groups, to be responsible for propaganda and statistical studies on a national level. But although they were seen as national co-ordinating bodies, the National Syndicates never realised their potential within the

---

110 *Memoria del Congreso celebrado en Barcelona los días 28, 29, y 30 de junio y 1º de julio de 1918* (Toulouse, 1957).

111 A. Monjo, *Militants. Participació i Democràcia a la CNT als Anys Trenta* (Barcelona, 2003), pp. 77–100.

USI because of distrust among syndicalists that they might threaten local autonomy. As a result, although the USI built a major national metalworkers' federation, it failed to establish strong industry-wide unions.[112]

So there were differences of emphasis within each syndicalist movement as it sought to create organisational forms that embraced workers across their respective trades and industries. The reasons for national differences in their organisation were varied and complex, and it is beyond the confines of this study to provide any general explanation which can account for the contrast between America, Ireland and Britain, on the one hand, and France, Spain and Italy, on the other, except to acknowledge that the different pace of industrialisation, in particular the concentration of ownership in industry and scale of production, as well as varying national labour traditions, were undoubtedly influencing factors.

Leadership Personnel

Finally, we can briefly consider another aspect of the syndicalist movement, the social class composition of its leading figures and their often charismatic personal style. According to Frederick Ridley most of the leaders of the CGT, far from being manual workers, in many cases led a white-collar life similar to that of a less prosperous bourgeois intellectual; one of the main exceptions from a genuinely working class background being Griffuelhes, who left school at 14 to apprentice as a cobbler. 'It is an old fact that revolutionary movements have been led by uprooted members of the very class against which they were directed'.[113] But while this broad assessment might accurately describe many of the key figures within the union, such as Pelloutier (journalist), Pouget (born into a middle-class family and became a shop assistant), Delesalle (publisher) and Rosmer (journalist), it fails to take sufficient account of other equally central leaders such as Yvetot (typographer), Jouhaux (apprenticed in numerous trades to finally become a match worker), Monatte (printing worker), Pataud (electrician) and Gaston Monmousseau (railway worker).

If anything, the leadership of Italian syndicalism, which had originated from within the Socialist Party, was relatively more bourgeois than in France. Many of the USI's chief labour organisers were journalists, university professors or lawyers who served apprenticeships as provincial secretaries in Chambers of Labour, including Arturo Labriola, Armando Borghi and Alceste DeAmbris,[114] But as in France the leadership role of important, albeit often unnamed, working class figures, particularly at regional level, should not be underestimated. This equally applies to Spain where, despite the influence of people like Joaquín Maurin and Andreu Nin (teachers), there was also leading CNT figures such as Buenaventura Durruti (railway worker) and Angel Pestaña (watchmaker).

In America, apart from resident intellectuals such as *Solidarity*'s editor Ben Williams, and the artist, poet and pamphleteer Ralph Chaplin, virtually all the IWW's

---

[112] Bertrand, pp. 38; 66–7; 94–7.

[113] Ridley, p. 258.

[114] C. Levy, 'Currents of Italian Syndicalism Before 1926', *International Review of Social History*, 45 (2000), p. 237.

leaders were self-educated skilled workers with a wealth of experience in different jobs, strikes and union organising; they included Bill Haywood (hard-rock miner) and St. John (printer, miner). In Britain, every one of the leading ISEL figures came from strong, usually skilled, working class roots, including Tom Mann and Jack Tanner (engineering workers), E.J.B. Allen (gas worker), Fred Bower (stonemason) and Charles Watkins (railway worker), as did the syndicalist-influenced leaders of the wartime engineering shop stewards' movement. And in Ireland, before establishing the ITGWU, Jim Larkin had left school at 11 and become a docker and foreman, while James Connolly had been a navy, builders' labourer and shipyard worker.

An often-stated characteristic feature of syndicalist leadership in all of these countries was the apparent spellbinding oratorical skills and fiery eloquence displayed by many of its individual figures, who voiced the anger and fighting spirit of the most militant workers, drew them together as a mass force and made them aware of their own power. For example, referring to the larger-than-life figure of Bill Haywood during the 1913 Paterson silk workers' strike, Carlo Tresca reflected:

> He would lift over the crowd his huge, powerful hand. He would spread the fingers as far apart from each other as possible. He would seize one finger after the other with his other hand, saying to his audience: 'Do you see that? Do you see that? Every finger by itself has no force. Now look'. He would then bring the fingers together, close them into a bulky, powerful fist, lift that fist in the face of the crowd, saying: 'See that? That's IWW'. The mass would go wild. Not the least factor in his success was his physical vigor, his unusual amount of vitality that throbbed in every one of his gestures.[115]

Similarly Tom Mann, who 'developed a winning pastiche', in which he flung himself on his knees in front of his audiences and reduced them to tears of laughter as he prayed to Parliament for the workers' salvation,[116] was regarded by many as one of the greatest platform speakers in British labour history. Bonar Thompson, a former syndicalist activist recalled:

> I have never heard anyone like Tom Mann. I have listened to him hundreds of times in all parts of the country. He was my ideal of what an orator should be. His personality in those days was like a human dynamo. Everything gave way before the tremendous torrents of oratory he let loose upon his audiences … He swept over the crowds like a whirlwind.[117]

And in Ireland, where Larkin's speeches were so powerful because he spoke bluntly and in bold terms. Countess Markievicz, who played an active part in the Easter 1916 Rising, wrote:

> Sitting there, listening to Larkin, I realised that I was in the presence of something that I had never come across before, some great primeval force rather than a man. A tornado, a storm-driven wave, the rush into life of spring, and the blasting breath of autumn, all seemed to emanate from the power that spoke. It seemed as if his personality caught up, assimilated, and threw back to the vast crowd that surrounded him every emotion that

---

[115] Cited in Kornbluh, p. 209.

[116] Foot, p. 213.

[117] Cited in B. Holton, *British Syndicalism 1900–1914* (London, 1976), p. 52.

> swayed them, every pain and joy that they had ever felt made articulated and sanctified. Only the great elemental force that is in all crowds had passed into his nature for ever.[118]

In many respects, this charisma displayed by many of the key syndicalist leaders, whose simple and powerful ideas inspired and activated the best young militants of its time, should not be understood as merely a reflection of personal qualities, but also has to be contextualised within the circumstances in which it emerged and flowered; it was, of course, very much a product of the movements themselves, in particular their sheer vibrancy and militancy in fighting for the establishment of revolutionary unionism in the face of enormous difficulties and opposition.

The syndicalist movement in every country attracted a remarkable selection of young revolutionary militants to its banner who provided an inexhaustible source of energy, dynamism and strength to the movement, even if their names often never appeared in their publications and scarcely ever in the speakers' lists at its congresses. It was the elementary class struggle which gave birth to such militants in their hundreds of thousands and which created the fighting material that were the soul of the movement, its nervous system and its blood vessels; they were the 'flower of a generation'.[119]

---

[118] Cited in D. Norman, *Terrible Beauty: Constance Markievicz* (Dublin, 1987), p. 83.

[119] J. Cannon, *The IWW: The Great Anticipation* (New York, 1956), p. 13.

Chapter 4

Internal Divisions

As will have already become clear there were always various internal ideological, strategic, tactical and organisational differences between syndicalists within each of the various movements. Such differentiation, and often bitter internal conflict, occurred (with no simple lines of demarcation) between different groups of leaders, between leaders and members and between members based in different geographical areas of their respective countries. Inevitably, from the outset there were many ideologically disparate elements operating inside each of the individual movements. For example, at the IWW's founding congress there were socialists, Marxists, anarchists, syndicalists and radical trade unionists. Likewise, both the CGT and CNT encompassed a myriad of ideological elements, from out-and-out anarchists to semi-reformist moderates. Indeed, the history of such movements is a record of continuous political quarrels between the various elements struggling for control. Other cleavages that emerged as the movements developed sometimes cut across ideological lines, but were equally divisive.

It is useful to document the main lines of division, bearing in mind that whilst many were replicated to varying degrees across different countries, others were distinctive to only some individual movements. The areas of division explored are: Ultimate Revolutionary Goals *versus* Immediate Day-To-Day Reforms; 'Boring from Within' *versus* 'Dual Unionism'; Political Action and the Relationship to Socialist Parties; Attitude towards the First World War; and Centralisation *versus* Local Autonomy

Ultimate Revolutionary Goals *versus* Immediate Day-To-Day Reforms

Undoubtedly one of the most common divisions arose from the different relative emphasis placed on obtaining immediate reforms *versus* ultimate revolutionary goals. The most well-known example of this occurred in France, where reformists and revolutionaries inside the CGT were locked in an often acrimonious struggle. The reformists were led by a powerful leadership, including Auguste Keufer (printers), Pierre Coupat (engineers) and Eugène Guérard (railwaymen), who represented a sizeable body of opinion within the Confédération. They were committed to practical activism and strikes to win material improvements in workers' conditions, but they eschewed what they considered to be the more violent forms of direct action, such as sabotage. And they viewed the strategy of continuous strikes, leading to a hoped-for revolutionary general strike, as both inexpedient and undesirable. 'I do not believe', Keufer wrote, 'that this ideal society will suddenly appear complete out of the revolutionary chaos, the general disorder for which strikes will have been the prelude, the preparation'.[1] By contrast, Victor Griffuelhes and the revolutionary syndicalists believed that since 'the … employer, the capitalist, can only prolong the existence of his prerogatives by keeping the … worker, subordinate', the struggle must continue until its ultimate cause – the exploitation of the workers – disappears; only a revolutionary overthrow of capitalism could accomplish such a task.[2]

Following the decisive defeat of a series of strikes in which the CGT had been centrally involved there was a *crisie syndicaliste*, with internal opposition to the revolutionary majority eventually leading in 1910 to Griffuelhes's replacement by Leon Jouhaux as general secretary. In the process, there was a retreat from direct action tactics and the adoption of a more pragmatic and moderate approach, highlighted in graphic relief when the Confédération abandoned its internationalist opposition to war and collaborated with the French government's war effort. The revolutionary syndicalist and anti-war minority mounted a continuing and growing challenge to the reformist leadership, which eventually exploded into a bitter internal schism in the post-war years.

The leadership of the Spanish CNT was likewise divided on a permanent basis, in this case between more moderate syndicalist elements on the one hand and more revolutionary anarcho-syndicalist (and anarchist) elements on the other. Initially the CNT adopted a 'pure' form of revolutionary syndicalism which extended from the (1907) foundation of the CNT's parent organisation *Solidaridad Obrera* to 1919. But this approach, personified by Salavador Seguí, became increasingly focused on obtaining immediate material and organisational gains and suggested much more preparation was necessary before a revolutionary overthrow could be contemplated. In attempting to promote a more moderate trade union policy within the CNT, Seguí controversially cut short a Barcelona general strike in 1919 and followed a policy of collaboration with the socialist UGT confederation. By contrast the anarcho-syndicalists, who resented the placing of 'bread and butter' issues ahead of opportunities to strike a blow at the bourgeois order, advocated revolutionary insurrectionism.

At the CNT's 1919 congress there was an attempted synthesis of the strategic and tactical principles of revolutionary syndicalism on the one hand, and anarchism on the other, with the adoption of 'libertarian communism' as the Confederación main goal. Over the next four years, amidst economic and political crisis, a revolutionary wave of struggles across Europe, the impact of the Russian Revolution and massive industrial unrest at home, the anarcho-syndicalists successfully took control of the CNT, backed by many of the new, radical elements who had emigrated from rural areas to Barcelona.

However, after the CNT's banning in 1924 the leadership fell back into the hands of more moderate syndicalist figures. It was only with the formation of the Iberian Anarchist Federation (FAI) in 1927, that the anarchists (including insurrectionary leaders like Buenaventura Durrutti and Juán Garcia Oliver) were to come back to the fore with the advent of the Second Republic in 1931 and the renewal of high levels of class struggle that followed.[3]

---

[1] Cited in J. Jennings, *Syndicalism in France: A Study of Ideas* (Oxford, 1990), p. 127.

[2] V. Griffuelhes, 'Le Syndicalisme révolutionaire' in 'Les Deux Conceptions du syndicalisme: Controverse', *Le Mouvement socialiste*, 146, 1 January 1905, pp. 1–17.

[3] A. Bar, *Syndicalism and Revolution in Spain: The Ideology and Syndical Practice of the CNT in the Period 1915–1919* (New York, 1981); G.H. Meaker, *The Revolutionary Left in*

Similar divisions between 'pure' revolutionary syndicalists and anarchists were apparent in Italy. Alceste DeAmbris, one of the USI's leading figures until 1914, shared the anarchists' conception of the overthrow of the Italian regime by a spontaneous rising, but believed a viable new order could not be created through barricades and violent insurrection, but only through a long, gradual process of industrial development and proletarian maturation. Anarchist tactics, it was argued, produced merely pointless revolts, which only appealed to peasants and declining bourgeois groups. The 'pure' syndicalists did not expect a general strike to overthrow the capitalist system in the foreseeable future and did not consider any of the strikes of the pre-war period (including the 'Red Week' general strike of 1914) to be definitive revolutionary episodes.[4] By contrast, the anarchists, such Armando Borghi, were much less trade union orientated than the 'pure' syndicalists, promoted political strikes rather than economic ones, and were more concerned with building revolutionary consciousness than in negotiating better conditions of employment.[5] Even after Borghi had taken over the helm of an increasingly anarchist-influenced USI from 1916, relations between 'pure' syndicalists and openly declared anarchists were rarely untroubled by disputes over doctrine and tactics.

In Ireland there were also severe tensions between Larkin and Connolly's notion of militant class struggle, as practised in the years leading up to the war, on the one hand, and the more moderate syndicalist stance exemplified by the increasingly bureaucratic leadership of William O'Brien (who assumed control after Connolly's death and Larkin's extended visit to America), on the other.

Likewise inside the IWW there was a continuing conflict as to whether the organisation should be a functioning labour union, combining the struggle for higher wages and better working conditions with a programme for revolutionary socialism, or a revolutionary cadre organisation that concentrated exclusively upon leading the working class to revolution. The national headquarters stressed the first, whilst many of the more anarchist-influenced members stressed the second, arguing that there was a contradiction between the goals of revolution and unionism, and that to concentrate on union activity would blind the workers to the final aim. Indeed from such a perspective it was felt that the IWW should abandon any pretence of being an economic organisation and devotes its energies exclusively to propaganda and agitation.[6]

'Boring From Within' *versus* 'Dual Unionism'

A second area of internal dissension within some syndicalist movements revolved around the argument as to whether to operate inside the reformist trade union movement or to build alternative revolutionary organisations in opposition to them. This dispute became manifest in the attempts that were made to challenge either the predominant 'boring from within' or 'dual unionist' strategies of different movements.

Spain, 1914–1923 (Stanford, Calif., 1974).

4 Cited in B. Riguzzi, *Sindacalismo e riformiso nel Parmense* (Bari, 1974), p. 129.

5 A. Borghi, *Anarchismo e sindacalismo. Conferenza tenuta il 3 aprile 1922 a Roma del Fascio Sindacale d'Azione Diretta* (Rome, n.d.), pp. 45–8.

6 *Solidarity*, 19 October 1912.

In France this was not really an issue for many years, given the syndicalists' successful 'boring from within' and conversion of the principal existing trade union confederation within the labour movement. Even after the CGT leadership had steered the organisation in a moderate direction from 1910 onwards, the revolutionary minority continued to fight from *within*, with the aim of eventually being able to secure majority influence. It was only in 1921, after the CGT reformist leaders had made refusal to disband the dissident tendency the excuse for wholesale expulsions, that a breakaway confederation (the CGTU) was eventually formed (see Chapter 5).

By contrast in America the IWW's 'dual unionist' strategy was subject to internal critique. Joseph Conlin has questioned whether the IWW was really a 'dual' union at all, on the basis that the Wobblies were not interested in seducing AFL locals away from their parent organisation but merely sought to organise the unskilled workers the AFL ignored.[7] Nonetheless, the fact remains the IWW was a *rival* national trade union simply in that it was *separate* from the AFL, and indeed many moderate socialists and trade unionists viewed it as a direct competitor of the AFL, a parallel union. Certainly, it was its 'dual unionism' (as well as unabashed radicalism) that Samuel Gompers, head of the AFL, emphasized in his virulent attacks on the IWW.

Yet by 1911 the evident difficulties that had been encountered in attempting to build Wobbly organisation led some elements within the IWW to suggest a different strategy. Most noticeable among the internal critics was William Z. Foster, a young IWW organiser who returned from a European trip convinced the Wobbly's belief in the efficacy of dual unionism was misguided. He asked the IWW to learn from the example of France where syndicalists had captured the CGT and from England where syndicalists had gained some success in attempting to 'bore from within' Trades Union Congress (TUC) unions.[8] He argued the IWW should disband its separate organisation so that its members could join the AFL and act as a network of militants within the various mainstream unions, fighting for their transformation into revolutionary bodies. Although the 1911 IWW convention rejected this alternative strategy, Foster formed his own Syndicalist League of North America (SLNA) and in the pamphlet *Syndicalism* outlined the rationale behind the 'boring from within' stance:

> Ever since its foundation the IWW has carried on a vigorous propaganda of the doctrine that the old conservative unions are incapable of evolution and must be supplanted by a 'ready-made' revolutionary movement. They have become obsessed with the notion that nothing can be accomplished in the old unions, and that the sooner they go out of existence the better it will be for the labour movement. As a natural consequence they, with rare exceptions, have either quit the old unions and become directly hostile to them, or they have become so much dead material in them, making no efforts to improve them. The result is a calamity to the labour movement. It has been literally stripped of its soul. The militants who could inspire it with revolutionary vigour have been taken from it by this ridiculous theory. They have left the old unions, where they could have wielded a tremendous influence, and gone into sterile isolation. They have left the labour movement in the undisputed control of conservatives and fakers of all kinds to exploit as they see fit …

---

7 J. Conlin, 'A Name That Leads to Confusion', in *Bread and Roses Too: Studies of the Wobblies* (Westport, Connecticut, 1969), p. 20.

8 *Industrial Worker*, 2 November 1911.

> The Syndicalist League of North America (SLNA) is an organisation of syndicalists, formed for the purpose of effectively propagating syndicalist tactics, principles, etc, among all groups of organised and unorganised workers. IT IS NOT A LABOUR UNION, AND IT DOES NOT ALLOW ITS BRANCHES TO AFFILIATE WITH LABOUR UNIONS. It is simply an educational league with the task of educating the labour movement to Syndicalism. The S.L. of N.A. plan of organisation, is somewhat similar to that of the Industrial Syndicalist League in England.[9]

But the IWW advocates of a separate revolutionary union responded by arguing that the alternative policy of infiltrating the AFL was impractical. Haywood declared it was virtually impossible for an unskilled worker to join the AFL because of 'a vicious system of apprenticeship [and] exorbitant fees'.[10] He said he would rather cut off his right arm than join the Federation and concluded that 'the 28,000 local unions of the AFL are 28,000 agencies of the capitalist class'.[11] Joseph Ettor also rebutted Foster and accused him of trying to save the AFL. 'We don't want to save the Federation any more than to save the nation', he wrote. 'We aim at destroying it.'[12] Haywood and Ettor rejected the validity of Foster's European examples, on the basis that both French and English labour movements already contained a significant proportion of sympathisers and supporters within their national union confederations and socialist parties prepared to co-operate with the 'borer', whereas in America neither the Socialist Party nor the AFL especially tolerated syndicalist influence. Moreover, the European syndicalists did not advocate a form of trade unionism at odds with the prevailing structure of their nations' labour movements, as was the case in America where the industrial unionism proposed by the IWW (politics and ideology excluded) was unacceptable to a dominant majority within the AFL.

Foster's SLNA never developed into more than a loosely connected propaganda organisation, and during its short life was unable to attract more than a minuscule membership, mainly in western and mid-western cities. A key problem was that the Wobblies' fortunes rose shortly after the League was launched, and with Foster's alternative body lacking support from any national IWW leader, it simply faded out of existence in the course of 1914, although it later metamorphosed into various similar named and marginally more influential guises over the next few years.[13]

During 1900–1912, before the foundation of the USI, Italian syndicalists were also in conflict with each other as to whether to seek to conquer the socialist-led trade union confederation from within or to withdraw and establish their own revolutionary confederation as a rival body, albeit continuing to operate from within the existing local unions, leagues, associations and Chambers of Labour. As we have seen, unlike France, many of the leaders of the Italian syndicalist movement had initially operated from *within* the Socialist Party. But as tensions between the reformists and

---

9 E. Ford and W.Z. Foster, *Syndicalism* (Chicago, 1912), pp. 45–6.

10 *Internationalist Socialist Review*, 14, March 1914, p. 546.

11 Cited in J.R. Barrett, *William Z. Foster and the Tragedy of American Radicalism* (Chicago, 1999), p. 50.

12 *The New Review*, May 1914, p. 283.

13 M. Dubofsky, *'Big Bill' Haywood* (Manchester, 1987), pp. 60–62 and *We Shall be All: A History of the Industrial Workers of the World* (Chicago, 1969), pp. 224–5; Barrett, p. 66.

revolutionary syndicalists had intensified inside the party, the reformists counter-attacked when a national congress of the main national trade unions was called in 1906 and agreed to set up the *Confererazione Generale del Lavro* (CGL) in imitation of the French CGT established a few years earlier.

The CGL was controlled from the outset by socialist moderates and organised on the principles of a centralised structure and the approval of political activity, notably co-operation with the Socialist Party. The syndicalists unsuccessfully opposed these developments, favouring local autonomy for the Chambers of Labour and a non-political stance. But they now faced a crucial dilemma. Should they split with the reformist CGL or attempt to capture it from within? At the 1906 Socialist Party congress, the majority of delegates sanctioned collaboration with bourgeois political parties. At this point, a number of leading syndicalists, led by Alceste DeAmbris, Michele Bianchi and Edmondo Rossini, called for an immediate break with both the Socialist Party and the CGL. Others, led by Arturo Labriola and Enrico Leone, argued that a split would weaken the working class movement and strengthen its opponents. For the next six years the syndicalists vacillated and no specific syndicalist organisation was formed in Italy until 1912. Most felt the struggle against the reformists could best be waged from within the existing socialist-led union confederation. But unlike their French counterparts Italian revolutionary syndicalists made virtually no headway within the CGL, and as anti-parliamentarist sentiment spread the more radical syndicalists began to search for a more suitable vehicle of direct action.

In late 1907 dissident syndicalists, DeAmbris and other delegates (who claimed to represent some 200,000 workers) decided to establish a *Comitato Nazionale della Resistenza* independent of the CGL, on the basis of seeking to defend local union autonomy and the propagation of direct action principles such as the general strike. DeAmbris had recently become secretary general of the Parma Chamber of Labour, the centre of syndicalist activity in Italy. The formation of the National Resistance Committee marked a rejection of the policy of attempting to conquer the CGL from within, though not all syndicalists were prepared to accept this course. The aim was to try to build up a new movement around a number of Chambers of Labour and local unions. The railwaymen, disgruntled with the CGL leaders, rallied to the movement, and to buttress membership of the National Resistance Committee DeAmbris invited the anarchists, represented by Armando Borghi, to join the new organisation. In the process DeAmbris and Borghi forged a link between anarchists and revolutionary syndicalist elements.

Yet the defeat of a general strike launched by the National Resistance Committee in Parma, and the subsequent wholesale expulsion of the syndicalists from the Socialist Party in 1908 strengthened the hand of those preferring the strategy of transforming the CGL from within. And for almost two years the syndicalists maintained their uneasy alliance with the CGL. Eventually in 1910, under the influence of Michele Bianchi, a dissident from inside the Bologna Chamber of Labour, they established a secret body, the *Comitato dell'Azione diretta,* which sought to co-ordinate the activities of the syndicalist organisations and to propagate their revolutionary principles within the CGL until sufficient strength could be mustered to challenge it openly. Friction between the syndicalists and the reformists grew ever more intense during the spring of 1912, such that the CGL executive finally pronounced support for the Committee as incompatible with CGL membership. Only now, with the Italian syndicalists effectively driven out of both the Socialist Party and the principal CGL structures, did they set up a new national labour confederation as an open rival of the CGL (although they continued as previously to operate within the existing local unions and Chambers of Labour) by joining with the railway workers' union and some other anti-reformist organisations, including those of anarchists and republicans.[14]

In Britain there were also divisions between different groups of syndicalist-influenced revolutionaries even before the foundation of the ISEL in 1910. On the one hand, there were those in the Socialist Labour Party (SLP) influenced by their American De Leonite counterparts. Believing in the need for a political party that could be elected to power, and industrial unions that would take over industry, the SLP advocated new revolutionary industrial unions to replace the existing reformist bodies. Despite its minuscule size in 1906 they formed the British Advocates of Industrial Unionism (BAIU), a propagandist organisation intended to pave the way for the construction of entirely new revolutionary unions modelled on the American IWW. In 1909 the BAIU was re-organised as the Industrial Workers of Great Britain (IWGB) and branches were set up in Scotland. Enjoying considerable support at the Singer sewing machine factory on the Clyde during a strike in 1911, the organisation was quickly suppressed.[15]

In America the policy of building entirely new revolutionary unions appeared to have relevance in a context where existing levels of trade union organisation were relatively low and where unskilled workers had been neglected by the predominately craft based AFL In Britain a higher proportion of workers were unionised and many unskilled workers had some prior experience of union membership and activity. In this situation 'dual unionism' was viewed by many as simply isolating militants from existing trade unionists in a highly sectarian fashion.[16] It was only during the First World War that a number of leading British SLP members (including J.T. Murphy, Tom Bell and Arthur MacManus), influenced by the development of the shop stewards' movement, transform their party's outlook and took a lead in mass struggles inside the engineering industry from within the existing unions.

On the other hand, there were individual figures such as E.J.B. Allen, national secretary of the SLP-BAIU branches, who became increasingly frustrated with the 'dual unionist' approach and began to see the need to adopt the alternative approach of reconstructing the existing unions on revolutionary lines. Following resignations and expulsions, Allen and his supporters left in 1908 to form the Industrialist League to propagate such a strategy. In 1910 the main grouping of British syndicalists around Tom Mann, who formed the ISEL, also adopted the 'boring from within' strategy and became involved in the amalgamation committee movements that aimed to

---

[14] See C. Levy, 'Currents of Italian Syndicalism before 1926', *International Review of Social History*, 45 (2000), pp. 209–50; J.A. Davies, 'Socialism and the Working Classes in Italy Before 1914', in D. Geary (ed.), *Labour and Socialist Movements in Europe Before 1914* (Oxford, 1989), pp. 182–230; C. Bertrand, 'Revolutionary Syndicalism in Italy 1912–1920', PhD, University of Wisconsin, 1970.

[15] R. Challinor, *The Origins of British Bolshevism* (London, 1977), pp. 99–104; Glasgow Labour History Workshop, *The Singer Strike, Clydebank 1911* (Glasgow, 1989).

[16] For an example of this process through the activities of one militant see T. Bell, *Pioneering Days*, (London, 1941).

unite the various existing unions into revolutionary industrial bodies. Likewise, the Unofficial Reform Committee in the South Wales Miners' Federation campaigned for the wholesale reconstruction of the miners' union from within.

But in 1913 an internal rupture occurred within the ISEL when Allen and Guy Bowman switched their allegiance to an essentially IWW position of 'dual unionism', and a rival syndicalist organisation, the Industrial Democracy League, was formed by dissidents determined to continue the position of the 'old' ISEL, although the damage had already been done.[17] The main body of British syndicalism lost its effectiveness, as a distinct organisational entity, even though ideologically and politically it continued to have significant influence inside sections of the pre-war union movement, notably within the independent left paper *The Daily Herald* (and network of *Daily Herald* Leagues established during 1912–1913) and the independent working class educational movement of the London-based Central Labour College and provincial Plebs League study groups network.

Political Action and the Relationship to Socialist Parties

A third issue of internal contention arose over the question of what attitude to adopt in relation to parliamentary political action and socialist parties. For example, it is of major importance that the Wobblies formally turned against political activity only gradually between 1905 and 1912. As we have seen some early activists maintained strong ties to both the Socialist Party and the Socialist Labor Party, although there were also anarcho-syndicalist opponents of political action and association with socialist parties. As a result, for the first three years of the IWW's existence there was an internal argument over the 'political clause' of its Preamble to the constitution, with the divergent views and conflicting ideologies of the heterogeneous elements sharply revealed.

The Socialist Labor Party's (SLP) leading intellectual Marxist figure, Daniel De Leon, who thought that the trade union movement ought to be the arm of a political movement under his party's influence, successfully moved a somewhat ambiguous amendment to the Preamble advocating political action, albeit specifically forbidding the IWW to affiliate with any political party:

> Between these two classes a struggle must go on until all the toilers come together on the political, as well as on the industrial field, and take and hold that which they produce by their labour through an economic organisation of the working class, without affiliation with any political party.[18]

This specific, if puzzling and contradictory, reference to political activity was designed by de Leon to avoid IWW affiliation with the rival reformist-led Socialist Party; at the same time it served as a means of increasing his own influence inside the IWW. Ironically, it was accepted by different elements within the new body (for varying reasons), but went too far in the direction of accepting political action for

---

17 See B. Holton, *British Syndicalism 1900–1914* (London, 1976), pp. 139–47.

18 Cited in J.L. Kornbluh (ed.), *Rebel Voices: An IWW Anthology* (Chicago, 1998), p. 13.

many delegates. In effect it represented a confused compromise between the anarcho-syndicalist ideas of Hagerty and Trautmann on the one hand, who emphasised that the IWW should primarily be an economic organisation based upon class struggle, and the view of the socialists, particularly De Leon on the other, who favoured political as well as economic action by the working class, including participation in parliamentary elections. Many IWW leaders and members fell somewhere in between these two positions. While technically committed to political activity, the IWW was unaffiliated with any party. The language of the clause was totally confused, but this was precisely its purpose – to make it acceptable to socialists of different persuasions as well as non-political syndicalists, all of whom could interpret it as they chose.

At the 1906 convention the question of political action was again thoroughly debated, with the more revolutionary elements renewing their fight to have the clause 'until all the toilers come together on the political as well as on the industrial field' cleansed from the taint of politics, with the removal of the words 'political as well as'. But the motion involving this change was emphatically opposed by the spokesmen of the SLP faction. Neither side was entirely successful. By way of compromise it was finally agreed that the clause containing the word 'political' should stand unaltered, but that an additional clause should be appended at the end of the Preamble. This new clause read: 'Therefore, without endorsing or desiring the endorsement of any political party, we unite under the following constitution.' Political action was still recognised and no less emphatically endorsed than before, but all political activities were now subject to very definite constitutional restrictions as to the relations between the IWW and political parties.

By the time of the 1908 convention De Leon and the SLP supporters within the IWW had been expelled, and the reference to political action in the Preamble deleted because of fears that De Leon was seeking to convert the IWW into a wing of the SLP (even though not all those who favoured the removal of De Leon were opposed to political action in any circumstances). The second paragraph of the new Preamble now read:

> Between these two classes a struggle must go on until the workers of the world organise as a class, take possession of the earth and the machinery of production and abolish the wage system.[19]

Thus, after three years of flirting with politics, the IWW formally adopted a basically anti-political attitude and an exclusive stress on direct action on the industrial front. The organisation became firmly under the control of leading anarcho-syndicalists, headed by St. John and Trautmann, although Haywood eventually took charge. Expelled from the Chicago Convention, De Leon founded his own rival IWW that set up headquarters in Detroit, although its influence was negligible and the organisation was dissolved in 1925.[20]

In France the reformist wing inside the CGT believed some sort of partnership between the unions and the newly unified Socialist Party was inevitable and that it

---

19 Ibid., p. 13.

20 P.F. Brissenden, *The IWW: A Study of American Syndicalism* (New York, 1919), pp. 168–9; P.S. Foner, *History of the Labor Movement in the United States: Vol. 4: The Industrial Workers of the World 1905–1917* (New York, 1965), pp. 34–99.

was necessary to combine trade union and political action. They sought to improve workers' conditions by supporting legislation on the eight-hour day, the right of civil servants to belong to trade unions, and a minimum wage. However, the CGT's 1906 congress approved by a near-unanimous majority the *Charte d'Amiens* co-authored by Griffuelhes and Pouget. The Charter was a manifesto of trade union autonomy from party rule and self-reliance in the revolutionary struggle to overthrow the wage system. Its significance was that it represented the culmination of the struggle against 'Millerandism' and the bourgeois parliamentary legislative program of social reform advocated by the Socialist Party, who had aspirations to bring the CGT under their political control. Yet the Charter proved to be no more than a brief pause in the continuing struggle for power with the reformists, and by 1909 Griffuelhes's revolutionary majority was in disarray and he was forced to resign. Strike defeats and the growing war threat pushed the more moderate syndicalist leaders towards acceptance of the need to co-operate with socialist politicians and government ministers.

The immediate post-war years produced a further twist in the increasing polarisation within the CGT. The by-now majority reformist leadership, composed of the general secretary Léon Jouhaux, assistant general secretary Georges Dumoulin, and metalworkers' secretary Alphonse Merrheim (who from 1916 had moved away from the revolutionary elements he had previously associated with), viewed the means to improve workers' position within capitalism and the Republic as being through close collaboration with the Socialist Party and pressure on parliament to secure reform legislation. By contrast, the rapidly growing revolutionary minority believed in the suppression of capitalism through the general strike and the institution of a producers' commonwealth. Such divisions (combined with arguments over what attitude to adopt towards the Bolsheviks) contributed to the eventual schism within the Confédération.

Attitude towards the First World War

The outbreak of the First World War in 1914 was to inevitably pose a serious acid test of the syndicalists' professed workers' internationalism, in a context in which the great majority of the Second International parties and the official leadership of the trade union movement renounced their prior internationalist pledges and rushed to support their respective governments' war drives. In fact in most countries syndicalists, more than any other ideological persuasion within the organised trade union movement, constituted an authentic movement of opposition to the war.[21] However, there were some exceptions to this general picture, notably in France and Italy, with bitter internal divisions on the issue.

In 1908 the CGT had openly threatened that any declaration of war should be met with a revolutionary general strike, although significantly this resolution was

---

[21] See W. Thorpe, 'The European Syndicalists and War, 1914–1918', *Contemporary European History*, 10:1 (2001), pp. 1–24. However, much of this opposition was reduced to general propaganda, as opposed to agitation in the workplace over concrete issues such as conscription that attempted to explicitly linked industrial militancy with 'politics'. See Chapter 9 and R. Darlington, 'Revolutionary Syndicalist Opposition to the First World War: A Comparative Reassessment', *Revue Belge de Philologie et d'Histoire*, 84:4 (2006), pp. 983–1003.

careful to commit the Confédération to no more than propaganda and to specify that the strike should be international. But the anti-patriotic and anti-militarist principles of the CGT were to be swept away overnight in 1914.[22] Once war was declared and conscription into the French armed forces had been announced, a wave of patriotism, a deep seated willingness to defend the Republic against external aggression swept the French labour movement and carried almost the whole of the CGT (and the Socialist Party) before it. Jouhaux argued that in the face of German militarism the democratic and republican traditions of France needed to be safeguarded; it was a war for civilisation, for progress and liberty against barbarism, a war of revolution and not reaction, truly in the 'revolutionary tradition' of 1792.[23]

On 4 August the president of the Republic urged all citizens to commit themselves to a *union sacrée* ('sacred union') in defence of France, a union that the CGT (and Socialist Party) willingly agreed to uphold for the duration. This involved support for a no-strike pledge and a programme of compulsory arbitration, with the CGT serving on various mixed commissions and Jouhaux becoming a 'commissioner of the nation'. In the process most union members of military age were called up without resistance. From 350,000 adherents in 1913, CGT membership collapsed in the face of military mobilisation to a mere 49,000 dues-payers by 1915, with the Confédération becoming a 'skeletal' organisation.[24]

There emerged a tiny internationalist and anti-war minority within the CGT. In December 1914 Pierre Monatte, the leader of the new generation of revolutionary syndicalists that had grown up around the paper *La Vie Ouvrière*, publicly resigned from the CGT executive. By the second year of the war, the opposition to the CGT had won over the powerful metal workers' union led by Alphonse Merrheim, who made speeches insisting 'their war is not our war'.[25] A group of *minoritaires* formed into a *Comité Défense Syndicalise* (CDS) which condemned the CGT majority for its collaboration with the government. In September 1915 Merrheim, accompanied by Albert Bourderon, head of the coopers' union, attended the conference of anti-war socialists held at Zimmerwald in Switzerland. Ultimately this group, along with others on the revolutionary wing formed the nucleus of an internationalist and anti-war minority movement within the CGT, albeit marginalised during the early stages of the war.[26]

The catastrophic bloodletting of the years 1914–1918, combined with the impact of the Russian Revolution, helped transform the situation more favourably during the last 18 months of the war. Above all the strike wave of 1917–1918 suggested the *union sacrée* consensus wore thin. Deteriorating working conditions, rising prices,

---

[22] R. Magraw, 'Socialism, Syndicalism and French Labour Before 1914', Geary, *Labour and Socialist Movements in Europe*, p. 96.

[23] Cited in Jennings, p. 162.

[24] See J. Horne, 'The State and the Challenge for Labour in France 1917–20', in C. Wrigley (ed.), *Challenges of Labour: Central and Western Europe 1917–20* (London, 1993), pp. 239–61.

[25] R. Magraw, *A History of the French Working Class, Vol. 2: Workers and the Bourgeois Republic* (Oxford, 1992), p. 155.

[26] B. Mitchell, 'French Syndicalism: An Experiment in Practical Anarchism', in M. van der Linden and W. Thorpe (eds), *Revolutionary Syndicalism: An International Perspective* (Aldershot, 1990), pp. 37–9.

profiteering and war weariness, all combined to reduce morale and encouraged growing numbers of workers to lend an ear to 'pacifist and Bolshevik' doctrines. In May–June 1918 there was a 200,000-strong metalworkers' strike, in which CDS militants played a key role channelling bread-and-butter issues into an anti-war protest, although their influence was defused by the arrest of strike leaders and transfer of a few hundred *mobilistés* to the trenches.[27] The immediate post-war years led to a further polarisation within the CGT between a reformist majority and a revolutionary minority, with the latter receiving a marked accession of strength from the Russian Revolution and the dangerously high social tensions that the war had generated.

In Italy the outbreak of war also created turmoil (albeit on a much less significant scale than in France) within the 100,000-strong USI. The Italian government, initially declared its neutrality, finally entered the war in May 1915 to join the Anglo-French-Russian alliance. It was a deeply unpopular decision that was opposed by parliament, the Catholic Church, the Socialist Party and its trade union confederation, the CGL. The Socialists became the largest political movement in a belligerent state to refuse to endorse the national war effort. As part of this process, the USI also immediately avowed opposition to war with its central committee urging on 8 August 1914 that if the government abandoned its neutrality all workers should respond with an insurrectionary general strike.[28] But the approaching war also reinforced a republican national tradition inside the Italian labour movement, with an active minority taking up the cause of national intervention on the side of the Entente.

Already in 1911, three leading syndicalist intellectuals, Arturo Labriola, Angelo Plivereo Olivetti and Paulo Orano had outraged most of their colleagues by advocating working class and socialist support for Italy's imperialist war with Turkey over Libya.[29] Now in August 1914, although the bulk of the USI remained firm in their anti-militarist and internationalist stance, a number of syndicalist leaders, including Alceste DeAmbris, Tullio Masoitto and Michele Bianchi, decided to support republican France against the absolute monarchies of Germany and Austria and to call for Italian intervention on the side of the Allied Powers. Such figures had witnessed the French CGT support the *union sacrée* and concluded that if their parent syndicalist organisation was in favour of protecting 'democracy' against the encroachment of the 'Hun', how could the Italian syndicalists do anything but follow their lead?[30] DeAmbris, the fabled syndicalist leader, threw out the challenge: 'Friends, I ask you a question: What will we do when western civilisation is threatened by the suffocating imperialism of Germany and only our intervention can save it? I leave the answer to you.'[31] He said the greatest menace to the revolutionary cause was not a war but rather the threat of a German victory which would destroy the

---

[27] R. Magraw, 'Paris 1917–20: Labour Protest and Popular Politics', in Wrigley, pp. 128–34.

[28] *L'Internazionale*, 1, 8 August 1914.

[29] Bertrand, pp. 52–7. See also C.L. Bertrand, 'Italian Revolutionary Syndicalism and the Crisis of Intervention: August–December 1914', *Canadian Journal of History*, 10: 3 (1975), pp. 349–67.

[30] Bertrand, 'Revolutionary Syndicalism in Italy 1912–1922', p. 125.

[31] *L'Internazionale*, 22 August 1914.

proletarian movement and leave the workers in the clutches of German exploiters.[32] Thus, the pro-war 'interventionists' asserted that while the syndicalists were anti-militarist they were not pacifist and that the war would provide the opportunity for a revolution that would destroy the liberal political system and monarchy.[33]

By contrast, the anarchist wing of the Italian syndicalist movement, led by Borghi, demanded that the USI adhere to its internationalism. For Borghi there was no compromise with pacifism, it meant a total anti-war stance without regard for the Italian nation or any other nation. And in September 1914 the USI executive voted to expel DeAmbris and his followers. But significantly the Parma Chamber of Labour, the largest section of the USI, voted to follow them on the path of intervention, with the Rome and Genoa Chambers of Labour (in which syndicalists were prominent) and the Maritime Union (an independent union) quickly joining them. And the *Unione Sindicale Milanese* (the fourth largest section of the USI) also broke with the Milan Chamber of Labour and voted to back the interventionists. After this demonstration of support, DeAmbris and his followers seized control of the official records, financial statements and membership lists of the USI, and quickly converted *L'Internazionale*, the principal newspaper of the Italian syndicalist movement, into a pro-interventionist organ.[34] Overall, they succeeded in taking almost one-third of the USI's membership, some 30,000 out of 100,000. Whilst the group was too small to be effective on a national scale, it was large enough to greatly limit the effectiveness of the USI, even though the bulk of Italian syndicalists confirmed their anti-militarism and internationalism.

In response to the interventionists, the USI executive selected Bologna as the union's new headquarters and appointed Borghi as secretary general. Borghi attempted to rebuild the Unione by launching an anti-war propaganda offensive via a new official journal launched in the spring of 1915, the internationalist *Guerra di Classe*. Nonetheless, Edmondo Rossoni, a long time syndicalist who had participated in the 1908 Parma general strike, wrote from America to express his support for DeAmbris[35] and the editor of the Socialist Party's daily paper (*L'Avanti!)*, Benito Mussolini, also began to write in favour of intervention. DeAmbris proceeded to establish hard-line groups, labelled *Fasci rivoluzionari d'azione* (Fasci), which increasingly violently attacked anti-war demonstrations. The combination of such interventionist attacks and government repression seriously undermined the USI's campaign to keep Italy out of the war, compounded by its refusal to engage in joint activity with the Socialist Party.

However, as the war progressed strikes broke out over wages, there were large anti-war demonstrations, and in August 1917 a spontaneous insurrectionary general strike erupted in Turin inspired by news of the February revolution in Russia. The economic strain of the war in Italy reached its height in 1918. As the cost of living increased and purchasing power plummeted, more and more workers responded by

---

32 *L'Internazionale*, 19 September 1914.

33 C.L. Betrand, 'Revolutionary Syndicalism in Italy', in van der Linden and Thorpe, *Revolutionary Syndicalism*, p. 146.

34 *L'Internazionale*, 19 September 1914.

35 *L'Internazionale*, 17 October 1914.

beginning to organise to defend themselves. For many the message of the Bolshevik revolution – immediate peace – appeared to offer the most compelling solution, and following the October revolution some 20,000 workers joined the Unione, drawn in part by Borghi's message that the Italians should 'Do as they did in Russia'. As a result, in the final phase of the war and the immediate post-war period the USI expanded rapidly; by the end of 1919 it had enrolled 305,000 members and was three times larger in 1919 than it had been in 1914 (although the socialist CGL exceeded this rate of expansion).[36] Nonetheless, the breakaway interventionists also took advantage of the situation, reviving an organisation *Unione Italiana Lavoro* (Italian Union of Labour) which has been set up in 1914 by DeAmbris and Bianchi after their expulsion from the USI, around the patriotic idea of 'national syndicalism'.[37] They were later to help, after the defeat of the factory occupations of 1920, to open the door to the rise of Mussolini's fascist movement.

Centralisation *versus* Local Autonomy

Although all syndicalist movements sought to reach a viable compromise between local autonomy and centralised control there were inevitably tensions on this issue, as with others. For example, in theory the CGT's central committee, with the general secretary at its head, was no more than the servant of the council and congress. Delesalle argued that the CGT was not 'a directing committee nor a workers' Senate but a simple correspondence bureau intended to put organisations in contact with each other'. Elsewhere he described the CGT as a 'registering office'. This, in turn, was an echo of Pouget's remark that the central committee of the CGT should be seen as a 'kind of switchboard'.[38] The idea was that the CGT would lack any executive authority, and instead of centralisation there would be 'the most absolute federalism'; the CGT would be no more than a grouping of independent unions, with no authority at the level of each constituent union.

However, in practice the officials of the CGT played a predominant role in policy making, even if in the last analysis, the CGT was a 'federation of federations'.[39] Thus, in place of a decentralised and skeletal structure which exuded a mistrust of administrators and bureaucracy, the moderate syndicalist figure Auguste Keufer sought to create a well-financed, efficient and competent system of administration for the *syndicats*, on the basis that they needed the requisite financial resources, higher membership fees and well-trained, permanent staff. For Keufer the model *syndicat* was to be composed not of a class conscious minority but of the mass of the workers in a particular trade. Only if this were the case would durable results be achieved.[40] Such an approach was fiercely rejected by the revolutionaries within the CGT, although with the shift towards a more moderate stance from 1910, and the

---

[36] *Guerra di Classe* 7 January 1920.

[37] D.D. Roberts, *The Syndicalist Tradition and Italian Fascism* (Manchester, 1979).

[38] Cited in Jennings, p. 27.

[39] F.F. Ridley, *Revolutionary Syndicalism in France: The Direct Action of its Time* (Cambridge, 1970), p. 76.

[40] Cited in Jennings, p. 129.

union's subsequent participation on numerous commissions during the war years, there were constant tensions evident between rival conceptions of the extent of centralism necessary for efficient organisation.

There were bitter divisions on similar issues in Ireland. In the pre-war years under Larkin's leadership the administration of the ITGWU had amounted to virtually to one-man governance. There was no executive and a proposed national convention of delegates never met. Up to 1917, the two general officers, the president and the secretary, who were supposed to be chosen by the members bi-annually, were actually elected annually by the No. 1 Dublin branch.[41] Whilst the union was engaged in such major battles as the Dublin lock-out such limitations in organisational democracy were not viewed as an issue of major concern. But after the war and under the new leadership of William O'Brien, it was a very different matter. Although initially a recovery in workers' confidence to strike provided an impetus for the re-emergence of the ITGWU with a phenomenal growth in union membership, the onset of economic slump and mass unemployment from 1920 onwards led to a further retrenchment. O'Brien made strenuous efforts as part of the 'One Big Union' model to augment officialdom at local level and strengthen central control, provoking a chorus of dissent as he increased his power within an increasingly bureaucratic union machine. Larkin, who returned to Ireland in April 1923, led a blistering attack on the leadership and made an ultimately unsuccessful attempt to re-capture control of the union.[42]

In Britain the early 1913 internal split within the ISEL had been created in part by the fact that it had no effective leadership structure to speak of beyond Tom Mann and a few of his confidantes. As one leading member pointed out, instead of possessing a formal membership and branch structure, the ISEL 'was made up of a small number of loosely organised groups and a large number of individuals scattered all over the country'.[43] Bitter criticism of the failure to organise the existing members, beyond regular speaker meetings and educational classes backed up by the sale of syndicalist literature and pamphlets, resulted in the re-organisation of the ISEL at its first AGM in early 1913 (more than two years after its birth).[44] *The Syndicalist* explained:

> Up to now the League has been more or less an amorphous organisation owing to the method of its inception. There were but few comrades who started it, and the need for a definite constitution, rules and so forth was not felt. We were all personal friends, and we just selected a committee of five and appointed a general secretary and president without giving definite duties to either, and let them get on with the work of spreading Syndicalist propaganda. Now, owing to the establishment of provincial groups and the increase of membership in every direction, it is desirable that the whole body of members should have a voice in saying what shall be done and how it shall be done.[45]

---

[41] E. O'Connor, *James Larkin* (Cork, 2002), p. 25–6.

[42] E. Larkin, *James Larkin: Irish Labour Leader 1876–1947* (London, 1965); O'Connor, pp. 70–79.

[43] *The Syndicalist and Amalgamation News*, January 1913.

[44] Ibid., March–April 1913.

[45] Ibid., February 1913.

Yet it was the decision to turn the ISEL into a fully-fledged formal organisation, complete with a constitution and branch structure, which contributed to its rapid splintering and disintegration by the autumn of 1913.

Finally in America during its early years the IWW was grounded, both implicitly and explicitly, on the basis of a centralised model of organisation. It was no accident that it campaigned for 'One Big Union'. Even the union's name – the 'Industrial Workers of the World' – declared clearly (even if the reality did not live up to the ambition) its intention to regroup the workers of the whole world into one single organisation. Yet the extent of centralised control inside the IWW became a source of bitter dispute. The 1905 convention had elected a seven-person General Executive Board (GEB) to conduct the affairs of the organisation, consisting of a National President, a National Secretary-Treasurer, and five other members. In its hands was placed the entire responsibility for the conduct of the affairs of the organisation between conventions, with full power to issue charters to all subordinate bodies – including industrial departments and local unions – to supervise and control the publication of the official organ *Industrial Worker* and elect its editor, and to call unions out on strike (although any agreement between unions and employers was subject to members' approval).[46]

From 1910 onward two distinct factions began to emerge: the 'footloose', migratory workers of the lumber camps, mines and wheat fields of the South and West; and the IWW of the immigrant workers in the great East Coast manufacturing industries. Each faction became identified with a different policy. The Easterners generally favoured greater centralization in the IWW organisation and more control of union activities from the centre to prevent the IWW dissipating its energy on perceived fruitless free speech fights and propaganda battles and to overcome its rapid turnover in membership. They were supported by people like Haywood, Ettor, Flynn and the majority of the General Executive Board. By contrast, the Westerners usually believed in less control and more autonomy from local branches. They favoured the abolition of the GEB and the post of general organiser and their replacement by a stenographer who would handle correspondence between locals. They were supported by anarchists like Carlo Tresca and James Rowan who resisted any sort of political control in principle.

While the Western Wobblies pressed for more autonomy and less control from the centre, the GEB believed that if the IWW was to grow it must transform itself from a purely propaganda and guerrilla body into an ordinary union, with all the responsibilities and compromises a permanent mass membership would impose. At the sixth IWW convention in 1911 the decentralisers made a serious challenge to the GEB's authority over members. Several amendments tried to minimise their power, but after much debate they were all defeated.[47] At the IWW's ninth convention in 1914 the centralisers further secured their victory and the union's 1916 convention was important for firmly reasserting the authority of the general headquarters under Haywood's leadership. All IWW administrative, printing and publishing operations were consolidated in Chicago. All the internal reforms adopted were aimed at

46 Brissenden, pp. 100–101.

47 *International Socialist Review*, 12, July 1911, pp. 300–302.

centralising the IWW's operations and making fieldwork subject to the discipline of elected administrators and the staff at national headquarters.[48] Nonetheless, the endless squabbles over the limitations to be placed on the leadership continued. Almost every issue of the *Industrial Worker* contained at least one article or resolution demanding decentralisation of the national administration and greater autonomy for Pacific Coast locals, and in 1919 anti-leadership elements successfully pushed the union to adopt a one-year maximum term provision for elected officers.[49]

Conclusion

Apart from internal tensions on all the different issues considered above, bitter divisions also emerged on the syndicalists' contrasting attitude towards the Russian Revolution, Bolshevism and the Communist International (which are explored in Part Two). Such internal ideological, strategic, tactical and organisational divisions were not unique to the syndicalist movement; most of the main socialist parties were bedevilled on similar lines, albeit usually with left-wing minorities confronting moderate leaderships, a process that was considerably accentuated by the impact of the First World War and the Russian revolution. Nor did such conflicts necessarily prevent united activity on many fronts between syndicalists of different persuasions, at least during periods of heightened class struggle. But clearly in the case of France the differences between reformists and revolutionaries had a dramatic effect on the substantive nature of the CGT in the years immediately before the First World War. And in other countries, with the ebb of revolutionary workers' struggle in the early 1920s the inherent divisions within the syndicalist movements were to take on a heightened form with debilitating effect. The next chapter explores the dynamic of such developments.

---

[48] Dubofsky, *We Shall Be All*, pp. 344–5; P. Renshaw, *The Wobblies: The Story of Syndicalism in the United States* (London, 1967), pp. 163–4; 173–4.

[49] Foner, *IWW*, pp. 144–5.

Chapter 5

Influence and Demise

Shortly after the demise of the movement internationally a number of historians developed a revisionist case against syndicalism suggesting its essential premise, that workers had an interest in overthrowing capitalism through revolutionary trade union activity, was fundamentally flawed. They argued that a combination of the untenable objective conditions within which syndicalism attempted to attract support and the unrealistic revolutionary policies it espoused, inevitably led to marginalisation of the movement to the fringes of the working class except for episodic periods.

Best known for their studies of American labour history, Robert Hoxie and Selig Perlman regarded the collapse of the IWW as evidence of an underlying conservatism among rank-and-file workers. Discounting any higher aspirations of the labour movement, they attempted to explain unionisation solely in terms of workers' material interest in protecting their jobs and raising wages. Whilst exceptional circumstances, such as a charismatic IWW leader or anger over repressive state policies, might allow militants to gain some influence for short periods, in the long-run unions adopted a business-like focus on jobs and wages that matched workers' own narrow concerns. Thus, Hoxie characterised syndicalism as a 'doctrine of despair' fundamentally at odds with the 'optimism' of American workers and concluded that the 'conditions are not here for its growth'.[1] Patrick Renshaw, a more recent historian of the IWW, has concurred with this view: 'the plain fact is that the American working class, in general, was just not interested in socialist theory with its millennial promises.'[2]

Peter Stearns has advanced similar arguments in relation to French syndicalism; French workers constituted a 'conservative, pragmatic labour force', sought limited and often traditional goals and most generally were simply not dissatisfied with their lot given the very limited nature of their expectations.[3] Syndicalism had little genuine mass influence and was a failure, either as instructor or stimulant to the working class. 'A cause without rebels', claims Stearns; a movement 'paralyzed outside the realm of theory', unable to generate among the French workers a revolutionary commitment to match its radical rhetoric.[4]

> The syndicalist minority was very small; many radical workers were not syndicalists; and the radical minority, of whatever stripe, dropped its effective radicalism surprisingly

---

[1] R. Hoxie, *Trade Unionism in the United States* (New York, 1920), p. 154; 160; 159; S. Perlman, *A Theory of the Labor Movement* (New York, 1928).

[2] P. Renshaw, *The Wobblies: The Story of Syndicalism in the United States* (London, 1967), p. 42.

[3] P.N. Stearns, *Revolutionary Syndicalism and French Labour: A Cause Without Rebels* (New Brunswick, 1971).

[4] Ibid., p. 102.

> quickly, because many grievances were satisfied or because tactical realities were recognised or because majority sentiment simply smothered it.[5]

Likewise in relation to the rise of the Irish trade union movement during this period, according to Dermot Keogh all that was at stake was the principle of the right to organise with a demonstration of merely trade union consciousness on the part of the workers. It was only employers' intransigence that made them turn to the likes of Jim Larkin for leadership.[6] And assessing the pre-war labour unrest in Britain G.D.H. Cole commented:

> The underlying movement was a mass movement of sheer reaction against the failure of either orthodox Trade Unionism or moderate parliamentarism to secure any improvement in working class standards of life. The theorists, working class and middle class alike, who sought to give this movement form and direction and to interpret its vague strivings into a new social gospel, never really captured the great mass of the working class. They might lead in this or that particular struggle, and might help to stir up troubles that would not have occurred without their impulsion. But the mass, as ever, was thinking not of Utopia and not even of the class war, but mainly of the immediate issues involved in each separate dispute. If a new temper was abroad, and the moderate leaders found their control of the movement seriously threatened, this did not imply a wholesale conversion of the British working class to revolutionary doctrines.[7]

Even though dismissive arguments about the potential radicalism of the American labour movement and its syndicalist protagonists have been refuted by generations of historians, and there have been some counter-challenges concerning French and British syndicalism,[8] the overall political significance of syndicalism in these countries and elsewhere internationally has clearly often been ignored or downplayed. So how valid is this attempt to suggest that the syndicalist movement's advocacy of revolutionary trade union activity was inevitably doomed to fail? Should we assess the movement's significance essentially only in terms of the attempt to secure immediate improvements in wages and conditions or did it have any potential wider and more radical resonance?

---

[5] Ibid., p. 95.

[6] D. Keogh, *The Rise of the Irish Working Class: The Dublin Trade Union Movement and the Labour Leadership, 1890–1914* (Belfast 1982), pp. 3–4.

[7] G.D.H. Cole, *A Short History of the British Working Class Movement, 1789–1947* (London, 1948), pp. 321–2.

[8] On America see R.S. Wilentz, 'Against Exceptionalism: Class Consciousness and the American Labor Movement', *International Labor and Working Class History*, 26 (1984), pp. 1–24; M. Shalev and W. Korpi, 'Working Class Mobilisation and American Exceptionalism', *Economic and Industrial Democracy*, 1 (1980), pp. 31–61; I. Katznelson and A. Zolberg, *Working Class Formation: Nineteenth Century Patterns in Western Europe and the United States* (New York, 1986). For France see G.C. Friedman, 'Revolutionary Unions and French Labour: The Rebels Behind the Cause: Or, Why Did Revolutionary Syndicalism Fail?', *French Historical Studies*, 20 (1997), pp. 155–81. For Britain see B. Holton, *British Syndicalism* (London, 1976).

Membership Levels and the Class Struggle

It is certainly true that even though syndicalist organisations sometimes grew rapidly during periods of upsurge in class struggle, when large numbers of workers were drawn into conflict with the existing order and established ideas, they remained almost everywhere *minority* movements (sometimes a smallish one as in Britain, sometimes a substantial one as in Italy) compared with their much larger reformist trade union adversaries. While actual membership figures are invariably difficult to determine with any degree of accuracy, we can briefly document overall membership trends in each country based on the available evidence.

In Britain, where the ISEL's appeal was essentially directed at activists *within* established unions, they performed a propaganda role and did not succeed in building a mass base. There were probably no more than a few thousand members at any one time, and sales of *The Syndicalist* only reached a peak of about 20,000 copies, although it was claimed two ISEL conferences in 1912 drew together delegates from unions, trades councils and amalgamation committees representing up to 100,000 workers.[9] During the war J.T. Murphy's pamphlet *The Workers' Committee*, which contained the syndicalist-influenced Shop Stewards' and Workers' Committee Movement's chief theoretical statement, reached a total sale of some 150,000 copies.[10]

By comparison in France, where it faced no reformist union rival, the CGT was able to build a national trade union centre that won the adherence of a much wider layer of workers, albeit containing sizeable (if initially minority) reformist elements. But while the Confédération's membership leapt from 122,000 in 1902 to 300,000 in 1908 during a time when strikes were relatively successful, its momentum was subsequently undermined amidst an employer and state counter-offensive which inflicted a series of important strike defeats. Internal divisions and the impact of war further exacerbated the decline, such that by 1915 the CGT had haemorrhaged to just 49,000 dues-payers. Only a revival of industrial militancy reversed the trend; by the end of the war there were 600,000 members, increasing to 1.2 million in 1919 and reaching a peak of 2.4 million in 1920, before falling off dramatically again in 1921, following internal schisms, to 1 million.[11] But even at its high point in the immediate post-war years the CGT never officially represented more than half the organised workers of France and at best one tenth of the industrial wage earners overall. [12] One historian has even estimated the hard-core revolutionary syndicalist cadre may not have numbered more than 2,000 if subscription to the organisation's theoretical journal is the barometer.[13]

---

9 *The Syndicalist and Amalgamated News*, November and December 1912.

10 J.T. Murphy, *New Horizons* (London, 1941), p. 135.

11 R. Magraw, *A History of the French Working Class, Vol. 2: Workers and the Bourgeois Republic* (Oxford, 1992).

12 Figures complied from M. Dubofsky, *Industrialism and the American Worker 1865–1920* (Arlington Heights, 1975).

13 Holton, *British Syndicalism,*, p. 210. This figure is unconvincingly derived from an estimated average circulation of the CGT's journal *La Voix du people* of about 5,000 copies, less than half of whom are assumed to be committed revolutionaries.

In Ireland, America, Italy and Spain syndicalists were able to build revolutionary alternatives to the existing national reformist trade union centres, in the process drawing into membership large numbers of previously unorganised workers who had often been neglected in the past by conventional unions. But even in the first three of these countries the numbers were limited in comparison to the size of the reformist-led unions and the workforce as a whole and membership gains were often short-lived. In Ireland the ITGWU grew from a mere 5,000 members at the beginning of 1911 to some 18,000 at the end, as a direct result of the upsurge in industrial unrest that swept the country that year. By the time of the 1913 Dublin strike and lockout the union claimed a membership of 30,000, although most historians accept substantially smaller figures of about 12-13,000.[14] At the height of the battle Larkin claimed sales of the union's weekly paper *Irish Worker and People's Advocate* neared 100,000 copies, although throughout the paper's life the average weekly sale was probably 20,000.[15] The devastating defeat of the Dublin dispute, combined with the impact of war, produced a collapse in union membership to about 5,000 members by 1916. While a revival of industrial militancy and growth of a mass movement for national independence from 1918 onwards encouraged a phenomenal growth to 100,000 during 1920–1923, membership rapidly declined again thereafter.[16]

In America for brief periods the IWW also involved many thousands of workers in their organisation. Nonetheless, one year after its 1905 foundation membership was down from 23,000 to 14,500 and, amidst internal faction fighting combined with the impact of economic depression, there continued to be a marked decline to 3,700 by 1908. It was not until 1909 that the Wobblies began to experience rapid growth arising from their free-speech campaigns and increased strike intervention, although before 1916 they never had more than 40,000 paid-up members. During 1916–1917 this leapt to 75,000 and it is estimated that by the end of the summer of 1917, at their height, they had between 125–150,000. But although there was a renewed post-war explosion of strike activity, massive state repression effectively put the Wobblies out of business as a functioning syndicalist organisation.[17]

In Italy the USI, which was founded at the end of 1912 with a membership of 80,000, grew in the course of 1913 to 101,000 members; the mass circulation of its weekly newspaper *L'Internazionale* increased accordingly. But in 1914 the emergence of the pro-war 'interventionist' grouping led to a split within the ranks of Italian

---

14 C.D. Greaves, *The Irish Transport and General Workers' Union: The Formative Years, 1909–1923* (Dublin, 1982), pp. 70, 82, 91; E. O'Connor, 'What Caused the 1913 Lockout? Industrial Relations in Ireland, 1907–13', *Historical Studies in Industrial Relations*, 19 (2005), p. 114.

15 J. Newsinger, '"A Lamp to Guide Your Feet": Jim Larkin, the Irish Workers, and the Dublin Working Class, *European History Quarterly*, 20:1 (1990), pp. 63–99.

16 E. Larkin, *James Larkin: Irish Labour Leader 1876–1947* (London, 1968), p. 71; 97–98; 236; C. Kostick, *Revolution in Ireland: Popular Militancy 1917 to 1923* (London, 1996), p. 32; 139.

17 P.F. Brissenden, *The IWW: A Study of American Syndicalism* (New York, 1919), p. 183, 357; M. Dubofsky, 'The Rise and Fall' of Revolutionary Syndicalism in the United States, in M. van der Linden and W. Thorpe (eds), *Revolutionary Syndicalism: An International Perspective* (Aldershot, 1990), p. 214.

syndicalism, with total membership of the USI declining to 48,000 by 1917. Only in the final phase of the war period and immediately afterwards, under the impact of an upturn in workers' struggle and the inspiration of the Russian Revolution, did membership levels recover, such that by the end of 1919 it had enrolled about 305,000. Membership then fall drastically again to 100,000 following the defeat of the occupation of the factories in 1920 and the rise of Mussolini to power in 1922.[18]

Finally in Spain, the CNT claimed about 26,000 members in 1911 (a year after its formation), expanded to 50,000 members in 1916 (overwhelmingly concentrated in Catalonia), and then grew spectacularly in the immediate post-war years to 791,000 by December 1920, again in the context of a huge rise in workers' militancy and the impact of the Russian Revolution. Yet by 1923, following a rapid decline in strike activity and massive state repression, the organisation was banned and driven underground with membership levels declining to a quarter of a million. Only with the advent of the Second Republic in 1931 and the explosion of class struggle and revolutionary uprisings that followed, was the CNT able to regain its previous mass influence, with membership leaping from around half a million in 1931 to 1.7 million by the outbreak of civil war in 1936.[19]

To recap, it is clear there was a direct relationship between the relative membership strength of syndicalist movements and the general level of class struggle, with membership levels fluctuating considerably within each country from one period to another. In general each individual syndicalist movement's period of maximum influence appears to have coincided with its highpoint in membership levels, although this was not always the case; 1906–1910 and 1920 in France, 1910–1914 (and 1917) in Britain, 1913 and 1918–1920 in Ireland, 1916–1917 in America, 1920 in Italy and 1917–1919 and 1936–1937 in Spain.[20] Obviously there was considerable variation in the extent of syndicalist influence, between, for example, British syndicalism with its few thousand loosely organised supporters intervening in some major industrial disputes on the one hand and hundreds of thousands strong CNT at the centre of the Spanish civil war and social revolution on the other.

It seems likely some workers may have readily subscribed to the *methods* of syndicalism (especially 'direct action') rather than necessarily the revolutionary *aims* of the movement. The immediate demands of the syndicalists, ostensibly a prelude to a revolutionary reconstruction of society, may have seemed to individual militants a more sensible strategy for securing reforms in the meantime than the activities of those in the labour movement dedicated to the mere attainment of such reforms and

---

[18] C.L. Bertrand, 'Revolutionary Syndicalism in Italy', in van der Linden and Thorpe, *Revolutionary Syndicalism*, p. 148; *L'Internazionale*, 12 December 1914; A. Borghi, *Mezzo secolo di anarchia 1898–1945* (Naples, 1954), p. 115; A. Gradilone, *Storia del sindacalismo, Vol. 3* (Milan, 1959), p. 109, 196.

[19] A. Bar, 'The CNT: The Glory and Tragedy of Spanish Anarchosyndicalism', in van der Linden and Thorpe, *Revolutionary Syndicalism*, p. 123, 125–6; A. Bar, *Syndicalism and Revolution in Spain: The Ideology and Syndical Practice of the CNT in the Period 1915–1919* (New York, 1981); A. Durgan, 'Revolutionary Anarchism in Spain: the CNT 1911–1937', *International Socialism* 2:11 (1981), p. 100.

[20] For a slightly different assessment see van der Linden and Thorpe, 'The Rise and Fall of Revolutionary Syndicalism', in van der Linden and Thorpe, *Revolutionary Syndicalism*, p. 5.

resistant to efforts to secure more fundamental change.[21] But while such workers may have been impressed by syndicalist ideas and tactics and prepared to try them out in the battle for immediate demands, only a small proportion of them were willing to join syndicalist bodies or adopt an explicit revolutionary commitment. In France a number of the large constituent unions that joined the CGT were actively reformist in character and adopted policies radically opposed to those of the revolutionary 'majority'. Finally, as in any organisation there were no doubt some disparities between the leadership and activists, on the one hand, and rank-and-file members on the other, in terms of degree of motivation for, participation in, and commitment to, revolutionary politics.

However, even if syndicalist organisations attracted only a minority of the workforce in the countries in which they operated, this was equally the case for their reformist adversaries. In fact, in the case of Spain and Ireland syndicalist unions did almost as well as their conventional counterparts and, in the case of France, they did better than them although many were (at a price) absorbed within the CGT itself. In practice *all* unions in the early twentieth century, whether they were syndicalist or otherwise, found it difficult to mobilise the *majority* of workers into the new institutions for collective action against their employers.[22] The fact that the vast mass of workers joined neither a syndicalist nor conventional union proves nothing about how they felt. It would surely be foolhardy to write off such workers as 'content' or 'moderate' simply because the number of militant activists was small. What it *does* suggest is that establishing union organisation was *generally* difficult, with employers and the state often willing to mobilise violent forms of opposition whenever unionism *of any variety* gained a significant degree of influence. If we were to accept the argument that the syndicalists' commitment to militant strike action and ultimate revolution was 'doomed to fail', how do we explain the fact that the more moderate approach of the reformist unions (and socialist parties) fared little better in terms of attracting the mass of workers, and was often itself subject to attack.[23] The answer to the more pertinent question of how well did syndicalism do compared with their contemporaries, is that they succeeded reasonably well.

In fact formal membership figures are not necessarily the best guide to syndicalist *influence*. To begin with, in every country syndicalists tended to place a very low priority on membership benefits and permanent structures. In France the syndicalists' anti-benefit culture meant that workers often had no individual interest in joining CGT unions or in remaining a member of a CGT union outside periods of heightened generalised conflict. But despite the fluctuating fortunes of the Confédération's membership at any given time, this did not necessarily reflect declining support given that thousands of workers read its papers, frequented the *bourses* and union headquarters, attended rallies and demonstrations and publicised union issues and

---

[21] V. Burgmann, *Revolutionary Industrial Unionism: The Industrial Workers of the World in Australia* (Cambridge, 1995), p. 129.

[22] G. Friedman, *State-Making and Labor Movements: France and the United States, 1876–1914* (Ithaca, New York, 1998), pp. 251–2.

[23] W. Preston, 'Shall This Be All? U.S. Historians Versus William D. Haywood *et al.*', *Labor History*, 11:3 (1971), pp. 440–41.

lent support to the CGT in all ways but financial.[24] In the process the CGT succeeded in attracting to the movement many of the most militant workers of the time.

In addition snapshot membership figures tend to underestimate the number of workers who moved in and out of syndicalist organisations. For example, on the basis of an annual average IWW membership turnover of 133 per cent, it has been estimated the Wobblies probably signed up four or five times its total membership at any one time, so that as many as 2–3 million probably passed through the organisation over the course of a few years, with millions more subject to its influence.[25] Of equal significance is the fact that syndicalists in every country invariably exercised an influence disproportionate to their formal numerical strength, notably in influencing the temper and scale of many strikes. For example, with reference to the CGT in France, Bernard Moss has commented:

> If they were 'active minorities' without followers in periods of social peace – periods of complacency, resignation or despair – they became leaders of masses during moments of social tension and conflict. During mass mobilisations – strikes, professional elections, political crises, and so on – they became the spokesmen for the usually 'silent majorities', including many of the normally moderate, apathetic, resigned, and perhaps even conservative workers. As ideological leaders, they gave clarity and consistency to what was at best the episodic class-consciousness of the majority.[26]

'Cause Without Rebels'?

Arguably the interpretation of strike militancy as direct action in pragmatic pursuit of demands on wages and conditions ignores the inherent anti-capitalist sentiment that was expressed during this period. Of course, it is undoubtedly true that many workers *were* reformist, conservative and apathetic. Many remained loyal to existing reformist trade union and socialist leaders and, as we have seen, only a minority (albeit larger in some countries than others) were attracted to membership of individual syndicalist organisations. However, the assumption that all 'real' workers were, by definition, 'pragmatists', essentially indifferent to radical ideas and that strike action was purely 'economistic' is wholly unconvincing.

Certainly, the implication that to show workers through trade unions 'only' struggle to satisfy their basic material interests in pay and conditions of employment is *ipso facto* to prove the non-existence of a revolutionary working class is untenable, as John Kelly has suggested.[27] First, it is wholly unrealistic to expect workers to be mobilised in struggle on anything other than their basis material interests. Second, this fact is wholly consistent with the likelihood of workers becoming class-conscious because their material interests can be shown to be incompatible with the major features of capitalism. And third, the pursuit of such material interests can help to

---

24 B. Mitchell, 'French Syndicalism: An Experiment in Practical Anarchism', in van der Linden and Thorpe, *Revolutionary Syndicalism*, p. 36.

25 Dubofsky, *Industrialism and the American Worker*, p. 103.

26 B.H. Moss, *The Origins of the French Labor Movement: The Socialism of Skilled Workers, 1830–1914* (Berkeley, Calif., 1976), p. 150.

27 J. Kelly, *Trade Unions and Socialist Politics* (London, 1988), p. 298.

create conditions of economic and political crisis in which a transition to a socialist society becomes more probable.

In reality, wage demands frequently disguised other fundamental grievances such as shorter hours, improved conditions, union recognition and control over work. In pursuing these immediate goals workers were often confronted with intransigent employers and hostile government officials, police and even troops, as well as by hesitant labour movement leaders anxious to channel demands within established channels. In the process, the established 'rules of the game' – piecemeal advancement by means of parliamentary action and institutionalised collective bargaining – was at the very least widely questioned and often subject to critique as a wholly insufficient means of advancing working class interests.[28] Even if the ideology of reformism was by no means destroyed it was nonetheless put under considerable strain in many respects. It was precisely for this reason that syndicalist movements, which represented both a reaction to and a rejection of the politics of gradualism in favour of revolutionary industrial struggle, could attract support in different countries amongst at least a sizeable minority of workers.

At the same time many strikes of the period – with their aggressive resistance to employers, defiance of magistrates, and clashes with police and troops – encouraged a process of radicalisation inside the working class that, whilst not necessarily revolutionary itself, signified the emergence of a political culture that was outside the formal consensus of the day. It was in this extraordinary context that syndicalism's insurgent trade unionism, whose cornerstone was to overturn the accepted order of things, could give hope and self-confidence to workers who had previously had to be content with survival on the employers' terms. The syndicalist movement gave organised form and inspiring voice to a determination to shift the balance of class forces in society in favour of the working class and offered the prospect of a new world where labour ruled.[29] Only on this basis can we understand, for example, the widespread appeal inside the American working class movement of IWW poet and song-writer Joe Hill's sardonic anti-capitalist ballads of class antagonism such as 'Solidarity Forever' and 'Workers of the World Awaken!' that according to Patrick Renshaw 'captured the imagination of a whole generation of workers'.[30] Such counter-politics stood for the celebration of working class solidarity and direct action and pointed in the direction of taking things a step further amongst the most militant workers, with demands for workers' control and fundamental political change to the existing political system.[31]

Such radicalisation was undoubtedly considerably further enhanced by the impact of war and the October 1917 Russian Revolution. The dynamic of war,

---

[28] N. Kirk, *Labour and Society in Britain and the USA: Vol. 2: Challenge and Accommodation, 1850–1939* (Aldershot, 1994), p. 108.

[29] J. Newsinger, 'Irish Labour in a Time of Revolution', *Socialist History*, 22 (2002), p. 4.

[30] Renshaw, p. 24.

[31] For an outline of such arguments with reference to Ireland and France respectively see E. O'Connor, *Syndicalism in Ireland* (Cork University Press, 1988), pp. 45–46; 186; R. Magraw, 'Socialism. Syndicalism and French Labour Before 1914', in D. Geary (ed.), *Labour and Socialist Movements in Europe before 1914* (Oxford, 1989), pp. 88–9.

with its multiple sacrifices and shifting relations between social groups, begged the question of whether the return to peace would mark a return to the status quo or to a changed social order.[32] And the impact of the Bolshevik revolution could be seen during many of the post-war strikes, as workers came to view the struggles for union recognition, higher wages, fewer hours and improved working conditions as part of a world-wide revolutionary movement in which they now had a chance to participate. In a memorandum to the Versailles Conference of 1919 the British Prime Minister Lloyd George wrote:

> Europe is filled with revolutionary ideas. A feeling not of depression, but of passion and revolt reigns in the breasts of the working class against the conditions of life that prevailed before the war. The whole of the existing system, political, social and economic, is regarded with distrust by the whole population of Europe. In some countries, like Germany and Russia, this unrest is leading to open revolt and in others, like France, England and Italy, it is expressed in strikes and in a certain aversion to work. All signs go to show that the striving is as much for social and political changes as for increases in wages.[33]

Such an analysis does not portray the *mass* of workers as ripe for revolution necessarily; certainly compared with the violent clashes between the old order and the forces of revolution in countries such as Italy and Spain, Britain remained relatively calm. But at the very least we will never understand how societies that were scarred by bitter and bloody industrial conflict managed to contain discontent and retain their essential stability if we deny the existence of class conflict, or the possibility that, in certain circumstances and among a wide layer of workers, such conflict created class consciousness and for some even a revolutionary commitment.[34]

We should not minimise the contribution of syndicalist (and other left-wing) activists to such working class radicalism. As Larry Peterson has suggested, in the post-war years there was the convergence of three forces – individual union militants, formal left-wing organisations (notably syndicalist bodies, but also socialist and later on communist parties) and mass unrest among industrial workers all converged in a general anti-capitalist movement. The role of left-wing organisations lent the movement its revolutionary ideology; the participation of union militants (whether or not members of such left-wing organisations) established a vital link between revolutionaries and the unions; and the unrest of workers provided the mass force to sustain and extend the movement.[35] The syndicalist element played an important role not only in trying to give organisation, leadership and coherence to the movement, but also in their simultaneous attempt to utilise workers' immediate issues of concern as the take-off point for a full-scale indictment of the capitalist

---

[32] J. Horne, 'The State and the Challenge of Labour in France 1917–20', C. Wrigley (ed.), *Challenges of Labour: Central and Western Europe 1917–1920* (London, 1993), p. 249.

[33] Cited in J.T. Murphy, *Preparing for Power* (London, 1972), p. 172.

[34] J. Jenson and M. Dubofsky, 'The IWW – An Exchange of Views', *Labor History*, 11:3 (1970), p. 371.

[35] L. Peterson, 'The One Big Union in International Perspective: Revolutionary Industrial Unionism, 1900–1925', in J.E. Cronin and C. Sirianni (eds), *Work, Community and Power: The Experience of Labor in Europe and America, 1900–1925* (Philadelphia, 1983), p. 68.

system and an exposition of the need for its revolutionary overthrow. The high level of class struggle and political radicalisation became a fertile breeding ground for the sowing of the syndicalist seed. For example, referring to the militant workers' struggle in Dublin in 1913, the British government's chief conciliator, Lord Askwith, acknowledged:

> ... the serious riots in Dublin, although founded on poverty, low wages and bad conditions, included a determination to establish ... 'one big union' and put into practice the doctrines of syndicalism. The influences ... [for] the overthrow of Capitalism, and revolution against existing authority, were all present.[36]

In the 1910–1911 South Wales coal dispute the syndicalist-influenced strike committee began by calling on workers to 'Down Tools' in support of higher wages and ended by calling on them 'To put an end to Capitalist Despotism and do battle for the cause of Industrial Freedom'.[37] And testimony to the widespread appeal of the IWW's explicit revolutionary unionism was provided by James Cannon:

> The IWW struck a spark in the heart of youth as no other movement in this country, before or since, has done. Young idealists from 'the winds' four quarters' came to the IWW and gave it all they had. The movement had its gifted strike leaders, organisers and orators, its poets and its martyrs. By the accumulated weight of its unceasing propagandistic efforts, and by the influence of its heroic actions on many occasions which were sensationally publicised, the IWW eventually permeated a whole generation of American radicals, of all shades and affiliations, with its concept of industrial unionism as the best form for the organisation of workers' power and its programme for a revolutionary settlement of the class struggle.[38]

Ironically, an important measure of syndicalism's influence within strike activity can be gauged by the level of fear it engendered and condemnation it received from employers and politicians, even if there was sometimes an element of exaggeration involved. For example, the IWW vexed employers, congressmen, cabinet members and American presidents. 'By World War 1 some Americans considered the Wobblies as great a threat to national security as German imperialists and Russian Bolsheviks. Neither before nor since has any group of labour radicals been as feared as the Wobblies.'[39]

In Britain even prominent official labour leaders such as Ramsay MacDonald and Philip Snowden, as well as Sidney and Beatrice Webb, published scathing attacks on the movement.[40] Ironically, although these parliamentary socialists confidently claimed there was nothing in the tradition or character of British labour that would permit syndicalism to gain a foothold, syndicalism was nonetheless

---

[36] G.R. Askwith, *Industrial Problems and Disputes* (London, 1974), p. 259.

[37] R.P. Arnot, *South Wales Miners: A History of the South Wales Miners' Federation: 1898–1914* (London, 1967), p. 273.

[38] J. Cannon, *The IWW: The Great Anticipation* (New York, 1956), p. 31.

[39] Dubofsky, *Industrialism and the American Worker*, p. 102.

[40] R. MacDonald, *Syndicalism: A Critical Examination* (London, 1912); S. and B. Webb, *What Syndicalism Means: An Examination of the Origin and Motives of the Movement with an Analysis of its Proposals for the Control of Industry* (London, 1912); P. Snowden, *Socialism and Syndicalism*, (London, 1913).

nervously viewed as a dangerous influence that could encourage workers into 'unnatural' social and political behaviour. Whilst MacDonald attempted to reassure his readers: 'Syndicalism in England is negligible, both as a school of thought and as an organisation for action', the extent of effort expended to prove it was negligible appeared to show otherwise.[41]

As Robert Price has suggested, pre-war British syndicalism was seen as a threat precisely because it came to represent an alternative extra-parliamentary set of policy prescriptions and strategies for labour at a time when all politics was in flux and such matters as the nature of political authority and accountability were open to debate.[42] Certainly, in its celebration of the spontaneity of direct action and its advocacy of strike activity as a weapon of revolutionary struggle to overthrow capitalism and replace it by workers' control of production, it challenged the existing industrial and political order as well as the authority structures of the mainstream labour movement. Whilst syndicalist-inspired voices were not the only ones raising doubts about the drift of labour politics, they were often treated as if they posed a more serious threat to British social democracy and orthodox trade unionism than any other group of the time.

It follows the experience of the international revolutionary syndicalist movement cannot simply be dismissed as some sort of irrelevant 'sideshow' as some historians have implied. Its explicit revolutionary aspirations proved to be of considerable appeal to a significant layer of workers because it expressed workers' rising level of organisation, confidence and class consciousness during what was, by any accounts, an exceptional period of industrial and political militancy. The postwar emergence of an international communist movement provided further evidence of the underlying process.

'Proto-Syndicalist' Revolt?

We can now consider the argument made by some historians that there was a broad 'syndicalist mood' of revolt or 'syndicalist impulse' inside the working class movement generally during this period. Thus, with reference to Britain, John Lovell has suggested: 'It was the mood of syndicalism, not the doctrine that made headway'.[43] Bob Holton has claimed that, whilst the British labour movement contained only a small hard-core of avowed syndicalist activists, there was a far wider 'proto-syndicalist mentality' in the evident mass strikes and anti-parliamentary ferment of the years 1910–1926.[44] By 'proto-syndicalist' he means the unofficial, insurgent, and expansive nature of many of the strikes. Holton points to the primary importance of direct action over parliamentary pressure as a means of settling grievances, and to mass support for industrial unionism to oppose employers, assert rank-and-file control over union leaders and fight to establish workers' control. Although not necessarily expressed in explicit revolutionary commitment, popular support for syndicalism

---

[41] A.W. Kirkaldy, *Economics and Syndicalism* (Cambridge, 1914), p. 101.

[42] R. Price, 'Contextualising British Syndicalism c.1907–c.1920', *Labour History Review*, 63:3 (1998), pp. 261–76.

[43] J. Lovell, *Stevedores and Dockers* (London, 1969), p. 156.

[44] Holton, *British Syndicalism*, pp. 209–10; see also B. Holton, 'Syndicalist Theories of the State', *Sociological Review*, 28 (1980), p.7.

was based upon the uplifting inspiration of fighting collective organisation, with many workers acting in a 'proto-syndicalist' manner on the basis of a feeling that they could change society through industrial rather than political action.[45]

Likewise David Montgomery has argued that autonomous self-activity, direct action at the point of production, and an emphasis on workers' control were all part of a diffuse 'syndicalist impulse' that defined the struggles of American workers for nearly two decades following the birth of the IWW.[46] Between 1909 and 1922 this 'new unionism' pushed strike activity to record levels, particularly in the immediate post-war years. Although the IWW set out to 'fan the flames' of this industrial and political unrest, it was much more widespread and diverse than the IWW could itself possibly embody. The direct action challenge to managerial authority was often to be found, ironically enough, within industries that were strongly unionised by the AFL, involving a contemptuous rank-and-file rejection of official AFL conservative practices. Samuel Gompers, AFL president, was forced to organise an 'All-American' committee of labour leaders to stage rallies against 'Bolshevism, IWWism and red flagism in general'. That industrial insurgency extended so far beyond the organisational boundaries of the IWW has led Montgomery to question 'the customary image of the IWW as representing conduct and aspirations far removed from the "mainstream" of American labour development'.[47]

Howard Kimeldorf has recently gone even further to argue that if syndicalism is viewed as a *practice* of resistance rather than a theory of revolution, then the IWW's 'industrial syndicalism' can be seen to have been a part of the American labour movement's mainstream, anchored in the same syndicalist waters as the AFL's 'business syndicalism'. Both waged the day-to-day struggle against the rule of capital by eschewing the political arena of legislative action in favour of the workplace and both preferred the immediacy of direct action at the point of production in pursuance of common objectives of extending their control over the job. The historical thrust of Kimeldorf's argument is that business syndicalism gave way to industrial syndicalism, not by the triumph of the IWW, but by the absorption of Wobbly practice into mainstream unionism as a result of 'situational' factors that appeared appropriate.[48]

Arguably the problem with this particular interpretation is that it effectively downplays the significance of syndicalism's distinctive ideological appeal and dilutes the central *revolutionary* component of the very term 'syndicalism' into something else entirely. To some extent even the use of terminology such as 'proto-syndicalism' and 'syndicalist impulse' is problematic given that a variety of material, ideological and political factors coalesced to provoke what might be more aptly described as the *zeitgeist* ('spirit of the age') of workers' industrial and political militancy of the period.

---

[45] Holton, *British Syndicalism*, pp. 118–19; 209–10.

[46] D. Montgomery, 'The "New Unionism" and the Transformation of Workers' Consciousness in America 1909–1922', *Journal of Social History*, 7:4 (1974), p. 509. See also *Workers' Control in America* (Cambridge, 1979), pp. 99–108, and 'What More to Be Done?', *Labor History*, 40:3 (1999), p. 361.

[47] Montgomery, *Workers' Control*, p. 91.

[48] H. Kimeldorf, *Battling For American Labor: Wobblies, Craft Workers, the Making of the Union Movement* (Berkeley, Calif., 1999).

Certainly we should not forget there was a logical and historical difference between the general movement of industrial and political unrest among workers generally, on the one hand, and the revolutionary syndicalist organisations and committed activists that tried to lead and influence them, on the other, which is liable to be obscured and confused with the use of terms that render them both as 'syndicalist'. Even though syndicalist activists attempted to provide organisation, leadership and ideological coherence to this broader workers' revolt, it was, of course, at no stage contained entirely within such a doctrine (or organization) and the use of fairly arbitrary (and partisan) terms that suggest otherwise is confusing.[49]

However, in so far as all these labour historians have attempted to recognise that syndicalism's appeal was much more widespread than mere organisational structures and formal membership figures would suggest, and was grounded on the distinctive *radicalism* of important minority sections of the American and British labour movement, they make a very valuable contribution to defending syndicalism from those who would write it out of working class experience as an aberration. It is true the strike militancy and political radicalisation of the period, in these countries as in others, often took place largely 'spontaneously', in conditions in which syndicalists were not even present. But it also seems clear that the experience of strike activity against employers, magistrates, police and military helped to generate a wider sympathy and interest in syndicalist ideas. At the very least, many of the most class-conscious workers knew of the efficacy of syndicalist practice even if they were not fully versed in the theory, and the sheer breadth of working class struggle affected – because it reinforced and seemed to confirm – syndicalist strategies, tactics and doctrine. Even if syndicalist activists did not in any sense cause the underlying material conditions that led to such militancy, they could sometimes play a central role in agitating around workers' grievances as part of a broader class struggle and urging them to seek redress through militant strike action and revolutionary union organisation. And even if syndicalists were only a distinct minority their ideological, political and organisational influence should not be dismissed, not the least because they were a product of a much broader radicalisation inside their respective working class movements.

Demise of the Syndicalist Movement

The syndicalist movement only survived as a powerful and influential current inside the international trade union movement for a brief period of about 20 years at the beginning of the twentieth century. Although the anarcho-syndicalism of the Spanish CNT was to play a prominent role in the Civil War in the 1930s, the bulk of the movement internationally effectively dissolved, split or was reduced to a shadow of its former self by the early 1920s. Apart from the explanations for decline specific to *individual* movements provided by different historians, Marcel van der Linden and Wayne Thorpe in a brief *comparative* overview have suggested two key factors were responsible internationally, namely the immediate problem of state repression and broader fundamental changes occurring in capitalist society generally (including the

[49] Peterson, p. 66, 68.

emergence of welfare states and of so-called Fordist accumulation patterns).[50] More recently van der Linden has signalled that any concrete analysis of the demise of particular movements needs to pay attention to additional contingent factors.[51]

What follows is an attempt to build on and considerably expand this tentative comparative overview, with an exploration of the potential objective and subjective features that need to be taken into account. These include: Structural Changes in the Labour Force; Employer and State Counter-Mobilisation and Ebb of Workers' Struggles; External Impact of Communism and Internal Schisms; and Prospects for Social Reform.

Whilst there was inevitably considerable variation between countries in the way such factors impacted, a general overview helps contextualise the demise of the movement on an international scale.

Structural Changes in the Labour Force

Some historians have argued that structural changes in the composition of the labour force brought on by rapid industrialisation meant that syndicalism was inevitably subject to extinction. In the case of France, Peter Stearns has emphasised the way the First World War accelerated the growth of large-scale heavy industry and mechanised factories (within the steel, engineering, chemical and electrical industries) employing a large per centage of semi-skilled labour, at the expense of small-scale, semi-artisanal consumer industries. The significance of this change, it is argued, is that it eroded the residual strength of craft groups and casual labourers at the heart of the old syndicalist labour tradition by paving the way for a more concentrated, homogeneous industrial proletariat that lacked contact with such pre-industrial revolutionary traditions. From this perspective, syndicalism can be regarded as being transitory, immature and backward when compared with the advanced German trade union movement which early on aligned with a mass social democratic party that channeled workers' grievances in a reformist direction.[52]

Likewise Edward Shorter and Charles Tilly, as well as Bob Holton, have suggested that what encouraged workers' resistance in a syndicalist direction in countries like France and Britain was the fact that to a large extent the workforce, particularly miners, craftsmen, dockers and agricultural workers, were as yet incompletely trained in routine capitalist factory discipline.[53] In other words, the assumption is that syndicalism represented a transitional form of labour movement activity, transitional between earlier capitalist craft methods and a second phase of factory-based mass

---

50 van der Linden and Thorpe, 'Rise and Fall', pp. 17–19.

51 M. van der Linden, 'Second Thoughts on Revolutionary Syndicalism', *Labour History Review*, 63:2, (1998), pp. 189–91.

52 See Stearns; and M. Collinet, *L'Ouvrier Francais: Essai sur la condition ouvrière 1900–1950* (Paris 1951).

53 E. Shorter and C. Tilly, *Strikes in France 1830–1968*, (Cambridge, 1974), p. 75; B. Holton, 'Revolutionary Syndicalism and the British Labour Movement', in W.J. Mommsen and H. Husung (eds), *The Development of Trade Unionism in Great Britain and Germany, 1880–1914* (London, 1985), p. 281.

production. The development of syndicalism can be viewed as a response to a particular stage of capitalist development, and hence its short-lived nature.

Arguably the attempt to characterise syndicalism as being pre-industrial, and to dismiss it as pre-modern, is unconvincing. As we have seen, despite the attempt to link different forms of labour politics to different occupational or skill groupings within the working class, it is important to note syndicalism appealed, in reality, to diverse groups of workers – skilled, semi-skilled and unskilled – depending on the circumstances. While it is true in France it proved to be particularly attractive to so-called 'artisans', it also won support from railway workers, building workers, as well as from skilled workers in small and medium-sized factories in the engineering and food industries. Kathryn Amdur has shown that although there were certain economic and political changes in the wartime and immediate post-war period, the survival and development of post-war syndicalism resulted in large part from the absence of vast economic and political transformations that would have made it truly outmoded. The war accelerated the growth and concentration of French industry, the recruitment of new sources of labour, and the active participation of the government in the economy. However, some of these changes had preceded the war, while others were undone, or at least slowed, by the post-war 'return to normalcy' and by the impact of economic recession in 1921. Neither the concentration of industry nor the recruitment of new groups of unskilled workers seriously challenged the predominance of skilled labour, on which the pre-war syndicalist movement had been firmly, although not exclusively, based.[54]

There is a similar problem with Eric Hobsbawm's designation of Spanish anarchism during the Civil War as 'primitive rebellion'.[55] The assumption made was that Spain was a predominately agrarian country, 'feudal' in its social structure, its proletariat 'undeveloped', its peasantry caught in a fever of 'millenarian' expectations. These 'primitive' features of Spain's development somehow accounted for the CNT's spectacular success in the 1930s compared with other industrially-advanced European countries. For Hobsbawm, anarchism was destined to collapse under the twin pressures of economic development and its own internal contradictions, whereupon it would be replaced by a more modern, urban-based, Marxist-led social movement. In fact, despite its trappings, Spain in 1936 was not quite the overwhelmingly agrarian and 'feudal' country we are led to believe. Certainly from the turn of the century to the coming of the Second Republic in 1931, Spain had undergone enormous economic growth with major changes in the relative weight of the agricultural and non-agricultural sectors. From 1910 to 1930 the peasantry declined from 66 per cent to 45.5 per cent of the working population, while industrial workers had soared from 15.8 per cent to 26.5 per cent and those in services from 18.1 per cent to 27.9 per cent. Indeed, the peasantry now formed

---

[54] K.E. Amdur, *Syndicalist Legacy: Trade Unions and Politics in Two French Cities in the Era of World War 1* (Urbana, Illin., 1986), pp. 8–12.

[55] E.J. Hobsbawm, *Primitive Rebels, Studies in Archaic Forms of Social Movement in the 19th and Twentieth Centuries* (Manchester, 1972), pp. 74–92.

a minority of the population, rather than its traditional majority and a substantial portion of this 'peasantry' owned land.[56]

Moreover, the Spanish case, as Chris Earlham has argued, reveals the limitations of Hobsbawm's 'stages of history' approach and 'the impossibility of establishing a cut-off point at which economic development provoked a definitive rupture with past modes of social struggle'.[57] That anarchism and the CNT 'were not an atavistic, exclusively pre-industrial movement, waiting to be superseded by capitalist modernisation' was shown by the ability of the CNT to establish its greatest strength among the industrial working class of Catalonia, not among the so-called 'millenarian' agricultural day-workers of the South. 'Spanish anarchism therefore adapted itself to urban struggles in the explosive circumstances provided by largely unmediated industrial relations.'[58]

All this is not to say that industrialisation and changes in the labour force in Spain, France or other countries, were insignificant, merely the assumption that it inevitably undermined syndicalism as a movement *per se* is questionable, at the very least unless this is related to *other* economic, social and political factors. By way of example, we can look at America, where it seems clear that in many respects the IWW *did* become a victim of changing technological development following World War 1. Thus, as more and more migratory workers took to the new motor cars and more families joined the annual migrations of harvest hands, the IWW's appeal to agricultural workers diminished proportionately.[59] The widespread use of the combine harvester in wheatfields also had the effect of reducing the total demand for low skilled labour and hence the size of the migratory army among whom the IWW had traditionally recruited. [60] Nonetheless as we have seen, whilst migratory workers – in lumber, agriculture and construction – formed the core of the IWW, the union also built a base amongst miners, longshoremen and seamen, as well as, albeit on a less stable and permanent basis, amongst factory workers in the textile, auto, rubber and power industries. But it seems likely the racial, ethnic, linguistic and religious heterogeneity of the working class during this formative period of American capitalism played a more important role in inhibiting the continuity of the syndicalist movement, than labour force structural changes as such.

There had been waves of immigration into the United States in the 50 years between 1870 and 1920, with the influx of more than 25 million men, women and children onto American shores, as well as a post-Civil War exodus of many of the 10 million-strong black population from the Southern states into the cities of the North

---

[56] M. Bookchin, *To Remember Spain: The Anarchist and Syndicalist Revolution of 1936* (Edinburgh, 1994), p. 45–6.

[57] C. Earlham, '"Revolutionary Gymnastics" and the Unemployed: The Limits of the Spanish Anarchist Utopia 1931–37', in K. Flett and D. Renton (eds), *The Twentieth Century: A Century of Wars and Revolutions?* (London, 2000), pp. 134–5.

[58] Ibid., p.135.

[59] M. Dubofsky, *We Shall be All: A History of the Industrial Workers of the World* (Chicago, 1969), pp. 447–448. See also J.L. Kornbluh (eds), *Rebel Voices: An IWW Anthology* (Chicago, 1998), p. 352.

[60] N.A. Sellars, *Oil, Wheat and Wobblies: The Industrial Workers of the World in Oklahoma, 1905–1930* (Norman, Oklahoma, 1998).

and West, due to the demands of an expanding economy hungry for labour. But such developments, at least in the short term, represented a tremendous obstacle to the formation of an American working class consciousness which in other capitalist societies at such a stage had provided a base for independent working class political parties.[61] This was because a large proportion of immigrants, perhaps the majority, saw their move to America as a temporary sojourn. Between 1900 and 1914 30 per cent returned to their homelands and, for those who stayed, the hope or dream of return was, perhaps, their dominant emotion.[62] In fact, the opportunity for building mass unions in the mass production industries only really came when restrictions on immigration had reduced the flow of unskilled workers and had allowed time for large-scale assimilation of those already in the country, and this was not until the 1930s. In addition, the CIO's subsequent success was dependent on being able to count on immense financial resources, millions of members and federal government encouragement, none of which were available to the IWW.[63]

Arguably to adequately explain the decline of the Wobblies and other syndicalist movements internationally it is necessary to consider a number of *other* economic, social and political factors which, despite variation between countries, underline the extent to which there was a rather more open-ended and less deterministic outcome than many commentators who have placed the primary stress on structural changes in the composition of labour force brought on by rapid industrialisation have tended to assume.

Employer and State Counter-Mobilisation and Ebb of Workers' Struggles

Undoubtedly one crucial factor helping to explain the demise of the syndicalist movement internationally was the impact of employers' and state counter-mobilisation, which was often combined in the early 1920s with the onset of economic slump and ebb of workers' struggles. Inevitably this process varied from country to country in the exact time-scale and manner in which it became manifest. In America unprecedented intimidation and outright violent repression were to be particularly significant in contributing to the IWW's demise, perhaps more so than in any other country. Even before the outbreak of war, the employers had regularly infiltrated spies into IWW locals, sacked the 'militant minority' among their workforce, took on 'scab' labour and persistently attempted to play diverse ethnic and religious groups off against each other. Local 'Citizens Alliances', organisations composed of local businessmen, lawyers, traders and other professional interests, were often utilised (particularly in mining areas) in a bid to destroy the Wobblies. And city, state and federal governments also consistently acted to defend employers' interests. During the 'free speech' campaign between 1908–1911 local governments passed laws banning the Wobblies, hundreds of whom were arrested and imprisoned, and they were often subject to attack by vigilantes organised by local businessmen. In 1915 the IWW songwriter Joe Hill had been executed on a trumped-up murder

61 D. Kennedy, 'The Decline of the Socialist Party of America 1901–19', *Socialist History*, 9 (1996), p. 15.

62 G. Kolko, *Main Currents in Modern American History* (London, 1976), p. 70.

63 Dubofsky, *We Shall Be All*, p. 482.

charge, with both the Idaho Governor and US President, despite an enormous defence campaign, refusing to pardon Hill or commute his sentence.

There was a similar extreme form of violent opposition to IWW-led strikes. During the 1912 Paterson strike 4,800 strikers were arrested and 1,300 sent to prison In 1917 in Bisbee, Arizona, during a strike by copper miners against wage cuts, 2,000 vigilantes had rounded up 1,286 IWW organisers, strikers and sympathisers at gun point, tried them in a 'kangaroo court' and deported them to the desert of New Mexico herded into a cattle train under armed guard. The protesters were then beaten up and left without food or water for 36 hours, only to be sent to a federal stockade and held without charge for three months before being released.

While such pre-war attacks had impeded, they had not prevented IWW efforts to sink significant roots inside the working class movement. But with America's 1917 entry into the war, followed by the Bolshevik revolution, the Wobblies were to become subject to a qualitatively more pronounced and systematic form of state repression. Even though IWW-influenced wartime strikes sought conventional labour goals and avoided the explicit question of opposition to the war, the state interpreted them as direct challenges to the war effort and the legitimacy of federal authority. The IWW were branded as 'German spies' and became a target for 'patriotic' violence by local vigilantes. In August 1917 in Butte, Montana, Frank Little, who had helped organise a strike by metal miners against the Anaconda Company, was dragged out of his bed by six masked men and hanged. In November 1919 an IWW lumberjack, Wesley Everest, was castrated and hung from a railroad bridge by a lynch mob in Centralia, Washington.

Individual states proceeded to use the excuse of the war to pass 'criminal syndicalism' laws making it illegal to advocate the overthrow of the state or the seizure of property as a means of accomplishing industrial or political reform. And in September 1917 the federal government finally raided IWW national, regional and state headquarters, seized tons of letters, newspapers, propaganda pamphlets and other documents, arrested over 100 of the Wobbly leaders (including Haywood) and put them on a show trial for violating the wartime sedition and espionage laws. The purpose of the raids, the United States attorney for Philadelphia acknowledged, was 'very largely to put the IWW out of business'.[64] The 1918 Chicago trial, which lasted five months (at that time the longest criminal trial in American legal history), led to Haywood and other defendants being sentenced to long prison terms.[65]

Despite the dramatic increase in union militancy that occurred across America in the initial post-war period, a 'Red Scare' claimed the labour unrest was essentially the product of left-wing ideologies sown by the Bolshevik revolution and brought into the American labour movement by 'outside agitators' who had their greatest influence among foreign-born workers. The subsequent so-called Palmer raids led to literally thousands of further arrests (not just of IWW members, but also anarchists, socialists and communists) and the deportation of many foreign-born militants, including many Wobblies. Even though a public defence campaign led to the release of all IWW political prisoners in federal jails by the end of 1923, and

---

[64] Cited in P.S. Foner, *History of the Labor Movement in the United States: Vol. 7: Labor and World War 1: 1914–1918* (New York, 1987), p. 299.

[65] Kornbluh, pp. 318–24; Renshaw, pp. 206–39.

post-war Wobbly organising efforts actually led to a steady increase in membership, the organisation was severely crippled by government attacks during the war and post-war period. As Haywood admitted in 1919, the IWW had been shaken 'as a bull dog shakes an empty sack'.[66]

According to James Cronin such methodical repression by the federal government destroyed, imprisoned or dispersed the leadership of the union (with Haywood's unanticipated subsequent defection to Moscow while convicted and out of prison on appeal proving to be an especially traumatic experience for the organisation). The imprisonment of many rank-and-file Wobblies, and not just the leaders, also had the effect of frightening others away from the organisation, for the convicts were not tried on the basis of any alleged specific acts but on the basis of their membership of the IWW. And it completely transformed the organisation and, to some extent, the *raison d'être* of the union, away from inciting, organising and directing industrial strikes into a legal 'defence committee', obliged to exert all its energies to trying to keep its members out of prison and to free by legal means those who had been imprisoned. Such repression directly contributed to the process by which the IWW was effectively put out of business as a functioning syndicalist organisation.[67]

Employer and state attacks also proved to be an important factor undermining support for the syndicalist movement in France. From the turn of the century the growing strike activity and CGT threat had prompted a hostile employer counter-mobilisation in defence of property. Employers' associations increasingly financed 'yellow' unions, imposed lockouts, imported blacklegs and hired gunmen to intimidate pickets.[68] Behind them stood the Republican state machine with its courts, police and troops. After assuming office in 1906 as president of the Council of Ministers, Georges Clemenceau swamped mining villages with 95,000 troops during a strike which followed a pit disaster in Courrières, and responded to the CGT's May Day general strike by arresting its leaders and sending 34,000 troops to Paris. Drawing the line against revolutionary agitation, governments led by Clemenceau (and Prime Minister and former socialist Aristide Briand) from 1906 to 1910 frequently deployed troops against strikes, conscripted participants into the army, and arrested leaders of the CGT for conspiracy.[69]

For example, in 1907 a syndicalist-led strike of dockers in Nantes St-Nazaire was broken when a cavalry charge left one dead and 21 wounded, with 18 leaders arrested, including Yvetot. In 1908 a demonstration of 4,000 Parisian workers in Villeneuvre-Saint Georges, in the Seine-et-Oise hinterland of Paris, was attacked by police, leaving four workers dead and 69 wounded. The arrest of the CGT leadership, including Griffuelhes, Pouget, Delesalle, Merriheim and Monatte followed. In 1909 a national postal workers' strike was put down by the use of troops and 300 workers were dismissed. In 1910 a national railway workers' strike saw the government

66 *One Big Union Monthly*, 1 (December 1919).

67 J.R. Cronin, *Bread and Roses Too: Studies of the Wobblies* (Westport, Conn, 1969), pp. 141–5.

68 Friedman, 'Revolutionary Unions and French Labour', pp. 177–81.

69 R. Magraw, 'Socialism, Syndicalism and French Labour'; B. H. Moss, *The Origins of the French Labor Movement: The Socialism of Skilled Workers, 1830–1914* (Berkley, Calif., 1976).

mobilise troops and treat unofficial action in the north-Paris rail depots as evidence of a revolutionary plot. Railway workers were conscripted into the army as reservists, 200 leaders were arrested, 3,300 activists sacked.

If the ferocity of such state repression won Clemenceau plaudits from the right as 'France's top cop' there is no doubt the CGT's retreat from a revolutionary to a moderate stance from about 1910, came in response to the strike defeats it suffered and the impact of such political repression.[70] The strong reformist elements within the Confédération claimed that revolutionaries had frightened the bourgeoisie, provoked state violence and encouraged strikes without adequate preparation.[71] On the basis of such a critique, moderates increasingly began to assume leadership positions and with the outbreak of war the CGT abandoned its revolutionary internationalism. Amidst a renewed post-war wave of industrial militancy and growth of CGT membership, the revolutionary minority within the Confédération's largest affiliate, the railway workers' union, succeeded in launching a national strike in May 1920 and called on the CGT to organise a general strike in support. Reluctantly, the CGT's reformist leadership called out other unions, although (in a clear bid to contain the revolutionary minority) only in three successive 'waves' rather than *en masse* as had been proposed. With such lackluster coordination from the top, abstentions were widespread and the strike crumbled. The CGT called for a return to work without obtaining any concessions and some 20,000 union members (including many leading militants) were subsequently sacked.[72]

This comprehensive defeat of the rail strike, effectively of both moderate and revolutionary variants of CGT unionism, marked the end of the immediate post-war era of labour militancy in France. The employer and state counter-offensive was facilitated by the onset of an economic recession, which significantly undermined the Confédération's bargaining position and disillusioned and discouraged many newer union recruits and less committed members. As a result, strike levels, which had often exceeded 1,000 per year in the 1900s, fell to an annual average of around 500 by the early 1920s.[73] At the same time there was a sharp collapse in union membership; from a peak of nearly 2 million in spring 1920 to barely 1 million by early 1921 (with the rail union losing 80 per cent of its 350,000 members). Such gloomy trends provided the background for the internecine feuding which proceeded to break out inside the organisation.

In Italy the USI was also confronted with fierce counter-mobilisation by the employers and the state. It was the failure of the September 1920 general strike and factory occupations to turn into a revolutionary struggle for power that led to the rise to power of Mussolini's fascist military dictatorship and the destruction of the syndicalist movement a few years later. In the wake of the 1920 set-back Italian workers quickly became demoralised as rising unemployment took away the gains of the *bienno rosso* industrial and political militancy. Sectors of employers (determined

---

70 Friedman, 'Revolutionary Unions and French Labour', p. 181.

71 See for example A. Keufer, *L'Éucation syndicale: Exposé de la méthode organique* (Paris, 1910).

72 A. Jones, 'The French Railway Strikes of January–May 1920: New Syndicalist Ideas and Emergent Communism', *French Historical Studies*, 12: 4 (1982), pp. 508–40; Horne, pp. 252–5.

73 Magraw, *Workers and the Bourgeois Republic*, p. 212.

to reassert their authority in industry) as well as the 'liberal' Prime Minister Giolitti (wanting a counterweight against the left) were offered the services of Mussolini and his newly-founded fascist movement to whom they provided funds. In November 1922 the fascists began to systematically attack USI offices in Milan and throughout northern Italy, arresting leaders and forcing others, such as Borghi, into exile.[74] The fascist offensive reduced the left to a state of semi-paralysis, and even semi-legality, and rode the tide of economic depression and unemployment against a working class already disarmed by political disillusionment after September 1920.[75] By early 1923, within two months of Mussolini's take-over, the USI had effectively been crushed, and was finally outlawed in 1925.

There was *not* a direct line of descent from syndicalism to fascism as some commentators have suggested.[76] Many of the members of the USI's pro-interventionist wartime breakaway, the UIL, should probably be termed populists rather than fascists. On the other hand, the fascists *were* able to integrate some syndicalists within their orbit and one of their leading figures, Edmondo Rossoni, was to become instrumental in the creation of the National Confederation of Syndicalist Corporations. This organisation was subsequently utilised to provide Italian employers with a docile working class by effectively eliminating open class conflict and initiating a long period of outward social peace.

In Spain 1919 marked the high point of the CNT's immediate post-war expansion of membership and influence. Although Spain became the first country in the world to legislate the eight-hour day (such was the pressure of the workers' movement), the Catalan employers took their revenge when they declared war on the Confederación by locking out 200,000 workers between December 1919 and January 1920. The lockout, which the moderate union leadership around Salvador Seguí refused to contest by the tactic of attempting to illegally enter and occupy the factories, seriously weakened the CNT. The employers combined their offensive by setting up anti-CNT unions, the so-called *sindicatos libres* ('free unions'). This initiated a bitter warfare between the CNT and the employers' organisations in Barcelona during 1921–1923, marked by a cycle of state terror by the police and army, and use of *pistoleros* in the pay of the employers, resulting in the murder of 21 leading Barcelona CNT members. This was followed by counter-anarchist terrorist attacks which only intensified the repression and further

---

[74] U. Fedeli,'Breve storia dell'Unione Sindacale Italiana, *Volontà*, 10 (1957), p. 654.

[75] G. Williams, *Proletarian Order: Antonio Gramsci, Factory Councils and the Origins of Communism in Italy 1911–21* (London, 1975), p. 292; T. Behan, *The Resistible Rise of Benito Mussolini* (London, 2003).

[76] For a completely unconvincing attempt to draw out the ideological affinities between the theoreticians of the CGT and French nationalist and proto-fascist movements, that concludes syndicalism was the incarnation on the left of a general anti-intellectual, anti-rational, existential wave, see Ridley, *Revolutionary Syndicalism in France*, pp. 191–238. For a more sober and critical assessment see T. Abse, 'Syndicalism and the Origins of Italian Fascism', *Historical Journal*, 25 (1982), pp. 247–58; D.D. Roberts, *The Syndicalist Tradition and Italian Fascism* (Chapel Hill, Carolina, 1979); D.D. Roberts, 'How Not to Think About Fascism and Ideology, Intellectual Antecedents and Historical Meaning', *Journal of Contemporary History*, 35: 2 (2000), pp. 185–211; J.J. Tinghino, *Edmoundo Rossoni: From Revolutionary Syndicalism to Fascism* (New York, 1991).

exposed the Confederación's militants to both legal and illegal sanctions. Mass trade union organisation was relegated to the sidelines as the initiative passed to small, often isolated, armed groups. And the murder of important moderate CNT leaders (including Seguí) and the arrest of many others effectively decapitated the union, with its ranks further depleted by the steady withdrawal of workers from the local unions.[77]

By 1923 the state had taken its toll on the CNT's ranks despite the incredible tenacity shown by the organisation. Days lost through strikes had fallen from its 1920 peak of 7.3 million to just over 3 million, while the number of armed attacks had increased tenfold. Primo de Rivera's *coup d'état* in September 1923 left the CNT in complete disarray. The organisation, with only 250,000 members (two-thirds less than in 1919) was banned once again the following year and driven underground (until 1930). Anarchist and CNT offices were closed, with many thousands of militants arrested. [78] Although the Confederación's fortunes were completely transformed with the Second Republic in 1931 and the outbreak of Civil War and workers' revolution in 1936, its leadership's short-lived experiment participating in the Popular Front government was quickly followed by the government's counter-revolutionary seizure of the Barcelona telephone exchange in May 1937 and the arrest of hundreds of CNT militants. The military defeat of the republican regime in 1939 put a final end to the revolutionary aspirations of the anarcho-syndicalists.

In Britain, employer and state repression was much less severe than in other countries. Nonetheless, by the spring of 1921 the brief post-war boom had turned into economic slump, with the rundown of munitions production and the unleashing of mass unemployment completely undermining the shop stewards' movement. It provided the opportunity for a reassertion of managerial authority and the victimisation of union militants. At the same time a series of workers' defeats (including the mines in 1921, engineering in 1922, and the docks in 1923) in which the power of the state was clearly deployed on behalf of the employers, put to an end the industrial militancy on which the syndicalist strategy had been built over the preceding decade.

In Ireland the onset of economic slump and mass unemployment also provided the conditions under which employers pressed for wage reductions to pre-war levels. This was backed by the new independent republican Provisional government and state forces (established following the granting of Irish independence in December 1921) and encouraged by a fiercely anti-union Catholic Church horrified by Bolshevism. The defeat of a dockers' strike in 1923 was followed by similar setbacks in other industries, leading to the collapse of the ITGWU in many small towns and on the land.

Inevitably the question arises: what was it about the syndicalist movement that caused it to be singled out for special attention by the authorities with all their weapons at their disposal in a number of countries? No doubt the conscious revolutionary intentions with which syndicalist used direct economic action (and the inherent revolutionary implications of many of the larger strikes) were viewed as more threatening to the employers and the state than the more moderate approach

---

[77] Bar, 'The CNT', p. 124.

[78] J. Casanoa, 'Terror and Violence: The Dark Face of Spanish Anarchism', *International Labor and Working Class History*, 67 (2005), pp. 87–90.

of their reformist counterparts. In other words, in many respects it was the direct challenge they laid down to capitalism, their encouragement of permanent militancy at the point of production and the rate at which their tactics appeared to be spreading among workers generally that prompted such a violent reaction.[79]

External impact of communism and *internal* schisms

Other crucial factors helping to explain the demise of the syndicalist movement internationally were the *external* impact of communism and its own *internal* schisms. As we have seen there were always various ideological, strategic, tactical and organisational differences between syndicalists within each of the various movements. But it was undoubtedly the political ramifications of the 1917 October Revolution which served to both underline and considerably deepen such divisive disputes. The seizure of state power by Russian workers under the leadership of the Bolshevik Party, and the subsequent formation of the Communist (Third) International in Moscow and of new affiliated revolutionary Communist Parties throughout the world, was to give a 'Leninist' perspective widespread support within the international workers' movement. Inevitably, the success of the revolution in Russia when revolutionary movements elsewhere had failed increased the attraction of the Russian model and the prestige of the Bolsheviks. In the process it exposed the differences between reformists and revolutionaries inside the international labour movement generally, leading to a fundamental split into rival social democratic and communist camps, with large numbers of radicalised members of socialist parties and mainstream trade unions being pulled towards the new communist parties.

In the process Bolshevism also posed a radical challenge to the syndicalist tradition itself and highlighted in graphic relief a number of apparent political limitations within this tradition. These included the following: the contradictory pressures between trying to build *both* revolutionary cadre organisations *and* mass trade unions; of reconciling the primary emphasis on *industrial* struggle to the subordination of *political* action; and of providing effective *centralized* organisation and leadership while being committed to *localism* and *autonomy*. Bolshevism was to offer an alternative set of political and organisational prescriptions that succeeded in attracting a significant layer, albeit a minority, of leading syndicalists (as Part Two examines). But it also had the effect of deepening and extending internal disputes between rival factions and generally contributed to the ultimate demise of the syndicalist movement internationally.

Although post-war IWW organising efforts led to a steady increase in membership, the organisation became severely crippled by the antagonisms and factionalism of the preceding years (exacerbated by state and employer repression). From 1920 to 1924 three issues sharply divided the IWW. First, there was the status of its political prisoners – with arguments over what attitude to adopt towards IWW prisoners who accepted individual clemency. Second, there was its relationship with the Communist Party at home and the Comintern and Red International of Labour

---

[79] Burgmann, p. 225.

Unions abroad – with disagreements over whether to participate within the rapidly developing communist movement. Third, there was the distribution of power within the IWW – with one tendency believing the solution to the Wobbly's problems lay with greater centralisation and accountability and another tendency insisting on increased decentralisation.

The destructive nature of these post-war disputes had an early manifestation when the IWW, caught up in the state indictment of 1917, voted to make all former Wobbly leaders ineligible for union office. This effectively severed the organisation from its past, decapitating the IWW even more ruthlessly than the government had been able to. Individuals ceased to pay dues and functioning locals withdrew affiliation. The culmination of this internecine wrangling came in a disastrous 1924 convention when what remained of the organisation split into two.[80] Ironically, according to Melvyn Dubofsky, this factional strife was in some respects more a result of organisational failure and frustration than it was of internal divisions over vital substantive issues of policy. 'Lacking flourishing affiliates or major industrial conflicts in which they could sublimate their hostilities, the frustrated [Wobblies] released their aggressions on each other. In the process they wrecked the organisation.'[81]

Meanwhile, after 1917 the Wobblies were being outflanked on the extreme left of the political spectrum by the Communist Party, which had emerged from a split in the radicalised Socialist Party. Inspired by the Bolshevik Revolution and the formation of the Comintern in Moscow, left-wing members of the Socialist Party (drawn largely from the foreign-language federations, especially East European elements) had tried to capture the party's machinery. About to lose control in the summer of 1919, the moderate leadership responded by expelling this left-wing opposition, albeit sacrificing two-thirds of the party's membership as a result. Two rival communist parties initially emerged, with few ideological differences between them, and both resolved to join the Comintern. Both emphasised dual unionism: while one called for the formation of 'One Big Union' as a rival to the AFL, the other considered it to be a major task to agitate for the construction of a general industrial union embracing the IWW and other independent unions (including militant unions of the AFL) and unorganised workers on the basis of revolutionary class struggle.

But the 'Red Scare' was in full swing just as both Communist Parties were established and many members became targets of vigilante attacks, with a number of the leaders of both groups arrested for conspiracy to overthrow the government. It is estimated more than 50,000 members dropped out of both Communist Parties during this repression. By 1920 membership had fallen from about 70,000 to 16,000, and both organisations were driven underground. Finally in May 1920 a unity convention was held at which the United Communist Party of America was formed, but which continued to oppose communists working within the AFL until convinced otherwise by Moscow.[82] The

---

80 S.D. Bird, D. Georgakas and D. Shaffer, *Solidarity Forever: An Oral History of the Wobblies* (London, 1987), pp. 15–16.

81 Dubofsky, *We Shall Be All*, pp. 466–7.

82 Foner, *Postwar Struggles*, pp. 237–53. The American Communist Party was set up by mainly foreign-language members, and the Communist Labor Party by left-wing English-speaking members (led by native-born John Reed and Benjamin Gitlow). The unified

combination of the new Communist Party's eventual decision to focus on capturing the mainstream AFL and the overall IWW rejection of Bolshevik overtures resulted in a fierce split between these two competing revolutionary organisations.

In the struggle for the leadership of the American left wing, the IWW was to rapidly lose ground to the communists, who attracted a significant layer of IWW leaders and activists. Haywood jumped bail and fled to Moscow where he became a fervent supporter of the Bolsheviks. Harrison George, another Chicago trial defendant, wrote a pamphlet called *Red Dawn* that was uncritically pro-Bolshevik and joined the Communist Party. George Andreytchine, a Bulgarian-born IWW who fled to Russia with Haywood in 1921, was also a convinced Bolshevik. Charles Ashleigh joined the party in prison, and other leaders who did the same included George Hardy, the seamen's organiser, Sam Scarlett, who joined in Canada, and Roy Brown of the lumber workers. William Z. Foster and four members of the executive board of his newly-named International Trade Union Educational League eventually also joined the Communist Party (Jack Carney, Jack Johnstone, Jay Fox and Joseph Manley), with Foster becoming the party's chairman. James Cannon also joined, although he later broke away to become a leader of the Trotskyist Socialist Workers Party. Elizabeth Gurly Flynn worked with the Communists from the mid-1920s through her International Labor Defence activity, and like many others, joined the party later in the 1930s. Earl Browder, who had been an activist in a local Kansas City group associated with Foster's Syndicalist League of North America, became general secretary of the Communist Party in the 1930s. Though accurate figures are impossible to tabulate, it is has been estimated that as many as 2,000 IWW members, or from 10 to 20 per cent of its total following at the time, may have joined the Communist Party.[83]

The majority of Wobblies rejected the proposal to affiliate with the Comintern and became increasingly critical of the Bolshevik regime. One of the chief circumstances operating against the transition to Bolshevism was the furious persecution of the IWW that coincided with the events and aftermath of the Russian Revolution. The imprisonment of literally hundreds of IWW activists inevitably 'cut them off from contact with the great new events, and operated against the free exchange of ideas which might have resulted in agreement and fusion with the dynamically developing left-wing socialist movement headed towards the new Communist Party'. Compelled to divert their entire activity into the campaign to provide legal defence for victimised members, many IWW activists had little time to assimilate the political implications of Bolshevism and retained their hostility to political action and political parties.[84]

As a consequence, despite the efforts made by the Russian Bolsheviks to attract them, the American communist movement was formed from another and apparently

---

communist party which finally emerged was originally called the Workers' Party of America, renamed the Workers' (Communist) Party in August 1925, and did not formally become the Communist Party, USA, until 1929.

[83] H. Draper, *The Roots of American Communism* (Chicago, 1989), p. 318. See also J.S. Gambs, *The Decline of the IWW* (New York, 1932), p. 89.

[84] Cannon, pp. 36–7.

less promising source, namely the Socialist Party.[85] Yet notwithstanding its initial difficulties, the subsequent growing influence of communism inside the American labour movement further sapped energy away from the IWW and (combined with the calamitous 1924 Wobbly split) sealed the fate of syndicalism as a major independent force on the left.

> Insofar as the human material was concerned, the advantages were all on the side of the IWW. Their militants had been tested in many fights. They had hundreds and hundreds of members in jail, and they used to look with something like contempt on this upstart movement talking so confidently in revolutionary terms. The IWW's imagined that their actions and their sacrifices so far outweighed the mere doctrinal pretensions of this new revolutionary movement that they had nothing to fear from it in the way of rivalry. They were badly mistaken.
>
> Within a few years – by 1922 – it became pretty clear that the Communist Party had displaced the IWW as the leading organisation of the vanguard. The IWW, with its wonderful composition of proletarian militants, with all their heroic struggles behind them, could not keep pace. They had not adjusted their ideology to the lessons of the war and the Russian revolution. They had not acquired a sufficient respect for doctrine, for theory. That is why their organisation degenerated, while this new organisation with its poorer material, its inexperienced youth who had seized hold of the living ideas of Bolshevism, completely surpassed the IWW and left it far behind in the space of a few years.[86]

Internal feuding also broke out inside the French labour movement in the post-war years, culminating in the 1921 schism inside the CGT. The annual congress of the Socialist Party (SFIO) at Tours in December 1920 marked a crucial turning point. The SFIO, despite the growing 'pacifism' of its left-wing minority had survived the war intact, although it underwent a massive radicalisation immediately afterwards. In the face of the impasse of its reformist policies combined with the enthusiasm generated by the Russian Revolution, it began to fall apart. The tumultuous party congress was confronted with deciding whether or not to join the Communist International. An overwhelming majority of delegates, especially the young and working class elements, opted to do so and renamed themselves the *Parti communiste française*; the anti-communist minority retained the old title. Out of 179,800 Socialist Party members 110,000 promptly joined the new French Communist Party, while the dissidents were scarcely able to muster 30,000.[87]

In the following year, the CGT also split when a sizeable minority of union members left to form an alternative confederation. Although the leadership of the CGT had emerged from the war with a markedly reformist stance, there had remained

---

[85] After suffering from factional infighting, clandestine activity and persecution the Workers' Party claimed an average membership of 12,058 for 1922 and 15,395 for 1923, although it is more likely these were maximum figures. See Draper, p. 391.

[86] J.P. Cannon, *The History of American Trotskyism: 1928–1938* (New York, 2003), pp. 37–8.

[87] See A, Kriegel, *Aux origines du communisme français, 1914–1920: Contribution á l'histoire du mouvement ouvrier français* (Paris, 1964); R. Wohl, *Franch Communism in the Making, 1914–1924* (Stanford, Calif., 1966), p. 82.

strong revolutionary syndicalist currents which approved of, and identified with, the Russian Revolution and the Bolsheviks. The defeat of the May 1920 attempted general strike, mounting employer intimidation and unemployment, combined with the political challenge of Bolshevism and the formation of the new Communist Party, now brought to a head a latent internecine conflict within the CGT.

The internal discord involved three rival factions. First, Leon Jouhaux's reformist group still commanded majority support amongst departmental federations, in the textile, mining, print and public service unions. Second, Pierre Monatte, editor of *La Vie ouvrière*, became the key spokesmen for a 'Syndicalist-Communist' faction which argued the time had come for syndicalists to collaborate with a genuine revolutionary party to present an effective counter-weight to the power of the capitalist state. In this, Monatte was influenced by contact with Trotsky, who claimed the French Communist Party was the logical heir to the revolutionary syndicalist tradition. A Committee for the Third International was formed, upon whose executive sat a wide variety of dissenting syndicalists, including Monatte and Alfred Rosmer.[88] Third, there was an 'anarcho-syndicalist' group, which rejected Monatte's concern with a *modus vivendi* with the Communist Party and talked only of the need for a split inside the CGT, a clean break with Jouhaux and a frank reliance on the militancy of 'active minorities'. Insofar as this third tendency expressed sympathy for Bolshevism, it involved an interpretation of Leninism as militant vanguardism and soviets as quasi-syndicalist instruments of workers' control.[89]

After the 1920 CGT congress, at which the socialist/reformist *confédéré* 'majority' won nearly 75 per cent of the delegates, the growing communist/revolutionary syndicalist *unitaire* 'minority' continued the struggle via an internal opposition, *Comités Syndicalistes Révolutionnaires*, eventually culminating in a split from the CGT in 1921 to form a separate confederation, the *Confédération Générale du Travail Unitaire* (CGTU). The new confederation, estimated to have about half-a-million members at the time of its foundation, initially grouped communists, anarchists and revolutionary syndicalists together. But after its own bitter battles and backed by the propagandist and practical support of Moscow, it soon came under the leadership of the group around *La Vie ouvrière* and became communist-controlled by 1923. A number of leading syndicalists joined the French Communist Party, including Monatte, Alfred Rosmer, Gaston Monmousseau, Pierre Sémard, Robert Louzon and George Verdier. According to Robert Wohl, Monmosseau, Sémard and other CGTU delegates to the second RILU Congress 'had gone to Moscow in November 1922 as defenders of the traditional ideas of French syndicalism. They came back Leninists'.[90] The Communist Party proceeded to build a network of communist groups within the CGTU.[91]

---

[88] C. Chambelland and J. Maitron (eds), *Syndicalisme Revolutionnaire et Communisme: Les Archives de Pierre Monatte, 1914–24* (Paris, 1968).

[89] Magraw, *Workers and the Bourgeois Republic*, pp. 192–3.

[90] Wohl, p. 344.

[91] The two organisations were reunited in 1936, after which the CGT became increasingly influenced by the Communist Party. A further split, this time involving the departure of

But many French anarcho-syndicalists and 'pure' revolutionary syndicalists were unable to accept the primacy of the party over the unions implied by Leninism. They viewed the Communist Party not as a revolutionary alternative to Socialist Party politics but an extreme version of the Socialists' stress on organisation and centralised political leadership and insisted on the need for local spontaneity and local autonomy within a federalist structure.[92] Believing that a middle ground might exist between the alleged comparable evils of the CGT and the CGTU, they formed another breakaway, the *Confédération Générale du Travail Syndicalist-Révolutionnaire* (CGT-SR) federations. As a result, the French union movement now become fragmented between the firmly reformist CGT, the pro-Communist but numerically weak CGTU and the smaller, but not insignificant, revolutionary syndicalist CGT-SR federations. Not surprisingly such schisms drove many thousands away from union activity within all three groupings and further undermined the strength of the French labour movement generally.

In Italy the USI, inspired by the example of the Russian Revolution initially supported the Comintern and in 1921 Nicolo Vecchi and Lulio Mari met with Red International of Labour Union (RILU) representatives in Moscow. Returning to Italy they recommended the USI accept the Bolsheviks' proposals. But the USI rebuked them and insisted on political independence. At the fourth congress of the Unione in March 1922 executive member Alibrando Giovanetti spoke against Vecchi's support for Bolshevik Russia and demanded total autonomy from all political parties. However two other important leaders of the USI leadership, Giuseppe Di Vittorio and Carlo Nencini, agreed with Vecchi and propagated the Bolshevik line; by June 1922 Vecchi's supporters numbered almost 30,000, approximately one-half of the total USI membership.[93]

Meanwhile the Italian Socialist Party, radicalised by its opposition to the war, the post-war labour militancy and the impact of the Russian Revolution, had by early 1920 split into three wings: the reformists (led by Filippo Turati), the centre-left (led by Giacinto Serrati) and the left (led by Amadeo Bordiga). The mutual recrimination within the Socialist Party over the failure to make greater capital out of the occupation of the factories in September 1920, combined with the revolutionary appeal emanating from Moscow, resulted in its own application for membership of the Comintern, formally accepting its stringent 'Twenty-One Conditions' drawn up by the Bolsheviks with the aim of keeping reformists out. However, at the party's Livorno congress in January 1921 Serrati refused to expel the reformists and a 'pure communist' tendency led by Bordiga broke away to form the *Partito communista italiano.* Unlike in France, the Italian Communist Party only succeeded in taking with them about a third of the Socialist Party membership, some 40,000 to 50,000. Nonetheless, the communists subsequently succeeded in attracting a layer of USI militants prior to Mussolini's seizure of power in 1922, even though the bulk remained aloof.[94]

---

the reformist right followed in 1948, when Jouhaux founded *Force Ouvrière*, leaving the communists in control.

92 Amdur, pp. 5–6.

93 *La Correspondence Internationale* (Berlin) 11 November 1922.

94 See. A. De Grand, *The Italian Left in the Twentieth Century: A History of the Socialist and Communist Parties* (Bloomington, Indiana, 1989).

In Spain the CNT became wracked by internal faction fighting in the immediate post-war years for similar reasons as elsewhere. The murder and imprisonment of important Confederación leaders placed the union in the hands of more radical activists and at its 1919 congress the CNT vowed to join the Comintern. This situation sparked off an internal confrontation of major significance for the subsequent evolution of the CNT as differences between the main ideological elements – 'pure' syndicalists, anarcho-syndicalists, anarchists and communist-syndicalists – increasingly became irreconcilable.[95]Although the communist-syndicalist group could not be compared in numbers and influence with either the 'pure' syndicalist or anarcho-syndicalist currents, they were able to gain an influence out of proportion to their numerical size in the Catalonian labour movement owing to the peculiar circumstances of state repression and the exceptional ability of its principal leaders Andreu Nin (who had only left the Socialist Party in December 1919), Joaquín Maurín and Hilario Arlandis. They shared with the anarcho-syndicalists an intense admiration for the Russian Bolsheviks, but differed from the majority of the *Cenetistas* (as rank-and-file CNT members were known) in that they also held Leninist values and were greatly pre-occupied with the need for centralised leadership and organisational discipline.

Nin and Maurín, both of whom had been marginal at the 1919 CNT congress, dominated the two most important committees of the union from the spring of 1921 until spring 1922. Nin was co-opted onto the clandestine National Committee, becoming acting general secretary and largely dominated the body, while Maurín was co-opted onto the Catalonian regional federation, in which he soon became the preeminent figure. The voice of communist-syndicalism was the journal *Lucha Social* of the Lérida regional federation (edited by Maurín), which because of the suspension of *Solidarida Obrera*, also became the chief organ of the CNT in Catalona. Nin and Maurín persuaded a local assembly to send them to Russia and, without any authority for doing so, they federated the CNT to the RILU.[96] However, the communist-syndicalists did not succeed in completely taking over a single union and its adherents, although some were highly placed, constituted only a relative handful among the legions of *Cenetistas*.

Moreover, by 1920 the anarcho-syndicalists' enthusiasm for the Russian Revolution had began to fade. The hard-line anarchists inside the CNT came out in full opposition to what they regarded as being a 'Bolshevik dictatorship' after learming of the alleged persecution of Russian anarchists, the suppression of the soviets, and the rise of a new bureaucratic state. Hatred of all governments and all authority constituted their reigning passion. By contrast, the anarcho-syndicalists accepted the dictatorship of the proletariat as a 'prophylactic measure' against the counter-revolution, but insisted it should be under the control of the *sindicatos* not in the hands of the Bolshevik party.[97] Angel Pestaña, the first editor of *Solidaridad Obrera* in 1916 and a leading figure in the CNT, returned to Spain from a visit to Russia with a damning account of developments. With the alleged subordination

---

[95] Bar, 'The CNT', pp. 124–5.

[96] G. Meaker, *The Revolutionary Left in Spain, 1914–1923* (Stanford, Calif., 1974), pp. 385–90.

[97] Ibid., p. 311.

of the CNT to the Communists (either in the Spanish Communist Party or the Comintern) unacceptable to the mass of Confederación members, Nin and Maurín's action was disavowed, with the CNT finally breaking with Moscow at its June 1922 congress.[98] The imposition of a military dictatorship in 1923 and subsequent banning of the CNT further diminished the pro-Bolsheviks' influence, although it did not overcome the internal faction fighting.

For Nin the trip to Moscow was decisive, and after a futile attempt to return to Spain he returned to Moscow and joined the Russian Communist Party. He was taken into the Secretariat of the Comintern, where he virtually became an assistant Secretary General of the RILU.[99] Maurin, who held a peculiar middle ground between revolutionary syndicalism and Leninism throughout 1921–1922, eventually joined the *Partido Communista Español* in 1923.[100] Other leading CNT figures that joined included Jesus Ibánez, national committee member from Asturias, and Hilario Arlandis from Levante. As in France and Italy, the Spanish Communist Party emerged from a split inside the radicalised Socialist Party. However, Maurin and the communist-syndicalists of Catalonia were never to achieve a close relationship with the so-called 'political Communists', the Spanish Communist Party members who were centered in Madrid and the North, and they maintained a nearly complete independence of the party.[101] In fact, there continued to be *two* communist movements: one political and centered in Madrid and the North, and one syndicalist, centered in Catalonia and Valencia. Not until December 1922 was there created, at the Comintern's behest, a true organisational linkage between them with the formation of *Grupos Sindicales Rojos* (Red Trade Union Groups).[102] The rump of the communist-syndicalists went on to form the Catalan Federation of the Communist Party and led a semi-autonomous life until they departed in 1930, eventually to form Maurin's Worker's and Peasant's Bloc (which in 1935 fused with Nin's Communist Left to form the POUM).

Significantly, despite the intense ferment generated by the Bolshevik revolution, the Spanish Communist Party, compared with its continental counterparts, failed to build a genuinely mass base inside the labour movement and there was nothing resembling the mass exodus of French syndicalists into the newly formed Communist Party during the early 1920s. As a result, it failed to outbid the CNT, at least until the Civil War, and the CNT (notwithstanding the external and internal pressures it faced) managed to survive with its forces intact, and to grow massively again in the early 1930s. Gerald Meaker has provided a number of explanations for such a distinct development.[103] On the one hand, the Communist Party was born late (April–November 1921) and thus came onto the scene after the post-war wave of revolutionary and pro-Bolshevik enthusiasm had passed its peak. This tardy arrival meant the new party encountered the full force of

---

[98] J. Garner, 'Separated by an "Ideological Chasm": The Spanish National Labour Confederation and Bolshevik Internationalism, 1917–1922', *Contemporay European History*, 15:3 (2006), pp. 293–326.

[99] P. Pagės, *Andreu Nin: Su evolución politica 1911–37* (Bilbao, 1975).

[100] A. Monreal, *El pensamiento politico de Joaquín Mauŕin* (Barcelona: 1984); Y. Riottat, *Joaquín Mauŕin, De l'anarcho-sindicalisme au communisme, 1919–1936* (Paris, 1997).

[101] *Lucha Social*, 19 November 1922.

[102] Meaker, pp. 422–7.

[103] Ibid., pp. 478–83.

repressive government measures while still in its formative phase, with the repeated imprisonment of party workers a formidable obstacle to organisational and recruiting activity. No less unfortunate for the new party was the relative indifference of the Comintern towards its fate, with Moscow's equally stubborn insistence on electoral and parliamentary tactics (against 'ultra-left' communist opposition) not immediately enhancing the popularity of the party among the masses of revolutionary-minded but anti-parliamentary workers and peasants.

On the other hand, Meaker has argued, there were also underlying structural causes, the most important of which was the relative slow pace of Spanish industrial development, which resulted in a labour movement both materially and ideologically retarded compared with similar movements elsewhere in Western Europe. The delayed development of the Socialist Party inhibited the appearance of a large and militant left wing whose conversion to Bolshevism might have ensured the success of the Communist Party. The CNT was in a similar condition of retarded evolution; organised only in 1911, and not really launched until 1914, the war had not transformed its economic base and the strong synthesis of anarchism and syndicalism, which harmonised remarkably well with the character and mentality of large numbers of workers, especially in Catalonia and the South, continued to command the loyalty of the great mass of the CNT supporters. The stability of the increasingly anarcho-syndicalist colouration of the CNT ideology was encouraged by the lack of any dramatic industrial transformation in Catalonia – by the continued presence of small factories, intransigent employers, unassimilated peasants and hostile state authority. If overt reformism had managed to conquer the CNT, no doubt the Communist ranks would have been correspondingly enlarged. Spanish participation in the war would also doubtless have had a disruptive effect. In fact, the blows needed to defeat and morally discredit the CNT would not come until the Civil War.[104]

In Ireland the ITGWU became wracked by internal ideological and organisational conflict from 1923 onwards. A chorus of dissent had begun to grow within the Transport Union as its post-1916 leader William O'Brien had increased his power and consolidated his position and that of other officials. Jim Larkin had returned from America in April 1923 hoping to recapture the union for its old militant traditions and made a searing attack on the leadership, including allegations of misappropriation of funds and subsequent maladministration. But united in their opposition to Larkin, the incumbent union executive suspended him as general secretary and secured an injunction to prevent him interfering with their duties at union headquarters. The ITGWU split deepened bitter personal recriminations on both sides and reflected two conceptions of what a trade union should be – a revolutionary or a reformist instrument for change. But with the Irish labour movement suffering a general counter-offensive by the employers, the attempt to build a *revolutionary* union organisation, as Larkin desired, was no longer tenable. After being expelled from membership of the ITGWU, Larkin's brother (Peter) launched a breakaway union, the Workers' Union of Ireland (WUI), in June 1924, which quickly won over two-thirds of the Dublin membership, along with 23 of 300 provincial branches. However, the great bulk of ITGWU branch officials, Dublin and county, stayed with the ITGWU. And the new union did not

[104] Ibid., pp. 482–3.

receive support from Moscow who opposed the creation of parallel revolutionary unions. The two rival unions were engaged in a whole series of bitter jurisdictional disputes and the Larkins were unable to stem the decline of influence of the new union, which itself increasingly adopted a reformist approach.[105]

Meanwhile, Larkin was won over to Bolshevism. Whilst in America he had joined the Socialist Party and helped organise its left-wing section in New York, aimed at transforming it into a communist party. He later joined the Communist Labor Party, the smaller of the two American CPs established after the expulsion of the left-wing of the Socialist Party, but was then arrested and imprisoned for three years under the state counter-offensive of the period. On his return to Ireland he attempted to form a political organisation, the Irish Worker League (analogous with the British *Daily Herald* League) in late 1923. Although viewed as a potential broad workers' party in which communists would play a central role, it won little support. He later traveled to Moscow to attend the Fifth Congress of the Communist International in July 1924, where he was elected to the Executive Committee of the Comintern. But despite his communist and pro-Soviet sympathies, Larkin could not bring himself to accept a formal relationship with the tiny group of Irish communists and blamed the Red International of Labour Unions for lack of financial support for the WUI.[106]

In Britain during 1920–1921 a number of the engineering shop stewards' movement leaders, following their wartime experiences and influenced by the inspiration of the Bolshevik Revolution, abandoned their previous syndicalist-type strategy and proceeded to play a highly influential role in the Communist Party of Great Britain. Indeed of the eight members of the National Administrative Council of the Shop Stewards' and Workers' Committee Movement who had been elected in August 1917, six had joined the Communist Party by January 1921.[107] J.T. Murphy and Tom Mann both attended congresses of the Communist International and subsequently played a key role in the Red International of Labour Unions. The transition was no doubt made easier by the fact that a number of the shop stewards' leaders had been members of one of the two Marxist parties (BSP and SLP) that merged with other revolutionary forces to create the new unified Communist Party. But even Mann, who had remained aloof from any party, had no apparent difficulty in reconciling communism and syndicalism. Of the Bolsheviks, he could simply say: 'They hold that parliament is outworn, and that the growing economic power of the workers must fashion new forces of political expression.' Of himself he stated: 'We should not rigidly adhere to past policies for the sake of consistency when these no longer make for perfect solidarity.'[108]

At first, the relationship between the party and the shop stewards' movement was left undefined. One group, led by Jack Tanner, advocated that the movement

---

[105] E. O'Connor, *Reds and the Green: Ireland, Russia and the Communist Internationals 1919–43* (Dublin, 2004).

[106] Larkin, pp. 231–65; E. O'Connor, *James Larkin* (Cork, 2002), pp. 80–93.

[107] These were A. MacManus (chair), G. Peet (secretary), J.T. Murphy (assistant secretary), T. Hurst, W. Gallacher and T. Dingley. See R. Darlington, *The Political Trajectory of J.T. Murphy* (Liverpool, 1998), p. 85.

[108] Tom Mann, *Russia in 1921* (London: n.d), esp. p. 15, 24, 38, 43; idem, *Tom Mann's Memoirs* (London, 1967), pp. 323–4.

should support the party as individuals but remain independent. The other group, led by Murphy and the Glasgow shop stewards (including Willie Gallacher and Tom Bell), were in favour of a closer connection. But a subsequent meeting with the Communist Party leadership overcame differences and agreed on the need for close co-operation between the two organizations.[109] A national shop stewards' conference in April 1921 ratified this alliance by accepting a constitution which effectively subordinated it to the political control of the party.[110] In the South Wales coalfield the main pre-war syndicalist militants also joined the Communist Party after 1920.[111] The British Bureau of the Red International of Labour Unions, set up with Russian money by Murphy and chaired by Mann, now worked as the chief industrial arm of the Communist Party. It effectively replaced the shop stewards' movement, which coalesced into a communist-led National Minority Movement that was to become a major influence inside the British working class movement in 1924–1925, even though the Communist Party (compared with its French and Italian counterparts) was miniscule with only about 5,000 members by the end of 1922.[112]

To recap, the general impact of the Russian Revolution and the specific intervention of the Bolsheviks contributed to the internal debates and schism that afflicted the syndicalist movement internationally. Although the establishment of new revolutionary Communist Parties only succeeded in attracting some, albeit prominent, syndicalists within its orbit, it helped to further marginalise the syndicalist movement generally.

Prospects for Social Reform

Syndicalist activists were also lured away from the movement during the post-war period by the prospects for social reform via official trade union and parliamentary channels. In countries such as Britain, America, Ireland and France there was the consolidation of parliamentary reformism, the widening of the socialist parties' electoral appeal, the increased role of the state in welfare measures, the extension of collective bargaining and industrial relations procedures, and improved working conditions. (In Spain and Italy, of course, such developments were less important in the short-term than other factors.)

Britain serves as a particularly vivid example of such broad social reform developments. The enormous growth in union membership immediately after the war from 2.6 million in 1910 to 8.3 million in 1920 (although it then fell to just 5 million by

---

109 R. Martin, *Communism and the British Trade Unions: A Study of the National Minority Movement* (Oxford, 1969), p. 18; Darlington, pp. 84–5.

110 B. Pribicevic, *The Shop Stewards' Movement and Workers' Control* (Oxford, 1959), pp. 142–3.

111 D. Egan, '"A Cult of Their Own": Syndicalism and the Miners' Next Step', A. Campbell, N. Fishman and D. Howell (eds), *Miners, Unions and Politics: 1910–47* (Aldershot, 1996), p. 29.

112 In 1922 the French Communist Party had 78,000 members (83,000 in 1925) and the Italian Communist Party had 24,000 (reduced to 12,000 in 1925 after Mussolini's seizure of power). See W. Kendall, *The Revolutionary Movement in Europe 1900-22* (London, 1969), p. 385.

1923), the series of amalgamations which led to the formation of giant general unions, and the progress of national collective bargaining as opposed to the pattern of district settlements that had prevailed before the war, encouraged the development of a layer of full-time union officials. With union strength on the shopfloor eroded by unemployment and strike defeats, the focus of power and influence within the unions shifted away from the rank-and-file to such full-time officials, who were increasingly able to assert their authority and channel working class discontent into formalised bargaining procedures. Rank-and-file activists, for lack of a viable alternative, now looked with renewed hope for reform through conciliation rather than direct action on the shopfloor.

At the same time, if at the beginning of the century parliamentary democracy lacked credibility in many countries, in the immediate post-war period there was significant political reform involving the extension of the franchise to much wider layers of workers and an accompanying rise in size and political influence of reformist labour and socialist parties, all of which helped to undermine syndicalism's appeal. For example in Britain, although electorally the Labour Party had made little progress between 1906 and 1914, post-war conditions produced a transformation in the party's fortunes. Two million more men *and* six million women were added to the electoral register for the 1918 general election, an election in which the Labour Party took 20 per cent of the vote, an enormous increase on the 6 per cent it received in 1910 (although only 57 Labour MPs were elected compared to 42 in 1910). But the real leap forward came in 1922 when its vote nearly doubled, from 2.2 to 4.2 million, and the number of parliamentary representatives rose from 57 to 142, making it the second largest party in parliament. In 1923 the party's vote increased slightly again to 4.4 million and 191 MPs, and in 1924 a minority Labour government able to have an impact on political power was formed, all of which considerably bolstered workers' faith in parliamentary action as opposed to syndicalist direct action.[113]

In the process the Labour Party was transformed into a mass membership party, growing from 2.5 million in 1917 to 3.5 million in 1919 and 4.4 million by 1920. In 1918 it amended its constitution so as to establish local Constituency Labour Parties across the country. It also adopted an explicitly socialist platform in Clause 4 of its constitution, composed by Sidney Webb, with a commitment to public ownership of industry. Even before the war David Lloyd George, Prime Minister from 1916 to 1922, had acknowledged the way in which the Labour Party acted as an effective defence mechanism of the existing order: 'Socialism', he said, meaning the Labour Party, would destroy 'Syndicalism – the best policeman for the Syndicalist is the Socialist':

> There is this guarantee for society, that one microbe can be trusted to kill another, and the microbe of Socialism, which may be a very beneficent one, does at any rate keep guard upon the other, which is a very dangerous and perilous one. I have, therefore, no real fear of the Syndicalist.[114]

---

[113] P. Foot, *The Vote: How It Was Won and How It Was Undermined* (London, 2005), pp. 241–3; J. Hinton, *Labour and Socialism: A History of the Working Class Movement 1867–1974* (Brighton, 1973), p. 117.

[114] D. Lloyd George, 5th series, *Hansard*, vol xxv, 19 March 1912, p. 1774.

Even in France where the Socialist Party lost about three quarters of its membership to the *Parti communisite français* at the congress of Tours in 1920, there was a steady recovery in fortunes during the 1920s.[115] As in Britain, the French state constructed an effective institutional apparatus to stabilise class relations, thereby having the effect of diminishing the influence of syndicalism. Meanwhile in America, growing prosperity, the end of mass immigration and the absorption of foreign labour, as well as the slow mitigation of the rigours of uncontrolled capitalist expansion in the 1920s, all undermined the basis for the IWW. While some employers continued to use authoritarian methods to crush any efforts to organise independent unions, the federal government used its vast powers to hasten the growth of welfare capitalism and encourage employers to improve working conditions. As a result, American industrialists such as Henry Ford developed elaborate paternalistic company welfare programmes that included modest insurance and pension plans, profit-sharing schemes and company-sponsored social activities, all designed to make workers loyal to and dependent on their benevolent employers. Given the prosperous business climate of the 1920s this carrot-and-stick strategy proved highly effective, with union membership declining from 5 million in 1920 to 3.5 million in 1923.[116] 'While IWW leaders [had] felt federal repression during [the war], their followers enjoyed eight-hour days, grievance boards and company unions. Put ... simply, reform finally proved a better method than repression for weakening the IWW's appeal to workers.'[117]

Conclusion

So a variety of factors combined in each country to contribute to the demise of the syndicalist movement internationally. Paradoxically, even though the reformist unions also suffered a loss of members amidst the strike defeats and economic recession, most in the long run survived and grew. By contrast:

> The reliance of the [syndicalist movement] on mass action and mass participation, its class struggle approach to limited demands for material improvements, and its consistent refusal to tighten its organisation for fear of deadening its dynamism with bureaucracy were all linked to its revolutionary orientation, and these factors mitigated against the survival of [syndicalist]-type unions in periods when workers were neither revolutionary nor militant.[118]

Van der Linden and Thorpe have suggested those syndicalist movements not already destroyed by state repression were faced with an unavoidable 'trilemma': three options, each of which would mean their demise: *Marginalisation*: hold on to its principles, in which case it would inevitably become totally marginalised; *Moderation:* change course fundamentally and adapt to the new conditions, in which case it would have to abandon its syndicalist principles; or *Dissolution:* disband or

---

[115] Membership of the Socialist Party increased from 50,000 in 1921 to 111,000 by 1925. See A.S. Lindemann, *A History of European Socialism* (New Haven, NY, 1983), pp. 239–41.

[116] P. Le Blanc, *A Short History of the U.S. Working Class* (New York, 1999), pp. 79–80.

[117] Dubofsky, *We Shall Be All*, p. 483.

[118] Peterson, p. 80.

merge into a non-syndicalist trade union organisation. The IWW (which still survives today) opted for the first alternative. The CGT, which in any case had abandoned its revolutionary trajectory, opted for the second. The ISEL opted for the third.[119] Of course, the CNT was an important exception.

In conclusion it should be noted that despite the retrenchment that occurred in individual countries, syndicalism as an international phenomenon remained on the scene, albeit a pale shadow of its former strength. The syndicalist urge towards international organisation, which had been temporarily diverted first by the war and then by the Bolshevik Revolution and Comintern, was resumed from December 1922. Delegates from 15 countries met in Berlin and founded the International Working Men's Association (IWMA) as a syndicalist alternative to both the reformist International Federation of Trade Unions and communist-dominated RILU. But not only had this new International come into being at a time when the post-war wave of revolutionary enthusiasm had already waned, but military dictatorship soon suppressed two of its most important affiliates in Italy and Spain, and inter-war economic crisis generally rendered the organisation ineffectual. Franco's victory in Spain in 1939, followed by the outbreak of the Second World War, sealed the IWMA's isolated fate.[120]

---

[119] van der Linden and Thorpe, 'The Rise and Fall of Revolutionary Syndicalism', p. 18.

[120] Thorpe, 'The *Workers Themselves': Revolutionary Syndicalism and International Labour, 1913–1923* (Dordrecht, 1989, pp. 237–68; G. Woodcock, *Anarchism* (Harmondsworth, 1979), pp. 252–5.

PART 2
The Transition to Communism

Part 2 Prologue

Following the relatively 'objective' examination of the dynamics of the syndicalist movement internationally provided in Part One, Part Two attempts to make a rather more 'subjective' assessment of the limitations of the syndicalist movement from a revolutionary Marxist perspective. Of course, in many respects the analysis and interpretation provided in Part One was *itself* informed by such Marxist political assumptions, although it was not always necessary for this to be explicitly reflected in the text. But in the chapters that follow the author has adopted a much more critical and disputatious approach than previously, of which the starting point of reference is pivoted on an alternative Marxist analysis.

Clearly, from a Marxist perspective there were a number of serious limitations in syndicalist theory and practice. In the past Marx and Engels had criticised the anarchist writings of Proudhon and Bakunin[1] and Lenin had polemicised against the 'economists' in the pamphlet *What is To Be Done*.[2] The controversy and debates that ensued at the Communist International added considerably to this literature, as did Lenin's political writings on revolutionary strategy and tactics,[3] Trotsky's discussions with French syndicalists aimed at trying to win them over to Marxism[4] and Gramsci's assessment of the revolutionary movement in Italy.[5]

What follows is an attempt to develop and extend this critique of syndicalism from a Marxist perspective. In the process there is an examination of: the attempts made by Moscow (via the Comintern and Red International of Labour Unions) to attract syndicalists into its communist ranks, and the arguments advanced by Lenin, Trotsky and others (as well as Marx and Engels before them); the positive (and negative) response by leading syndicalists internationally to the Russian Revolution, Bolshevism and attempt to build communist trade union and political organisation; the contrast between syndicalist and communist traditions and the degree of synthesis that emerged within the new revolutionary communist parties that emerged; the limitations in syndicalist strategy and tactics that contributed to the ideological and political transition to communism; and the overall strengths (as well as notable weaknesses) of the alternative Bolshevik and communist tradition.

The first chapter explores Moscow's embrace of syndicalism. Subsequent chapters examine in thematic fashion five specific (although interrelated) theoretical and practical limitations of the syndicalist tradition from a communist perspective: These relate to: Trade Unionism; Union Bureaucracy; Economics and Politics; State and Revolution; and Leadership and the Party.

---

[1] K. Marx, F. Engels and V.I. Lenin, *Anarchism and Anarcho-Syndicalism* (New York, 1972).

[2] V.I. Lenin, 'What is to be Done?', *Selected Works*: *Vol. 1* (Moscow, 1970).

[3] V.I. Lenin, 'The State and Revolution', *Selected Works Vol. 2* (Moscow, 1970).

[4] L. Trotsky, *Marxism and the Trade Unions* (London, 1972).

[5] A. Gramsci, *Selections from Political Writings 1910–1920* (London, 1977).

he analysis situates the ideological and political tensions of syndicalism within : historical context in which they became apparent and were advanced both by communists as well as by newly converted syndicalists themselves. But Part Two also goes beyond the debates held at the time to draw out more explicitly, occasionally with the benefit of historical and political hindsight, some of the unresolved issues and themes of both traditions. In the process it seeks to contribute to our broader understanding of the relationship between trade unionism and revolution. The final chapter assesses the problematic nature of the syndicalist-communist fusion, with the carrying over of syndicalist influences into the new communist parties that emerged.

Chapter 6

Moscow's Embrace

Revolutionary syndicalists across the world received the news of the October 1917 revolution with jubilant enthusiasm and their newspapers rushed to declare solidarity with it. It was viewed as the first phase of a revolutionary process that would have a domino effect on other countries. Bill Haywood told fellow IWW leader Ralph Chaplain: 'The Russian revolution is the greatest event in our lives. It represents all that we have been dreaming of and fighting for all our lives. It is the dawn of freedom and industrial democracy. If we can't trust Lenin, we can't trust anybody.'[1] In Italy Armando Borghi recalled: 'We made [the Russian Revolution] our polar star. We exulted in its victories. We trembled at its risks … We made a symbol and an altar of its name, its dead, its living and its heroes'.[2] 'To do as in Russia' (*Fare come in Russia*) became the watch-word of Italian revolutionary forces. A similar 'Russian fever' rapidly spread across cities in Spain, where scores of 'pro-Bolshevik' meetings and demonstrations were held from autumn 1918 through to 1919, with a rash of 'Bolshevik' journals appearing (such as *El Maximalista* in Barcelona), many of which emanated from anarcho-syndicalist quarters. CNT national committee member Manuel Buenacasa acknowledged: 'the immense majority of us considered ourselves true Bolsheviks', and saw in Bolshevism 'the revolution we dreamed of.'[3]

At least in its early forms the syndicalists could detect the basis of a close kinship between their own conceptions and the shape the Russian revolution appeared to be taking. Thus, an IWW publication concluded a month after the revolution that 'in broad essentials, the now famous Bolsheviki stand for about the same thing in Russia as our IWW stands for in America'.[4] The Bolshevik emphasis on political action and the necessity of capturing the institutions of the state went against IWW insistence that only economic activity was important. But although the soviets and the formation of the Bolshevik government were 'admittedly political [and] not the establishment of a society of labour based on the principles of industrial administration', this was regarded in the face of military invasion and blockade as being necessary 'for the time being'.[5] The important point was that organs of working class self-government

---

1 R. Chaplain, *Wobbly: The Rough and Tumble of an American Radical* (Chicago, 1948), p. 298. See also W.D. Haywood, *Bill Haywood's Book: The Autobiography of William D. Haywood* (New York:, 1929), p. 360.

2 A. Borghi, *L'Italia tra due Crispi: cause e conseguenze di una rivoluzione macata* (Paris: n.d. [1924], p. 91.

3 M. Buenacasa, *El movimiento obrero español, historia y crítica, 1886–1926* (Paris, 1966), p. 89.

4 *Defense News Bulletin*, 8 December 1917.

5 *Industrial Worker*, 4 May 1918.

were in control of the factories, the capitalists had been expropriated and the land distributed to the long-suffering Russian peasantry.

In France, although the leadership of the CGT had emerged from the war with a markedly reformist stance, a growing (albeit varied) internal minority opposition movement became dedicated to enrolling the union's support for the Bolshevik Revolution and the Communist International. Former CGT secretary Victor Griffuelhes emerged in 1917 as a strong supporter, his pro-Bolshevik stance emanating from a belief that the new Russian regime was centred on the soviets and thus derived from the French syndicalist blueprint for the producers' commonwealth. 'The soviet – i.e. the union – [is] in charge of production under the direction of national soviets – i.e. the national federations – and under the inspiration of a grand soviet composed of delegates from the national soviets – i.e. the CGT'.[6] Likewise, the new-style 'pure' syndicalist faction of the CGT revolutionary minority (many of whom were anarchist inspired), greeted the October revolution as both a vindication of the theory and practice of pre-war revolutionary syndicalism and a guide and inspiration for the revolution in France they fervently believed was possible.[7] The communist-syndicalist faction of Pierre Monatte and Alfred Rosmer displayed the greatest sustained enthusiasm, with *La Vie Ouvrèire* remarking: 'What therefore is the Russian Revolution if not a revolution of a syndicalist character?'[8] The journal was to carry numerous articles exploring the parallels between the *syndicats* and the soviets and the manner in which power had been turned over exclusively to the producers, its location transferred from the state to the factory.[9]

In Britain, the passion with which J.T. Murphy and other shop stewards' leaders took up and developed the idea of soviet power was to be explained in part by the way in which they saw a direct parallel between their own wartime practice of independent rank-and-file organisation via the Workers' Committees and the Russian soviets. In Ireland, the ITGWU's infatuation with Bolshevism was reflected in meetings organised to express support for the revolution and a good deal of pro-Soviet writing, including translations of articles by Bolshevik leaders. When sections of the Irish labour movement attempted to emulate the Russian example in 1919, with 'soviets', mostly short-lived, established in a number of towns including Limerick.[10] *Voice of Labour* published an article reflecting the opinions of the whole ITGWU leadership, which declared:

> To-day the Soviet idea is sweeping westward over Europe ... The Soviet has shown itself the only instrument of liberation in Europe...Ireland's best and most effective answer is the immediate establishment of the Soviets, the instruments which will bring about the dictatorship of the Irish proletariat.[11]

---

6 V. Griffuelhes, 'A propos d'un livre', *Le Journal du Peuple*, 30 August 1919.

7 See D. Reid ' Guillaume Verdier et le Stndicalisme rèvolutionnaire aux usines de Decazeville 1917–1920', *Annales du Midi*, 166 (1984), p. 196.

8 Cited in C. Chambelland (ed.), *La Lutte syndicale* (Paris, 1976), p. 159.

9 J. Jennings, *Syndicalism in France: A Study of Ideas* (London, 1990), p. 175.

10 L. Cahill, *Forgotten Revolution: Limerick Soviet 1919* (Dublin, 1990).

11 *Voice of Labour*, 1:73, 12 April 1919.

Despite initial approval of the Russian Revolution by syndicalists *generally*, as more news began to filter through there was growing apprehension about the role of the Bolsheviks. Such anxiety was compounded by the way in which communism became an important battle ground between the various competing tendencies within the syndicalist movement. Nonetheless, against the backcloth of revolutionary upheaval across Europe, a number of leading syndicalist figures from different movements across the world made the journey to Moscow so they could personally assess the situation in Russia first hand.[12] In the process they participated in the important debates about strategy and tactics that were to be conducted at the congresses of the Communist International (Comintern) and Red International of Labour Unions.

The Comintern and Red International of Labour Unions

With the outbreak of war and collapse of the Second International into nationalism and reformism, Lenin had unsuccessfully campaigned at anti-war international socialist meetings in Zimmerwald (1915) and Kienthal (1916) for a new, genuinely revolutionary International that could pull together the left wings of the labour and socialist parties.[13] Of course before October 1917 the Russian Bolsheviks had possessed only marginal influence within the European and American left; but as architects of the one enduring socialist revolution their status was inevitably transformed and it now became possible to make Lenin's aspiration for a new International a reality. As *successful* revolutionaries, the Bolshevik's authority to offer strategic guidance to help foreign revolutionary counterparts (including those from the syndicalist tradition) became hard to challenge, although many did question their key arguments. But to *sustain* the achievements of revolution within an isolated and economically backward country such as Russia, Lenin argued, would be impossible without revolution fairly rapidly spreading to the rest of the world (notably Germany).

Such hopes that the Russian Revolution could be spread were not unrealistic. During 1918–1920 the inspiration of the Russian Revolution, combined with the conditions of economic and political crisis that accompanied the end of the First World War, produced a wave of revolutionary struggle that swept across the world. In November 1918 a revolution in Germany overthrew the Kaiser and brought the Social Democrats to power. This was followed in January 1919 by the unsuccessful Spartakus rising in Berlin. In the spring of 1919 the short-lived Hungarian and Bavarian republics were formed, and in the summer Italy embarked on its *bienno rosso* and factory council and occupation movement. It was the first international revolutionary situation since 1848, and was far and away the most powerful challenge

[12] Among those syndicalist movement leaders who visited Moscow were: Victor Griffuelhes, Gaston Monmousseau and Alfred Rosmer from France; Bill Haywood, William Z. Foster and George Williams from America; Joaquin Maurin, Andreu Nin and Angel Pestaña from Spain; Armando Borghi, Nicolo Vecchi and Lulio Mari from Italy, Jim Larkin from Ireland; Tom Bell, Willie Gallacher, Arthur MacManus, Tom Mann, J.T. Murphy, Jack Tanner and David Ramsey from Britain.

[13] W. Thorpe, *'The Workers Themselves': Revolutionary Syndicalism and International Labour, 1913–1923* (Dordrecht 1989), pp. 94–5; 100–101.

to world capitalism ever presented by the world working class. The formation of the Communist (or Third) International in March 1919 was both a product of this dramatic situation and a response to it.[14] The Second Congress of the Comintern met in Moscow in the summer of 1920 'in a mood of all-conquering faith and hope'. J.T. Murphy recalled:

> It was an intoxicating period for those who, such as myself, had become absorbed by the question of the workers' revolution. It appeared to us that events were sweeping us forward to that goal at a tremendous speed. All around us capitalism appeared to be on the retreat before the advancing workers. Now it seemed clear that the Russian revolution was no mere national event peculiar to Russia, but was the beginning of the World Revolution. Had it not already swept Germany into the throes of revolution? Were not thrones tumbling down and crowns rolling in the dust? Was not this tremendous wave of mass action in Britain but the prelude to revolutionary storms that would grow in force and power?[15]

The Comintern set itself the task of winning over that section of the international working class that was disillusioned with social democracy by encouraging and sponsoring the building of revolutionary communist parties of the Bolshevik type in every country. Unlike the Second International, which had been a loose federal body allowing more or less complete independence for its national sections and embracing a wide range of different political tendencies, the Comintern aimed to be a single centralised world party and exclusively communist, that is revolutionary Marxist. The form of organisation reflected a conception of the world as a single battlefield on which the class war was to be waged with one army and one high command; its aim was to create a unified general staff of what was assumed to be the impending world revolution.[16] The Comintern was to be, as the Hungarian revolutionary Marxist intellectual Georg Lukacs put it, 'The Bolshevik Party – Lenin's concept of the party – on a world scale'.[17]

Achieving the transformation of the Comintern into a mass force was not a simple operation. The problem was that without winning over as many as possible of the leftward moving rank-and-file of the old socialist parties who still remained loyal to their organisations, the new International could not hope to exert a revolutionary influence. But the socialist parties' 'centrist' leaders, who preached a radical rhetoric, had to be prevented from entering the International and infecting it (by the imposition of extremely stringent 21 conditions of admission) and politically discredited to detach supporters from their influence. At the same time the Comintern aimed to draw together all the existing revolutionary communist tendencies, uniting them into parties that embodied the Bolshevik experience. That meant engaging in a much more friendly debate with groups whose often ultra-left 'errors' – such as refusing to participate in bourgeois parliaments or reactionary trade unions – were put down to their youth and inexperience.

---

[14] For some general background material see E.H. Carr, *The Bolshevik Revolution 1917–1923, Vol. 3* (London, 1966); D. Hallas, *The Comintern* (London, 1985); A. Rosmer, *Lenin's Moscow* (London, 1971).

[15] *New Horizons* (London, 1941), p. 83.

[16] J. Molyneux, *Marxism and the Party* (London, 1978), p. 86.

[17] G. Lukacs, *Lenin* (London, 1970), p. 59.

But the Bolsheviks also wanted to harness the revolutionary potential of that section of the labour movement which lay beyond the boundaries of the communist and socialist parties and mainstream trade unions. The revolutionary syndicalists, along with anarchists and associated anti-parliamentarians, fell into this category. Thus, Trotsky's invitation to the Comintern's founding congress proclaimed the necessity of forming:

> … a block with those elements in the revolutionary workers' movement who, although they do not formerly belong to socialist parties, now stand by and large for the proletarian dictatorship in the form of Soviet power. Chief among these are the syndicalist elements in the workers' movement.[18]

It was necessary to win over those whose disgust at the opportunism of the reformist parties had led them to reject the need for a revolutionary political party in favour of revolutionary trade unionism. Therefore the call from Moscow to all revolutionary workers' movements and groups to send representatives to the Comintern was directed not only at political organisations but also at workers' organisations and trade union bodies, including syndicalist organisations. In response, the IWW's General Executive Board initially expressed support and voted unanimously to 'provide for the representation of the IWW as a constituent member of the Third International',[19] although no one actually attended the founding Congress from the IWW. The USI's central council voted to affiliate to the Comintern, a decision which was endorsed by its Parma congress in December 1919. Likewise the CNT sent a group of delegates, headed by Andreu Nin and Joaquín Maurin, to Moscow where they pledged the Confederación's support, with the CNT's Madrid Congress provisionally agreeing to affiliate in December 1919.[20]

Yet the central means by which the Bolsheviks sought to win over the syndicalists was via the construction of a subsidiary organisation of the Comintern, the Red International of Labour Unions (RILU), a new revolutionary *trade union* International that operated alongside the more party-structured Comintern. Significantly, according to Reiner Tosstorff, the launch of such a decisive initiative 'stemmed from coincidence rather than calculation'.[21] Although it was clear the Comintern needed to develop an organisational form through which it could reach trade union militants, in particular those influenced by various forms of syndicalism, the specific character it was to adopt only took shape when other alternative options presented themselves as being either unwanted or unviable. At the Cominern's Second Congress in July–August 1920 there were delegations from a wide range of labour organisations, and during its deliberations the Russians started talks with left-wing supporters of the

---

[18] Cited in J. Degras (ed.), *The Communist International, 1919–1943: Documents: Vol 1* (London: 1956), p. 3.

[19] *Industrial Worker*, 30 October 1920.

[20] *Memoria del Congreso celebrado en el Teatro de la Comedia de Madrid, los días 10 al 18 de diciembre de 1919* (Barcelona, 1932).

[21] R. Tosstorff, 'Moscow Versus Amsterdam: Reflections on the History of the Profintern', *Labour History Review*, 68:1 (2003), p. 81. See also *Profintern: Die Rote Gewerkschaftsinterntionale, 1920–1937* (Paderborn, 2004), pp. 165–73.

reformist-led and Amsterdam-based International Federation of Trade Unions (IFTU) from Britain and Italy. Agreement was reached on the foundation of a new international trade union council whose task would be to convene an international congress of revolutionary trade unions. A number of syndicalist representatives proved willing to support this agreement, giving a real fillip to the proposed initiative.[22] However, expectations differed: whereas the left reformists from Amsterdam hoped that the initiative would produce reinforcements to buttress their influence inside the IFTU, the syndicalists were determined to take this opportunity to realise their long-cherished idea of achieving a revolutionary alternative to the IFTU.

As firm antagonists of the Amsterdam International, the Bolsheviks decided to concentrate their efforts on establishing close relations with the syndicalists, with whom they had already declared themselves in favour of a common struggle during the First World War. They now explicitly sought to pull syndicalist organisations across the world around the Comintern orbit. Initially Grigory Zinoviev, President of the Comintern, had proposed it should 'revive the tradition of the First International', whereby trade unions as well as political parties could affiliate.[23] But this was hardly a plausible proposal given the Comintern was simultaneously attempting to impose 21 stringent conditions for admission on affiliates. Even though the USI and CNT had voted to join the Comintern, it seemed unlikely many other trade union bodies would do so. And the subsequent suggestion by Zinoviev that the 21 conditions might not apply to unions, would have created a situation whereby there were effectively two classes of affiliates in the International, those who accepted the conditions and those that did not. So this meant accepting that any revolutionary trade union body would have to be structurally distinct rather than a mere section of the Comintern. On this basis the Bolsheviks now decided to set up a new full-blown trade union International that could unite not only communist trade unions and communist minorities in reformist trade unions, but also independently-organised radical unions and syndicalist bodies.

Such a new 'Red' trade union International, it was hoped, could simultaneously rival the 'yellow' IFTU. Despite the Amsterdam International's recent growth, the authority of its reformist leaders had been severely damaged by their conduct during the war in renouncing prior internationalist commitments. And on the expectation of renewed social explosions and working class revolutions in the coming few years, a new 'Red' International, it was believed, could woo national trade unions (either wholesale or substantial sections) to break from their allegiance to the IFTU and affiliate to Moscow. Thus, an invitation to all revolutionary unions who supported the Comintern's programme to attend a conference to decide how to structure and launch the new trade union International was sent out, and a Provisional International Council of Trade and Industrial Unions was elected, composed of Alexander Lozovsky (Russia) as president and the syndicalists Tom Mann (Britain) and Alfred Rosmer (France) as vice-presidents charged with organising the founding congress the following year in May 1921. J.T. Murphy helped draft its first manifesto which called upon trade unionists to choose between Moscow and Amsterdam:

---

22 See Thorpe, *Workers Themselves*, pp. 128–49.

23 J. Riddell (ed.), *Workers of the World and Oppressed Peoples, Unite! Proceedings and Documents of the Second Congress 1920* (New York, 1991), p. 85.

> The world is now divided into great divisions and WE MUST MAKE OUR CHOICE as to which camp we belong. On the one side is the capitalist class with its ... 'yellow' Amsterdam International ... On the other side is the Communist International and all that is loyal and true to the working class.[24]

The appeal was an inviting one for the syndicalists, for they had long urged the establishment of a genuinely revolutionary labour International, and were consequently reluctant to turn their backs on the proposed Bolshevik-sponsored body, despite apprehensions about yielding political control and sacrificing their autonomy. The inaugural congress of the Red International of Labour Unions took place in July 1921 (parallel with the Comintern's Third Congress) with 380 delegates from 41 countries, composed of a variety of different syndicalist currents and the trade union fractions of communist parties (representing minority groups within the unions).[25]

At this and subsequent RILU and Comintern congresses during 1920–1922 a conscious and determined attempt was made to win over the syndicalists to the Bolshevik conception of the revolutionary process. In part, this involved pointing out what both syndicalist and communist traditions had in common and engaging in patient fraternal persuasion. Nonetheless, the Bolshevik leaders also proceeded to conduct a series of sharp arguments with the syndicalists. Apart from the issue of whether or not revolutionaries should participate in parliamentary activity, there were three other main formal debates; these related to (a) whether revolutionaries should stay inside the existing reformist unions to win them to their cause or set up new revolutionary union bodies to replace them; (b) the nature of the organisational and political ties between RILU and the Comintern; and (c) whether a revolutionary political party was necessary.

Although Bolshevik resolutions on such matters were formally won within congress sessions (despite vigorous minority opposition) the arguments that ensued were to highlight the underlying fundamental tensions between syndicalism and communism. As a result, many of those syndicalist leaders initially attracted to the achievements of the Russian Revolution quickly became disillusioned and rejected the Bolsheviks' overtures, ultimately unable to accept the insistence on the central role of a vanguard political party and the establishment of a centralised state power within the revolutionary process. Indeed, most syndicalist bodies generally continued to strongly oppose any connection with political movements, expressing concern that the RILU would simply become a subordinate appendage of the Comintern, and likewise that the trade unions would be transformed into mere subsidiary organisations under the control of the communist parties.[26] For example, when USI

---

24 *Solidarity*, 7 January 1921.

25 *Résolutions et statuts adoptés au ler congrès international des syndicates révolutionnaires – Moscou: 3–19 juillet 1921* (Paris, 1921), p. 17.

26 See E.H. Carr, *Socialism in One Country, 1924–1926, vol. 3, part 1* (London, 1964) and *The Bolshevik Revolution, 1917–1923* (London, 1966); Thorpe, *Workers Themselves*; 'Syndicalist Inrternationalism Before World War II', in M. van der Linden and W. Thorpe (eds), *Revolutionary Syndicalism: An International Perspective* (Aldershot, 1990), pp. 14–260; 'Syndicalist Internationalism and Moscow, 1919–1922: The Breach', *Canadian Journal of History*, 14:1 (1979), pp. 199–234; Tosstorff, 'Moscow Versus Amsterdam', pp. 79–97.

representatives Nicolo Vecchi and Lulio Mari returned to Italy after the RILU's founding Congress and recommended that Italian syndicalists join the new body, the majority of the leadership rebuked them, agreeing to support an International but insisting on political neutrality. Alibrando Giovanetti complained: 'The dictatorship of the proletariat has become the dictatorship of a few party leaders' and demanded total autonomy from all political parties.[27]

In France, with the eventual expulsion of the revolutionary minority from the CGT in December 1921, and the formation of the *Confédération Générale du Travail Unitaire* (CGTU), the 'pure' anarcho-syndicalist group who initially gained the upper hand attempted to completely sabotage efforts to affiliate to the Comintern or the RILU, insisting on trade union independence from any political organisation. In response the RILU decided at its Second Congress in November 1922 to give up the 'organic' connection that had been established between RILU and the Comintern, with its reciprocal representation in the leading organs. From now on, the RILU would be structured as a separate organisation, but linked to the Comintern by fundamental political agreement.[28] Such a compromise proved to be a pyrrhic syndicalist victory given that communist influence was crucial and news of the decision elicited a storm of protest from many syndicalists in France, as elsewhere across the world. But with the RILU now emphasising its independence, the CGTU, which had increasingly come under communist influence, soon declared its readiness to affiliate.[29]

In Spain, a CNT plenum also forcefully rebuked its delegation to the Comintern by adopting a resolution that stood in sharp contrast to that passed in Moscow.[30] Angel Pestana, who had from the outset (in contrast to Maurin and Nin) been instinctively wary of any subordination of the unions to the party and RILU to the Bolsheviks, returned from the RILU Congress with the news of the alleged persecution of Russian anarchists, the rise of a 'party dictatorship' and the suppression of the Kronstadt sailors' insurrection. His reports caused a general revulsion among Spanish anarchists and syndicalists, and at its Saragossa Conference in 1922 the CNT reasserted its faith in 'libertarian communism', and decided to withdraw its affiliation from the Comintern.

Similarly before the end of 1921 the IWW had repudiated the RILU. Over the strenuous objections of the most anti-communist Wobblies, they had agreed to send George Williams as delegate to the RILU Congress, although he was instructed to stand firm on all issues dividing syndicalists from Bolsheviks.[31] When Williams returned to America he submitted a very hostile report: 'I am convinced that a truly economic international of revolutionary industrial unions cannot exist with headquarters in Moscow without being dominated by the Communist International. It is a physical impossibility.'[32] The General Executive Board unanimously endorsed his proposals

---

[27] *Guerre di Classe* (Bologna) 25 March 1922.

[28] J.T. Murphy, *The 'Reds' in Congress: Preliminary Report of the First World War Congress of the Red International of Trade and Industrial Unions* (London, 1921).

[29] G. Lefranc, *Le Mouvement Syndical sous la Troisième République* (Paris, 1967); M. Dreyfus, *Historie de la C.G.T.* (Brussels, 1995); Thorpe, *Workers Themselves*, pp. 226–35.

[30] *Lucha Social*, 27 August 1921.

[31] *Industrial Worker*, 4 June 1921.

[32] *The First Congress of the Red Trades Union International at Moscow, 1921: A Report of the Proceedings by George Williams, Delegate from the IW* (Chicago, 1921).

and rejected affiliation with the RILU, which it described as 'not only undesirable both absolutely impossible'.[33] A formal statement explained the reasons for its decision: the condemnation of IWW policies; the advocacy of working inside the mainstream union movement; the political character of the RILU dominated by Communists determined to liquidate the IWW for refusing to submit to its autocratic discipline; and the impossibility of collaboration between the IWW and the American Communist Party.[34]

Notwithstanding such opposition, a significant layer of prominent pre-war and wartime syndicalists, profoundly influenced by the nature of the October 1917 Revolution, *did* unceremoniously abandon their previous philosophy to embrace the main tenants of Bolshevism.[35] Most responded by joining the new revolutionary Communist Parties that were subsequently established in their respective countries and which were to rapidly supersede syndicalist organisations. The ideological and political evolution from syndicalism to communism was to be dramatic amongst these leading figures. For example, Lenin's pamphlet *The State and Revolution* (1917) was characterised by Joaquin Maurin of the CNT as: 'the doctrinal bridge which linked Bolshevism with syndicalism and anarchism.'[36] Similarly, Lenin's *'Left-Wing' Communism: An Infantile Disorder* (1920) made a significant impression on J.T. Murphy; it was 'one of the most profound pieces of writing on revolutionary theory in relation to questions of strategy and tactics ever written', influencing his own political development 'more than any other book in the armoury of revolutionary Socialism and Communism'.[37]

Under the combined force of Russian experience, prestige and argument, Murphy and other syndicalist-influenced British shop stewards' leaders, including Willie Gallacher and David Ramsey, found all their ideas 'on politics and life in general' were 'completely shaken up'. If before arriving in Moscow they had already come to an appreciation of the soviet as the chief agency of socialist revolution and of the need for the working class to conquer state power, they now embraced the idea of a disciplined, centralised party, working in an organised way in the trade unions and providing an alternative political leadership to the official leaders of the movement. As Murphy remarked:

> My experience in … Russia … had shown me the real meaning of the struggle for political power. Instead of thinking that a Socialist Party was a mere propaganda organisation for the dissemination of Socialist views I now saw that the real Socialist Party would consist of revolutionary Socialists who regarded the party as the means whereby they would lead the working class in the fight for political power. It would be a party such as Lenin had described.[38]

---

[33] *The IWW Reply to the Red Trade Union International* (Moscow) *by the General Executive Board of the Industrial Workers of the World* (Chicago, n.d [1922]), p. 23. See also *Industrial Solidarity*, 17 December 1921.

[34] Ibid., pp. 31–5.

[35] For a detailed account of this political conversion to communism by one leading British syndicalist figure see R. Darlington, *The Political Trajectory of J.T. Murphy* (Liverpool, 1998).

[36] Cited in Thorpe, 'Syndicalist Internationalism', p. 203.

[37] *New Horizons*, p. 118.

[38] *Preparing for Power* (London, 1972), pp.159–60.

Likewise in America a number of IWW figures recognised in Bolshevism the rounding out and completion of their own revolutionary conceptions, and joined the Communist Party. Bill Haywood expressed their trend of thought succinctly in an interview he gave to Max Eastman, published in *The Liberator*, April 1921:

> 'I feel as I'd always been there', he said to me. You remember I used to say that all we needed was fifty thousand real IWW's, and then about a million members to back them up? Well, isn't that a similar idea? At least I always realised that the essential thing was to have an organisation of *those who know*.[39]

That it needed the impact of the 1917 Russian Revolution under the leadership of the Bolshevik Party, and the subsequent intervention of the Comintern, to act as a catalyst to cause important syndicalist elements to fuse together into the new communist parties should not diminish the importance of their *own* theory and practice in encouraging such developments. This needs to be insisted upon because some historians have suggested they were essentially an *externally*-imposed formation. For example, in relation to Britain Walter Kendall has argued that the Communist Party 'was an almost wholly artificial creation which wrenched the whole course of the [labour] movement's left wing out of one direction and in another'.[40] In fact, Murphy and his shop steward comrades became convinced that Russian ideological and organisational conceptions were right not merely because the Bolshevik Revolution had proved their efficacy, but also because they appeared in many respects to fit their own positive and negative experiences in the shop stewards' movement. It was this that led them to abandon their previous syndicalist tradition and return home to build a new communist party along the Bolshevik-type lines agreed in Moscow.[41]

Existing Literature on the Comintern

Before examining some of the central issues on which the transition from syndicalism to communism pivoted, it is useful to briefly make an assessment of the general literature on the history of the Comintern (and RILU), much of which arguably has suffered from the political distortions of the cold-war epoch. Thus for many anti-communist historians, the Comintern was from the beginning manipulated in authoritarian fashion by the Russian leaders who imposed their will from the top down.[42] Invariably such histories fail to distinguish between the Leninist and Stalinist phases, although it is clear there was a considerable contrast between the relatively lively and open debate of the early congresses and the later straightjacket period from 1924 onwards. Moreover the stress which is placed on the manipulative aspects of even the early years of the Comintern, during which there was a determined effort to win over the syndicalists, is arguably not so much wrong as one-sided.

---

[39] Cited in J.P. Cannon, *The IWW: The Great Anticipation* (New York, 1956), p. 37.

[40] W. Kendall, *The Revolutionary Movement in Britain 1900–1922* (London, 1969), p. xii.

[41] Darlington, *Political Trajectory*, pp. 54–86.

[42] For example, see R. Aron, 'Préface' to B. Lazitch, *Lénine et la IIIe internationale* (Neuchâtel, 1951).

Wayne Thorpe, whose political sympathies are clearly with the syndicalists rather than the Bolsheviks, has made a valuable contribution to our understanding of the repudiation of the Bolshevik tradition by the majority of those within the syndicalist movement.[43] However, he has also tended to emphasise the alleged authoritarian intervention of Russian leaders who engaged in 'dogmatic condemnation' of syndicalists.[44] But as Ian Birchall has pointed out, the problem with this depiction is that it treats the Russians as if they were a homogeneous bloc, when in fact there was a huge gulf in the leadership style adopted towards the syndicalists by different figures within the Comintern in its early years. In particular, there was a contrast between the relatively comradely approach of Lenin and Trotsky aimed at trying to win over the syndicalists through fraternal argument on the one hand, and the bureaucratic sectarian bullying of Zinoviev and Karl Radek on the other.[45]

The forthright position taken by the Bolsheviks on the role of a revolutionary communist party and its relationship to the trade unions probably made a sharp confrontation between the communists and syndicalist delegates inevitable. But the French syndicalist, Alfred Rosmer, recalled that prior to the Second Comintern Congress, the Bolshevik leader Nikolai Bukharin had reprimanded a Spanish delegate who had spoken of waging 'a pitiless struggle against the anarchists', telling him: 'It's not a question of "fighting" them, but of discussing frankly and cordially, seeing if we can work together, and only abandoning the attempt if there is an irremovable obstacle'.[46] Rosmer, given his background in forging close personal and organisational contacts between syndicalists from various countries in the pre-1914 period via the paper *La Vie ouvrière*, had a particular role to play in this process. Rosmer worked alongside the Bolsheviks in Moscow with the aim of drawing in syndicalists from across the world. But the task of doing so was undoubtedly made considerably more difficult by some of the manipulative leadership practices evident in the Comintern.

For example, Zinoviev bluntly declared on the eve of the Second Comintern Congress that the assembly 'will have to put an end to all syndicalist prejudices' on such questions as the role of the communist party. 'It will have to separate the Communist wheat from the Syndicalist weeds'.[47] He proceeded to introduce the debate on the role and structure of communist parties with a speech notable for its triumphalism and ultimatory style, informing the syndicalists they were the

---

43 Thorpe, *Workers Themselves*.

44 Thorpe, 'Syndicalist Internationalism and Moscow', p. 221.

45 See I. Birchall: 'The "Reluctant Bolsheviks": Victor Serge's and Alfred Rosmer's encounter with Leninism', in C. Barker, A. Johnson and M. Lavalette (eds), *Leadership and Social Movements*, (Manchester, 2001), pp. 44–59; 'The Success and Failure of the Comintern', in K. Flett and D. Renton (eds), *The Twentieth Century: A Century of Wars and Revolutions?* (London, 2000), pp. 117–32; 'Alfred Rosmer and the RILU', Paper presented to London Socialist Historians Group Conference, Institute of Historical Research, University of London, 6 May 2000; 'Alfred and Marguerite Rosmer', Paper presented to New Socialist Approaches to History Seminar, Institute of Historical Research, University of London, 2 April 2001.

46 A. Rosmer, *Lenin's Moscow* (London, 1971), p. 61.

47 *Communist International*, no. 11-12, June–July 1920, pp. 2133–4.

'bearers of bourgeois ideology'.[48] Such a patronising approach merely provoked the indignation of those it was meant to persuade. Rosmer later summed up the damage he believed Zinoviev had done to the International:

> Zinoviev is the supreme demagogue, incapable of any constructive effort or of any organisational work. When the history of the Comintern is written, it will be seen that he bears the main responsibility for the lamentable way it has worked ... It is he who aroused and maintained for so long the distrust of syndicalists and serious militants with regard to the Comintern, by the way he shouted his mouth off in speeches marked equally by the absence of ideas and the triviality of form, revealing total failure to understand the labour movement in Europe.[49]

Meanwhile, the committee considering the trade union question was headed by Radek (secretary of the executive of the Comintern and concerned especially with German affairs), who viewed syndicalism as 'a transitional disease of the revolutionary workers' movement'.[50] CNT leader Angel Pestaña was later to describe Radek, not without justification, as an '*antisindicalista rabioso*'.[51] Even Rosmer, who accepted the Bolshevik policy, considered this section of the theses to be 'formulated so curtly and brutally that it could not convince, only provoke'.[52]

Yet all this stood in stark contrast to the approach adopted by Lenin and Trotsky. In '*Left-Wing' Communism* Lenin had sharply criticised the 'ultra-left' approach of those revolutionaries (including the IWW) who spurned participation in parliamentary elections and refused to operate inside the existing reformist unions. But he also devoted great efforts, despite competing demands on his time, to patiently win over such revolutionaries. For example, after only two days in Moscow, J.T. Murphy was invited to meet Lenin in the Kremlin, where he found not a 'hard, ruthless fanatic' who sought to overwhelm him with the force of authority, but a man who convinced him by his powers of reasoning.[53] The meeting lasted for an hour, during which Lenin asked a range of questions about the trade unions, the shop stewards, the Labour Party and the different trends of opinion in the ranks of the socialist groups in Britain:

> I gave him an account of the Shop Stewards' Movement and he was alarmed when I told him of our conception of the role of a political party. He set himself to explain the kind of

---

48 Riddell, p. 144, 146.

49 A. Rosmer, 'La Liquidation du "Putschisme"', *La Rèvolution prolètarienne*, no. 14, 1926, in *Revolutionary History*, 7:4 (2000), p. 111.

50 *Second Congress of the Communist International: Minutes of the Proceedings, Vol. 2* (London, 1977), p. 72.

51 Cited in Thorpe, *Workers Themselves*, p. 139.

52 Rosmer, *Lenin's Moscow*, p. 74.

53 *Workers' Life*, 20 January 1928. Whenever a delegate from abroad arrived in Moscow it was the practice to arrange a conversation with Lenin. Despite his many responsible duties as chair of the Council of Peoples' Commissars and Bolshevik Party leader, Lenin displayed a keen interest in the workers' movement abroad. For example, he arranged similar meeting to Murphy's with Tom Bell (*Pioneering Days*, London, 1941, p. 219), Willie Gallacher (*Last Memoirs*, London, 1966, pp. 153–4) and Harry Pollitt (*Serving My Time*, London, 1940, p. 139).

> party he thought was necessary to lead the workers in the struggle for power and later gave much attention to this question when he met other shop stewards.[54]

Such arguments were further reinforced at the debates that took place within the Congress sessions and commissions in which Lenin (and Trotsky) played a leading role, and in the informal discussions which went on until late at night between the foreign delegates. Rather than insulting and denouncing the syndicalists, Lenin sought to draw them closer by pointing to what they had in common with the Bolshevik tradition in terms of the need for activist leadership, at the same time recognising that many syndicalists were anti-party because of their experience of corrupt parliamentary organisations. For example, his attitude towards the IWW was extremely fraternal.

> … in the present instance, particularly as regards the Industrial Workers of the World in the U.S.A. … we are dealing with a profoundly proletarian and mass movement, which in all essentials actually stands by the basic principles of the Communist International. The erroneous views held by these organisations regarding participation in bourgeois parliaments can be explained … by the political inexperience of proletarians who are quite revolutionary and connected with the masses.[55]

Trotsky too sought to conciliate rather than to estrange, explicitly characterizing syndicalism as a *revolutionary* tendency inside the international working class movement compared with the outright reformists who wished to pull the Comintern rightwards. While the likes of Scheidemann (the German social democratic leader) might formally accept the principle of the 'party', Trotsky insisted he had more in common with 'American or Spanish or French syndicalists who not only to wish to fight against the bourgeoisie but who, unlike [the reformists], really want to tear its head off'. Recalling his days in Paris during the war he commented:

> I had the opportunity of personally observing … that the first audacious voices against the war – at the very moment when the Germans stood at the gates of Paris – were raised in the ranks of a small group of French syndicalists. These were the voices of my friends – Monatte, Rosmer and others … I felt myself a comrade among comrades in the company of [these] and others with an anarchistic past.[56]

Undoubtedly manipulative leadership practices existed in the Comintern from the beginning, and anti-communist historians have been able to make great play of them. But arguably it was only after 1923 and the Fourth Comintern Congress that they began to become dominant, amidst the complete subsiding of the international revolutionary wave of struggle, the isolation of the Russian revolution, the death of Lenin and the rise of a state bureaucracy around the figure of Stalin. Until then the congresses had been a relatively genuine forum for debate and development of revolutionary strategy and tactics. Only afterwards did the negative critique of

---

54 Murphy, *New Horizons*, p. 129.

55 V.I. Lenin, 'Theses on the Fundamental Tasks of the Second Congress of the Communist International', *Collected Works: Vol. 31* (Moscow, 1966), p. 200; Riddell, pp. 168–71.

56 L. Trotsky, *The First Five Years of the Communist International*, vol. 1 (New Park), p. 98.

syndicalism clearly begin to prevail over the positive appreciation of the movement, although by then it was so far merged with the critique of the Left Opposition and 'Trotskyism' as to lose its specific point.[57]

Another problem with Wayne Thorpe's particular analysis of 'the breach' between syndicalism and Moscow is that his focus on the syndicalists' increasing critique of the apparent dictatorial nature of Bolshevik state power inside Russia means he either only touches on, or completely ignores, a number of other substantive issues of contention that also need to be taken into account in any comprehensive evaluation of the limits and potential of the two competing revolutionary traditions. In particular, he fails to adequately outline and assess the central arguments that underpinned the Bolsheviks' alternative approach, and thereby account for what *attracted* a significant layer of syndicalists to communism.

Other explicitly politically-informed literature on the Comintern and the relationship between communism and syndicalism has also been handicapped with important weaknesses. Official Communist or Stalinist historiography, as practiced in Moscow and within their respective satellite parties internationally, was traditionally dominated by a deferential justification of every twist and turn of the Russian bureaucracy.[58] Paradoxically the attempt made recently by some British historians to flip the coin over and suggest individual national communist parties had considerable political autonomy from the Comintern is equally unconvincing.[59] Even within much of the dissident Trotskyist tradition, that justifiably has emphasised the distinction between the early years of the Comintern and its later Stalinist degeneration, severe problems have persisted. There has been a romanticisation that suggests the 'first four congresses' of the Comintern, those dominated by Lenin and Trotsky, provided some sort of 'model school' of 'correct' strategy and tactics, with all its inadequacies and contradictions effectively removed.[60]

It is only more recently that a more nuanced revolutionary Marxist analysis has begun to emerge, produced by those sympathetic to, but not uncritical of, the early years of the Russian revolution and Communist International and who make a sharp

---

[57] The gulf between the relatively fraternal attitude towards the syndicalists in the early years of the Comintern and the outright Stalinist contempt that later predominated is vividly illustrated in the book *Marx and the Trade Unions* by Alexander Lozovsky (London, 1935).

[58] See R. Palme Dutt, *The Internationale* (London, 1964).

[59] There has been a lively debate on this topic between those who attempt to uncover the British Communist Party's *independence* from Moscow and those who document the extent of political *dependence*. For the independence position see A. Thorpe, 'Comintern "Control" of the Communist Party of Great Britain, 1920–43', *English Historical Review*, vol. 113, no. 452 (1998), pp. 637–68. For the alternative, and undoubtedly more convincing, dependence interpretation see J. McIlroy and A. Campbell, 'New Directions in International Communist Historiography', *Labour History Review*, 68:1 (2003), pp. 3–7. There is a useful summary of the debate by J. Newsinger 'Review Article: Recent Controversies in the History of British Communism', *Journal of Contemporary History*, 4: 3 (2006), pp. 557–72.

[60] G. Novak, D. Frankel and F. Fedlman, *The First Three Internationals: Their History and Lessons* (New York, 1974).

distinction with its later Stalinist development.[61] Such work, while recognising the qualitative advance in revolutionary theory and practice made by the early communist tradition compared with the syndicalist tradition, also acknowledges the ramshackle and improvised quality of much of the early Comintern (in which the pressures of ultra-leftism and reformism repeatedly threatened to drag the organisation off course) and the fallibility of the Bolsheviks.

Synthesis of Traditions?

The shift from syndicalism to communism proved to be a complex and contradictory process. Clearly ex-syndicalists did not simply abandon their syndicalism when they joined their respective communist parties. While specific aspects of the earlier syndicalist movements (notably the anti-party doctrines) were unceremoniously abandoned, other features (workplace organisation, industrial unionism and direct action) were often carried over into the new communist parties (See Chapter 12).[62] Indeed as Larry Peterson has argued, the experiences of *both* industrial militants *and* revolutionary Marxists in Europe and North America at the end of the First World War led them, in different ways, to a re-evaluation of their tactics, goals, ideologies and organisations, resulting in a 'new synthesis of politics and economics'[63] (of revolutionary socialism and industrial struggles) within the Communist International. This synthesis, it is suggested, grew out of both the failures and successes of the industrial movements (of which syndicalism was a central component) during the years 1917–1920. On the one hand, there was a critical reconsideration of the limitations of purely economic tactics by industrial militants and a new unavoidable awareness of the power of the capitalist state; industrial organisation, militant strike tactics and economic strength were now viewed as being simply not enough. On the other hand, there was a new, more positive attitude of revolutionary Marxists towards the importance and potential strength of industrial and trade union struggle to the revolutionary movement, with recognition of the need to unite political forms

---

[61] For example see J. Hinton and R. Hyman, *Trade Unions and Revolution: The Industrial Policies of the Early British Communist Party* (London, 1975); P. Broué, *Historie de l'internationale communiste* 1919–1943 (Paris, 1997); T. Cliff, *Lenin*: *Vol. 4: The Bolsheviks and the World Revolution* (London, 1979); Birchall, 'The Success and Failure'.

[62] This is a process vividly outlined, for example, in the case of French communism by R. Wohl, *French Communism in the Making, 1914–1924* (Stanford, Calif., 1967). Such continuity within Britain is documented in a number of sources, including: L.J. McFarlane, *The British Communist Party: Its Origin and Development until 1929* (London, 1966); M. Woodhouse, 'Syndicalism, Communism and the Trade Unions in Britain, 1910–1926', *Marxist*, 4:3, 1966; J. Klugmann, *History of the Communist Party of Great Britain: Formation and Early Years 1919–1924, Vol. 1* (London, 1968); M. Woodhouse and B. Pearce, *Essays on the History of Communism in Britain* (London 1975); Hinton and Hyman; R. Challinor, *The Origins of British Bolshevism* (London, 1977); T. Cliff and D. Gluckstein, *Marxism and Trade Union Struggle: The General Strike 1926* (London, 1986).

[63] L. Peterson, 'Revolutionary Socialism and Industrial Unrest in the Era of the Winnipeg General Strike: The Origins of Communist Labour Unionism in Europe and North America', *Labour/Le Travail*, 13 (1984), pp. 115–31.

of struggle with the economic militancy of workers. In other words, starting from widely differing positions, these two sides of the workers' movement converged in the course of the struggles of these years.

One of the main factors underpinning the success of the Communist International in establishing its hegemony over the revolutionary left, Peterson has argued, lay in its ability to reinterpret radically the Marxist view of industrial and trade union struggles, to devise a programme and organisation to translate this new view into practice and thereby to attract and incorporate into the communist movement the most dynamic elements of the industrial movements from before 1920. From this perspective, the Comintern was attractive to syndicalists, for example, not just because the success of the Bolshevik Revolution offered them an alternative or because the syndicalists recognised the need to overthrow the capitalist state, but also because the Comintern incorporated much of the programme of the industrial militants into their own communist approach to revolution. Through their participation in the Comintern and RILU the industrial militants saw to it that key elements of their approach were accepted as integral parts of the Communist programme.

Most important was the acceptance by Marxists, for the first time, of an *industrial* component in their strategy for revolution, which comprised a whole series of specific tactics and positions; these included: (a) an uncompromising position in favour of industrial unionism; (b) the organisation of both party and unions based on factory units; (c) emphasis on rank-and-file action; (d) the encouragement of various kinds of extra-union factory councils, rank-and-file committees, and shop stewards' groups; and (e) the active exploitation of industrial unrest for the achievement of both short-term and long-term political goals. Specifically, the Communists advocated a wide range of militant tactics in industrial movements. Hence they included unofficial strikes as important tactical weapons; they advocated use of the sympathetic strike, the expansion of local strike movements to other areas and industries to help create unity of action; they encouraged mass participation in industrial movements through such means as factory assemblies and mass picketing; and they advanced a wide range of demands that went well beyond the narrow economic issues of 'bread and butter' unionism, from immediate economic demands over wages and hours to issues of workplace rules and industrial control, and onto explicitly political questions. Moreover, the Communists cultivated the growth of *workers'* parties under *workers'* leadership, thereby overcoming the objections of many industrial militants towards the domination of social democratic parties by intellectuals of bourgeois origins.

Finally, the Comintern, radically redefined the relationship between the party and the trade unions. This involved changing the relative weight of the two organisations and the structure of their interrelationship. On the one hand, the communists insisted on the leading role of the party over the unions, thereby rejecting the organisational autonomy of unions: the party was to be the decisive and dominating force. On the other hand, the communists attempted to incorporate the rank-and-file leaders of the industrial movements into the structure of the party itself: thereby subjecting such workplace militants to party discipline, but also giving them a say in formulating policy and simultaneously injecting the Communist Party directly into industrial struggles; in the process they re-orientated the entire structure of the party towards industrial action through the creation of factory cells, communist fractions in trade unions and a wide range of industrially-based movements and organisations.[64]

Peterson recognises that each country underwent a different realignment on the left to form new, hybrid communist parties. For example, in France when the revolutionary minority within the CGT left to form the CGTU they inevitably had a profound long-term impact on the structure of French communism, as the new Confédération came under Moscow's influence. Likewise in Britain the convergence of communism and industrial militancy was made easier by the fact that a disproportionate number of Communist leaders came from the SLP, the one Marxist party that had consistently advocated industrial unionism before 1917 and that had been most active in the shop stewards' movement during and after the war. By contrast, in America although the Comintern's programme, tactics and organisation concerning industrial movements converged with that of the 'boring from within' strategy as practiced by the ex-IWW industrial organiser, William Z. Foster, the American communists did not directly carry on the work of the IWW and, in turn, the latter retained their hostility to political parties and refused to engage in a working relationship with the communists.

In making an assessment of Petersons' contribution it is clear his central argument, that there was a *synthesis* of the two traditions of the militant industrial movement (including syndicalism) and revolutionary Marxism, is essentially both justified and accurate. It provides a very important corrective to those commentators, including Wayne Thorpe, who have, by contrast, emphasised the extent to which the syndicalist tradition was rejected wholesale by the communist tradition. It helps to reframe our appreciation of the process by which the communist tradition was not merely transplanting something born in Russia, but evolved out of the earlier industrial movements of which syndicalism had been an important component. Nonetheless, arguably there are a whole series of qualifications and limitations to the analysis which we also need to take into account. To begin with it does not examine in any detail the central points of dispute between the two traditions, the tensions and contradictions that prevented the *bulk* of syndicalists in every country from being won over. Notably, there was the communist critique of trade union autonomy from political parties, and the syndicalist hostility towards the building of a revolutionary vanguard party. In the absence of consideration of such arguments based on antagonistic positions, there is a danger of Peterson presenting the impression of a relatively unproblematic convergence, whereas, of course in reality, there were also formidable divergences, if not incompatibilities.

While both traditions were undoubtedly present in the final mixture that was produced, they were weighted rather differently, with the Marxist contribution much more substantial. It included the need to link up the industrial struggle with an explicit political strategy; to provide a centralised leadership inside the working class movement; to group together the most class-conscious workers into an interventionist revolutionary political party that directed its members' activity within the unions; to view the seizure of state power via insurrection as a prerequisite of the revolutionary overthrow of capitalism; and to view the role of the soviet (rather than the unions) as the economic and political nucleus of a future workers' state. It is

---

[64] Ibid., pp. 123–5.

clear the sheer extent of such Marxist ideas and practice meant that in many respects the transition from syndicalism to communism involved much more of a *break* with past syndicalist ideas and practices than a process of continuity. And it was precisely because this was the case that only *individual* syndicalists, and a minority of them at that, made the leap, rather than any syndicalist *body* as a whole (the only exception to this was the French CGTU, which having split from the CGT, was finally won over to communism from 1923 onwards).

Peterson's analysis also does not really take sufficient account of the extent to which Lenin and the Bolshevik Party's distinctive experience of struggle within Tsarist Russia profoundly influenced and shaped subsequent Communist International and RILU policy with reference to trade unions and industrial struggle, with *both* positive *and* negative consequences. Ironically, although in its early years the Comintern was a power-house for the development of revolutionary strategy and tactics, and drew on a wealth of Russian experience in many fields, trade unionism was not one of these areas.[65] The trade union policies of Lenin and the Comintern struggled to make concrete what had until then been an abstract analysis within the Marxist tradition. They were underpinned by the Marxist conception of the necessity and desirability of class struggle (of which strikes were the primary expression) and of trade unionism as a means of collective resistance to capitalism that could both improve immediate wages and conditions and develop the overall confidence, organisation and class consciousness of workers. But the relationship in practice between communists and non-communist trade unionists was not something that had previously been developed by Marx, Lenin or any other revolutionary socialist.

As a consequence, while the Comintern and RILU congresses affirmed the importance of revolutionaries working within the existing reformist-led trade unions so as to win them to a revolutionary course, there was, as we will see, little detailed practical guidance provided. Moreover, not only was the question of how to overcome the problem of the union bureaucracy barely touched upon, but a good deal of confusion was to be generated by the establishment of a Red International of Labour Unions. Yet the inadequacies of Russian Bolshevik theory in relation to trade union work were understandable in many respects given the Tsarist repressive context in which it emerged, with underdeveloped levels of reformist organisation in terms of both trade unions and political parties. The Bolsheviks probably developed as sophisticated a view of communist work within western European and North American mass reformist and bureaucratic trade union organisations as could be expected of a party for which, in the words of Fernando Claudin, 'the decisive forms of struggle' had been 'extra-parliamentary, and the role played by the trade unions … an extremely modest one'.[66]

Despite such limitations, there *were* undoubtedly some very important advances in the Marxist analysis of the relationship between revolutionaries and trade unions made within the Comintern during its early years. Certainly, on many aspects, the strategy and tactics developed within its early congresses represented a qualitative leap from previous ideas and practices. And, perhaps inevitably so authoritative

---

65 Cliff and Gluckstein, p. 42.

66 F. Claudin, *The Communist Movement* (Markham, 1975), p. 104.

was the Russian Bolshevik Party, because of its role in leading the only successful workers' revolution, that its trade union directives were to have a decisive impact on the subsequent trajectory of a number of the syndicalist movement's most prominent figures. Even though Peterson is justified in highlighting the important element of absorption of the syndicalist tradition, it would be mistaken to underestimate the extent to which the Comintern's programme and policies, based to a large extent on Bolshevik practice, *superseded and transformed* this tradition, albeit with some accompanying confusion and limitations.

While the above qualifications in no way invalidate the validity of Peterson's general notion of a synthesis and realignment on the left, which succeeded in creating a qualitatively new understanding of the relationship between socialism and industrial action, it does mean it is necessary to explore in more detail the tensions, complications and contradictions involved in both traditions and in the transition from syndicalism to communism.

Chapter 7

Trade Unionism

In Russia the trade unions had only come into existence with the revolutions of 1905 and 1917, although individual workers' associations and unions had fought to establish themselves previously. In conditions of illegality even the economic class struggle had become highly politicised, and the unions were structured on industrial lines that tended to avoid the dangers of bureaucracy to a large extent. They proved themselves capable of uniting masses of workers and joining in the revolutionary struggle, albeit initially under Menshevik influence.[1] By contrast, in Europe and America the rise of trade unions had been very much part of the 'normal' expansion of capitalism over many years. Although craft unions had sometimes fought fight bitter battles against employers to achieve economic security, they had tended to restrict themselves to narrow immediate issues and felt no need to generalise their struggle politically or seek to overthrow capitalism. They had also produced a layer of bureaucratic officials who were a conservative block on workers' struggle. It was precisely such limitations which had encouraged the development of revolutionary syndicalist movements in a number of countries. Such differences in the nature of Russian trade unionism compared with the West were not ignored by Lenin:

> The Mensheviks of the West have acquired a much firmer footing in the trade unions; there the craft-union, narrow-minded, selfish, case-hardened, covetous, and petty-bourgeois 'labour aristocracy', imperialist-minded, and imperialist-corrupted, has developed into a much stronger action than in our country.[2]

Nonetheless, Lenin and the Comintern leaders believed that following the impact of war and the Russian Revolution, and within a context of mass industrial unrest, the upsurge in trade union membership and political radicalisation, there had been a qualitative shift in emphasis within many western trade unions. Increasingly the ability of the capitalist system to permit trade unions even limited and temporary gains was being eroded, leading many union members to demand and initiate a more radical response despite the attempted restraint of their leaders. This meant the existing unions could in principle serve a key role in revolutionary class struggle:

> At a certain stage of the development of the capitalist contradictions, the trade unions turn from organs of resistance against separate employers, into organs of attack against the capitalist system as a whole …

---

1 V.E. Bonnell, *Roots of Rebellion: Workers' Politics and Organization in St. Petersburg and Moscow, 1900–1914* (Berkley, Calif., 1988).

2 V.I. Lenin, '"Left-wing" Communism: An Infantile Disorder', *Selected Works*, vol. 3 (Moscow, 1971), p. 316.

> The more acute the struggle between labour and capital becomes, the clearer becomes the aim of the revolutionary wing of the labour movement. The trade unions must transform themselves from organs of self-defence within the capitalist system to organs for the overthrow of the capitalist rule, and the establishment of the Dictatorship of the Proletariat.[3]

The role of syndicalists in explicitly attempting to radicalise trade unions into instruments of revolution was viewed as a welcome, albeit limited, reflection of this overall process. But although the Comintern leaders acknowledged, and sometimes enthused about, the potential revolutionary role of trade unionism, they also stressed their limitations and argued that on their own trade unions could not be the vehicle of capitalism's abolition. Hence the insistence on the importance of *political* methods of struggle and political parties. As we shall see in subsequent chapters, the Comintern leaders insisted that while trade unionism's maximum economic weapon, the strike (or general strike) could win improvements in wages and working conditions, it could never overthrow a *social régime*. That would require the political conquest of state power via an insurrection, with the soviet (rather than the trade unions) the chief organ of workers' power. In the process a revolutionary vanguard party was needed that would not only supplement but also transcend the trade unions. By contrast, the syndicalists, although aware of the imperfections of existing trade union forms of organisation, nonetheless believed that reconstructed revolutionary unions could provide both the main agency for the transformation of society as well as the instrument by which a new society could be governed.

The contrast between syndicalist and communist conceptions of the relationship between revolutionaries and the trade unions, and the inherent tensions within the whole concept of revolutionary unionism, can be explored within two different areas: namely the specific debate within the Comintern and RILU as to whether to fight inside the existing reformist unions or break away to form alternative revolutionary bodies; and the more general problem of the inbuilt pressures of reformism on even revolutionary union bodies. The related problem of the union bureaucracy is examined in Chapter 8.

Conquering the Existing Unions

The Bolshevik leaders propagated within the Comintern the pressing need for revolutionaries across the world to 'conquer the trade unions', to win over the mass of leftward-moving workers within the *existing* reformist trade unions to the battle to overthrow capitalism.[4] This required revolutionaries joining such unions in all countries, immersing themselves in the day-to-day economic struggles of workers, proving themselves to be the best fighters on trade union matters, and using this to politicise the trade union struggle so as to win the majority of workers to the necessity of workers' revolution. But it also meant opposing the setting up of *separate*

---

3 *Resolutions and Decisions of the Second World Congress of the Red International of Labour Unions, 19 November to 2 December 1922* (London, 1923).

4 *Second Congress of the Communist International: Minutes of the Proceedings, Vol. 2* (London, 1977), p. 69.

revolutionary unions. As the *Theses on the Trade Union Movement* adopted at the Second Comintern Congress declared:

> All voluntary withdrawals [from the existing unions], every artificial attempt to organise special unions ... represent a grave danger to the Communist movement. It threatens to hand over the most advanced, the most conscious workers to the opportunist leaders, playing in to the hands of the bourgeoisie ... Communist[s have to learn to be] not only preachers of the ideas of communism, but also the most determined leaders of the economic struggle of the labour unions. Only in this way will it be possible to remove from the unions their opportunist leaders, only in this way will the communists be able to take the lead in the trade union movement and make of it an organ of the revolutionary struggle for communism.[5]

Likewise an entire chapter of Lenin's *Left-Wing Communism*, aimed primarily at the 'ultra-left' within the communist movement but also at those in the syndicalist tradition, insisted that revolutionaries had to 'learn how to work legally in the ... most reactionary of trade unions'.[6] To withdraw from the official unions 'because of the reactionary and counter-revolutionary character of the trade union top leadership' and set up small but revolutionary unions was 'the greatest service Communists could render the bourgeoisie'. Communists should establish communist groups in all the trade unions, help construct factory committees, win support for radical demands and aspirations, and dislodge the 'opportunist' leaders, thereby bringing the mass trade union bodies under communist leadership.[7]

Robust opposition to this policy of permeating the existing reformist unions was mounted by British shop stewards' delegates to the Comintern. Willie Gallacher commented it was 'simply nonsense and ridiculous to talk of conquering the old trade unions with their ossified bureaucracy'. Emphasising the significance of the powerful independent shop stewards' movement that had been built up in Britain, Gallagher insisted:

> One can bring the masses into motion through agitation under the flag of a left-wing trade union organisation not only inside but also outside these trade unions. We have been active in the British trade unions for 25 years without ever having succeeded in revolutionising the trade unions from inside.[8]

Likewise American communist delegates (including John Reed), echoing the arguments of their IWW counterparts, insisted it was the impossibility of progressing within the existing AFL organisations that made dual unionism necessary; to work within the 'reactionary' AFL would only corrupt the fighting spirit of the revolutionary workers. They protested that the Comintern's policy of effectively only 'permitting' IWW unions to organise in those industries in which no AFL union operated (such as lumber and agriculture) threatened to strike a death blow to the IWW's very existence as an alternative central revolutionary union body. But at the Third Comintern Congress in July 1921, the fight against 'dual unionism' was

5 *Second Congress*, pp. 279–80.
6 *'Left-wing' Communism*, p. 295.
7 *Second Congress*, p. 281.
8 Ibid., p. 167.

continued and deepened in a context in which original optimistic expectations of rapid communist advance had been confounded by the partial stabilisation of the European capitalist economy, the ebbing of working class struggle and the continued strength of reformism. Working class retreat had been symbolised by the failure of the premature offensive known as the 'March Action', launched by the German Communist Party, and the failure of the French, Italian and British Communist Parties to win mass support. This meant, it was argued, that the task of revolutionaries was not to immediately prepare to seize state power, but to attempt to increase their influence inside the working class movement, starting first and foremost from *within* the old trade unions.

As a result, the Comintern came out much harder against the IWW's strategy, despite the protests of Bill Haywood,[9] and at the contemporaneous founding RILU Congress a resolution on the questions of tactics was approved over the objections of George Williams:[10]

> The IWW, an independent organisation in America, is too weak to take the place of the old labour unions … Therefore, the question of creating revolutionary cells and groups inside the American Federation of Labor is of vital importance. There is no other way by which one could gain the working mass in America than to lead a systematic struggle within the unions.[11]

While many of the points raised by Gallacher, Haywood, Williams and others were viewed by the Comintern leaders as 'ultra-left', underestimating the potential for, and importance of, consistent work by revolutionaries within the existing reformist unions, the searching points these critics raised concerning the difficulty of combating the reformist trade union bureaucracy within more advanced countries appeared to be simply ignored by their Russian comrades.[12] Yet significantly, on the basis that there was no Comintern insistence on the dissolution of the CNT, and a rather ambiguous attitude was adopted towards the USI, syndicalist (and communist) delegates from Spain and Italy to Moscow raised little formal objections to the policy. No doubt the Comintern leaders took into account two features. First, although in both countries separate revolutionary union confederations vied for the allegiance and organisation of workers in competition with the existing reformist-dominated bodies, the relative size of both syndicalist bodies vis-à-vis their reformist counterparts was comparable (something which, of course, was in marked contrast to the dwarfing of the IWW by the AFL and the shop stewards' movement by TUC unions). Second, the Spanish and Italian syndicalists *did* essentially operate inside the existing unions and Chambers of Labour at local level. Meanwhile, in France, the revolutionary syndicalist minority remained committed to fighting for influence *inside* the reformist-led CGT,

---

9 *The Third Congress of the Communist International* (London, 1922), pp. 141–2.

10 *The First Congress of the Red Trades Union International at Moscow, 1921: A Report of the Proceedings by George Williams, Delegate from the IWW* (Chicago, 1921).

11 *Resolutions and Decisions of the First International Congress of Revolutionary Trade and Industrial Unions* (Chicago, 1921), p. 30.

12 T. Cliff and D. Gluckstein, *Marxism and Trade Union Struggle: The General Strike of 1926* (London, 1986), p. 44.

rather than (for the moment at least) advocate a conscious breakaway; and in Ireland although the ITGWU had originated from a breakaway from a British-dominated union, it had no real competitor.

Nonetheless, by the end of 1922 the RILU was campaigning in Spain for communist oppositional minorities in both the CNT and the socialist-led confederation (and independent unions) to co-ordinate their activities within mixed Councils of Action, with the aim of creating one trade union centre which would unite all workers and propagate the principles and methods of the Red International. Likewise in Italy, it advocated the need to conduct a persistent struggle for the unification of all trade union organisations, with the adherents of the RILU creating Alliances of Labour with local branches as a transitional form of unity.[13] Ironically in France the mass expulsion of the revolutionary syndicalist minority inside the CGT and regroupment of those excluded into a new confederation, the CGTU, demonstrated in sharp relief some of the tensions inherent in the Comintern's policy of conquering the existing unions.

Ambiguities of the Red International

The establishment of the Red International undoubtedly proved to be problematic as far as Moscow's attempted embrace of the syndicalists was concerned. Quite apart from the argument over the nature of the relationship between the new trade union International and the Comintern, there was the ambiguous nature on which the RILU was set up. J.T. Murphy claimed that had there been the slightest suggestion of 'splitting' the trade unions, it would not have received support from within the British trade union movement.[14] Yet as Jack Tanner justifiably pointed out, it was highly inconsistent to urge communists and syndicalists alike to stay inside the old, reformist Amsterdam unions on a *national* level, whilst at the same time attempting to break them from Amsterdam in favour of an alternative revolutionary trade union body based in Moscow on an *international level*.[15] Indeed, those revolutionaries who were to become active in organisations belonging to the Amsterdam International were to be accused by their opponents of double membership: they belonged to two different, antagonistic, bodies. The strategy was to prove confusing for communists and syndicalists alike.

But there was a much more fundamental fault-line underlying the entire RILU project, which also undermined Moscow's wooing of the syndicalist movement. As we have seen, the strategy of attempting to be an official mass trade union International committed to communism had depended on the hope that, in the short term, trade unions could be conquered wholesale or substantial sections split off. It assumed that within conditions of massive economic and political crisis the unions could be turned into instruments of revolutionary struggle, with union leaders either forced to change by pressure from below or being replaced by communists. In other words, RILU was quintessentially an organisation based on the assessment

---

13 *Resolutions and Decisions of the Second World Congress of the RILU* (London, 1923), pp. 13–14.

14 J.T. Murphy, *New Horizons* (London, 1941), p. 158.

15 *Second Congress*, p. 81.

of the period as being one of profound radicalisation and revolutionary potential. Only at the Fifth Comintern Congress in 1924 did Zinoviev belatedly admit that no sooner had the RILU been created than a decline in revolutionary workers' struggles occurred, with developments 'much slower than we had anticipated'.[16] The retreat was such that as early as the end of 1921 the Comintern felt it necessary to adopt new 'united front' tactics which required the RILU to actually attempt to co-operate with the very Amsterdam International it had initially been set up to destroy.

Notwithstanding its grandiose membership claims, Moscow was primarily only able to bring party trade union fractions into the new International, with many existing national trade union centres remaining loyal to Amsterdam.[17] Although the Italian socialist-led confederation flirted with the RILU it never actually joined it. With the exception of the CGTU it only really succeeded outside Western Europe, in countries with low industrialisation and repressive regimes which tended to force workers' economic organisations to ally more closely with their respective communist parties than in the West.[18] As Reiner Tosstorff has noted:

> The original conception of the RILU as an alliance of Communists and syndicalists was ended soon after its foundation. Either the syndicalists withdrew out of fundamental opposition to Communist ideas, or they joined the Communist Parties in various countries. A separate syndicalist current within the RILU ceased to exist after its Second Congress in 1922. The RILU became a unitary, politically homogeneous organisation … almost automatically tied to the resolutions of the Comintern and the Soviet party which increasingly dominated it.[19]

Despite such tensions within Comintern and RILU policy, what assessment can be made of the IWW's refusal to abandon the strategy of dual unionism? Undoubtedly one of the crucial weaknesses of the Wobblies was their failure to take with them from the outset any mass trade union body, besides the Western Federation of Miners which anyway soon left them. While they succeeded in building a credible revolutionary union organisation in certain industries and work contexts, their gains were generally limited and often of a transitory nature. Moreover, if in the past, during a relatively more 'peaceful' period of development, IWW attempts to operate within the AFL had proved impossible, the situation was considerably transformed under the impact of war and post-war economic crisis, exemplified by the influx of over 2 million new workers into the AFL's ranks and the growing willingness of union members in a variety of different important industries to engage in strike action. Ironically,

---

16 *International Trade Union Unity* (London, 1925), pp. 17–18.

17 J.T. Murphy, *The 'Reds' in Congress: Preliminary Report of the First World Congress of the Red International of Trade and Industrial Unions* (London, 1921), p.8; Cliff and Gluckstein, p. 47; R. Darlington, *The Political Trajectory of J.T. Murphy* (Liverpool, 1998), p. 94.

18 R. Tosstorff, *Profintern: Die Rote Gewerkschaftsinterntionale, 1920–1937* (Paderborn, 2004).

19 Tosstorff, 'Moscow versus Amsterdam: Reflections on the History of the Profintern', *Labour History Review*, 68:1, p. 84. From November 1922 to 1927 the communists unsuccessfully attempted to bring about a merger of the RILU and the Amsterdam International, before pushing it into a disastrous Stalin-inspired ultra-left phase during 1928–1934, and then finally winding up the discredited International in 1937.

despite the formidable obstacles presented by the AFL's reactionary leadership, the membership of AFL unions contained the majority of class-conscious workers in America. Indeed Socialist Party members, who had chosen *not* to ignore the AFL, succeeded in making some political advances in AFL affiliates such as the United Mine Workers. In other words, there may have been possibilities, at least in certain AFL unions, for IWW members to have built some influence from within, had they made a determined attempt. Instead, the IWW's fear that the Cominern's strategy necessarily implied dissolution of the IWW itself meant they were not prepared to countenance the possibility of combining revolutionary work in the old reformist unions with work from the outside in revolutionary bodies where appropriate. Even so, the British shop stewards' leaders and the American communists, as well as a sizeable layer of rank-and-file IWW members, were eventually to come around to accepting this strategy and attempting to practically implement it within their respective countries.

Such an outcome vindicated the 'boring from within' approach of the American syndicalist dissident William Z. Foster, whose central argument had been that it was necessary for a 'militant minority' of syndicalists to bore within the AFL unions in order to push them along the revolutionary road that workers' struggle was propelling them. He had pointed to the craft unions in the building trades, metalworking, railroad, and garment industries as obvious candidates for amalgamation, and envisaged 'proto-industrial' federations of craft unions that would increase organised labour's strength until it would be in a position to overthrow capitalism. Towards this end Foster had set up the Syndicalist League of North America (1912–1914), the International Trade Union Educational League (1915–1917) and the Trade Union Education League (from 1920).

Significantly, by adopting such a 'boring from within' approach Foster's supporters were relatively successful in winning influence in local labour movements (mainly in Chicago) and creating alliances with a broad range of progressive trade unionists (although there were probably only around 2,000 members of Foster's organisation).[20] Foster proved to be a brilliant organiser and strike strategist, leading strike movements of unskilled workers in the meat-packing (1918) and steel (1919) industries in which, despite resounding defeats, many thousands of workers were unionised against the fierce opposition of employers. Such campaigns represented the first national efforts to unionise unskilled workers in basic industry, a project the AFL had studiously avoided up to this point and the IWW had not managed either, despite its vigorous efforts. In the process of creating centralised structures that were equal to the task, Foster and his colleagues also took a giant step beyond craft unionism and towards industrial organisation.[21]

When in 1921 the Comintern opened its international campaign for minority movements inside the existing unions, Foster and a number of his supporters rapidly moved towards communism, and the Trade Union Education League became from

---

[20] E.P. Johanningsmeier, *Forging American Communism: The Life of William Z. Foster* (Princeton, 1994), p. 71.

[21] E.P. Johanningsmeir, 'William Z. Foster and the Syndicalist League of North America', *Labor History*, 30:3 (1989), pp. 329–53; idem,. *Forging American Communism*; J.R. Barrett, *William Z. Foster and the Tragedy of American Radicalism* (Chicago, 1999).

1922 onwards the American section of RILU with Foster as the main director of the Communist Party's trade union activities. In effect, Foster's style of syndicalism, which foreshadowed ideas and strategies later embodied in the early American Communist Party, probably made it easier for many IWW members, as well as those syndicalists not attached to the Wobblies, to embrace communism. On this basis the Comintern's advice to syndicalists and communists alike not to isolate themselves from the mass of organised workers, but join the existing reformist unions so as to build them up and inspire them with the spirit of militant struggle, appeared well founded. But there were also problems inherent in the 'boring from within' approach which need examination.

Contradictory Roles

From Moscow's perspective there was undoubtedly a general underlying tension at the heart of the syndicalist conception of revolutionary unionism itself, albeit one which was not explicitly formulated by Comintern leaders at the time. This concerns the inherent contradiction between the syndicalist conception of unions as the chief instruments for revolutionary change, on the one hand, and the pressure of reformism and the structural tendencies to incorporate trade unions within capitalism as permanent bargaining agents and mediators of conflict, on the other. In other words, the problem that confronted the syndicalists, and which arguably they never satisfactory resolved, was how, in practice, to combine their declared aims of conducting a state of permanent war against capitalist society with the pursuit of immediate and limited improvements for workers.

Nowhere was this to become more apparent than in France where the CGT come under constant pressure to adapt to their circumstances, to interpret 'direct action' not necessarily as the revolutionary general strike but as merely the use of industrial force to wrest concessions from the capitalist system. Thus, although the most pressing demands of the *syndicats* (such as agitation for the 8-hour day) were promoted as steps towards emancipation and the partial expropriation of the capitalist class, in practice they increasingly became pursued for their own sake, as ends in themselves rather than as episodes in a permanent revolution. The CGT's leadership, unwilling to sacrifice their often expressed revolutionary ideals, were forced to interpret reformist activity so that it fitted into their own philosophy. As the historian Louis Levine commented in 1912: 'The struggle for immediate gains is a necessity which they must make a virtue of while waiting for the hoped for final struggle.'[22] As a consequence, the revolutionary syndicalism of the pre-war CGT was transformed from 1910 onwards into the advocacy of social amelioration through collective bargaining and legislation.

It was not only the successive defeat of a number of large-scale CGT-led strikes from 1906 onwards, that sapped workers' fighting strength and contributed to the

[22] L. Levine, *The Labor Movement in France: A Study in Revolutionary Syndicalism* (London, 1912), p. 201.

stagnation in CGT membership, which encouraged such a transformation.[23] The CGT also began to change as a result of employers' more conciliatory initiatives, with the widespread extension of collective bargaining arrangements to most major industries encouraging a number of Confédération leaders, who had previously opposed collective agreements as contrary to class war, to turn to vigorous advocacy of negotiation.[24] Indeed the prospect of potentially fruitful negotiations helped to dampen union militancy and increasingly prevented strikes from breaking out altogether. In the process the CGT's affiliates built up their organisational resources, including formal strike funds, and attempted to develop a more professional union leadership. The CGT leadership's willingness in 1914 to participate in the *union sacrée* further encouraged the abandonment of a class and revolutionary perspective in favour of a national corporatist approach.

However, there is little real evidence that among those who held aloft the revolutionary syndicalist flag within the CGT, and who subsequently split away to form the CGTU, there was any serious questioning of the contradictory pressures that appeared to impact on even revolutionary unionism within capitalism. The assumption was that the trajectory of the syndicalist movement in France had been an exception, compared with elsewhere; that the early years of the CGT (and the new CGTU project) led by 'genuine' revolutionaries proved the efficacy of revolutionary unionism. It was the question of union *leadership* that was central, not the nature of trade unionism under capitalism as such. Such an analysis also underpinned the Comintern leaders' policy of communists 'capturing' the unions and thereby turning them into genuine revolutionary bodies. In other words, arguably *both* syndicalist *and* communist traditions underestimated the powerful reformist impulse of trade unionism generally.

If reformist pressures on the IWW were nowhere near as marked this did not mean there were not similar underlying tensions at work. As James Cannon was later to argue:

> one of the most important contradictions at the heart of the IWW was its attempt to combine the dual role of being *both* a revolutionary organisation *and* a trade union.[25] Two different tasks and functions which at a certain stage of development required separate and distinct organisations were assumed by the IWW alone; and this duality effectively hampered its effectiveness in *both* fields.[26]

---

[23] B. Mitchell, *The Practical Revolutionaries: A New Interpretation of the French Anarchsyndicalists* (New York, 1987), pp. 499–500.

[24] Confédération Générale du Travail, *XVIII(e) congrès national corporatif XII(e). Compte rendu des travaux (Le Havre, 1912)*, p. 305. Statement by Renard, president of the Textile Federation.

[25] J.P. Cannon, *The IWW: The Great Anticipation* (New York, 1956), p. 15. A similar argument has been advanced by many subsequent writers, including P.S. Foner, *History of the Labor Movement in the United States, Vol. 4: The Industrial Workers of the World 1905–1917* (New York, 1965), pp. 462–472 and A.S. Kraditor, *The Radical Persuasion, 1890–1917: Aspects of the Intellectual History and the Historiography of Three American Radical Organizations* (Baton Rouge, Louisiana, 1981), pp. 26–33.

[26] Cannon, p. 16.

On the one hand, the IWW's leadership of numerous strikes demonstrated its genuine commitment to the improvement of workers' immediate conditions and the redress of specific grievances. And in attempting to build revolutionary trade unionism, IWW agitators utilised immediate issues of concern as the take-off point for a full-scale indictment of the capitalist system and projection of the need for the revolutionary overthrow of capitalism. On the other hand, the problem which confronted the Wobblies was that if they were to build a functioning industrial union they would have to recruit masses of workers, many of whom might not (at least for some time) understand or agree with their revolutionary programme. Such non-revolutionary workers would join the IWW for essentially the same reasons they might join AFL-affiliated unions (albeit on the basis of a much more militant stance): to obtain higher wages, better working conditions and shorter hours. Of course in practice the Wobblies *did* make a real attempt to encourage *any* worker who wanted union organisation to join the IWW, regardless of their views on any other question. And on occasion, around different strikes and campaigns in various localities, an all-inclusive *mass* membership was attained.

But the underlying dilemma was reflected in the way the IWW's activity tended to be sporadic, flaring up wherever there was a strike or free speech campaign, but dying down and moving elsewhere just as quickly, leaving little trace of any permanent organisation behind. One contemporary observer of the Wobblies noted: 'No one uses the word "organisation" oftener and practices it less.'[27] In effect, outside of strike periods, IWW leaders were not directly concerned with the bread-and-butter shopfloor questions or meeting management on a day-to-day basis to negotiate for better conditions. As a result after every strike IWW membership tended to settle down again to the die-hard revolutionary cadre united on the basis of principle, and stable union organisation was not maintained to protect the economic interests of their erstwhile followers. The problem was created by the conjunction of *agitational* and *organisational* motives in the same body of strategy; the former dictated that strikes were used as an instrument of propaganda to instill revolutionary sentiments; the latter emphasised their use as means of building and then maintaining a functioning trade union apparatus.[28] The two functions were confused and activities that were logical and necessary on a trade union front were rejected because they conflicted with revolutionary aims.

For example, a consequence of the IWW's refusal to engage in conventional trade union procedures by signing collective bargaining agreements with employers was that the stability of the union became impossible: 'If the IWW could not negotiate with employers, how could it raise wages or improve working conditions? If it could offer its members nothing but perpetual industrial warfare, how could it maintain its membership, let alone increase its ranks?'[29] Ironically, while the refusal to sign agreements was justified, in part, as a means of keeping

---

[27] J.G. Brooks, *American Syndicalism* (New York, 1913), p. 175.

[28] A. Kornhauser, R. Dubin and A.M. Ross (eds), *Industrial Conflict* (New York, 1954), p. 29.

[29] M. Dubofsky, *We Shall Be All: A History of the Industrial Workers of the World* (Chicago, 1969), p. 165.

the employers off balance, experience proved it had the opposite effect of enabling them to use it to their advantage by rationalising their own resistance to any form of collective bargaining. While the IWW advocated the permanent mobilisation of workers to wage the class struggle, many workers were not prepared to enlist in a permanent confrontation with their employers; they wanted what collective bargaining and agreements could obtain. Other IWW practices which also made for union instability were the refusal to agree to the check-off (which could have guaranteed a stable income and job control through steady membership) and its low initiation fees and dues, all of which kept union funds pitifully small and undermined its ability to conduct a prolonged organising drive.

In other words, although the IWW could sometimes lead successful militant strikes, it found it difficult to combine the dual roles of being *both* a revolutionary organisation *and* a trade union. Although for brief periods they succeeded in building a mass membership in certain workplaces and locations, it was always temporary, rising and falling with the level of workers' militancy. None of the great struggles left the IWW with a continuing organisation, particularly in the mass production industries of the East. For example, at the end of the Lawrence textile workers' strike in 1912 the IWW had recruited 16,000 new members into the union 'local', but a few months later membership had dwindled to about 700.[30]

In partial recognition of the problem the 1916 IWW convention marked a decisive change in the history of the organisation. Experience of industrial disputes had shown that if the IWW was to grow it must transform itself from a purely revolutionary propaganda and guerrilla body into an ordinary union, with all the responsibilities and compromises a permanent mass membership would impose. As a result, the flamboyant agitators, strikes leaders and propagandists of its past were replaced by less well known but more effective labour organisers. The Wobblies increasingly addressed themselves to the problem of how to secure higher wages and shorter hours, improved conditions of work and job security and said less and less about the revolution to come 'in the sweet bye-and-bye'.

For example, with the formation of the Agricultural Workers' Organisation (AWO) in 1915 the IWW began to make a significant move away from its previous style of organising amongst migratory labourers, in which it had concentrated on spreading propaganda through free speech campaigns and the promotion of spontaneous strikes. Unable to improve working conditions or build a permanent union base merely through such methods, the Wobblies now introduced a higher union initiation fee and attempted to establish job control in many farm districts where employers observed union wage rates and hours under collective bargaining contracts. The AWO leaders realised the only way to recruit the lumber worker was 'by showing him the immediate necessity of the union and its ability, not to display him a picture of an ideal state in the dim, distant future, but to produce the "goods" here and now'.[31] This organising approach was subsequently generalised across the rest of the IWW, thereby contributing to the spectacular growth of union membership that occurred.

[30] Foner, p. 349.

[31] Cited in Dubofsky, *We Shall be All*, p. 334.

Such a move contained its own potential problems, given that by sanctioning union recognition and collective bargaining as a means of improving its members' lives, there was the danger of forsaking revolutionary goals and adhering to the well-established AFL pattern. In practice, unlike their French counterparts, Bill Haywood and other Wobbly leaders displayed no inclination of making peace with American capitalism. But while they were still dedicated to the concept of revolution, they increasingly came to realise that in order to build durable unions they would have to grapple with the contradiction of leading the organisation into a working relationship with employers, public officials and society with whom they claimed to be at loggerheads on principle.[32] It was only America's entry into the war and the wave of state repression that was unleashed against the IWW which prevented this evolving process from deepening and potentially resulting in the establishment of long-tenured officials and a permanent union bureaucracy. Even though such a trend is unlikely to have gone as far as that of the CGT in France, it could possibly have resembled the way the CIO of the 1930s later turned out to be.[33]

According to Melyvn Dubofsky a central dilemma was that if the IWW operated primarily as a *revolutionary organisation*, it was likely to gain only a few recruits and possess little effective shopfloor industrial power. But if it operated primarily as a *trade union* and moderated its stance so as to draw in wider layers of workers, it would threaten its revolutionary fervour.[34] Arguably, the latter is more convincing than the latter. Yet undoubtedly the irony was that in the long run any success the IWW had in fulfilling one function undermined their efforts to fulfill the other, and trying to combine them had the effect of undermining its effectiveness in both fields.

A vivid illustration of the pressure of reformism affecting syndicalist practice within America was to be seen in terms of William Z. Foster's trajectory within the AFL as part of his 'boring from within' strategy. In 1916 Foster had written a treatise entitled *Trade Unionism: The Road to Freedom*, which was the only formal statement of policy issued by his new organisation at the time, the International Trade Union Educational League (ITUEL). In this booklet, he had apotheosised the function of American trade unions. Regardless of whether they were organised along craft or industrial lines, or whether or not there was any degree of class consciousness among their members, the trade unions were by their 'very nature driven on to the revolutionary goal'.[35] As Edward Johanningsmeier has explained, the logic of Foster's position was to imply that, if trade unions were moving automatically towards revolution, then it was possible to work for purely trade union ends without compromising radical goals. Thus, Foster's syndicalism gradually emerged reformulated as a structuralism in which the rhetorical importance of revolution became secondary.[36] For example, during the 1919 national steel strike, in which Foster played a central militant leadership role, his syndicalist philosophy and association was even publicly denied and he refused to criticise the

[32] M. Dubofsky, *'Big Bill' Haywood* (Manchester, 1987), p. 93.

[33] J.R. Conlin (ed.), *At the Point of Production: The Local History of the IWW* (Westport: Conn., 1969).

[34] *We Shall be All*, p. 334.

[35] W.Z. Foster, *Trade Unionism: The Road to Freedom* (Chicago, 1916).

[36] *Forging American Communism*, pp. 88–9.

conduct of moderate AFL officials. Ironically, it was at the very point of his highest visibility in American life as a radical with a political identity that he came closest to disappearing. 'I have no teachings or principles' he pleaded. 'I apply the principles of the American Federation of Labor as best I understand them'.[37]

Meanwhile, even in countries such as Spain, where the CNT wanted to maintain a constant war with the employers and government, there were significant (albeit less marked) reformist pressures to accommodate to the system. While syndicalist and anarcho-syndicalist activists were able to fire worker enthusiasm and mobilise wide-ranging support, their all-or-nothing tactics also sometimes resulted in a series of total defeats and invited state repression. Such setbacks strengthened the hands of more moderate syndicalists who won influence on the basis that they should concentrate on the improvement of working conditions rather than being carried away by premature revolutionary adventures, with the overthrow of capital postponed to sometime in the future. Likewise they successfully insisted that to gain or maintain a mass membership, the CNT had to forego its principles and accept collective agreements with employers. This tendency towards negotiation led to the emergence of a nascent union bureaucracy inside the post-1916 CNT, with anarcho-syndicalists elements resenting the willingness of moderate syndicalists to respond to the conciliatory overtures of the government and enter into a dialogue with the bourgeois enemy. However, such pressures towards reformism were counteracted by the fact that the CNT often found itself confronting employers and political authorities too recalcitrant to buy them off with concessions, particularly in the immediate post-war context and Civil War period. In such circumstances, union organisers remained much more militant than their reformist socialist counterparts and it proved almost impossible to control Confederación bodies that grew at breakneck speed and were flooded by previously non-unionised and radicalised workers. A similar process of reformist and bureaucratic pressures being undermined by combative circumstances operated in Italy. Even so in both countries, as elsewhere, the existences of such tensions underlined the limitations of trade unionism as a self-sufficient instrument of revolution.

Strengths and Limitations

In conclusion the Communist International's explicit and implicit critique of the syndicalist conception of revolutionary unionism undoubtedly contributed to the overall ideological and political process of reflection that led key syndicalist figures towards communism. Certainly the Comintern appears to have been justified in pointing out to syndicalists, particularly the IWW, the need to operate inside the existing unions. Not only did such unions contain a significant section of the working class movement but, in conditions of economic and political upheaval, their members were being radicalised, thereby opening up serious opportunities for revolutionaries to win influence. But the Comintern, or at least important elements within it, notably Zinoviev and Radek, were also insensitive in their handling of the issue and failed to provide sufficient concrete guidance that took into consideration

---

[37] *Trade Unionism*, pp. 142–3.

varying circumstances in different countries. And while the Red International of Labour Unions project was thought to be a useful and necessary means of pulling militant trade unionists towards revolutionary politics, it also confused matters enormously both in terms of encouraging syndicalists to work alongside reformist-influenced workers in order to win them over politically and in cementing syndicalist-communist united activity against the conservative leaders of the labour movement.

Underlying such dilemmas was the fundamental question of the limitations of revolutionary unionism *per se*. Ironically the Comintern's emphasis on the insufficiency of trade unionism as an instrument of revolution was considerably undermined by its own ambiguity on whether the unions *could* be transformed into revolutionary bodies under the correct (communist) leadership. While in general theoretical terms there was an understanding of the changing nature of trade unionism under capitalism in different contexts, the contradictory nature of such organisations, at one and the same time agencies of *both* conflict *and* accommodation, appears to have eluded them. As a consequence, the crucial problem of how to challenge and overcome the conservative and counter-revolutionary role of the trade union bureaucracy was also not satisfactorily resolved, as Chapter 8 explores.

Chapter 8

Union Bureaucracy

The dilemmas of union officialdom were recognised by a variety of different commentators within and outside the labour movement internationally during the early twentieth century. In Britain, the Webbs were one of the first to draw attention to the growth of a layer of full-time officials: 'a shifting of the leadership in the trade union world from the casual enthusiast and irresponsible agitator to a class of permanent salaried officers expressly chosen out of the rank and file of trade unionists for their superior business capacity'.[1] The development of what they termed a trade union 'bureaucracy',[2] a 'Civil Service of the Trade Union world',[3] was viewed as being a direct result of the spread of national collective bargaining and conciliation machinery which accompanied the expansion in trade union membership and moves towards union amalgamation that occurred. But if the Webbs were broadly supportive of such union officialdom, others were much more critical.

Rosa Luxemburg, drawing on her experience of the German labour movement, developed a theory of the bureaucratic and conservative nature of trade union officials:

> The specialisation of professional activity of trade union leaders, as well as the naturally restricted horizons which is bound up with disconnected economic struggles in a peaceful period, leads only too easily, amongst trade union officials, to bureaucratism and a certain narrowness of outlook ... There is first of all the over-valuation of the organisation, which from a means has gradually been changed into an end in itself, a precious thing, to which the interests of the struggles should be subordinated. From this also comes that openly admitted need for peace which shrinks from great risks and presumed dangers to the stability of the trade unions, and further, the over-valuation of the trade union method of struggle itself, its prospects and its successes.[4]

Likewise Antonio Gramsci, sharing the widespread contempt for this stratum of full-time professional trade union officials held by many industrial militants in Italy, focused on their collective bargaining function, which perpetuated an 'industrial legality' developed in the accumulated compromises with the employers, to explain their profound conservativism: 'These men no longer live for the class struggle,

---

[1] S. and B. Webb, *History of Trade Unionism 1666–1920* (London, 1919), p. 204.

[2] S. and B. Webb, *Industrial Democracy* (London, 1920), p. 28.

[3] Webbs, *History of Trade Unionism,* p. 466.

[4] R. Luxemburg, *The Mass Strike, the Political Party and the Trade Unions* (London, 1986 [first published 1906]), pp. 87–8.

no longer feel the same passions, the same desires, the same hopes as the masses. Between them and the masses an unbridgeable gap has opened up.'[5]

There were varying assessments as to the extent to which the limitations of trade union officialdom could be overcome by workers' struggles. On the one hand, Robert Michels, a former member of the German Social Democratic Party, developed a pessimistic' iron law of oligarchy' thesis, concluding that because of their need to develop an effective system of internal administration trade unions (and all voluntary democratic organisations) tended towards an oligarchical style of government, with power and influence exercised by a minority over the majority. The practical implications was that little could be done by grassroots union members to change this situation even if they wanted to, and syndicalist organisations themselves were not immune from such oligarchical tendencies.[6] By contrast, Rosa Luxemburg, emphasising the explosive potential spontaneous militancy of the working class (as displayed in the 1905 Russian Revolution), optimistically predicted that even if bureaucratic and conservative trade union officials attempted to restrain the struggle, the upsurge of the masses would ultimately sweep them aside.[7]

In Tsarist Russia, Lenin and the Bolsheviks' experience of reformist and bureaucratic leadership within trade unions, in the context of fierce state repression of independent workers' organisations, had been very limited. Nonetheless, the Comintern was very much aware of its obstruction to the transformation of the unions into revolutionary bodies:

> The old trade union bureaucracy ... breaks up the powerful stream of the labour movement into weak streamlets, substitutes partial reformist demands for the general revolutionary aims of the movement, and on the whole retards the transformation of the struggle of the proletariat into a revolutionary struggle for the annihilation of capitalism.[8]

Despite such obstacles the Comintern assumed, like Luxemburg, that in the context of revolutionary workers' struggles ushered in the wake of October 1917, the trade unions could be transformed into instruments of revolutionary struggle – with union leaders either forced to change by pressure from below, or driven out and replaced by communists.[9] However, beyond broad appeals to organise 'communist cells within trade unions' and to support factory committees that could fight 'the counter-revolutionary tendencies of the trade union bureaucracy',[10] there was no detailed practical guidance provided. Significantly, there was an insistence on the possibility, even more the imperative necessity, of being able to completely transform the

---

[5] A. Gramsci, 'Officialdom', *Selections from Political Writings, 1921–1926* (London, 1978), p. 17.

[6] R. Michels, *Political Parties: A Sociological Study of the Oligarchical Tendencies of Modern Democracy* (New York, 1962; [first published 1915]), pp. 317–24.

[7] Luxemburg, pp. 79–80.

[8] 'Theses of the Trade Union Movement, Factory Committees and the Third International', *Second Congress of the Communist International: Minutes of the Proceedings, Vol. 2* (London, 1977), pp. 278–9.

[9] Karl Radek's speech proposing the trade union theses, *Ibid.*, pp. 74–5.

[10] Theses of the Trade Union Movement, p. 281.

existing unions and win them over to communism *before* the revolution had even taken place. As Alexander Lozovsky's told the Second Comintern Congress:

> Before the October revolution we transformed the factory committees, not by verbal propaganda, but by deeds. We will yet transform the trade unions before the social revolution, for the trade unions must become the organs of this revolution.[11]

Ironically such an analysis appeared to considerably underestimate the damaging effect the trade union bureaucracy could have on the mass struggle and their central role in defusing a revolutionary situation. For example, in the 1918–1919 German revolution the Social Democratic Party-influenced trade union leaders who opposed the mass movement from below had not been swept away. Instead they had sprung to the head of the movement with the clear intention, and evident success, of pushing back the revolutionary tide. Even in Russia, where the unions had been very young and the bureaucracy relatively weak, it needed the victory of the October revolution to break the power of the right, the Mensheviks, inside them.[12]

Meanwhile, revolutionary syndicalists in every country also mounted a critique of trade union officialdom and sought to challenge its bureaucratic and conservative influence. But it was the specific theoretical and practical contribution made by British syndicalism that was to be one of the most insightful and pioneering, not only in relation to other syndicalists but also to other political traditions within the labour movement internationally. The historically deep-rooted and long-established roots of union bureaucracy in Britain combined with the predominant unofficial character of the labour unrest that swept the country, with its open hostility to the existing union leadership and collective bargaining machinery, provided the specific context within which such a development took place. As J.T. Murphy commented: 'To be "agin" the officials was as much a part of the nature of the syndicalist-minded workers of that time as to be "agin the Government" was a part of the nature of an Irishman.'[13] Also of crucial significance was the tactical decision made by the mainstream British syndicalist trend to operate inside the existing reformist trade union movement, and thereby grapple with the practical task of attempting to directly confront the union bureaucracy. It was the fruit of such practical experience which facilitated a more sophisticated analysis of the problem and ways of challenging it than produced by others elsewhere.

By contrast in America, the issue of union bureaucracy was of much less direct concern given the IWW's 'dual unionist' approach of attempting to build an entirely separate revolutionary union. The Wobblies clearly recognised the problem of bureaucracy within the trade unions, and castigated the leaders of the craft-based AFL unions. But believing the existing power of officials was an insurmountable obstacle to reconstruction, they imagined they could wish these difficulties away by setting up their own incorruptible revolutionary industrial union body. In both Italy and Spain the alternative 'boring from within' strategy' was applied essentially

---

[11] *Second Congress*, p. 89.

[12] T. Cliff, 'Introduction', *The Mass Strike* (London, 1987), pp. 9–10; P. Broue, *The German Revolution, 1917–1923* (Chicago, 2006) V.E. Bonnell, *Roots of Rebellion: Workers' Politics and Organisation in St. Petersburg and Moscow 1900–1914* (Berkeley, Calif., 1988).

[13] J.T. Murphy, *New Horizons* (London, 1941), p. 81.

at a *local* level, within locally-based craft unions and Chambers of Labour, rather than inside the existing national union confederations. In counter-posing their own rival revolutionary confederations, it meant relations between Italian and Spanish syndicalist bodies and the bureaucrats inside the reformist-dominated unions and confederations were conducted essentially from the outside. This meant, as in America, there was little detailed consideration of the theoretical and practical problems of union bureaucracy and how its restraining influence might be overcome.

In France, although revolutionary syndicalists were initially successful in capturing control over a sizeable section of CGT unions, the Confédération leadership as a whole, and its supporters holding official positions in some of the largest unions and federations, moved a considerable way from 1910 onwards towards abandoning direct action in favour of accommodating to the employers and the state. Even though there remained a sizeable revolutionary minority in open conflict with the CGT leadership, they subsequently broke away to form an alternative union, with the CGTU shortcircuiting the experience of confronting union officialdom. Likewise, in Ireland, faced with an ITGWU which had developed bureaucratic trends that stymied the previous militant approach, the breakaway Workers' Union attempted unsuccessfully to resolve the problem by simply avoiding it.

In all these countries syndicalists vigorously denounced the domination of the trade unions by bureaucratic and reformist officials and helped to encourage independent militant workers' activity. British syndicalism's contribution to tackling the problem of the union bureaucracy – notably via the leadership of the wartime Shop Stewards' and Workers' Committee Movement – was to be particularly significant and went beyond the Comintern's conceptions. We can explore the nature of this contribution, and in turn consider some of the ambiguities in Moscow's approach.

Putting Pressure on Union Officials

In highlighting the fundamental conflict of interests between the union bureaucracy and rank-and-file workers, pre-war British syndicalists criticised the way in which union officials acted as a brake on workers' struggles, 'betrayed' their members in strikes and prevented a decisive challenge to the employers and the capitalist class.[14] Like Gramsci and Luxemburg, they drew attention to the collaborationist logic of formalised collective bargaining which encouraged union officials to concentrate on improving workers' material conditions within the framework of capitalist society, rather than to seek to transform society through revolution.[15] In the process a connection was made between the structural features of trade union consolidation (for example, recognition by employers and the state, achievement of social prestige, and acquisition of organisational assets) and the adoption of bureaucratic and conciliatory policies[16].

Yet British syndicalists also proposed practical measures, notably mass rank-and-action and control from below, to overcome the union officials' stranglehold.

[14] E.J.B. Allen, *Revolutionary Unionism* (London, 1909) p. 9.

[15] J. Radcliffe, *The Syndicalist*, October 1912.

[16] B. Holton, *British Syndicalism 1900–1914* (London, 1976), p. 204.

They were confident it would be possible to radically transform the structures and procedures of trade union organisation (towards industrial unionism) as a means to wrest effective power away from bureaucratic officialdom and encourage unions to adopt revolutionary objectives. While open as to whether the sought for amalgamation of unions would be supported by union officials, they insisted it would depend primarily on rank-and-file action, which was likely to involve direct conflict with the officials. More generally, emphasis was placed on rank-and-file democracy, decentralisation of union power and mass participation as the chief means by which the rank-and-file could assert control over the official apparatus of the unions and direct it to their own ends.[17] A devastating critique of union officialdom in *The Miners' Next Step* pamphlet (1912), published by the Unofficial Reform Committee (URC) within the South Wales Miners Federation, campaigned for a union executive composed of lay members, with all officials excluded; the executive's role reduced to merely administrative functions; and all initiatives for new proposals, policies and tactics for the union to be in the hands of the membership.[18]

If during the pre-war years industrial militants in Britain had been inclined to look with varying degrees of disfavour upon *individual* trade union leaders for their timidity and conservatism, the syndicalists, in a new departure, identified the *entire layer* of officialdom as necessarily a problem for workers in struggle with their employers. Such a critique earned them support from grassroots militants whose own experiences inclined them to a similar viewpoint. In contrast to Michels' pessimistic assumptions, it seemed that syndicalists were more than justified in stressing the potential for rank-and-file democratic control over officials; even if incorporation and bureaucracy might be powerful tendencies, they were not inevitable trends that were impossible to offset by pressure from below.

Nonetheless the pre-war British syndicalist tradition was also confronted by some difficult dilemmas. One of these was the danger of co-option into the union machine arising from the attempt to capture official union positions. Significantly, the URC confined its attention to agitation among the rank-and-file with the aim of pressurising the existing union leaders into the adoption of specific policies.[19] As supporters of the unofficial movement in South Wales wrote: 'we ought to be a "ginger group" constantly attempting to galvanise the executive committee into life and focusing their efforts in the direction of our programme.'[20] They assumed conciliatory trade union officialdom could effectively be offset by greater rank-and-file pressure and control, and by changes in the structure and procedures of the existing union.[21] They hoped eventually to supplant the bureaucratic machine with their own democratic one.

---

[17] W.F. Hay, *The Industrial Syndicalist*, November 1910.

[18] *The Miners Next Step*, South Wales Unofficial Reform Committee (Tonypandy, 1912 [reprinted London, 1973]).

[19] M. Woodhouse, 'Marxism and Stalinism in Britain', in M. Woodhouse and B. Pearce, *Essays on the History of Communism in Britain* (London, 1975), p. 31.

[20] Cited by M.G. Woodhouse, in 'Rank and File Movements amongst the Miners of South Wales 1910–26', D Phil thesis, University of Oxford, 1970, p. 149.

[21] Holton , pp. 204–205.

However, in practice while the URC successfully channelled rank-and-file struggle into the miners' union as a counter-weight to the union bureaucracy, its orientation on reforming the union machine and on getting militant candidates elected to office on the executive committee, meant it was not immune from the problem of bureaucracy. As Tony Cliff and Donny Gluckstien have commented:

> Rank-and-file agitation threw up new and vigorous combative forces but the structure of the union creamed off the best of them, isolated them from their bases and dropped them into the bureaucratic mire at the top. A union official's origins in a militant syndicalist movement could not give them a lifetime inoculation against bureaucracy.[22]

The element of truth in this was to be seen in the way some of the leaders of the unofficial movement attacked their 'spokesmen' on the union executive, notably the former protagonist of the movement, Noah Ablett. As C.L. Gibbons, one of the authors of *The Miners' Next Step* wrote:

> They were pledged to abstain from supporting reactionary politics … they were to keep revolutionary policies and militant policies to the fore; they were to force the executive committee to take action along lines laid down by the militant section in the coalfield. Have they done this? Unhesitatingly we answer 'No'. They have ceased to be revolutionary, except in words. In the matter of deeds they are not to be distinguished from members of the openly reactionary majority on the EC.[23]

Willie Gallacher, reflecting back on his long years of experience inside the British labour movement, raised an important point at the Second Comintern Congress about the practical difficulties posed by Moscow's blanket slogan 'conquer the unions':

> Every time we succeeded in making one of our own comrades an official of the trade unions, it turned out that, instead of a change of tactics taking place, the trade unions corrupted our own comrades too. We have often made our comrades into big trade union officials, but we have seen that nothing can be achieved for communism and the revolution through such work.[24]

The underlying dilemma was that in practice no trade union under capitalism could fully escape the pressure of its environment. It had to operate in a contradictory fashion, responding to its members' demands in struggle and yet still seeking to preserve itself as a defensive organisation within capitalism. The problem was that (as we saw in Chapter 7) the day-to-day pressure to bargain and negotiate with employers in different industries and workplaces necessarily pushed trade unionism, *including revolutionary trade unionism*, in the direction of bureaucracy and reformism.

---

22 Cliff and Gluckstein, p. 76.

23 Cited in Woodhouse, 'Marxism and Stalinism in Britain', pp. 32–3.

24 *Second Congress*, p. 167.

Amalgamation and Industrial Unionism

Another dilemma was the paradox at the heart of the successful campaigns – in which British syndicalists played a prominent role – to forge the amalgamation of different societies into one large industrial National Union of Railwaymen (NUR) in 1913, and to create a 'Triple Alliance' between the miners, railway and transport workers' unions in 1914.[25] While amalgamation and industrial unionism were certainly of use if the existing unions were to be encouraged to adopt aggressive revolutionary objectives, they could also be seen as necessary for quite different reasons.

In practice the amalgamation of the different railway workers' unions into a single organisation with a 'model' industrial structure, the NUR, did not lead to a fighting union.[26] Union officials agreed to amalgamation partly because it had long become manifest that competition between unions for members weakened their power for effective negotiation in the face of federated employers' organisation; partly as a means to increase bargaining leverage within the industry; and partly because their support (however belated) for industrial unionism also proved tactically useful as a means of staving off rank-and-file challenges to their position. But despite a formally highly democratic structure, the NUR was still dominated by full-time union officials and proved as willing to compromise and behave 'responsibly' as its sectionalist predecessors.[27]

Similarly, while on the face of it the 'Triple Alliance' of miners, railway and transport workers' unions amounted to a significant step towards industrial unionism, for the officials involved it had nothing at all to do with the syndicalist aim of fostering working class militancy with the aim of overthrowing capitalism. In practice, the existence of an entrenched union bureaucracy that acted as an agent of class collaboration was a far more fundamental problem than sectionalism or the problems of union structure on which the syndicalists tended to concentrate attention. At the Comintern's Second Congress Karl Radek pointed out the limitations of the syndicalist emphasis on industrial unionism:

> ... what we are dealing with is a new fetish. It is claimed that the old craft unions can no longer serve the revolution, that industrial unions are the highest and most perfect thing. That is a completely metaphysical position. It has already been proved in practice that reactionary industrialism is possible. If the workers organise themselves in industrial unions in order to reach agreements with the capitalists, then there is nothing revolutionary in that, while it is on the other hand possible that trade union organisations that are even more backward than the craft trade unions will unite in revolutionary struggles if they are

---

[25] J. Hinton, *Labour and Socialism: A History of the Working Class Movement 1867–1974* (Brighton, 1983), p. 92.

[26] See P. Bagwell, *The Railwaymen: The History of the National Union of Railwaymen*, London, 1963); P. Bagwell, 'The New Unionism in Britain: the Railway Industry', in W.J. Mommsen and H-G. Husung (eds), *The Development of Trade Unionism in Great Britain and Germany, 1880–1914*, (London, 1985), pp. 185–200; D. Howell, *Respectable Rebels: Studies in the Politics of Railway Trade Unionism* (Aldershot, 1999).

[27] D. Howell, 'Taking Syndicalism Seriously', *Socialist History*, 16 (2000), p. 40.

> filled by revolutionary spirit … Our attitude towards industrial unions is progressive. We want to support them, but we cannot make a shibboleth out of them.[28]

Undoubtedly British syndicalists concurred with the sentiment that 'revolutionary spirit' was more important than trade union structure, but the tensions between the two were nonetheless real. The problem was that, assuming the union leadership would automatically be forced through sheer pressure from below to adopt a militant posture or be removed from office, they concentrated their propaganda efforts on emphasising the revolutionary possibilities of the Triple Alliance. By contrast, relatively little effort was devoted to warning rank-and-file workers of the danger of the union bureaucracy attempting to use the Alliance to defuse action from below.

Action Independent of Union Officials

It was not until the First World War, when the shop stewards' movement built rank-and-file organisations capable of fighting independently of the union bureaucracy, that a way out of this critical dilemma was discovered.[29] Significantly, the leadership of the movement devolved onto a number of leading syndicalist-influenced militants, some of whom had been involved in the pre-war amalgamation movement, who were prepared to defy both the trade union bureaucracy and the state. A handful of these activists (including Arthur MacManus, Tom Bell, Willie Gallacher and J.T. Murphy) were members of revolutionary socialist parties, either the SLP or the BSP, whilst others (including W.F. Watson and Jack Tanner) were non-aligned union militants. But all of them in their theoretical outlook and practical activity carried forward the main features of the pre-war syndicalist tradition. Wartime experiences now led these engineering shop stewards' leaders to make important advances on this syndicalist tradition.

In particular they came to believe it was doubtful whether the sectional interests of unions and their bureaucratic leaders could ever be overcome and unlikely that the goals of the unions could be transformed, merely through amalgamation of official structures. Instead they advocated militants taking the initiative to construct the new industrial unionism from below, in the workshops. In the past, Murphy explained, amalgamationists had 'sought for a fusion of officialdom as a means to the fusion of the rank-and-file. We propose to reverse this procedure'.[30] They campaigned for the establishment of workshop committees, composed of shop stewards representing all workers irrespective of union, craft or gender. The spread of such workshop organisation, linked by local Workers' Committees, from engineering to the rest of industry, it was argued, would ensure an all-encompassing *class* organisation on a national scale. Murphy later distinguished between two phases 'of our development as revolutionary agitators in the trade union movement':

---

[28] *Second Congress*, p. 72.

[29] Hinton., p. 93.

[30] J.T. Murphy, *The Workers' Committee: An Outline of its Principles and* Structure (Sheffield, 1917 [republished London, 1972]), p. 18.

> The first phase [pre-war] was that of propagandists of industrial unionism, amalgamation of the unions, ginger groups within the various organisations. The second [wartime phase] was characteristically the period of action, the attempt to adopt industrial-unionism principles to the immediate struggle, and to take on the direct responsibility for the conduct of the fight against the bosses and the state.[31]

Even more significantly the shop stewards' leaders also developed the critique of trade union officialdom, by advocating the theory of independent rank-and-file organisation as an effective counter to the bureaucratisation of trade unionism. The most sophisticated exposition of this theory was contained in J.T. Murphy's pamphlet *The Workers' Committee*. The pamphlet began with identifying the existence of a separate stratum of trade union officials who had become removed from the rank-and-file: 'One of the most noticeable features in recent trade union history is the conflict between the rank and file of the trade unions and their officials.' He continued: 'Everyone is aware that usually a man gets into office on the strength of revolutionary speeches, which strangely contrast with those of a later date after a period in office.'[32] Murphy pointed to both the material and social pressures that could make union officials become bureaucrats:

> Now compare the outlook of the man in the workshop and the man as a full-time official. As a man in the workshop he feels every change; the workshop atmosphere is his atmosphere, the conditions under which he labours are primary ... But let the same man get into office. He is removed out of the workshop, he meets a fresh class of people and breathes a different atmosphere. Those things which were once primary are now secondary ... Not that he has ceased to feel interested, not that he has become dishonest, not that he has not the interests of labour at heart, but because human nature is what it is, he feels the influence of new factors, and the result is a change of outlook.[33]

Murphy explained that the growth and consolidation of this stratum of union official meant 'a desire for their own security, a permanent office or a parliamentary career, and a "cushy" government job becomes more attractive as the days pass'.[34] Acknowledging, as had *The Miners' Next Step*, that the passivity of ordinary trade unionists reinforced such bureaucratic tendencies, he argued the need for every rank-and-file member to become activity involved in union affairs so as to make officials act as delegates on behalf of the rank-and-file rather than allowing them to '[speak] and [act] as if the workers were pliable goods, to be moulded and formed according to their desires and judgement'.[35]

At the same time, Murphy saw the need to concentrate on developing, both *within* and *outside* official union structures, rank-and-file organisations that would be capable of fighting independently of the bureaucracy where necessary.[36] The Workers'

---

31 *The Worker*, 19 March 1921.

32 *The Workers' Committee*, p. 13.

33 Ibid., p. 13.

34 J.T. Murphy, *Compromise or Independence? An Examination of the Whitley Report With a Plea for the Rejection of the Proposals for Joint Standing Industrial Councils*,(Sheffield, 1918), p. 9.

35 *The Workers' Committee*, p. 14.

36 *Solidarity*, March 1917.

Committees, created on the Clyde, in Sheffield and elsewhere across the country, were seen as the model of organisation required. They represented the establishment of a situation of 'dual power' between trade union officialdom and the independent organisation of the rank-and-file. Although this rank-and-filist approach arose from the immediate necessities of wartime conditions it contained within it a solution to the theoretical problem of union bureaucracy and sectionalism that had confounded the pre-war syndicalist movement. Significantly, the shop stewards' strategy marked the progress from 'pressure upon the officials' to 'action in spite of the officials'.[37] The approach was summed up by the famous Clyde Workers' Committee statement: 'We will support the officials just so long as they rightly represent the workers, but we will act independently immediately they misrepresent them.'[38]

Such an approach was quite different from that which had been advocated by the pre-war Unofficial Reform Committee which had the objective of reforming trade unionism through the official machinery. Reflecting the practical achievements of the wartime engineering shop stewards' movement, Murphy pointed to the possibilities of independent rank-and-file organisation based in the workshops rather than in the union branches as the most appropriate form of organisation and effective counter to the bureaucratisation of the unions. As a result, *The Workers' Committee* proposed a complete national structure that, unlike *The Miners' Next Step*, was an *alternative* source of authority to the existing unions and their leadership. Whereas the miners' activists had aimed at *reforming* officialdom, the engineering shop stewards attempted to *bypass* it where necessary.[39]

Because the value of participation in the official union machinery necessarily appeared to be limited to the shop stewards' leaders, no organised effort was made to capture trade union positions:

> If we centre our activities on capturing the trade union movement, instead of capturing [the workshop organisations] we will be captured by the Official movement…A man is governed by his environment, and we should very definitely oppose any member taking any office in a trade union that will take him away from the shop or his tools.[40]

The stewards were content to rely on putting pressure on trade union officials from the strongholds of independent rank-and-file organisation, confident that if the officials failed to respond to this pressure the existing unions would eventually be 'thrown off' and replaced in all their essential functions by the Shop Stewards' and Workers' Committees.

So it was the practical realities of building workshop organisation that led the militant shop stewards to reject both the 'amalgamation' and 'dual unionist' traditions of pre-war British syndicalism.[41] Instead of seeking to either *reform* or *replace* the existing unions they concentrated on developing within official structures rank-and-file organisations

---

[37] J.T. Murphy, *Preparing for Power* (London, 1972 [first published 1934]), p. 111.

[38] Clyde Workers Committee leaflet in the Beveridge Collection, British Library of Political and Economic Science, section 3, item 5.

[39] Cliff and Gluckstein, pp. 70–71.

[40] J.T. Murphy, *Solidarity*, June 1918.

[41] J. Hinton, *The First Shop Stewards' Movement* (London, 1973) pp. 280–86.

that were capable of fighting independently of the bureaucracy if necessary; a rank-and-file movement that walked on two legs, official and unofficial.[42]

'General Staff of Labour'

During 1919 some British trade union leaders, riding the massive post-war wave of workers' militancy and political radicalisation, moved significantly to the left and began to talk the language of 'direct action', of the political general strike to force parliament to respond to trade union demands. Thus, several unions threatened to take direct action to enforce the nationalisation of the mines, the ending of conscription and the withdrawal of troops from Russia and Ireland. The renewed emphasis placed on the dormant 'Triple Alliance', the replacement of the old ineffective TUC Parliamentary Committee by a General Council, and the direct action rhetoric generally created fertile soil for the revival of syndicalist illusions in the revolutionary potential of trade unionism. A wide layer of union militants now began to look to the leaders of the Triple Alliance to initiate a general strike and final confrontation with the power of capital. In the event, the Triple Alliance remained as ever dominated by the union bureaucracy's desire to *contain* rather than to *lead* militancy, and where this was not possible to keep industrial disputes within the bounds of trade union sectionalism rather than broaden the struggle to challenge the state.

However, whilst Murphy and the other stewards appreciated the revolutionary possibilities of a general strike, it was a virtue of their political development that, compared with the pre-war syndicalist tradition, they approached the rhetoric of 'direct action' during 1919–1920 with caution, developing a clear analysis of the inadequacy of left-wing union officials as leaders of a potentially revolutionary situation. Murphy now developed an even more refined analysis of union officialdom. First, he explained that centralised collective bargaining under capitalism necessarily involved the creation of a 'big specialised official army' who, because of the need to strike bargains with employers, took on certain disciplinary functions over their members on behalf of the employers and tended 'to run the organisation in oligarchical or caucus fashion' detached from democratic control.[43] Second, he argued collective bargaining produced a leadership incapable of seeing beyond compromise with capitalism:

> When it is remembered that Trade Unions are limited, constitutionally to narrow channels of activity, and that officialdom is a product of this limited activity, it is only to be expected

---

[42] After the war, in the context of the Russian Revolution and revolutionary turmoil throughout Europe, including massive labour unrest in Britain, the stewards extended the concept of rank-and-file independence to the idea of the seizure of state power by the Workers' Committees, which were now conceived of as embryonic 'soviets', the economic and political nucleus of a future workers' state similar to that which existed in Russia. Although the revolutionary optimism on which the shop stewards' experience rested was quickly undermined by the collapse of the movement after the war, it nevertheless marked a major advance on the pre-war 'pure' syndicalist conception of trade unionism and the problem of union bureaucracy.

[43] *The Socialist*, December 1919.

> that the official leaders are essentially conservative in outlook and action. Today they have a nineteenth century psychology with which to face twentieth century problems. We have entered an era of revolution, demanding revolutionary leadership: we get in response pathetic appeals to do nothing which will disturb the equilibrium of the existing order. Issues are confined to narrow channels. Sectionalism becomes a virtue to them and class action a dreadful nightmare.[44]

Murphy explained that because their whole function was to negotiate, trade union officials came to view collective bargaining procedures not as a temporary truce but as a permanent peace with capitalism: 'The whole machinery of the trade unions is constitutionally directed into channels of adaptation … to the capitalist system.'[45]

> Trade unions … are organised bodies for the modification of the existing system, accepting the capitalist idea of society. They simply bolster up or modify part of the capitalist system itself …
>
> I do not mean for a moment that these organisations will not play a part in the destruction of capitalism, but the revolutionist does recognise the limited part which they will play … performing what I would call a conservative function, continually modifying the outlook of the workers by their limited scope.[46]

He warned against the illusion that the formation of a TUC General Council could lead the revolution:

> The call comes for a General Staff for the labour hosts [the General Council], and again the principal thought impressed is conservative and reactionary. The General Staff of officialdom is to be a dam to the surging tide of independent working class aspirations and not a directing agency towards the overthrow of capitalism.[47]

From this argument it followed that the only way to finally defeat the bureaucratic and collaborationist tendency of trade unionism was to overthrow capitalism. It was acknowledged that, in a period of revolutionary upheaval, it might be possible for the workers to replace collaborationist leadership with revolutionaries and to remould the structure of unions on industrial lines. However, unless the revolution was successfully carried through (by the Workers' Committees), the same tendency to bureaucracy and collaboration would rapidly assert itself amongst the new leadership. Even the achievement of industrial unionism and the replacement of the branch by the workshop as the basis of the union could not guarantee democratic control over the officials. Independent rank-and-file organisation, not the reconstruction of trade unionism as a whole, was the key to working class advance, with the perfection of industrial unionist structures proving to be a post-revolutionary task. Despite the fact many industrial militants continued to exaggerate the possibilities of the left trade union bureaucracy and industrial unionism during 1919–1920, Murphy and the other stewards' leaders pointed out that irrespective of 'reconstruction', the trade

---

44 *The Worker*, 20 December 1919.

45 *Solidarity*, December 1919.

46 J.T. Murphy, *The Trade Unions: Organisation and Action*,(Oxford, 1919), p. 19.

47 *Solidarity*, December 1919.

unions and their bureaucratic leaders would continue to operate as the machinery of compromise with capital until the revolution was accomplished.

Such an analysis marked a further major advance on the pre-war syndicalist tradition. The government's subsequent ability to ride out the post-war industrial crisis of 1919–1920 without confrontation as a direct result of the unwillingness of the union leadership to engage in confrontation with the state, and the collapse of the Triple Alliance on 'Black Friday' 15 April 1921 when the miners were left to fight alone, was to confirm the value of such an analysis.

Comintern Ambiguities

Nonetheless the idea that the highly developed trade unions of western Europe and America *could* be transformed into institutions of revolution, with union leaders either forced to change by pressure from below or replaced by revolutionaries *before* a victorious socialist revolution and conquest of state power had been enacted, was given an important fillip by the 'conquer the unions' policy emanating from the Communist International.[48] Ironically, despite his 'ultra-left' stance towards the AFL unions, the American communist Louis Fraina was undoubtedly justified in pointing out that the trade union bureaucracy was strong enough to hold on to its position right up to the moment of revolution, and would be in a position to paralyse the movement unless an independent rank-and-file movement organised against it:

> Our objections to Comrade Radek's Theses [on the trade unions] … concern above all his conception of the nature of unions … one could draw the conclusion … that what we have to do is to capture the trade union bureaucracy. We do not find there any indication or instructions on the formation of special organisations (for example trade committees, shop stewards, etc) as instruments in the struggle against the bureaucracy and to mobilise the masses for action.[49]

In fact, the Comintern (and RILU) *did* advocate that communists should endeavour to render factory committees as: 'the nuclei of the trade unions and to support them in proportion as the unions overcome the counter-revolutionary tendencies of their bureaucracy, as they consciously become organs of the revolution.'[50] But there was no detailed exposition or consideration of how this could be done, let alone any serious integration of the experience of the syndicalist-influenced British shop stewards' movement in attempting to overcome the problem of union bureaucracy. Moreover, the notion that the union bureaucracy could somehow be removed or the official machinery wrested from their control *this side* of a workers' revolution that completely transformed social relations was reinforced. As Fraina remarked:

> We are of the opinion that it is not the tying-down of the bureaucracy that must be emphasised but the liberation of the masses to proceed independently of the bureaucracy … I do not quote this as an argument against work in the unions but as an argument

48 Cliff and Gluckstein, pp. 52–3.
49 Ibid., p. 77.
50 *Second Congress*, p. 284.

> against the idea of tying down the bureaucracy. We must fight against this bureaucracy in the unions; it will only be possible to tie them down or finish them off during the revolution or after it.[51]

The subsequent formation of the Red International of Labour Unions was to further accentuate the notion of capturing the official union apparatus. Likewise the onset of mass unemployment and dramatic shift in the balance of class forces towards the employers that occurred in Britain during the early 1920s encouraged a switch of emphasis from the workplace to capturing official union positions.[52] Under the influence of its Moscow guardian, the tendency of placing faith in the left wing of the TUC General Council increasingly became entrenched inside the newly formed Communist Party (which absorbed many of the pre-war syndicalist activists and wartime stewards' leaders).[53]

In retrospect such a perspective completely undervalued the special role of the union bureaucracy and its deep roots inside the labour movement. Certainly, the idea that the union leadership might play a central role in strangling any revolution at birth was absent in official Comintern pronouncements and discussions. Lenin and Trotsky did not appear to fully appreciate the full ramifications of the more deeply rooted nature of the trade union bureaucracy in countries such as Britain compared with Russia. There is no real evidence that even Murphy, despite his own pioneering analysis of the need for rank-and-file organisation to counter the treachery of union officials, raised any objections to the notion that the unions and their leaders could be won to communism wholesale, although the relative weakness of the British Communist Party and the British Bureau of the RILU actually made such a grandiose objective purely academic.

---

[51] Ibid., p. 78.

[52] Cited in 'Anarcho-Syndicalism in Britain, 1914–30', *A History of Anarcho-Syndicalism*, Unit 14, www.selfed.org.uk, p. 23.

[53] The establishment of an Anglo-Russian Trade Union Committee aimed at fostering international trade union unity between Russian and British trade unions, also contributed to the process by which the British Communist Party looked favourably towards the TUC General Council acting as a 'General Staff of Labour' in the 1926 General Strike.

Chapter 9

Economics and Politics

The syndicalist movement's attempt to correct the perceived failings of the *political* representation of the working class, by insisting on the primacy of the *industrial* struggle and militant trade unionism, was to be the subject of fierce Comintern critique.[1] Such an orientation, it was claimed, involved at best the subordination of political issues to the industrial struggle and at worst a rejection of politics. Of course, in many respects, the division of 'economics' and 'politics' in the early years of the twentieth century, reflected the real experience of many workers within capitalism. As objects of exploitation in the workplace, they could readily understand the need for collective economic organisation, such as trade unions, to fight back against the employer. However, when it came to broader political issues, which did not seem so directly relevant to workers' immediate situation, the need for generalised class-wide politics and organisation was not nearly so obvious.[2] But this division of economics and politics was not merely a simple reflection of workers' condition under capitalism. If this *had* been the case, the division might have been easily and spontaneously overcome either when the First World War forced workers to consider problems far wider than their individual workplace, or when the intervention of the state in industrial struggles showed the close link between political and economic issues.

The problem was compounded by the fact that sectional trade unions and parliamentary labour parties had grown up which had built their very structures upon the separation of economics and politics.[3] Trade union leaders, whose chief focus was on industry, feared attack if they politically challenged the state during strikes. Therefore, they attempted to ensure trade unions were merely concerned with the *economic* struggle, such as wages and conditions. Conversely, reformist politicians, with a constituency-based organisation, feared losing votes if they were involved in strikes. Therefore, they attempted to ensure *politics* was merely concerned with winning parliamentary elections, the job of a party. In other words, reformist organisations essentially aped their adversary; they reflected back capitalism's own demarcation between economic and political questions. For example, in Britain a division of labour operated, with the trade unions fighting on the economic front, the parliamentary Labour Party on the political front. The two 'wings' of the labour movement complemented each other, each devoting itself to its specific problems.

---

1 See *Second Congress of the Communist International: Minutes of the Proceedings: vols 1 and 2* (London, 1977).

2 D. Gluckstein, *The Western Soviets: Workers' Councils versus Parliament, 1915–20* (London, 1985), p. 57.

3 A. Callinicos, *Socialists in the Trade Unions* (London, 1985), pp. 14–15.

Because under 'normal' day-to-day conditions within society reformist trade unions and political parties provided the capacity, however limited, to resist capitalist power and to achieve material reforms, they succeeded in attracting workers' loyalty. Yet at the same time, these forms of organisation, particularly during the social crises of 1910–1921, often acted to demobilise their supporters, to contain protest and opposition within the existing framework of capitalist society. The division between economics and politics tended to encourage the belief that the class struggle between capital and labour was a non-political, economic and social issue, and that workers' interests were best served through negotiation and parliamentary reform than through the revolutionary transformation of society.

From the Comintern's point of view this separation of economics and politics was both misleading and very damaging. Lenin argued that (in Tsarist Russia, as in the developed bourgeois democracies of advanced capitalism) politics was not about parliament and elections, but *class* power. The capitalist state existed to defend the economic system through which workers were exploited; there was no separation of economics and politics (certainly not for the capitalist class). It followed that while trade union struggle which limited itself to the economic field might achieve a temporary victory, because the capitalist class remained in control of the economy and the state, it could always make a counter-attack.[4]

Likewise Rosa Luxemburg had warned the separation of economics and politics had the effect of 'depoliticising' trade union struggles and of channelling union politics into the safe conduit of parliament. She compared trade unionism to the 'labour of Sisyphus', who in Greek legend was condemned for all time to push a huge boulder up a hill only to watch adversaries roll it down again.[5] As a consequence, no trade union organisation, however militant, was enough to defeat capitalism. Workers' struggles could only decisively deal with the power of the capitalist class if they *broke out* of the confines of trade unionism; only by ignoring the division of economics and politics and by making their target the capitalist state could the working class hope to win a lasting victory.

On the basis of such an analysis, there was a serious Comintern critique of the theory and practice of syndicalism, for failing to provide a lead to workers' struggles by explicitly linking industrial agitation with socialist politics. Alexander Lozovsky, the head of the RILU, argued, the fundamental defect in the syndicalists' exclusive emphasis on the industrial struggle was their inability to discern 'the politics of the economy'. Ironically, this failure to connect industrial agitation with socialist politics was by no means something peculiar to syndicalism, as even many pre-war Marxists had conceived politics as a set of ideas existing in abstraction from the daily struggle against capitalist exploitation. But it was the syndicalists' exclusive orientation on the industrial struggle and denial of 'politics' and political organisation which received the most critical attention by the Comintern.

Such a critique had to some extent been pre-figured in Lenin's conception of the relationship between spontaneity and political consciousness and organisation,

4 V.I. Lenin, 'The State and Revolution', *Selected Works Vol. 2* (Moscow, 1970).

5 R. Luxemburg, 'Social Reform or Revolution', *Selected Political Writings* (New York, 1971 [originally published 1908]), p. 105.

outlined in the pamphlet *What is to be Done?* (1902). Of course, in some respects in Tsarist Russia the relationship between economics and politics had been very close, with all workers' associations and trade unions prohibited and strikes regarded as a criminal (and sometimes even a political) offence.[6] Yet Lenin had conducted a merciless attack on the theoretical and political tendency within the Russian Social-Democratic Party known as 'economism'. Against those who believed that arguing 'politics' with workers was a waste of time and who resisted placing the political fight against Tsarism at the centre of their activity, Lenin answered that socialists who only spoke about pure trade union issues to workers both patronised them while simultaneously failing to challenge bourgeois ideology within the working class. The task of socialists was to:

> *convert* trade unionist politics into Social Democratic struggle, *to utilise* the sparks of political consciousness which the economic struggle generates among the workers, for the purpose of *raising* the workers to the level of *Social-Democratic* political consciousnesses.[7]

That meant, Lenin argued, that socialists should not strive to be the 'trade union secretary' but the '*tribune of the people*' who would 'react to every manifestation of tyranny and oppression, no matter where it appears';[8] not limiting themselves to so-called economic or trade union issues, but being at the forefront of broad *political* struggles by every downtrodden section of society. He insisted the spontaneity of the masses' struggle had to be supplemented by a nationwide Social Democratic (i.e. revolutionary Marxist) party that sought to develop class consciousness, lead political class struggle against the state and encourage political organisation. Similar arguments were now applied by the Comintern leaders against the syndicalists.

Subordination of Politics to the Industrial Struggle

As we have seen, whilst many syndicalists dismissed 'political action' they were (by adopting a narrow definition of political action) basically rejecting or minimising what they saw as the dead-end of electoral and parliamentary politics advocated by the dominant wing of labour and socialist parties. This did not mean collaboration was necessarily ruled out between syndicalists and those socialists and parties that themselves rejected parliamentarism. Moreover, syndicalists were practically involved in a variety of directly political issues, despite their protestations to be 'non-political'; and they were inescapably 'political' in their commitment to the overthrow of the capitalist economic and political system and to the establishment of a collectivist society based on working class democracy. As James Cannon was to point out in relation to the IWW:

> The professed 'non-political' policy of the IWW doesn't stand up very well against its actual record in action. The main burden of its energies was devoted to agitation and

6 V.I. Lenin, 'What is to be Done?', *Selected Works: Vol. 1* (Moscow), p. 208.
7 Ibid., p.177.
8 Ibid., p.183.

> propaganda – soap-box speeches, press, pamphlets and songbooks – against the existing social order; to defence campaigns on behalf of imprisoned workers; and to free-speech fights in numerous localities. All these activities were in the main, and in the proper meaning of the term, political.[9]

However, the solution to all political problems, syndicalists believed, could be found in the workplace, where political differences were subordinated into the economic need for all-out collective struggle against the employers; militant and class-wide forms of trade unionism could bring a new political clarity and overcome sectarian divisions. As James Connolly (who was involved with both the IWW and the ITGWU and heavily influenced by syndicalist ideas), explained in a 1909 pamphlet given a title appropriate for its syndicalist message *The Axe to the Root:*

> As political parties are the reflex of economic conditions, it follows that industrial unity once established will create the political unity of the working class. Political division is born of industrial division. I feel that we cannot too strongly insist upon this point.[10]

Moreover, political power was dependent upon and secondary to economic power within capitalist society. This meant no political revolution would be possible until the industrial unions were in a position to take over the decisive industries. 'The fight for the conquest of the political state is not the battle, it is only the echo of the battle. The real battle is the battle being fought out every day for the power to control industry.'[11] Industrial organisation and the struggle for both immediate and eventual revolutionary ends was viewed as *primary*, political issues as *secondary*:

> The power of this idea to transform the dry detail work of trade union organisation into the constructive work of revolutionary socialism, and thus to make of the unimaginative trade unionist a potent factor in the launching of a new system of society cannot be overestimated. It invests the sordid details of the daily incidents of the class struggle with a new and beautiful meaning, and presents them in their true light as skirmishes between the two opposing armies of light and darkness.[12]

From a communist point of view a key dilemma here was the syndicalist assumption that workers' consciousness was shaped by the form of industrial organisation they adopted. If workers were organised in industrial unions then class consciousness would permeate upwards; spontaneous militant industrial struggle would automatically

---

[9] J.P. Cannon, *The IWW: The Great Anticipation* (New York, 1956), p. 16.

[10] J. Connolly, 'Socialism Made Easy', *Selected Political Writings* (New York, 1974 [originally published 1914]), p. 268.

[11] Ibid., p. 280.

[12] Ibid., p. 275. However, it should be noted Connolly, unlike the syndicalists generally, also stressed the need for electoral activity by a socialist political party to accompany direct action in the workplace. During the early years of the century Connolly played a leading role in attempting to build revolutionary socialist parties in both Britain and Ireland. During his seven-year stay in America he was first an organiser for Daniel de Leon's Socialist Labor Party and then a prominent figure in the Socialist Party. On his return to Ireland in 1910 he became a leading member of the Socialist Party of Ireland. Like Jim Larkin, as well as building the ITGWU, he supported the campaign for an Irish Labour Party.

produce the unity of the working class and in the process transform workers' conceptions in a revolutionary direction. The assumption was that a *trade union* view of the world and *socialist* consciousness were one and the same. It reinforced the view that political issues outside the sphere of economics and narrow trade union activity barely warranted discussion by syndicalists.[13] In contrast the communists pointed out, in line with Lenin's earlier analysis, that while industrial unionism and collective workplace struggle *could* undoubtedly show workers, through their own experience, the need to unite against a particular set of employers, and begin to break down divisions on the basis of craft, section, race and gender, it did not *automatically* overcome the ideological and political divisions that existed between workers (for example, between strategies for reform or revolution) or necessarily clarify the political role of the capitalist state.

From the Comintern's perspective the problem was that in 'normal' conditions of relative capitalist stability the working class was far from homogeneous. *Trade union* consciousness inevitably lagged behind *political* or *class* consciousness, because trade unions, by their very nature, accepted into their ranks *all* workers irrespective of their ideas. This meant trade unions necessarily reflected the unevenness inside the working class. It followed that revolutionary trade unionism which tried to encompass all such diverse trends and maintain working class unity, by avoiding political issues often faced the pressure to adapt to the prevailing mood, to build on the lowest common denominator necessary to attract mass support. The more successful the unions were in organising the greatest number of workers, the greater the potential weaknesses arising from differentiation, from uneven consciousness. Differentiation became more of a hindrance to class unity, not less, the longer it was ignored and backward ideas not challenged. It would only be by actively engaging with and challenging the ideological and political divisions that debilitated the working class movement that real unity could be fashioned. This required not a mythical conception of class unity, but a dialectical approach that recognised the working class as a 'differentiated unity'.[14]

With the benefit of historical hindsight one example of the limitation of the subordination of ideological and political questions was the way in which British syndicalists who intervened in the 1911 Liverpool transport strike thought it was possible to ignore the political and religious issues in the city – in particular, the sectarianism between Catholic and Protestant workers – and concentrate on trade unionism and industrial struggle. Yet whilst the strike clearly demonstrated the power of a mass, spontaneous strike wave to restructure political life, with no revolutionary current (including the strike committee's chairman Tom Mann) willing to face religious and political issues and to challenge the existing sectarian 'common sense' of workers, it had the same effect as the Independent Labour Party's kowtowing to existing prejudice: it left Liverpool politics in the hands of 'Tory Democracy', the Irish Nationalists and right-wing Labour Party and trade union leaders.[15]

---

[13] K. Allen, *The Politics of James Connolly* (London, 1990), pp. 71–4.

[14] G. Lukács, *History and Class Consciousness: Studies in Marxist Dialetics* (London, 1971).

[15] J. Smith, 'Labour Tradition in Glasgow and Liverpool', *History Workshop Journal*, 17 (1984), pp. 40–42.

A more generalised communist critique of the syndicalist movement arose from the way they appeared to simply write off the politics of reformism, rather than attempting to combat it by political means. Despite its rejection in principle of the politics of reformism, syndicalism's primary emphasis on the industrial struggle meant that in practice it effectively failed, it was argued, to provide a consistent *political* alternative to the reformist leaders of the trade unions and socialist parties. Clearly the leaders of reformist parties and unions had a vested interest in maintaining a separation of politics and economics as one of the chief means of protecting their own organisations, and in turn protecting capital from trade union militancy and workers' revolution. But reformism was not just something imposed from the outside on workers by conservative labour movement leaders, it also represented the political expression of the contradictory ideas of the mass of workers who, even though they might challenge the existing system through union struggles, could also take for granted many of the ideas it inculcated into them. Thus, particularly in periods of 'social peace', or the aftermath of defeat, the virtues of militant struggle might not seem apparent, and the politics of reformism – of *negotiating* for individual pieces of the cake in preference to *fighting* for overall control of the bakery – could fit the experience of many workers.

This was not a static situation; there would always be a minority (including syndicalist activists) who made the connection between trade union struggle over immediate economic issues and the ultimate need for revolution and who, during the general periods of labour unrest, could begin to gain a mass hearing. Indeed, as Luxemburg in her pamphlet *The Mass Strike* had pointed out, in periods of general strikes and revolutionary upheaval, when the struggle over living and working conditions touched on fundamental issues of control over production and society, the distinction between 'political' and 'economic' issues could break down and the two could be fused in an entirely new and dynamic fashion. Thus, examining the 1905 Russian Revolution, Luxemburg drew attention to the way in which not only did economic strikes rapidly pose political demands, but strikes over political demands set off waves of economic strikes, with both methods drawing new layers of workers into collective struggle for the first time and coalescing into a revolutionary movement for the overthrow of the Tsarist regime.[16]

Nonetheless, even in these exceptionally favourable conditions, reformist leadership still had to be challenged *politically* and large bodies of workers won to *new* kinds of independent revolutionary ideas and action if the movement was not to be contained within the framework of the existing capitalist system. In short, a breach with the destructive consequences of reformist leadership depended on whether an alternative political perspective, that challenged reformism, was clearly articulated and a different lead offered.[17]

Positive confirmation of such an approach was provided by the experience of the 1917 October Revolution, which demonstrated that the process by which the working class was drawn to a revolutionary political consciousness was not

---

16 R. Luxemburg, *The Mass Strike, the Political Party and the Trade Unions* (London, 1986 [first published 1906]), pp. 50–51.

17 C. Barker, 'Perspectives', in C. Barker (ed.), *Revolutionary Rehearsals* (London, 1987), pp. 232–8.

automatic. Although their self-activity prepared the way for new ideas, workers did not spontaneously free themselves from the reformism of the Mensheviks and Social Revolutionaries. The alternative ideas of revolutionary Marxism had to be introduced by a Bolshevik organisation, which successfully challenged the attempt to restrain the movement within the confines of the bourgeois provisional government and its imperialist war effort. *Negative* confirmation was provided by the outcome of the 1918 German Revolution, when Social Democratic and Independent Socialist leaders, who opposed the mass movement from below, were able to retain control of the movement, and in collaboration with the Imperial General Staff to crush the revolutionary left.[18] In short, even during a mass revolutionary strike wave, there was a necessary *political* fight to be waged inside the workers' movement against reformism, which in turn required the *political organisation* of the growing numbers won to the idea of revolutionary change (see Chapter 11).

Opposing the First World War

An important paradox of the syndicalist emphasis on industrial struggle to the subordination of politics, the Comintern leaders alleged, was that the revolutionary union movement from below which they encouraged inevitably was confronted by the opposition of a state which even in syndicalists' own eyes was a thinly disguised 'executive committee of the bourgeoisie'. For example in France, as Frederick Ridley has pointed out:

> In any extensive strike movement, not to speak of a general strike, the syndicalists were bound to come into conflict with the forces of the state, acting as the defenders of capital. The revolutionary character of the direct action they proposed made this all the more inevitable. Whether they wished it or not, the workers were thus drawn into a form of action which, even if economic in origin and purpose (i.e. concerned with relations between workers and employers), could not but break those bounds and become political (i.e. involve relations between government and governed).[19]

In January 1920 Zinoviev made a similar point in an *Appeal to the IWW*:

> The word *politics* is to many members of the IWW like a red rag to a bull – or a capitalist ...
>
> This is using the word politics in too narrow a sense. One of the principles upon which the IWW was founded is expressed in the saying of Karl Marx, 'Every class struggle is a political struggle'. That is to say, every struggle of the workers against the capitalists is a struggle of the workers for the *political* power – the state.[20]

Paradoxically the more 'non-political' the syndicalists tried to be and the more they tried to avoid parliamentary politics, the more they were bound to involve

---

[18] P. Broué, *The German Revolution, 1917–1923* (Chicago, 2006).

[19] F.F. Ridley, *Revolutionary Syndicalism in France: The Direct Action of its Time* (Cambridge, 1970), p. 92.

[20] J. Riddell (ed.), *Workers of the World and Oppressed Peoples, Unite! Proceedings and Documents of the Second Congress 1920: Vol. 1* (New York, 1991), p. 323.

themselves in the wider field of political action in rivalry with the reformist parties and in conflict with the state. To that extent there was an internal contradiction in syndicalist doctrine.[21] The most graphic illustration of this contradiction, and of the syndicalists' subordination of politics to the industrial struggle, was revealed in their attitude towards the First World War, when despite formal public declarations of opposition, they refused in a number of countries to agitate against the war for fear of introducing politics and division into the working class.[22] Although this was not an issue formally commented upon within the Comintern congresses, it is worthy of consideration in so far as it underlines the general problem.

For example, as we have seen, in America the IWW from the outset adopted a principled position of opposition to the war on the basis that it was a purely capitalist struggle for economic leverage that no worker should support. Neither the outbreak of the war in Europe nor the subsequent intervention of the United States caused the IWW to change their approach, despite fierce state repression. Unlike elsewhere the war initially provided the occasion and opportunity for the IWW to flourish. Against the background of a tight labour market and an economy in which prices rose more quickly than wages, there was an increase in labour unrest. In the process the Wobblies were able to mount successful organising campaigns and expand their membership massively, such that by September 1917 they had between 125,000 and 150,000 paid up members.[23]

Yet the war years also exposed the limitations in the IWW's approach to politics and the state. While they were able to play a leading role as strike leaders in some crucial war industries, their rejection of 'political action' meant they ended up doing little in practice to effectively oppose the war, apart from advising workers to wage the class war at home even while bloody military battles dragged on overseas. Thus, they did little concretely to oppose the draft, to explicitly disrupt production in the workplace so as to prevent war materials being manufactured or transported, or to build a national anti-war movement. Their ambiguous stance was a reflection of their syndicalist refusal to explicitly link industrial activity with political ideas and organisation. Thus, when the IWW began to discuss what to do when Congress declared American participation in the war, a West Coast Wobbly recommended they call a 24-hour protest general strike. Better to go to prison, he said, than to wage a capitalist battle. However, *Solidarity's* editor opposed such a response:

> In case of war we want One Big Union … to come out of the conflict stronger and with more industrial control than previously. Why should we sacrifice working class interests for the sake of a few noisy and impotent parades or anti-war demonstrations. Let us rather get on

---

[21] Ridley, p. 93.

[22] R. Darlington, 'Revolutionary Syndicalist Opposition to the First World War: A Comparative Reassessment', *Revue Belge de Philologie et d'Histoire*, 84:4 (2006), pp. 983–1003.

[23] M. Dubofsky, 'The Rise and Fall of Revolutionary Syndicalism in the United States', in M. van der Linden and W. Thorpe (eds), *Revolutionary Syndicalism: An International Perspective* (Aldershot, 1990), p. 214; P.S. Foner, *History of the Labor Movement in the United States: Vol. 7:Labor and World War I: 1914–1918* (New York, 1987).

> with the job of organising the working class to take over the industries, war or no war, and stop all future capitalist aggression that leads to war and other forms of barbarism.[24]

Similarly, when a member of the IWW wrote to Haywood asking for advice, first having proposed that the organisation declare a nation-wide general strike if Congress declared war, Haywood offered neither support nor counsel. Finally, when a declaration of war was made by the national IWW office, under Haywood's guidance, it demanded the Wobblies play down anti-war propaganda and concentrate upon 'the great work of ORGANISATION'. The most militant member of the IWW leadership, Frank Little advised members to 'stay at home and fight their own battles with their own enemy – the boss'. But Haywood advised: 'Keep a cool head; do not talk. A good many feel as you do but the world war is of small importance compared to the great class war ... I am at a loss as to definite steps to be taken against the war.'[25] When the United States enacted a general conscription law in 1917, and the Wobblies were faced with the choice of whether or not to register when their draft boards beckoned, Ralph Chaplin used the pages of *Solidarity* to advise members to mark their claims for exemption 'IWW opposed to war'. But he was overruled by Haywood who stressed it was a matter of *individual* conscience and choice. In the event, roughly 95 per cent of the eligible Wobblies registered with their draft boards and most of those served when called.[26] Whilst the IWW was quite serious about continuing the class struggle as the war went on, unlike the conservative AFL who collaborated with the government, they were not prepared to actively take up the political issue of the war for fear of losing support amongst workers and providing the government with the pretext to use the war emergency to repress their organisation.

Yet however much the IWW-influenced strikes sought conventional labour goals, the American state interpreted them as direct challenges to the war effort and the legitimacy of federal authority. As long as members of the IWW refused to renounce their commitment to revolution or to change their practices at the workplace, the ruling class became increasingly alarmed by their successes on the industrial front and began to whip up huge anti-IWW hysteria as the US prepared to enter the war in the spring of 1917. The Wobblies were branded as 'German spies' and became a target for 'patriotic' violence by local vigilantes. Nonetheless, strikes continued and a broad-based anti-war movement subsequently developed which provided opportunities to link workers' economic grievances with political opposition to the war. Instead the IWW chose to ignore this 'political' anti-war movement, even though the Socialist Party began to grow by attracting to its revolutionary wing a new layer of activists who *did* want to campaign in opposition to the war. Ironically, the IWW's disavowal of 'politics' made the government's task of isolating it much easier and the organisation suffered heavy state repression that it was ill-prepared to survive.

In Britain as the war progressed militancy in the munitions factories constituted a major problem for the government, with the powerful engineering Shop Stewards'

---

[24] *Solidarity*, 17 February 1917.

[25] Cited in P. Renshaw, *The Wobblies: The Story of Syndicalism in the United States* (London, 1967), p. 217.

[26] M. Dubofksy, *'Big Bill' Haywood* (Manchester, 1987), p. 100.

and Workers' Committee Movement spearheading resistance to employers and the government. The shop stewards' leaders adopted a position of opposition to the imperialist war and were committed to the overthrow of the state that prosecuted it. In the process, they led unofficial and illegal rank-and-file strikes that threatened to disrupt the flow of arms, irrespective of government attacks and the pro-war policies of the trade union and Labour Party leaders. For example, in 1916 they led a successful strike of 12,000 Sheffield workers to prevent the conscription of an engineer in breach of the government's pledge to exempt those employed on munitions work, and in May 1917 led a national strike by 200,000 engineers against an attempt by the government to extend 'dilution' (the substitution of less skilled for skilled labour). In the process, a network of Workers' Committees, representative of workshop organisation and committed to the revolutionary goals of workers' control of production and abolition of capitalism, was established across the country.

But although they rejected the pro-war policies of the trade union and Labour Party leadership, the shop stewards' leaders did not offer an alternative policy of their own. Unlike the Russian Bolsheviks, they refused to agitate *politically* against the war on the shopfloor, albeit from a minority position. Instead, they argued the issue was beyond the Workers' Committees' bounds and that they should limit themselves to issues of wages and conditions. They felt that maximum unity to win militant action on immediate industrial issues was more important than the broader, more hotly disputed political questions of the war which threatened to puncture such unity. They remained satisfied to act merely as delegated representations of industrial discontent.[27]

This approach was highlighted in sharp relief by the publication of J.T. Murphy's pamphlet *The Workers' Committee*, the chief theoretical statement to emerge from the National Administrative Council of the shop stewards' movement.[28] Despite being written in 1917, the pamphlet made absolutely no mention of the war and the political issues it raised. Instead, it reduced the immense economic and political problems that lay behind the growth of the Workers' Committees to the level of simple industrial organisation. Ironically, even those shop stewards' leaders who were members of revolutionary socialist parties acted no differently. No doubt as members of the Socialist Labour Party or British Socialist Party, Murphy, Gallacher and others denounced the war at party meetings, but they made no attempt to propagate their views publicly amongst the rank-and-file in the factories for fear of losing support, remaining content to merely defend workers against the threats to their organisation brought about by the war. In effect, they wore two hats, one reserved for their party activities, the other, a shop steward's hat, to be worn as a representative of the rank-and-file, many of whom were, initially at least, pro-war.

In other words, the British shop stewards' leaders, influenced by the syndicalist conception of the primacy of industrial struggle in the battle to overthrow capitalism, restricted themselves to narrow trade union struggle, convinced that in this way they

---

[27] B. Pribicevic, *The Shop Stewards' Movement and Workers' Control* (Oxford, 1959); J. Hinton, *The First Shop Stewards' Movement* (London, 1973).

[28] J.T. Murphy, *The Workers' Committee: An Outline of its Principles and* Structure (Sheffield, 1917 [republished London, 1972]).

were preparing for the establishment of workers' control of production. The central question, they believed, was the building of workshop organisation and to delay its progress by introducing *political* issues into the trade union struggle was both unnecessary and foolish.

In many respects every issue workers faced, and every industrial dispute over wages and conditions of work, was inherently profoundly political, since they all arose directly as a result of the government's determination to win outright victory in the war. As a consequence, the extreme political circumstances of the war, and the abject failure of the trade union and Labour Party leaders to defend workers in the face of an all-out attack by employers and the state, opened possibilities for a class-wide agitation for militant trade unionism that fused immediate economic issues with a political challenge to the war.[29] In the event, as Murphy and others later acknowledged, relying simply on the industrial struggle had the effect of handing the political initiative to the 'patriotic' reformist labour leadership, isolating the movement to the engineering industry and limiting its overall potential.

So to recap, although they gained significant influence and were able to lead important workplace struggles, the syndicalists' tradition of treating politics as something external to the workplace and shopfloor unrest as simply an economic issue in both America and Britain effectively undermined the impact of their principled internationalist opposition to the war. By contrast, the stance adopted by Lenin and the Bolsheviks in Russia, it was justifiably claimed, was to have considerably more success, albeit in very different circumstances.

Lenin, the Bolsheviks and the War

Amidst mass patriotic fervour and the abandonment of opposition to war by the majority of labour leaders, only tiny radical left groupings of the socialist movement internationally, apart from the syndicalists, stood in principled opposition. For example in Britain, the revolutionary Marxist John Maclean made an isolated attempt to link the economic strikes waged by the Clyde Workers' Committee with a fight against the war, and in Germany Rosa Luxemburg, Clara Zetkin and Karl Liebknecht also attempted to mount outright opposition. But the consistent record of resistance to the war made by Lenin and the Bolsheviks in Russia was to be particularly significant.

Lenin argued that the war was an imperialist conflict; that the betrayal of the main socialist parties signalled 'the ideological collapse of the Second International', a body socialists should break away from; and that the key task for the Bolsheviks was to agitate for the working class to end the war through revolution and the overthrow of Tsarism, to 'turn the present imperialist war into a civil war'.[30] Crucially, this

---

[29] Gluckstein, *Western Soviets*, pp. 59–89; Cliff and D. Gluckstein, *Marxism and the Trade Union Struggle*, pp. 63–9; R. Darlington, *The Political Trajectory of J.T. Murphy* (Liverpool, 1998), pp. 41–6.

[30] V.I. Lenin, 'The War and Russian Social Democracy', *Selected Works: Vol. 1* (Moscow, 1970), pp. 656–7.

meant adopting a 'revolutionary defeatist' strategy of encouraging workers in every country to fight their own governments whatever the military consequences:

> A revolutionary class cannot but wish for the defeat of its government in a reactionary war, and cannot fail to see that the latter's military reverses must facilitate its overthrow … the socialists of *all* the belligerent countries should express their wish that all their 'own' governments should be defeated.[31]

In many respects such 'revolutionary defeatism' was an unambiguous and more hard-line political strategy than the 'class war continues' stance adopted by the syndicalists, even if the latter implicitly threatened similar practical consequences. Clearly, objective circumstances meant it was potentially far easier for Russians to dissociate themselves completely from any obligation to defend their Tsarist state than it was for most Europeans. After all, in Russia there was no bourgeois democracy, no legally recognised political parties or trade unions and the alienation between socialism and the labour movement on the one hand, and the state on the other, was more total than anywhere else.[32] Yet the revolutionary defeatist strategy also flowed from Lenin's distinctive application of Marxist politics that directly linked the dynamics of monopoly capitalism to imperialism and war. From this analysis came the insistence that 'politics is concentrated economics',[33] that workers' struggles could only decisively deal with the power of the capitalist class if they ignored the false division between economics and politics and made their target the capitalist state.

Such revolutionary defeatist arguments against the war were deeply controversial and even many Bolsheviks initially rejected Lenin's radical standpoint. However, after a few months of ideological confusion, more and more Bolshevik groups began to adopt this stance against the war In the process, unlike the syndicalists, the Bolsheviks conducted widespread propagandist and agitational activity not only among workers and peasants, but also inside the armed forces, with the specific aim of encouraging soldiers' mutinies. When the initial political stupor inside the labour movement gave way from mid-1915 to a revival of militant strike activity, the Bolsheviks were increasingly able to give a voice to the mounting industrial and political opposition to the war and the Tsar which eventually exploded into the revolution of February 1917.[34] The stance adopted by Lenin and the Bolsheviks also contributed to a re-groupment of the radical left internationally around conferences of anti-war socialists held in Zimmerwald and Kienthal in Switzerland in 1915 and 1916. The call to reject the Second International and break away immediately from the existing socialist parties with their millions of adherents for a completely new International was a prospect that initially daunted all but the most uncompromising western revolutionary socialists. Yet as popular disaffection with the war grew in other more economically and politically advanced countries it proved possible for the Bolsheviks to help spearhead the international revolutionary opposition to it among growing socialist forces.

---

31 Cited in T. Cliff, *Lenin: Vol. 2: All Power the Soviets* (London, 1976), p. 4.

32 N. Harding, *Lenin's Political Thought: Vol. 2: Theory and Practice in the Socialist Revolution* (London, 1981), p. 39.

33 Lenin, *'State and Revolution'*, pp. 283–75.

34 Cliff, *Lenin, Vol 2*, pp. 22–48.

While the subsequent October 1917 revolution was caused obviously by a *variety* of economic, political and social factors, Lenin's theory of revolutionary defeatism, explicitly linking industrial and political forms of protest, undoubtedly proved to be a major contributory factor. In the process the Bolshevik Revolution spurred on revolution in Germany and mass strikes and anti-war movements elsewhere across the world, from which new revolutionary Marxist forces emerged.

Mirror Image

In conclusion, from the Comintern's point of view although syndicalism clearly represented a significant step forward from parliamentary reformism – with its emphasis on workers' power in the workplace – the exclusive emphasis on the industrial struggle meant that in practice it represented the mirror image of reformism, with its separation of economics and politics. Failing to grasp (as did many revolutionaries well beyond the syndicalist tradition during this period) the importance of connecting industrial agitation and socialist politics, they made no sustained attempt to engage in ideological or political struggle over broader questions – such as religious sectarianism, women's suffrage, or the war – connecting them to the limitations of trade unionism and the need for a revolutionary political alternative. The inability to consistently challenge and provide an organised revolutionary political pole of attraction to that of the reformist party and trade union leaders meant it effectively left the door open to such reformist (as opposed to revolutionary) politics to predominate. This could only have been different if syndicalists had adopted a general political approach as well as a commitment to militant rank-and-file activity; engaging in open political propaganda and intervention on national and international political issues as well as in strikes and other workers' struggles.

The impact of the Russian Revolution and the intervention of the Comintern, combined with domestic experiences, helped encourage a layer of syndicalists on a political trajectory that led them gradually away from a strictly industrial orientation and toward a greater concern with state power and politics. The argument between syndicalism and communism on the dynamics of the revolutionary process, notably the question of state power, is the subject of the next chapter.

Chapter 10

State and Revolution

Syndicalists were also subject to Comintern critique for failing to consider in any detail or outline any concrete plan of how the ultimate revolutionary overthrow of the capitalist state and establishment of workers' control of industry and society was to be achieved in the face of violent resistance by the capitalist class. In the utopian novel *How We Shall Bring About the Revolution* the leading French syndicalists, Emile Pataud and Emile Pouget, had sketched out the dramatic scenario of a general strike leading to a popular mass uprising that successfully paralysed the forces of the government and the state, overthrew the capitalist system and replaced it with workers' power. But they provided no explicit strategic contribution as to how this would come about.[1] Instead, in France as elsewhere, syndicalists generally tended to assume the general strike would be the ultimate form of direct action that would somehow inevitably lead to social revolution, and it was counter-posed to the need to engage in day-to-day political activity.

The centrality of the general strike in the Russian Revolution of 1905 had led to a reassessment of its role in the transition to socialism inside the labour movement internationally. For the reformists of the Second International, who before 1905 has assumed 'politics' excluded direct action such as the general strike, it was now conceived of as a limited one-off set-piece to be used defensively to protect workers' right to organise against capitalists. But it was viewed as a weapon of last resort, not to be utilised as an alternative to the parliamentary road to socialism. By contrast, emphasising the potential explosive militancy of the working class, Rosa Luxemburg viewed the general strike as one of the most effective means of bringing the *masses* into struggle and turning the working class into a revolutionary force.[2] Lenin also, despite often being viewed by many later commentators as highly dismissive of workers' self-activity and revolutionary potential, in many respects placed both at the core of his understanding of the nature of the Russian Revolution, a conception that had been profoundly enriched by the experience of 1905.[3] Similarly, Trotsky, who was chairman of the Petrograd Soviet in 1905, envisaged a central role for the general strike in the revolutionary process.[4]

But from the Comintern's perspective the fundamental strategic premise of many syndicalist advocates of the general strike, that workers' economic power

---

1 E. Paturd and E. Pouget, *How We Shall Bring about the Revolution: Syndicalism and the Co-Operative Commonwealth* (London, 1990 [first published 1909]).

2 R. Luxemburg, *The Mass Strike, the Political Party and the Trade Unions* (London, 1986 [first published 1906]).

3 V.I. Lenin. 'Strike Statistics in Russia' *Collected Works, Vol. 16* (Moscow, 1963), pp. 395–421.

4 L. Trotsky, *1905* (Harmondsworth, 1973).

would effectively offset coercive state institutions, had been falsified in practice in successive industrial disputes that witnessed political authorities engage in repressive violence. Such coercion by the American state led Charles E. Ruthenberg, Cleveland Socialist and later secretary of the Communist Party, to observe:

> The trouble with the IWW theorising is that it overlooks entirely the fact that in the very process of organising industrial unions and carrying on their strikes they run into opposition to the organised power of capitalism as embodied in the state. It is an illusion to think that the capitalists will fail to use their state power to check the development of these unions and defeat them in their strikes.[5]

In the process of coming to terms with the centrality of state power, and the likelihood of intervention to settle any general strike by military force, some Wobblies were prepared to acknowledge the general strike would probably be merely the *prelude* to social revolution, which would have to be defended by violent means. Likewise in Spain, where the experience of state violence and repression of the CNT was acute and ever present, there were those within the Confederación who accepted the anarchist Errico Maletesta's judgment that while the general strike seemed to be 'an excellent means for starting the social revolution', syndicalists must be on their guard 'against falling into the disastrous illusion that the general strike makes armed insurrection unnecessary'.[6]

Yet despite such acknowledgement there was no explicit consideration of how the anticipated fierce physical resistance from the state would be broken, nor was there any strategy for the seizure of power. Instead, there remained an assumption that the struggle for workers' control would be largely confined to the industrial sphere alone, at the point of production. As Richard Hyman has commented: 'The notion of an integrated structure of capitalist economic-political-cultural domination, requiring a similar integrated revolutionary challenge, found no place in their analysis'.[7]

In this chapter we can examine the Comintern's critique of the syndicalist conception of the general strike and dynamics of revolution: notably their insistence on the need for the conquest of state power, the role of soviets in the revolutionary process; and the unions' post-capitalist role. In addition, the activity of the CNT in the Spanish Civil War is briefly assessed.

Conquest of State Power

Marx and Engels had argued that the capitalist state was the most concentrated single form of political power at the disposal of the capitalist class; it was a product of class antagonism and an instrument of class domination: 'Political power, properly so called, is merely the organised power of one class for oppressing another'.[8]

---

5 Cited in P.S. Foner, *History of the Labor Movement in the United States: Vol 4: The Industrial Workers of the World 1905–1917* (New York, 1965), p. 141.

6 E. Malatesta, 'Syndicalism: An Anarchist Critique', G. Woodcock (ed.), *The Anarchist Reader* (Glasgow, 1977), p. 223.

7 R. Hyman, 'Foreword', C.L.C. Goodrich, *Frontier of Control* originally published in 1920] (London:, 1975), p. xiv.

8 K. Marx and F. Engels, *The Communist Manifesto* (Harmondsworth, 1972), p. 105.

Therefore, the working class could only triumph by overthrowing the capitalist state. But, drawing from the experience of the 1871 Paris Commune, Marx and Engels had also insisted that workers' control of production would be impossible until *after* the overthrow of the capitalist state and the conquest of political power by the working class.[9] The *Communist Manifesto* declared: 'the first step in the revolution by the working class is to raise the proletariat to the position of the ruling class'.[10] Therefore, instead of the conquest of the political state being the 'echo of the battle' as James Connolly had suggested, Marx and Engels set this question before the working class as the first fundamental task of the revolution, ridiculing the 'roundabout way of a general strike to achieve its goal'.[11]

Similarly, Lenin explained that whilst capitalist economic and ideological power was usually sufficient to head off revolutionary working class challenges, there were always 'special bodies of armed men' – the army, police and security services – waiting in the background. Therefore, the organised might of capital could only be defeated as a result of workers organising to overthrow the existing state machine. But this meant that the collective strength which workers possessed at the point of production had to be directed at the conquest of political power concentrated in the capitalist state. Socialism could only be achieved if workers were prepared to 'break up and smash the ready made state machinery', and replace it with a workers' government that could crush the resistance of the bourgeoisie.[12] Unlike the syndicalists, who identified the general strike with social revolution, Lenin viewed it as only one important element of modern revolution, which would still require a revolutionary seizure of state power. Likewise, on the basis of the experience of the 1905 Russian Revolution, Trotsky explained the general strike inevitably posed, but did not automatically resolve, the question of state power:

> In the struggle it is extremely important to weaken the enemy. That is what a [general] strike does. At the same time a strike brings the army of the revolution to its feet. But neither the one nor the other, in itself, creates a state revolution. The power still has to be snatched from the hands of the old rulers and handed over to the revolution ... A general strike only creates the necessary preconditions. It is quite inadequate for achieving the task itself.[13]

The Second Comintern Congress reaffirmed the view that while general strikes could win concessions from the capitalists, they could not make them give up their economic and political power, which could only be removed by the working class seizing state power:

> Any strike at all that spreads over the whole country becomes a threat to the bourgeois state and thus takes on a political character. Every attempt to overthrow the bourgeoisie and to destroy its state means carrying out a political fight. Creating a proletarian state apparatus

9 K. Marx, *The Civil War in France* (Moscow, 1970).

10 *Communist Manifesto*, p. 104.

11 F. Engels, 'The Bakunists at Work: An Account of the Spanish Revolt in the Summer of 1873', in Marx, Engels, Lenin, *Anarchism and Anarcho-Syndicalism* (New York, 1972), p. 132.

12 V.I. Lenin, 'The State and Revolution', *Selected Works Vol. 2* (Moscow, 1970).

13 *1905*, p. 119.

> for administration and for the oppression of the resisting bourgeoisie, of whatever type that apparatus will be, means conquering political power.[14]

Trotsky directly challenged the French syndicalists to undergo a 'thoroughgoing review of their theory and practice' on the question:

> It is quite self-evident that a continued 'denial' of politics and of the state by French syndicalism would constitute a capitulation to bourgeois parties and to the capitalist state. It is not enough to deny the state – it is necessary to conquer the state in order to surmount it. The struggle for the conquest of the state apparatus is – revolutionary politics. To renounce it is to renounce the fundamental tasks of the revolutionary class.[15]

As J.T. Murphy acknowledged, the importance of workers seizing state power *before* control of production could be secured was something the Shop Stewards' and Workers' Committee movement only belatedly recognised:

> The shop stewards did not discuss it. Had this question been clearly understood then a totally different attitude would have developed on the question of union organisation and 'control of industry'. It would have been realised that the unions will never be reorganised to control industry until the working class has conquered political power. Every step in the direction of industrial unionism is of value to the extent that it facilitates the massing of the workers for common action in defence of their economic conditions against the increasing pressure and exploitation of the capitalists, but 'workers' control of industry' with 'workers' ownership of industry' is utterly impossible. The change of ownership is a political question, indeed the outstanding political question of our time, involving a complete and fundamental change in the relation of classes.[16]

The fact that the state was a centrally organised body that commanded forces of repression meant it could retain the initiative even during a general strike, throwing the general strike into a means of *defence* rather than *attack*. Only if the general strike progressed to the level of an insurrection to seize state power, could it prevent an inevitable counter-attack that would paralyse the unions. Evidence of this was provided during the mass strike and wave of factory occupations that swept Italy in September 1920, as one million workers took over the running of the factories, with factory councils springing up across the country.[17] Even though workers took control over production the capitalist class still maintained a firm grip over the institutions of political state power, including the army and police. In effect, only the *substance* of the capitalist class's power was taken away from them, not the *structure*. As a result, two irreconcilable forces found themselves locked in mortal combat. But the balance

---

14 'Theses on the Communist Parties and Parliamentarism', *Second Congress of the Communist International: Minutes of the Proceedings: Vol 2* (London, 1977), p. 53.

15 L. Trotsky, 'On the Coming Congress of the Comintern', *The First Fives Years of the Communist International: Vol 1* (New York, 1972), p. 93.

16 J.T. Murphy, *Preparing for Power* (London, 1934 [republished London, 1972]), p. 159.

17 See P. Spriano, *The Occupation of the Factories: Italy 1920* (London, 1975); G. Williams, *A Proletarian Order: Antonio Gramsci, Factory Councils and the Origins of Communism in Italy 1911–21* (London, 1975).

of class forces could not remain at a point of equilibrium for an indefinite period of time, and a clash became inevitable.

As Gramsci explained, a general strike and the taking over of the factories only possessed the possibility of workers' power; it was not workers' power itself, nor did it automatically lead there. Therefore, the key question became that of state power.

> Power remains in the hands of capital; armed force remains the property of the bourgeois state; public administration, the distribution of basic necessities, the agencies disposing of credit, the still intact commercial apparatus all remain under the control of the bourgeois class.[18]

This meant it was necessary to shift the focus of struggle to such centres of capitalist power, to generalise workers' economic struggle into a political battle to overthrow the government and towards the seizure of state power. Gramsci attacked the strategy of the USI:

> It is essential that the workers should not be able to believe for one instant that the communist Revolution is as easy to accomplish as the occupation of an undefended factory. These events, on the contrary...show up with blinding clarity the ... anarcho-syndicalist utopia ... what good would the occupation of the factories in the sense given it by the anarchists be, if there is not – or if one does not energetically organise – a political-economic centre (the workers' State) which unites one factory to another; which transforms the banks, to assist working class management; which breaks, whether by physical sanctions or by rationing, the sabotage of the counter-revolutionaries? And how could the workers at the same time be in the factory and on the streets to defend their conquests, if there is not a State organisation to train a loyal and well-positioned armed force, ready in all circumstances and for all eventualities?[19]

Without such a seizure of state power the danger was, Gramsci warned, the workers' movement would itself be destroyed and control of the factories restored to the capitalist class.[20] In the mass strike of April 1920, during what was the prelude to the September confrontation, Gramsci wrote what could have been an epitaph for Italian syndicalism:

> Turin is a garrisoned fortress. It is said that there are 50,000 soldiers in the city, that artillery is drawn up on the hills, that reinforcements are waiting on the outskirts of the town and armoured cars in the city ... If there was still someone in our midst who cherished illusions, if any of our workers still thought it right and proper to limit the scope of revolutionary and insurrectional action to the factory or the town, if anyone found difficulty in making that last step to the point where power in the factory can be seen as just one element in relation to State power – if such doubters, such deluded people still existed, then this lesson was for them.[21]

While the Socialist Party and its associated union leaders opposed an armed revolution and seizure of state power, the USI naively assumed the workers' revolt would inevitably bring down the state, but made no preparations themselves among

---

[18] A. Gramsci, 'The Occupation', *Selections from Political Writings, 1910–1920* (London, 1977), p. 327.

[19] Ibid.

[20] Spriano, p. 72.

[21] 'Turn and Italy', *Selections*, pp. 182–4.

the workers for an engagement with the forces of the state. When the factory occupations eventually petered out, often amidst bitter recriminations, the employers quickly re-established their authority. The Hungarian Marxist Georg Lukács spelt out the weaknesses of Italian syndicalist strategy:

> *The general strike alone, the tactic of folded arms, will not enable the working class to defeat the bourgeoisie.* The proletariat must resort to armed uprising … the power of the capitalist state remained unimpaired. During the entire movement *not a single step* was taken in the direction of shaking that power, such a step was not even attempted.
>
> The explanation lay and lies primarily in the syndicalist ideology of the workers. The great and fatal flaw in syndicalist thinking is that it localises the antagonism between labour and exploitation, centering it on the *immediate area of exploitation*, the factory. Hence it confronts the workers only with the capitalists, not with the capitalist state. Thus it is … incapable of perceiving correctly the dilemma of the workers' situation. Which is namely: *either they must abandon the factories*, which represents in any event, no matter what the conditions, a victory for the capitalists; *or they must topple the capitalist state by force of arms in order to be able to retain the factories they have seized.*[22]

In an article entitled 'From Syndicalism to Communism' Tom Mann later acknowledged the way British syndicalists were forced to confront the need for the working class seizure of state power:

> The experience of the war and after the war has shown conclusively that we can no longer think simply of an industrial struggle, and industrial organisation alone is not enough. Whatever is done by industrial organisation, the organised State machine will continue to function, and beyond question will be used by the plutocracy in any and every conceivable form against the workers. The dominant ruling capitalist class, the plutocracy, has complete control of that highly efficient machine for class purposes; the interests of the community are ever secondary to the maintenance of power by the master class, and that machine will continue to be theirs until it is wrested from them by the workers.[23]

Transitional Workers' State

The differences between syndicalists and communists were not confined to the question of whether the working class needed to seize state power, but also to how the transition to a classless society would occur following any revolutionary triumph. Marx had advocated the need for a 'dictatorship of the proletariat', a transitional period between a workers' revolution and the achievement of full communism, during which time the working class would have to arm and organise itself against the threat of counter-revolution through the establishment of a workers' state.[24] Similarly Lenin

---

[22] G. Lukács, 'The Crisis of Syndicalism', Kommunismus, vol. 1, no. 40 [1920], *Political Writings, 1919–1929: The Question of Parliamentarism and other Essays* (London, 1972), pp. 81–6.

[23] *Labour Monthly*, August 1922, pp. 206–207.

[24] K. Marx, 'Critique of the Gotha Programme', in K. Marx and F. Engels, *Selected Works* (Moscow, 1970), p. 327.

insisted the experience of the Russian Revolution had demonstrated that the capitalist state had to be replaced by a new and transitional form of workers' state, founded on workers' councils, so as to crush the resistance of the bourgeoisie.[25] Both Marx and Lenin argued that having overthrown the 'bourgeois state', the new workers' state would endure only so long as class antagonisms persisted, before eventually 'withering away'. As exploitation of labour was replaced by social co-operation, and new democratic forms of control exercised by the majority of society became fully developed, there would be the abolition of any specialised apparatus of coercion, and the disappearance of the state and of classes in the highest stage of full communism.

In January 1920 Zinoviev sent a long letter to the IWW in which he took note of the Wobbly's opposition to 'the State in general' and declared: 'We, Communists also want to abolish the State'. However, Zinoviev insisted that, temporarily, 'a State, the Dictatorship of the Proletariat', was necessary in order to 'destroy the capitalist state, break up capitalist resistance and confiscate capitalist property in order to turn it over to the whole working class in common'. Once this was accomplished, and all class divisions were done away with, the letter continued, 'the proletarian dictatorship, the state automatically disappears, to make way for an industrial administrative body which will be something like the General Executive Board of the IWW'.[26]

By contrast, as we have seen, syndicalists did not see the state as simply an instrument of the capitalist class, they regarded it as an independent and oppressive body in itself, and drew no distinction between a 'bourgeois' and a 'proletarian' state. Genuine revolution, for syndicalists, required not only the overthrow of capitalism but also the immediate overthrow of *all* forms of state power. Thus, at the CNT's December 1919 congress Eleuterio Quintanilla refuted the necessity of a 'proletarian dictatorship' to destroy the power of the privileged classes in Russia: 'A revolution that is placed in the hands of a government, no matter how revolutionary it might be, is always a danger for the revolutionaries themselves, is always a danger for the revolution itself.'[27] The key difference between the syndicalist and Bolshevik conception of revolution, he pointed out, was whether power was being wielded by the *syndicats* and not by political parties from the old state machinery even though their intentions were revolutionary. Likewise, Angel Pestana, who travelled to Moscow, bitterly criticised what he believed to be the Bolshevik regime's dictatorial character:

> We have seen how the dictatorship of the proletariat ... operates, and we have seen the people groaning under the most atrocious tyranny, enduring the most horrific persecutions, subject to the foulest exploitation. And who was it that was tormenting, ridiculing and vilifying the people? The bourgeoisie? No. A party that was thrown up by the revolution and that claims to govern in the name of the most vilely oppressed class ... Dictatorship of the proletariat? Dictatorship of those who have taken the proletariat for a long-suffering mule upon which they can rise with confidence.[28]

---

25 *State and Revolution.*

26 P.S. Foner, *History of the Labor Movement in the United States: Vol. 8: Post-War Struggles 1918–1920* (New York, 1988), p. 232.

27 A. Bar, *Syndicalism and Revolution in Spain: The Ideology and Syndical Practice of the CNT in the Period 1915–1919* (New York, 1981), chapter 3 [no page reference provided].

28 Cited in I. de Llorens, *The CNT and the Russian Revolution* (London, n.d), p. 13.

Nonetheless, Alfred Rosmer, who became a leading figure in the RILU, reflected the views of those syndicalists who were prepared to acknowledge that the experience of the October Revolution required a complete reappraisal:

> As far as the anarcho-syndicalists were concerned ... the dictatorship of the proletariat, hitherto a theoretical question, was now posed as a concrete problem – in fact, as the most urgent problem. Yet this transitional period, this passage from capitalism to socialism, had never been studied in depth; in fact, when the issue had come up as an obstacle in discussion, it had been evaded. The transition had been seen as a leap from capitalist society into an ideal society to be constructed at leisure ...
>
> The bourgeoisie, even a feeble bourgeoisie like the Russian one, did not let themselves be overthrown so easily. They too were capable of sabotage when they were threatened. They found support from outside, for the bourgeoisie of the whole world rushed to their aid. Far from being able to get down to work in peace, the revolutionaries had to prepare for war, and for a terrible war, since the attack came from all sides ... All the moral and material resources of a country already drained and exhausted by war had to be thrown into war for three years. It was an unforgivable illusion to expect things to happen differently and more easily elsewhere. The struggle would be even more bitter, since everywhere else the bourgeoisie was stronger.[29]

Soviets

The installation of *soviet* power in the 1917 Russian revolution, and subsequent emergence of similar soviets elsewhere, inevitably exercised a powerful influence on the syndicalist movement. Such new institutions of working class power, which could play a central role in the revolutionary process and provide the institutional basis for a new working class state, both inspired syndicalists and presented a considerable challenge to their existing conceptions of revolutionary unionism. The Comintern argued that it was these democratic workers' organisations, rather than the trade unions, that needed to take power from the capitalist class and break up their state, as had happened in October 1917.

The Russian Revolutions of 1905 had given birth to the soviet. Formed first as a strike committee by striking St. Petersburg print workers, it grew into a body made up of delegates elected from different workplaces across the city, cutting across the sectional lines which trade unions reflected, and basing itself on the power of workplace organisation.[30] The soviets reappeared on a mass scale when the February 1917 toppled the Tsar. This time they included not only the workers in all the major cities but also the millions of soldiers who had rebelled against Russia's involvement in the First World War. Because of this, the soviets directly challenged the ultimate source of state power – the monopoly of armed force. And not only did the soviets command the support of many soldiers, but they created their own workers' militia, the Red Guard. The Provisional Government which replaced the Tsar found itself confronted by what was effectively an alternative workers' government – which began

---

[29] A. Rosmer, *Lenin's Moscow* (London, 1971), p. 20.

[30] See Trotsky, *1905*; P. Glatter (ed.), 'The Russian Revolution of 1905: Change through Struggle', *Revolutionary History* [special edition] 9:1 (2006).

to control food supplies and transport, implement the eight-hour day and stop press censorship. The expression that Lenin and Trotsky used to describe this situation, in which *two* governments existed alongside each other, was 'dual power'.

Inevitably, there could not be any permanently agreed division of authority between these two powers. Each was by its nature fundamentally hostile to the other. Either the Tsar's government and the capitalist class would move against the workers' soviets to restore their monopoly of force, or the soviets would overthrow the government and take power themselves. Although the period of dual power lasted eight months it was ended in October 1917 when the soviets, led by the Bolsheviks, seized power from the Provisional government. Thus, born as an organ of workers' struggle, the soviet developed into an organisation of workers fighting *for* power, and eventually was transformed into a form of organisation of workers *in* power.[31]

Soviets (or workers' councils) became a central feature of the revolutionary movements in Germany (1918–1920), Hungary (1919) and Italy (1920).[32] Inevitably such developments obliged syndicalists internationally to reconsider, to a greater or lesser extent, their advocacy of trade unions as the main vehicle of revolution. At the Second Comintern Congress Alexander Lozovsky made it clear that communist enthusiasm for the building of factory committees or 'works-councils' in the advanced countries of the West, on the basis that they could be transformed into soviet-style organs of workers' power, did not diminish the continuing importance of the trade unions in the revolutionary process, (despite the experience of the Russian trade unions).[33] But Karl Radek explained why the organ of proletarian dictatorship after the revolution had been accomplished had to be the *soviets*, and not the unions:

> I should only like to say a few words to point out what difference exists between this [communist] conception of the functions of trade unions after the conquest of political power by the proletariat and the syndicalist conception. The syndicalists have conceived the development of socialism in this way: that after the proletariat has overthrown the bourgeoisie through general strikes it organises itself in the great trade unions into a federation of trade unions and that this federation would lead economic life by free agreement with the communists, without a proletarian state. We think this conception is wrong. First of all the proletariat cannot take power without setting up the proletarian state as an organ with whose help the proletariat is to break the resistance of the bourgeoisie. And secondly the running of economic life is neither a thing that every trade union can sort out for itself, nor is it a thing that can be regulated by free agreement between the trade unions ...
>
> Besides the organisations that consider their tasks from the standpoint of one branch of industry, the working class must defend the interests of the whole of the proletariat in the form of its proletarian state. The economic plan and its execution must be forcibly subjected to the pressure of the interests of the whole of the proletariat. For this reason we see here [in Russia] how ... the regulative side of the state organisations has taken the

---

31 T. Cliff, *Lenin: Vol. 2: All Power to the Soviets* (London, 1976).

32 D. Gluckstein, *The Western Soviets: Workers' Councils versus Parliament 1915–1920* (London, 1985).

33 *Second Congress*, p. 89.

> form predominately of soviets; that is to say that the trade unions participate in running the economy through the general organs of the state.[34]

Such an analysis underlined the contradiction at the heart of the syndicalist assumption that in a new post-revolutionary society control of industry would be exercised by the unions. The obvious dilemma was that as an organ of industrial administration the unions' role would be largely incompatible with their character as organisations designed to represent and protect workers' interests independently of management. As Sidney and Beatrice Webb pointed out: 'In short, Syndicalism, by making the Trade Union into an employing authority, necessarily destroys its utility as a Trade Union.'[35] It would be structurally impossible for the unions to perform *both* functions. Only when the demand for workers' control was subsumed into a theory of the struggle for soviet power could the confusion among syndicalists become resolved.[36]

The Russian soviet model became particularly influential among Italian engineering workers in the militant industrial city of Turin. During the war unofficial structures of workplace representation, known as 'internal commissions', had arisen as a means of expressing workers' immediate work-related grievances and obtaining remedies from the employer. In 1919–1920 Gramsci grasped the interrelation of the day-to-day struggle in the factories via these new institutions and the creation of the embryo of a future workers' state (as existed in Bolshevik Russia). The small revolutionary socialist group around the paper *Ordine Nuovo* (New Order) encouraged the transformation of the internal commissions into 'factory councils' that would take over more and more powers from management. By learning to manage the productive process in their own factories, workers could develop the competence and ambition to control the economy as a whole:

> Today the internal commissions limit the power of the capitalist in the factory and perform functions of arbitration and discipline. Tomorrow, developed and enriched, they must be the organs of proletarian power, replacing the capitalist in all his useful functions of management and administration.[37]

Thus, not only was the factory council movement that subsequently developed within the factories of Turin viewed by Gramsci as an essential instrument for preparing the revolution, it was also 'the model of the proletarian State' within a future socialist society.[38]

In a polemic against the syndicalists, Gramsci argued that the USI were wrong to maintain that unions were capable of being instruments of workers' revolution. He said this confused a marketing organisation of labour within capitalism (the trade

---

[34] Ibid., pp. 161–2.

[35] *The Crusade*, August 1912.

[36] We should note that in the extreme circumstances of civil war and threat of counter-revolutionary overthrow, both Lenin and Trotsky briefly argued in favour of the militarisation of labour and the subordination of trade unions to the state provoking a major trade union debate inside the Bolshevik Party. See I. Deutscher, *Soviet Trade Unions: Their Place in Soviet Labour Policy* (London, 1950).

[37] A. Gramsci and P. Togliatti, 'Workers Democracy', *Selections*, p. 66.

[38] 'Unions and Councils', ibid., p. 100.

unions) with an organisation for running production in a socialised economy (the workers' councils). Because the function of a union was to affect the terms and conditions of the sale of labour to the employers, he argued, it was an organisation specific to a capitalist society; hence their bureaucratic and conservative tendencies. By contrast, the factory councils were spontaneously revolutionary precisely because they were organisations specific to the activity of production (not wage earners), were not subject to a bureaucracy external to the workforce and represented the negation of 'industrial legality'.[39] Gramsci displayed contempt for the 'pseudo-revolutionary' syndicalists, who refused to 'prepare' for revolution and whose greatest error was to 'regard as a permanent fact, as a perennial type of association the Trade Union, in its present form and with its present functions' – a form dictated by capitalist society, and therefore unable to supercede it.[40]

The USI agreed with Gramsci's views on the limits of the existing bureaucratised and reformist unions (notably the metalworkers' union, FIOM), but insisted that when they advocated 'revolutionary unionism' they were referring to a completely different form of organisation entirely. At the same time, Gramsci acknowledged that, although the two institutions had to be kept separate, the growing importance of the factory councils would help to transform the character of existing unions, dissolving their bureaucracy, creating industrial-based forms and encouraging a revolutionary spirit.[41]

Initially the USI looked warily on the rise of the factory councils. At the *Unione*'s National Congress of 1919 Armando Borghi admitted the idea had merit, but was concerned because the movement had started in Turin, a centre of reformism. He was unable to accept the role of the Socialist Party (even the Gramsci section) in the factory councils.[42] Both Alibrando Giovanetti and Niccola Vecchi also expressed doubts as to whether the factory councils could produce a revolution and warned they could quickly become tools of the government. While they expressed sympathetic support for the councils, they continued to insist the USI would remain the instrument of revolution, with the councils training the workers to run things after the revolution.[43] Yet the USI's attitude underwent considerable transformation as a direct result of the experience of the factory occupation movement of April and September 1920. The Italian syndicalists' traditional support for direct action at the economic rather than the political level,

---

[39] See, 'Unions and Councils' and 'Syndicalism and the Councils', *Selections*, pp. 98–102 and 109–13; *Soviets in Italy* (Nottingham, 1969), pp. 15–17.

[40] A. Gramsci, 'La Conquista dello Stato', *Ordine Nuovo*, 12 July 1919; see also 'Unions and Councils'; 'Trade Unions and the Dictatorship'; and 'Syndicalism and the Councils', *Selections*, pp. 98–113. Ironically, the idea that as part of the offensive against capital, the factory councils could take over the functions of management, even *before* a revolution, led to some criticism of Gramsci for ignoring the power of capital in the state (as had the syndicalists). But in the lead up to and during the period of the factory occupations of 1920 he re-worked his initial ideas about the factory councils, registering more clearly the significance of political organisation beyond the factory walls, and the corresponding need for the conquest of political power, if workplace control and soviet-style democracy was to be sustained.

[41] M. Clark, *Antonio Gramsci and the Revolution That Failed* (New Haven, 1977), pp. 64–8.

[42] *Guerra di Classe*, 6 December 1919.

[43] *Guerra di Classe*, 7 January 1920; 13 December 1919.

their opposition to reformism unionism, and desire for revolution, converged to make the leaders of the USI actively campaign in support of the factory councils on the basis that they aimed at taking possession of the factories and managing them directly.[44] Paradoxically, in some respects, the independent, democratic organisation of the councils and their orientation to direct action and workers' control made them a living approximation of anarcho-syndicalist ideals. In the process the USI played a prominent role and often underestimated role in the factory council movement.[45]

Yet even if workers' councils or soviets of some kind were an indispensable mechanism for the shift of real power away from the capitalists and the state into the hands of the workers, the Comintern insisted that alongside this form of popular power was also needed a revolutionary political party which soviets argued for and organised to realise their full potential as the democratic structures of a new form of working class government an armed insurrection to actually effect the seizure of state power (see Chapter 11).

Spanish Civil War

The Spanish Civil War was to provide powerful evidence of the limitation of syndicalist strategy in relation to the capitalist state. Again although this was obviously beyond the comintern's 1920s deliberations it is worthy of brief consideration here as illustrative of the problem. Within the main Republican controlled areas of the country such as Catalonia and Andalusia, the anarcho-syndicalist CNT regarded the crisis as an opportunity to carry through a social revolution. Factories and railways were taken over by workers' committees and in hundreds of villages the peasants seized the land and established collectives. A new social order was enforced under the authority of a myriad of rank-and-file armed detachments. Many of these were influenced by the CNT, others by the Communist Party and the Trotskyist-influenced POUM. In Barcelona and other parts of Catalonia, the CNT called upon workers to maintain their control over the factories as the real source of capitalist power, with the functions hitherto performed by capitalist entrepreneurs or by the state now performed by revolutionary committees of the workers themselves. And in Andalusia, the traditional home of rural anarchism, the CNT encouraged the collectivisation of villages and factories, with the *Guardia Civil* chased away or killed, and the transformation of village *syndicats* into popular assemblies in which everybody could participate directly in the affairs of the community.[46]

With the disintegration of the army in the republican-held areas of Spain, the bourgeoisie appeared to be finished. In Barcelona especially during the early months of the civil war, a situation of 'dual power' existed, with the official Catalan government, under the leadership of Luis Companys, dependent on the networks of revolutionary committees, in which the CNT and its conscious minority, the FAI, were highly influential.[47] There was nothing to prevent the workers' committees from seizing *de jure* the power which they already exercised *de facto*. But warning against the deceptions of 'politics' and emphasising

---

44 A. Giovanetti, *Guerra di Classe*, 6 December 1919.

45 Clark, p. 34; 145–6; Williams, pp. 193–9.

46 R. Alexander, *The Anarchists in the Spanish Civil War: Vol 2* (London, 1999).

47 D. Guerin, *Anarchism: From Theory to Practice* (New York, 1971), pp. 128–9.

the primacy of the 'economic', the CNT-FAI *Information Bulletin* published an article entitled 'The Futility of Government' which suggested the economic expropriation taking place would lead *ipso facto* to the 'liquidation of the bourgeois state, which would die of asphyxiation'.[48] Satisfied it could make its revolution simply by seizing the means of production and confident in its power amongst the workers and peasants in republican areas, the CNT and FAI saw no danger in allowing the fragments of the bourgeois state to survive. Determined to retain their independence and to stand by their principles, they refused to take part in government or to become involved in politics.

Yet the necessity of winning the war against Franco meant there needed to be one centralised nation-wide leadership with the authority to deploy resources across many different fronts. For Trotsky, by now in exile from Stalinist Russia, this sharply posed the need for the CNT to take the initiative and lead a full-blown social revolution, involving the overthrow of the Republican government and the seizure of state power. The choice was between leaving the capitalist state intact and thereby risking the danger of paving the way for Franco's victory, or building an alternative workers' state structure in Catalonia – directly controlled by the working class and based on workers' councils – which could attempt to weld together the fragmented militias into a united revolutionary military command that could both break the fascists' coup *and* overthrow the capitalist state.

However, anarcho-syndicalist opposition to *all* forms of government led them to renounce the conquest of state power by the working class. They continued to call upon workers to turn their backs on the state and seek control of the factories as the real source of power; they believed that with the ultimate source of power (property relations) being secured, the state's power would collapse, never to be replaced. As Felix Morrow later commented:

> The Spanish anarchists thus failed to understand that it was only the collapse of the state power, with the defection of the army to Franco, which had enabled them to seize the factories and that, if Companys and his allies were allowed the opportunity to re-construct the bourgeois state, they would soon enough take the factories away from the workers. Intoxicated with their control of the factories and the militias, the anarchists assumed that capitalism had already disappeared in Catalonia.[49]

Ironically, when the Catalan government admitted its impotence in the battle against Franco and offered to dissolve, effectively handing power over to the revolutionary forces, the CNT turned them down. Yet as the desperate need for centralisation of the war effort intensified, the CNT underwent a complete 180-degree about-turn in September 1936. They now abandoned their cardinal principle of opposition to all governments and the state, agreeing to three of their members serving in a Catalan regional government dominated by pro-capitalist forces. A few weeks later, in early November, the CNT and FAI entered the central Madrid-based Popular Front government, with four of the most respected leaders taking ministerial posts in the previously despised bourgeois liberal administration of Francisco Largo Cabellero.[50]

---

[48] Ibid., p. 128.

[49] F. Morrow, *Revolution and Counter-Revolution in Spain* (New York, 1974), p. 102.

[50] Juan Peiró became Minister of Industry and Juan López Sánchez became Minister of Commerce. The two anarchist members of the government represented the more militant wing

They justified their new stance by claiming the government was a regulating instrument and that the state had ceased to be an oppressive force against the working class. But within a year of this compromise having been made, this alleged 'non-oppressive' government had sent troops in Barcelona to suppress a workers' uprising. The CNT urged its supporters to lay down their arms, stood by while revolutionaries from the POUM were persecuted, and allowed for the dissolution of the militia. There were some subsequent attempts from within the anarchist movement by the *Amigos de Durruti* ('Friends of Durruti'), a dissentient libertarian affinity group which emerged in the spring of 1937, to renew the original tactical and strategic perspectives of the CNT and the FAI. Recoiling against the 'collaborationist' Popular Frontism of the anarchist hierarchy, they called for the complete disarming of the state's armed forces and for a 'revolutionary junta' to take power based on the CNT, the socialist UGT and elected workers', peasants' and soldiers' assemblies. In short, a section of the anarchist movement finally grasped the importance of the struggle for state and therefore political power. But the Friends of Durruti group was far too small to make other than a marginal impact.[51]

Ironically, having rejected the conquest of state power, the state first incorporated, and then rejected the CNT. The consequence was both the eventual destruction of the world's largest ever anarcho-syndicalist movement and the defeat of the Spanish Revolution itself. Trotsky commented:

> The anarcho-syndicalists, seeking to hide from 'politics' in the trade unions, turned out to be, to the great surprise of the whole world and themselves, a fifth wheel in the cart of bourgeois democracy ...
>
> To renounce the conquest of power is voluntarily to leave the power with those who wield it, the exploiters ... It is impossible to wage war and to reject victory. It is impossible to lead the masses towards insurrection without preparing for the conquest of power ...
>
> In opposing the *goal*, the conquest of power, the Anarchists could not in the end fail to oppose the *means*, the revolution.[52]

Related to the problem of the conquest of state power was the Comintern's insistence on the need to provide centralised leadership inside the working class movement; the divergences and convergences between syndicalist and communist traditions on this subject is examined in the next chapter.

---

of the movement and were leading members of the FAI. One was Garcia Oliver who became Minister of Justice, and the other was a representative of the purest intellectual anarchism, Federica Montseny, who became Minister of Health.

[51] C. Earlham, '"Revolutionary Gymnasitics" and the Unemployed: The Limits of the Spanish Anarchist Utopia 1931–37', K. Flett and D. Renton (eds), *The Twentieth Century: A Century of Wars and Revolutions?* (London, 2000), p. 154.

[52] L. Trotsky, 'The Lesson of Spain', *The Spanish Revolution 1931–9*, (New York, 1973), pp. 315–16. Although Trotsky placed the overwhelming responsibility for the defeat of the Spanish revolution on the shoulders of the Communist Party and its Popular Front policies, combined with the ineffectiveness of the CNT's strategy, he was also scathing about the role of the POUM.

Chapter 11

Leadership and the Party

The final problematic area of syndicalist philosophy and practice, from the Comintern's perspective, related to the question of leadership inside the working class movement and the role of an organised revolutionary party in the struggle to overthrow capitalism. The experience of consistent 'sell-outs' at the hands of the official labour leaders in both the trade unions and reformist political parties encouraged syndicalists to look to develop rank-and-file workers' own organisation and confidence on the shopfloor to counteract this betrayal. They stressed the creativity and spontaneity of working class activity from below, from the most limited local campaign to the ultimate revolutionary general strike, effectively by-passing the existing labour movement leaders. In the process, syndicalists in Britain even went so far as to publicly repudiate the whole notion of 'leadership' altogether. By contrast, in most other countries they emphasised the role of a conscious vanguard minority that would provide the 'catalyst and motor force' for workers' activity by guiding and inspiring the more passive majority in the unions.[1] But syndicalists everywhere insisted on neutrality towards, and independence from, political parties, and displayed outright antipathy towards the new revolutionary communist parties that emerged in the wake of the Russian Revolution. This chapter explores the communist critique of the syndicalist movement's conception of the relationship between revolutionaries and the working class movement.

Repudiation of 'Leadership'

In conducting a systematic propaganda campaign inside the existing reformist trade unions in Britain, aimed at transforming them into industrially-structured revolutionary bodies, Tom Mann made it clear he did not think this entailed making the ISEL a *mass* membership syndicalist organisation. Instead, the key to success was to influence the minority of active trade unionists:

> There are three million trade unionists in the United Kingdom. Of these, one third may be counted as of serious importance – i.e., the other two-thirds are relatively passive. It is the active third that counts. It is of more importance to the revolutionary movement that the active one million of trade unionists shall be influenced aright than six times that number of others ... The ISEL need not strive to obtain an enormous membership, but it must be equal to reaching the rank-and-file of the trade unionists.[2]

---

[1] W. Thorpe, *'The Workers Themselves': Revolutionary Syndicalism and International Labour, 1913–1923* (Dordrecht, 1989), p. 17.

[2] *The Syndicalist*, January 1913.

But while pre-war British syndicalists saw themselves as playing a crucial role in propagating the anti-capitalist message and encouraging militant rank-and-file action, they tended, unlike in other countries, to publicly recoil from the idea of providing practical day-to-day leadership inside the working class movement.[3] Indeed, as an article in *The Times* noted, there was open hostility towards the very idea of 'leaders': it 'professes to do without them'.[4] Significantly, the deficiencies of official labour leaders were blamed not merely on poor direction and wrong-headed policies, but on the very institution of leadership itself. As the authors of *The Miners' Next Step* wrote:

> Leadership: implies power held by the Leader. Without power the leader is inept. The possession of power inevitably leads to corruption. All leaders become corrupt, in spite of their own good intentions. No man was ever good enough, brave enough or strong enough, to have such power at his disposal, as real leadership implies.[5]

From the fact that shopfloor workers tended to become corrupted once they were elected to full-time union office, they concluded 'the remedy is not new leaders'; *all* leaders, whether from official *or* unofficial sources, were bound to stifle the independence and initiative of the rank-and-file. As J.T. Murphy later explained in *The Workers' Committee* pamphlet produced by the wartime shop stewards' movement:

> It matters little to us whether leaders be official or unofficial, so long as they sway the mass, little thinking is done by the mass. If one man can sway the crowd in one direction, another man can move them in the opposite direction. We desire the mass of men and women to think for themselves, and until they do this no real progress is made, democracy becomes a farce.[6]

Degenerate politics, it was argued, occurred wherever a centralised organisation created an authority over and above the rank-and-file, with betrayal intrinsic to the nature of leadership and organised power. As a result, the ISEL (notwithstanding its success in pulling together a network of union militants across different industries) was marked by its decentralised, localised and diffuse character. It had neither a formal membership nor a branch structure, or even a leadership structure to speak of beyond Tom Mann and a few of his confidantes.[7]

Likewise the wartime shop stewards' movement remained a localised movement with only a loose national structure, never more than a federation of autonomous groups of militants. The central body of the movement, the National Administrative

---

[3] M. Woodhouse, 'Marxism and Stalinism in Britain, 1920–26', in B. Pearce and M. Woodhouse (eds), *A History of Communism in Britain* (London, 1975), pp. 31–55.

[4] 'Syndicalism in England: Its Origin and History', *The Times*, 16 April 1912, reprinted in *The Syndicalist*, May 1912.

[5] *The Miners Next Step*, South Wales Unofficial Reform Committee (Tonypandy, 1912 [reprinted London, 1973]), p. 13.

[6] J.T. Murphy, *The Workers' Committee: An Outline of its Principles and Structure* (Sheffield Workers' Committee, 1917 [republished London, 1972]), p. 17.

[7] G. Simpson, *The Syndicalist and Amalgamation News*, January 1913.

Council (NAC), held no executive power and was intended to function as little more than a reporting centre for the local committees, with no policy initiatives being taken independently of the membership. The movement had no paid officials, organisers or offices. Murphy expressed the shop stewards' antipathy towards 'leadership':

> One of the first principles of the shop stewards' movement and workers' committees, they obey the instructions of the rank and file and not *vice versa*. This repudiates the charge of the press and those good clear-thinking people who refer to those wicked shop stewards who bring men out on strike. Shop stewards do not 'bring' men out on strike, the shop stewards' duties do not involve 'leadership'. As a matter of fact the whole movement is a repudiation of leadership.[8]

The very act of leadership involved 'acting as if the workers were pliable goods, to be moulded and formed according to [the leaders'] desires and judgement'.[9] Instead, Murphy emphasised the self-activity and revolutionary potential of the working class. The spontaneity of the movement made powerful centralised organisation and leadership unnecessary; all that was needed was a loose body with local autonomy and democratic control to stimulate the rank-and-file along the right lines.

Of course in many respects the British shop stewards' leaders were a victim of a hidden contradiction in their own thought and action. Clearly they *did* provide a form of informal (organic) leadership to workers, particularly when they suggested initiatives that involved workers taking strike action, often independent of full-time union officials. As Murphy later acknowledged:

> It is quite true that the shop stewards and I very definitely were repeatedly frustrated and inhibited by the 'rank and file policy of administration' instead of excessive authority to lead. But we did lead...and we did move masses into action against the war ... every one of the wartime strikes were engendered and developed by the anti-war socialists and syndicalists who were seizing upon any and every grievance arising from the conduct of the war.[10]

On the other hand, ideological considerations and experience of the trade union and reformist party leaders led them to reject the idea of leadership focused within a formal (structured) organisation as reactionary. Yet in many respects the lesson of the strikes in which they became involved, combined with the extreme concentration of economic and political power in the hands of the state, was that without some form of centralised organisation there was the danger of the movement wasting its strength and exerting its massive power to limited purpose. Their 'anti-leadership' convictions meant they effectively reduced the movement to the level of spontaneity and undermined the basis for effective co-ordinated action.[11] As Murphy was to concede:

---

[8] *Solidarity*, July 1917.

[9] *Workers' Committee*, p. 14.

[10] Cited in R. Darlington, *The Political Trajectory of J.T. Murphy* (Liverpool, 1998), p. 48.

[11] See J.T. Murphy, *Preparing for Power* (London, 1972 [reprint of 1934 edition]), pp. 141–4; B. Pribicevic, The Shop Stewards' Movement and Workers' Control 1910–1922 (Oxford, 1959), pp. 100–102; W. Kendall, *The Revolutionary Movement in Britain 1900–22* (London, 1969), pp. 160–61; Darlington, pp. 46–9.

> Of all theories that played into the hands of every reactionary executive, none has been more effective than this [anti-leadership theory]. It represents a complete abandonment of all responsibility for leaders to lead. Arising out of distrust of existing leaders, it fostered still further distrust, and at the same time gave them a first class excuse for not leading. This theory … diffused the energies of the revolutionaries and made their movement into a ferment rather than an organised force fighting for a new leadership.[12]

'Conscious Minority'

It was not only in Britain where the perceived need to counteract the trend towards bureaucratic union leadership encouraged a strong emphasis on rank-and-file self-activity and decentralised forms of organisation. Ironically without firm leadership the IWW drifted aimlessly in its early years, before strong individuals like Bill Haywood, who centralised general headquarters in 1916, and Walter Nef, who constructed a tightly-knit and carefully administered Agricultural Workers' Organisation, came to the helm.[13] Yet even though the IWW, compared with syndicalist movements elsewhere, became a relatively centralist body, the organisation remained, as we have previously seen, deeply divided between those supporters in the East who favoured some central co-ordination and direction and those in the West who demanded less central control and more autonomy for local branches.

CGT organisation was very much a reflection of the decentralised structure of French trade unionism; its Confederal Committee was viewed not a directive organ, but merely an advisory body, and *syndicats* in disagreement with its policy could continue membership without conforming to its views. In Spain the CNT adopted a federalist system of organisation that sought to allow the greatest degree of local initiative and decision-making. To co-ordinate this loose national structure, CNT annual congresses elected a National Committee which was expected to confine itself primarily to correspondence, the collection of statistics and aid to prisoners. Elected each year from a different locality, with no individual serving more than one term, and all delegates subject to immediate recall by the members, the National Committee and all of the CNT's bodies were managed by committees of ordinary unpaid workers, with the general secretary and the regional secretaries the only paid officials. Likewise in Italy the idea of local autonomy and decentralisation pervaded USI organisation and activity.

In May 1921 the Spanish Communist-Syndicalists around Joaquin Maurin and Andreu Nin, who briefly captured control of the CNT, acknowledged the extent to which local autonomy had made the development of united action on a national scale almost impossible, in particular hampering the ability of the CNT to co-ordinate workers' action in the post-war wave of struggles. Their journal *Lucha Social* lamented:

> The labour movement has been characterised these last years by a dispersed, atomistic, and undisciplined activity. What happened was very sad. When one of the great capitals

---

[12] *Preparing for Power*, p. 97.

[13] For example see M. Dubofsky, *We Shall Be All: A History of the Industrial Workers of the World* (Chicago, 1969), p. 482.

> [of Spain] was at white heat, the rest were cold ... All [struggles] were isolated combats, impregnated with an excess of localism that made a unified [revolutionary] movement impossible.[14]

Influenced by the dynamics of the Bolshevik Revolution, Nin and Maurin advocated the need to strengthen centralised organisation and leadership and de-emphasise spontaneity and localism inside the CNT.[15] However, the Communist-Syndicalist tendency's influence, which anyway could not be compared in numbers and influence with the anarcho-syndicalist and 'pure' syndicalist currents, proved to be short-lived, and the pull towards local autonomy and initiative was soon reasserted.

Even so, as in Britain, leadership and central direction *was* displayed within syndicalist movements, despite decentralised forms of organisation. For example in Spain there were periods of time when repression and sudden turns in events led to the suspension of annual or regional CNT congresses, with important policy-making decisions being taken by plenums of leading committees or 'congresses' that were little more than patchwork conferences. In such circumstances, as Murray Bookchin has documented, there were always 'influential militants' – the more informed, experienced, 'strong' and oratorically gifted individuals – who tended to exercise directive power at all levels of the organisation, albeit this did not prevent individual bodies acting autonomously, occasionally against the directives of the superior committees.[16] Moreover, not surprisingly, the Catalan organisation (and more specifically that in Barcelona) – by far the largest section of the CNT – effectively controlled the union throughout the main part of its history.

In addition, it is of major significance that syndicalist movements in Spain, France, and America went much further than their counterparts in Britain in advocating the need for a so-called 'conscious minority' to provide theoretical and practical leadership inside both the syndicalist movement specifically and the working class movement generally. For example, in France, in recognition of the fact that the CGT was not composed exclusively of revolutionary workers, syndicalists sought to nurture an 'active minority' (*minorité agissante*) of revolutionary militants who would gain influence within its leading committees. This 'vanguard within a vanguard', it was conceived, would play a crucial role convincing members of the need for revolutionary change and protecting the organisation from becoming reformist. Thus, although Pierre Monatte and Alfred Rosmer and the grouping around *La Vie ouvriére* had no intention of forming a party or a faction, they clearly regarded the near 2,000 subscribers to their syndicalist journal as a nucleus which could raise the political and cultural level of union activists and develop a leadership cadre inside the Confédération.[17] The tutelary and inspirational role of such a conscious minority within the CGT would also provide leadership to the rest of the working

---

[14] Cited in G.H. Meaker, *The Revolutionary Left in Spain, 1914–1923* (Stanford, Calif., 1974) p. 391.

[15] Ibid., pp. 390–91.

[16] M. Bookchin, *To Remember Spain: The Anarchist and Syndicalist Revolution of 1936* (Edinburgh, 1994), p. 33.

[17] A. Rosmer, 'Il y a quarante ans', *La Révolution prolétarienne*, January 1951, pp. 1–3.

class generally, thereby helping to goad the relatively inert masses into action and spearheading the future revolution.

Of course, French trade unionism was very different and had far fewer members than in Britain; and to some extent it was because French unionism was much less inclusive that the notion of an 'active minority' giving leadership to the unorganised masses appeared both an inevitable and necessary process.[18] Perhaps for similar reasons some elements within the IWW subscribed to the same viewpoint, although not all Wobblies favoured the doctrine. Thus, the *Industrial Worker* stated 'We are the militant minority of the working class'.[19] The duty of this 'militant minority' was to promote solidarity and class-consciousness among the workers, fostering in them a revolutionary spirit. It was 'the real driving force in the labour movement of every country';[20] the 'advance guard of an emancipating army' separated from the main body of troops, and 'compelled to wage guerrilla actions while awaiting reinforcements from the main army of the proletariat'.[21] Likewise, despite sharp disagreements with the IWW over overall strategy, William Z. Foster's Syndicalist League of North America, essentially a propagandist body operating inside the existing unions, also wrote of the crucial vanguard role played by the syndicalist 'militant minority'.[22]

In Spain the decentralised structure of CNT organisation provided the context for a Bakunin-type semi-secret society of 'invisible pilots' who aimed to direct the revolution. Thus, in 1927 when the anarchists thought they might lose control of the CNT to the reformist trend, they established the Iberian Anarchist Federation (FAI), determined to 'keep an anarchist soul in a syndicalist body'.[23] The FAI was based on *grupos de afinidad* (affinity groups), consisting of up to 12 determined anarchist revolutionaries, drawn to each other not only by common social principles but also by common personal proclivities, or 'affinities'.[24]Although by no means a politically homogeneous organisation, the FAI was united in the pursuit of a set of common goals to inspire and guide the CNT and the affinity groups were viewed as the basis for a vanguard movement avowedly dedicated to the achievement of 'libertarian communism'. Like the CNT, the FAI was structured along confederal lines, linked together by a Peninsular Committee whose tasks, at least theoretically, were merely administrative. It had no bureaucratic apparatus, no membership cards or dues, and no headquarters with paid officials, secretaries and clerks.

---

18 This tradition of minority unionism has persisted in France; for example, in 1968, out of 10 million strikers only 3 million were unionised.

19 *Industrial Worker*, 3 October 1912.

20 *Solidarity*, 5 November 1912; *Industrial Worker* 3 July 1913; *Voice of the People*, 9 October 1913.

21 J.P. Cannon, *The IWW: The Great Anticipation* (New York, 1956), p. 30.

22 E.C. Ford and W.Z. Foster, *Syndicalism* (Chicago, 1990 [reprint of 1912 edition]), pp. 43–4.

23 R. Carr, *The Civil War in Spain 1936–39* (London, 1986), p. 15.

24 M. Bookchin, *The Spanish Anarchists: The Heroic Years 1868–1936* (Edinburgh, 1998), p. 197. See also R. Alexander, *The Anarchists in the Spanish Civil War: Vol 2* (London, 1999); J. Perirats, *Anarchists in the Spanish Revolution* (London, 1990).

Most writers on the Spanish labour movement seem to concur in the view that, with the departure of the moderate syndicalists in the early 1930s, the CNT fell under the complete domination of the FAI, effectively becoming an *anarcho*-syndicalist body. Certainly the FAI, with its commitment to revolution and to libertarian communism, helped to raise the political consciousness of the average CNT member. Moreover, it quickly established an ascendancy over the CNT so that a very small anarchist minority held all its important posts and dominated its bureaux and committees. While it was never able to completely rid the CNT of reformist elements, it gained a considerable following within the Confederación. It has been estimated that from 1934 to 1936 membership was around 10,000 and at its height in the Civil War about 30,000.[25] In other words, for all its anarchist rhetoric of rejection of authority and leadership, it was no secret that the FAI effectively guided CNT policy during the 1930s. The decentralised structure of the Confederación provided the context within which the Peninsular Committee walked a thin line between an administrative bureau and a Bolshevik Central Committee directing its supporters.[26]

Parallels with Bolshevism

The syndicalist theory of the leading role of a 'revolutionary minority' was, according to the Bolsheviks, in essence an uncompleted theory of a revolutionary workers' party. At the Second Comintern Congress, Jack Tanner, editor of the British shop stewards' paper *Solidarity*, related how the most conscious and able minority of the working class within the shop stewards' movement could, on their own, direct and lead the mass of workers in the struggle for everyday demands as well as revolutionary battles. There was no need for any special type of Bolshevik party.[27] Lenin replied:

> If Comrade Tanner says he is against the Party but in favour of a revolutionary minority of the most determined and class conscious proletarians leading the whole proletariat, then I say that in reality there is no difference between our points of view. What is the organised minority? If this minority is really class conscious and able to lead the masses and give an answer to every question that stands on the agenda, then it is actually the Party … If Comrade Tanner and the other comrades from the Shop Stewards Movement and the IWW recognise – and we see every day in every discussion that they really do recognise – that the conscious Communist minority of the working class can lead the proletariat, then they must admit that this is the meaning of all our resolutions Then the only difference between us is that they avoid the word 'party' …[28]

---

[25] First figure from G. Brenan, *The Spanish Labyrinth: An Account of the Social and Political; Background of the Spanish Civil War* (Cambridge, 1988), p. 184; second figure from Bookchin, *To Remember Spain*, p. 23.

[26] A. Durgan, 'Revolutionary Anarchism in Spain', *International Socialism*, 2:11 (1981), pp. 93–110.

[27] *Second Congress of the Communist International: Minutes of the Proceedings: Vol. 1* (London, 1977), pp. 61–2; A. Rosmer, *Lenin's Moscow* (London, 1971), pp. 68–71.

[28] *Second Congress*, p. 69; Rosmer, *Lenin's Moscow*, pp. 68–9.

Trotsky reiterated the parallel between the French syndicalists and the role of a communist party:

> The French syndicalists, in defiance of the traditions of [bourgeois] democracy and its deceptions, have said: 'We do not want any parties, we stand for proletarian unions and for the revolutionary minority within them which applies direct action' …
>
> What does this minority mean to our friends? It is the chosen section of the French working class, a section with a clear programme and organisation of its own, an organisation where they discuss all questions, and not alone discuss but also decide, and where they are bound by a certain discipline.[29]

The Second Comintern's *Theses on the Role of the Communist Party in the Proletarian Revolution* underlined the point:

> The revolutionary syndicalists often talk about the great role of the determined revolutionary minority. Well, a truly determined minority of the working class, a minority that is Communist, that wishes to act, that has a programme and wishes to organise the struggle of the masses, is *precisely the Communist Party*.[30]

In other words, because syndicalism understood and preached the leading role of the 'revolutionary minority' that vigorously waged a struggle for influence over the trade unions, it represented in practice the *embryo* of a revolutionary party, irrespective of its incomplete and undeveloped outlook. As Trotsky insisted with reference to the French syndicalists:

> It is my contention that your entire past activity was nothing else but preparation for the creation of the Communist Party of the proletarian revolution. Pre-war revolutionary syndicalism was a Communist Party in embryo. Conversely, active participation in the building of a genuine Communist Party means the continuation and development of the best traditions of French syndicalism.[31]

Yet after 1917, it was argued, the essence of this practice had found its full development and completion in the establishment of revolutionary communist parties.

Ironically, although initially attracted by syndicalism's stress on 'direct action', many working class militants subsequently dropped out of activity in the absence of general politics that could sustain their commitment once the level of industrial struggle had died down. For example, the Wobblies excelled in rushing around the country to wherever a strike was taking place, and leading the struggle in a militant and inspirational way. But they would then leave for action elsewhere, failing to grasp the importance of political organisation and understanding to ensure more than a tiny number of workers would stay changed after the strike ended. Relating their militant style of trade unionism to the level of class struggle meant that they effectively *rose* and *fell* with that struggle. This made it very difficult for them to build permanent

---

29 *Second Congress*, p. 73; 'Speech on Comrade Zinoviev's report on the role of the party', L. Trotsky, *The First Five Years of the Communist International, Vol. 1* (New York, 1972), pp. 98–9.

30 *Second Congress*, p. 93.

31 *First Five Years*, p. 160.

organisation, to sustain them and their periphery, during the 'downturn' in industrial militancy that often followed in particular workplaces.

By contrast, the Bolsheviks – with their notions of centralisation, leadership, organisation and discipline – had succeeded in building a political party that was not only able to withstand a period of brutal repression following the defeat of the 1905 revolution, but to maintain a hard core of committed activists that was in a position to provide revolutionary leadership once the level of struggle began to rise again from 1912 onwards, and to steadily build a genuinely mass organisation in the revolution of 1917. They had understood that any advance in class *consciousness* would prove temporary unless it was embedded in *political organisation.* If the problem with the Wobblies was that they fell between the two stools of building a trade union and a revolutionary organisation, the French syndicalists faced a similar dilemma according to Trotsky: 'they were too indefinite for the role of a party and too small for the role of a trade union.'[32]

Vanguard Party

As we have seen, the vast majority of syndicalists identified political parties with parliamentarism, opportunism and betrayal; at best they were unnecessary, at worst they were a positive handicap to the working class. Even those syndicalists who *did* accept the need for a socialist party, essentially viewed them as an auxiliary propaganda outlet for purely industrial activity, accompanied by occasional participation in elections. As J.T. Murphy later acknowledged: 'None of us saw the political party as anything other than a propaganda body for the spread of Socialist ideas.'[33] 'Before 1917, the revolutionary socialist parties "preparing the day" were not conceived of as parties of insurrection. Rather did we conceive ourselves as "John the Baptists of the New Redemption".'[34]

Of course, this was not an oversight that was peculiar to syndicalists but was part of the limitation of all pre-1917 revolutionary Marxists, including Luxemburg, Gramsci and Trotsky.[35] Moreover, although Lenin was building a 'new type' of Bolshevik party in Russia the significance of this did not become generally apparent until workers seized power in the October revolution. Understanding the different

---

32 L. Trotsky, 'The Anarcho-Syndicalist Prejudices Again!' [May 1923] *Marxism and the Trade Unions* (London, 1972), p.32.

33 J.T. Murphy, *New Horizons* (London, 1941).

34 *New Reasoner*, Winter 1958/9.

35 Luxemburg and her supporters in the Spartacus League had remained part of the reformist German Social Democratic Party even after it supported the First World War. Gramsci had remained a member of the Italian Socialist Party, albeit supporting the factory council movement in Turin. Neither left to establish communist parties on the Bolshevik model until after they had reassessed their experiences in the light of the Russian Revolution, outbreak of revolution in Germany in November 1918, and revolutionary crisis that engulfed Italy in 1920. Trotsky during the years leading up to 1914 was a 'conciliationist', advocating and working for the unification of the Mensheviks and Bolsheviks within the Russian Socialist Democratic Party, until his return to Russia in May 1917 when he finally joined the Bolsheviks.

context in which Bolshevism emerged is important, before we proceed to consider the arguments that were held with the syndicalists.

The extreme backwardness of the productive forces compared to Western Europe, the severity of Tsarist rule and the absence of parliamentary democracy meant there was little scope for the reformist model of a broad-based socialist party representing the whole of the working class.[36] Instead, Russian Marxists were forced to organise in the workplace rather than on the geographical lines of parliamentary constituencies, and Tsarist repression meant even the economic class struggle became highly politicised. But in addition to such objective conditions, the conscious role played by revolutionaries, above all Lenin, in turning small propaganda and agitation circles together into a national, centralised revolutionary party was also significant. It transformed an apparent organisational division between two factions (Bolsheviks and Mensheviks) within one party in 1903 into what effectively became two completely separate parties with fundamental differences in political perspective about the nature of the coming revolution and the respective roles of the working class and bourgeoisie within it.

This was to be of enormous importance, particularly as in other countries many revolutionaries (such as Rosa Luxemburg) had remained organisationally trapped in the left-wing of broad reformist or 'centrist' social democratic parties (for example in Germany the Communist Party was not founded until after the outbreak of revolution in November 1918). By contrast, in Russia a clear break had been made and an independent revolutionary party had existed for 14 years before its triumph. It would be wrong to imagine that Lenin grasped the full significance of what he was doing from the beginning; in fact he did not advocate a break with the Second International until 1914 and even then did not call for revolutionaries outside Russia to form their own parties. But it was his understanding of the need to combat reformism, not only ideologically, but also organisationally, that was to be crucial to the process. Thus, prior to 1917 the practice of Bolshevism had already emerged, even if the theory, which separated the Bolsheviks from other groups on the left in Russia and in Europe more generally, still awaited its final completion.[37]

From a syndicalist perspective Lenin's insistence on the need for a revolutionary socialist party negated the Marxist claim that socialism could only come through working class self-emancipation. But in response, Lenin insisted that while socialism could indeed only come from below, the sectional and fragmented nature of workers' struggle against capitalism also made the need for a vanguard party necessary if a revolution was to be accomplished. It was precisely because of the inherent unevenness in organisation, struggle and consciousness inside the working class movement that only a minority of workers would become revolutionaries, at least until there was a fully revolutionary situation. But there was always a *militant minority* that became convinced by its experience that the system had to be transformed as a whole, and that the direct methods of struggle employed by the working class were the most effective means of doing so. The key question was how

---

[36] J. Molyneux, *Marxism and the Party* (London, 1978) p. 38; 65–9.

[37] J. Molyneux, 'The Birth of Bolshevism', *Socialist Worker*, 4 April 1987; M. Haynes, 'The British Working Class in Revolt: 1910–1914', *International Socialism*, 2: 22 (1984), p. 103.

to organise such a minority so that they could become the lever which could raise the combativity of the *entire class*?

Lenin's response was to argue that 'a sharp distinction must be made between the concepts of 'class' and 'party'. Instead of attempting to 'represent' the working class as a whole, it was necessary to fuse 'it's most advanced, most class-conscious and therefore it's most revolutionary part'[38] into a revolutionary party. Such a *vanguard* party should seek to encourage workers self-activity, whilst at the same time fighting to raise the general level of political consciousness of those it influenced, linking the immediate aspirations of workers to the central political aim of the need to overthrow the system.[39] It was not to be a leadership that issued commands from above and expected the working class to follow, but which took the best of what was invented by workers themselves in struggle and then generalised that experience. Thus, when in 1905 the Petrograd working class spontaneously created soviets, Lenin and the Bolsheviks, (after initially opposing them) had rapidly changed their model of revolution.[40]

Leading Role of the Party in the Revolution

Within the early congresses of the Comintern and RILU Lenin and other Bolshevik leaders made every effort to win over the syndicalists to the need for a revolutionary party on the basis that it was 'indispensable for the fulfilment of the historical mission which is placed upon the [working class] – the destruction of the bourgeoisie':[41]

> The Communist International rejects most decisively the view that the proletariat can carry out its revolution without an independent political party …
>
> The class struggle demands … the centralisation and common leadership of the different forms of the proletarian movement (trade unions, co-operatives, works committees [etc]) … Only a political party can be such a unifying and leading centre. To renounce the creation and strengthening of such a party, to renounce subordinating oneself to it, is to renounce unity in the leadership of the individual battle units of the proletariat who are advancing on the different battlefields. The class struggle of the proletariat demands a concerted agitation that illuminates the different stages of the struggle form a uniform point of view and at every given moment directs the attention of the proletariat towards specific tasks common to the whole class. That cannot be done without an centralised political apparatus, that is to say outside of a political party … [The syndicalists] do not see that without an independent political party the working class is a rump without a head.[42]

---

38 *Second Congress*, pp. 91–2.

39 T. Cliff, *Lenin: Vol. 1: Building the Party* (London, 1975); N. Harding, *Lenin's Political Thought: Vol. 2: Theory and Practice in the Socialist Revolution* (New York, 1981).

40 Ibid., pp. 159–68.

41 *First Five Years*, p. 98.

42 *Second Congress*, pp. 92–3.

Recognising that the collapse of the Second International and betrayal of the socialist parties had reinforced the syndicalists' antipathy towards political parties, Zinoviev insisted they appreciate the difference between *reformist* and *revolutionary* parties:

> We say to our comrades from the ranks of the syndicalists … that the sign of the times does not consist in the fact that we should negate the Party. The sign of the epoch in which we live … consists in the fact that we must say: 'The old parties have been shipwrecked; down with them. Long live the new Communist Party that must be built under new conditions' …
>
> No formless workers' union, living from hand to mouth, can show the working class the correct path, but a party that embraces the best out of the working class … It is for us a matter of organising the vanguard of the working class so that they can really lead the masses in this struggle.[43]

The problem was that in the absence of a revolutionary party led by the more advanced workers, the mass of the working class would follow or acquiesce in some *other* kind of lead. The vacuum had to be filled and if the advanced workers lacked the cohesion and confidence to provide an organised *revolutionary* pole of attraction – if they were not able to act as a *party* – then the vacuum would always be filled by default by those *reformist* forces who offered a strategy of working within the system and accommodating to it. Even after the February 1917 Russian revolution, it was pointed out, when workers had broken with past traditions by creating new institutions of power, the soviets, they had still remained loyal to those who had led them in the past. Thus, at first the two main reformist parties, the Mensheviks and Social Revolutionaries, had a majority of delegates in the soviets, with the Bolsheviks only a minority. The Bolshevik Party had set themselves the task of winning the workers' and soldiers' soviets to the goal of overthrowing the Provisional government, and it was the Bolsheviks' arguments, and their own experience, which convinced Russian workers of the necessity of this second revolution. By the late summer and early autumn of 1917 the Bolsheviks had gained a majority in the soviets, and it had become possible for the revolution to be accomplished in October 1917.[44]

In response, the syndicalists protested that the Bolshevik seizure of state power had not been a genuine revolution. CNT leader Angel Pestaña stressed the spontaneous mass character of a revolutionary uprising, not the guiding role of a revolutionary party; the February 1917 Russian Revolution was one thing, he argued, the Bolshevik Revolution quite another. He dismissed as gratuitous, as belied by history, the claim that revolution everywhere required the existence of communist parties. Political parties did not make revolutions; they merely organised coups, 'and a *coup d'état* is not a revolution' Pestaña insisted. History demonstrated

---

[43] Ibid., pp. 50–52.

[44] By contrast the foundation of the German Communist Party on the Bolshevik model only occurred in December 1918 *after* the revolution had broken out; faced with the near impossible task of attempting to build a revolutionary party from scratch in the course of a revolutionary situation, it ended up veering from right to left and back again. See P. Broué, *The German Revolution 1917–1923* (Chicago, 2006); C. Harman, *The Lost Revolution: Germany 1918 to 1923* (London, 1982).

that 'from the French Revolution of 1789 onward revolutions were made without parties'.[45] Trotsky responded by shouting out: 'You're forgetting the Jacobins!'[46] After being triggered off by a spontaneous uprising in 1789, the transition from the semi-republican government of Gironde to the revolutionary one of 1792, which overthrew feudal property relations, had not been carried out by the unorganised masses without any party, but under the decisive leadership of the Jacobin Party.

Similarly, although the Russian Revolutions of February 1917 had also started out as a spontaneous act without the leadership of a party, the October Revolution had been organised in practically all its important particulars, including the date, by the Bolsheviks. During the zigzags of the revolution between February and October – including the June demonstration, the July Days and subsequent orderly retreat and the rebuff of the rightist Kornilov putsch – the mass of workers and soldiers had gradually come under the influence and leadership of the Bolshevik Party. Such a party had been essential to raising the revolution from its initial stages to its final victory. It had provided the centralised organisation and leadership that the working class movement required to match the general staff of the ruling class concentrated in the capitalist state and ultimately resting on its repressive apparatus.[47] It had required the existence of a revolutionary socialist party to co-ordinate, plan, consciously synchronise and continuously shape the intervention of the leading elements in the 'spontaneous' mass struggle to make possible the overthrow of the regime.

It was true, it was pointed out, that if revolutionary parties were necessary to *lead* workers' revolutions, they did not *create* them, only the mass upsurge of the working class could do that. In the words of Trotsky: 'Without a guiding organisation the energy of the masses would dissipate like steam not enclosed in a piston-box. But what moves things is not the piston or the box, but the steam'.[48] Nonetheless, despite the necessity of winning majority influence within the soviets to ensure the active support of the majority of workers for revolutionary politics, the conquest of state power required an *insurrection* that could not be carried out by the soviets, which organised all workers, both advanced and backward. Ultimately the act of armed insurrection demanded much more decisiveness, a resolute leadership that could plan the action and decide on the exact day and manner of carrying it out. Lenin repeated Marx and Engels' proposition that 'insurrection is an art', requiring the right balance between political leadership, and military and technical planning.[49] So it was that the Bolshevik Party had organised the October 1917 insurrection, albeit not directly in its own name but via the channel of a Revolutionary Military Committee established by the Petrograd Soviet and headed by Trotsky.[50]

Despite the greater significance of the ('war of manoeuvre') ideological struggle against capitalist ideological hegemony in Western Europe compared with Russia,

---

45 Cited in Thorpe, p. 136.

46 Rosmer, *Lenin's Moscow*, p. 69.

47 T. Cliff, *Lenin: Vol. 2: All Power to the Soviets* (London, 1976).

48 Cited in A. Callinicos, *The Revolutionary Road to Socialism* (London, 1983), p. 47.

49 V.I. Lenin, 'Marxism and Insurrection: A Letter to the Central Committee of the R.S.D.L.P. (B), *Selected Works: Vol. 2* (Moscow, 1970), pp. 381–4.

50 Cliff, *All Power to the Soviets*, pp. 335–79.

Gramsci was also later to insist that a direct assault on capitalist power via armed insurrection ('war of position') was still the 'decisive moment of struggle', with the 'modern prince' (revolutionary party) an essential central, co-ordinating and generalising body.[51] Likewise Joaquín Maurin recognised the necessity of a 'revolutionary apparatus' that could determine the precise moment for a revolutionary assault.[52]

Union Autonomy from the Communist Party

After the Second Comintern Congress Trotsky conducted a vigorous campaign to win French syndicalists to communism. He argued that in fighting for trade union 'autonomy' or neutrality from politics the pre-war French syndicalists had effectively fought for independence from the capitalist class and its reformist socialist parties, which had represented a 'struggle against opportunism – for a revolutionary road'. However, the First World War had subsequently proved that their previous justifiable hostility to the reformist socialist parties in no way guaranteed that all syndicalists would remain independent from the capitalist state. Thus, the CGT had collapsed into patriotism and accepted government office. More significantly, post-1917 French syndicalists had transformed their notion of 'autonomy' of the trade unions from reformist socialist parties into an absolute principle, to mean autonomy from *all* political parties, including the newly established revolutionary communist parties affiliated to the Comintern. By doing so, Trotsky argued, they effectively proposed the 'dissolution of the revolutionary vanguard into the backward masses, that is, the trade unions'. In effect, autonomy, which had once had a revolutionary content before 1917, had effectively become reactionary after the best syndicalist militants had gone over to the communist party and the remaining syndicalists had come to view it as their most dangerous opponent.[53]

At the Third Comintern Congress held in June 1921 Trotsky attempted to deal with the syndicalist fears that if they aligned themselves they would run the risk of seeing the unions transformed into mere subsidiary organisations under the control of the communist parties:[54]

> Those who recognise that the proletariat urgently needs the ideological and political leadership of the vanguard, united in the Communist Party, thereby recognise that the party must become the leading force inside the trade unions as well …

---

51 A. Gramsci, *Selections from the Prison Notebooks* (London, 1971).

52 *Lucha Social*, 29 April 1922.

53 L. Trotsky, 'Communism and Syndicalism', *Marxism and the Trade Unions* (London: New Park, 1972 [first published October 1929]), pp. 35–50.

54 See E.H. Carr, *Socialism in One Country, 1924–1926, vol. 3*, part 1 (London, 1964) and *The Bolshevik Revolution, 1917–1923*, vol. 3 (London, 1966); Thorpe, *Workers Themselves*; W. Thorpe, 'Syndicalist Internationalism Before World War II', in M. van der Linden and W. Thorpe (eds), *Revolutionary Syndicalism: An International Perspective* (Aldershot, 1990); 'Syndicalist Internationalism and Moscow, 1919–1922: The Breach', *Canadian Journal of History*, 14:1 (1979), pp. 199–234; R. Tosstorff, *Profintern: Die Rote Gewerkschaftsinterntionale, 1920–1937* (Paderborn, 2004) and 'Moscow Versus Amsterdam: Reflections on the History of Profintern', *Labour History Review*, 68:1 (2003), pp. 79–97.

> Naturally this does not mean that the trade unions become subject to the party organisationally, or from the outside. The trade unions are organisationally independent. Within the trade unions the party wields the influence it gains by its activity, by its ideological intervention, by its authority. But to say this is to say that the party must strive in every way to increase its influence over the trade unions; it must deal with all the questions arising in the trade union movement; it must give clear answers to them and carry out its views through the Communists functioning in the trade unions, without in the least violating the organisational autonomy of the unions.[55]

As on the other main issues of contention we have considered, a number of leading syndicalists in France and elsewhere finally made the break with their past traditions to accept the Bolshevik party model: a new type of revolutionary political party that would be capable of providing centralised leadership inside the working class movement. The final chapter assesses the syndicalist-communist fusion within such parties during the 1920s.

---

[55] L. Trotsky, 'Speech at a General Party Membership Meeting of the Moscow Organisation, July 1921', *The First Five Years of the Communist International: Vol. 2* (New York, 1972), p. 34.

Chapter 12

Syndicalist-Communist Fusion

The syndicalist movement not only made a considerable and enduring contribution to the explosive wave of working class struggle that swept the world during the first two decades of the twentieth century (as well as in Spain during the 1930s), but was itself a direct expression of workers' rising level of organisation, confidence and class-consciousness during this period. The movement displayed a powerful and inspiring capacity to mount uncompromising anti-capitalist forms of struggle which challenged both the structures of managerial authority within the capitalist enterprise and the legitimacy of 'democratic' state power within society generally. In the process it provided a devastating critique of the prevailing versions of political labourism and state socialism, as well as of bureaucratic and conservative trade union officialdom. It antipathy to capitalism and vision of an alternative society raised fundamental questions about the need for new and democratic forms of power through which workers could manage society themselves. According to the Webbs:

> We must recognise that the Syndicalists are trying to express what is a real and deep-seated feeling in millions of manual working wage earners, which cannot and ought not to be ignored. The workman refuses any longer to be a mere instrument of production: a mere 'hand' or tool in the capitalist enterprise. He claims the right … to be … not merely a means to someone else's end. And with this in mind he refuses … to be satisfied with continuing, for all time, to merely be a wage-earner serving under orders, without control over his own working life.[1]

Undoubtedly, syndicalism's chief contribution was their development of revolutionary strategy and tactics within the trade unions. Although Marx, Engels and Lenin and Trotsky had made pioneering efforts to understand the nature of trade unions, they lacked practical experience of mass reformist unions and, not surprisingly, left many questions unanswered. By contrast, although Luxemburg and Gramsci went somewhat further, the syndicalists, approaching the problem as shopfloor activists, were able to draw out some essential features of the dynamics of trade unionism within capitalist society. In particular British syndicalism (reflected in both the ISEL and wartime shop stewards' movement) not only theorised the nature of the trade union bureaucracy and the conflict between the rank-and-file and union officialdom, but also demonstrated a distinctive practical means to overcome the officials' hold. The model of independent rank-and-file organisation they developed, which in certain circumstances has the potential to develop into workers' councils or soviets,

---

[1] S. and B. Webb, *What Syndicalism Means: An Examination of the Origin and Motives of the Movement with an Analysis of its Proposals for the Control of Industry* (London, 1912).

went much further than the Comintern had conceived at the time, and has arguably retained its relevance to the contemporary world.

Despite the failure of the syndicalist movement to achieve its ultimate objectives, this in no way invalidates its influential contribution in propaganda and action to the international revolutionary movement, one that produced some of the most audacious and imaginative working class fighters of the early twentieth century. Assessing the impact of the ITGWU in Ireland Emmett O'Connor has commented:

> As a revolutionary force it lacked the means of sustenance, the power of articulation, and was reliant on a convergence of [structural and contextual] factors. Judged in this context, syndicalism amounted to little more than a passing thunderclap, a distant Irish echo to the tumult of post-war Europe. However, as a technique of mobilisation, it achieved remarkable success and had a formative influence on the structure of the Labour movement ... If syndicalism may be criticised as being amorphous, incoherent, and transitory, then the Irish movement was virtually a caricature of syndicalist inefficacy. And if the real accomplishment of syndicalism lay in its power to inspire discontent among the working masses, and its capacity to generate and sustain direct action with a method of agitation, then post-war Ireland must be regarded as a minor but brilliant illustration of syndicalist capability.[2]

In addition, despite its subsequent demise, syndicalism bequeathed an enduring legacy for future generations of trade union and political activists in many countries. For example in America it seems likely that without the IWW the massive renewed outburst of industrial struggle that swept the country during the 1930s, with its highly successful mass union recruitment drive among unskilled and foreign-born workers in the mass production industries carried out by the newly formed Congress of Industrial Organisations (CIO), would have been very different and certainly less effective. As James Cannon commented, the IWW was a 'dress rehearsal' for the CIO in the same manner that the failed 1905 revolution in Russia had been a dress rehearsal for the revolutions of 1917. His view that 'the CIO became possible only after and because the IWW had championed and popularised the notion of industrial unionism in word and deed' is supported by detailed studies which document the way many of the organisers in the auto and steel unions, often at local level, were ex-Wobblies.[3] The sit-in tactic that was used to such dramatic effect in the CIO organising drives was inspired directly from the IWW. In 1906, more than three decades before the factory occupation at the General Motors plant in Flint, Michigan in 1937, the IWW had led a sit-in at a General Electric plant in Schenectady, upstate New York, to protest at the dismissal of three workers. The 1906 strike, like so many Wobbly efforts, was lost, but its lessons about militant direct action at the point of production lived on. Meanwhile, even to this day the IWW song 'Solidarity Forever' has remained the American labour movement's classic anthem. Likewise in other countries the syndicalist tradition has been viewed with considerable admiration by future generations of union and political activists; its valuable contribution to the

---

[2] E. O'Connor, *Syndicalism in Ireland* (Cork, 1988), p. 191.

[3] J.P. Cannon, *The IWW: The Great Anticipation* (New York, 1956), p. 5; S. Bird, D. Georgakas and D. Shaffer, *Solidarity Forever: An Oral History of the Wobblies* (London, 1987), p. 80.

growth and subsequent development of respective labour, socialist and communist movements widely acknowledged.

Nonetheless, as we have seen, it would be mistaken to only acknowledge syndicalism's tremendous contribution and latent possibilities. With the benefit of historical and political hindsight it is possible to observe its in-built limitations and weaknesses. In many respects, its efficacy as a strategy for the revolutionary transformation of society, can be seen to have been overtaken by a more developed and richer Marxist tradition. Of course, there were a number of commonalities between the two traditions, such as the advocacy of revolution from below and the self-emancipation of the working class, the antipathy displayed towards reformist socialist party and trade union leaders, and the attempt to transform the unions into revolutionary bodies. And to some extent the revolutionary Marxist tradition was *itself* refined as a result of the influence of syndicalism, notably with the placing of trade union struggle at the very core of the communist project (thereby also building on the prior Bolshevik experience). But the Marxist tradition also crucially pointed to a number of crucial limitations within the syndicalist tradition, including: the need to link the industrial struggle to political issues of a broader nature and to direct such struggles towards the conquest of state power via insurrection; the need for a revolutionary political party that provided centralised leadership inside the working class movement; and the insufficiency of unions compared to soviets as the chief agency of revolution and organ of workers' power.

This Marxist critique of syndicalism, which reached its zenith with the Russian Revolution and the establishment of the Comintern and RILU, was further enriched by subsequent theoretical work and practical experience. In the process a number of the most prominent syndicalists made the leap to communism. Clearly, as we have seen, the experience of October 1917 and the direct intervention of the Bolsheviks were a decisive factor in the emergence of communist parties and the transition from syndicalism to communism that was made by a layer of leading syndicalist activists. The success of the Russian Revolution, when revolutionary movements elsewhere in Europe had failed, undoubtedly increased the attraction of the Russian model and the prestige of the Bolsheviks. And the intervention of Lenin and the Comintern leadership in the affairs of the different revolutionary movements across Europe and beyond was vital for the creation of communist parties and the shaping of their policies, tactics and organisation.

But we should not underestimate the extent to which communist ideas and organisation *also* developed out of various strands in the *domestic* situation in each country: these included pre-war workers' struggles, the impact of the First World War, the post-war economic and social crisis, the spring-tide of workers' struggle and its ebb, the discrediting of social democracy, the development of radical left currents within reformist socialist parties, *and* the experience, both positive and negative, of revolutionary syndicalist movements. In fact such domestic influences were not only important in the emergence of the new communist parties, but also in terms of their subsequent early development. With reference to Britain James Hinton has noted:

> It is doubtful whether, by the time of the formation of the communist parties in 1920–21, any substantial proportion of its members or leaders had really grasped the Bolshevik idea

> of the party or would have approved of it had they done so. In this sense they carried their syndicalism over into the new party.[4]

Indeed the new revolutionary communist parties that emerged were fraught with ideological, political and organisational limitations, which to some extent at least were compounded by the carrying over of syndicalist influences into the new parties. This meant it took several years to transform them into combat organisations orientated to workers' struggles. Had they been established prior to 1918 or 1919 it might have been possible to have taken advantage of the unprecedented industrial and political struggles that swept the world. But by 1920 and 1921 the working class was on the retreat and the subjective weaknesses of the revolutionaries who came together in the new communist parties compounded the disadvantages of the objective situation created by their belated formation. This meant the parties spent their formative years during the 1920s trying to turn themselves into parties of the Bolshevik-type, along the lines laid down at the Comintern, in conditions not at all favourable to their growth or expanding influence. A brief exploration of such developments follows.

The Syndicalist-Communist Fusion

In France, the Socialist-turned-Communist Party, according to Franz Borkenau, was far from being really revolutionary: it was 'a coalition of left-wing and centrist groups ... [an] unwieldy and hybrid political formation ... an unstable compound of conflicting elements'; and the party's most prominent leaders were out-and-out reformists willing to affiliate to the Comintern only because it was popular.[5] A factional struggle was to ravage the new Communist Party from its formation in December 1920 until the beginning of 1923. On one side stood the partisans of the Comintern (including Souvarine Loriot), who defended Moscow's policy of strict discipline and ideological unity, the subordination of the unions to the party, and a united front with the socialists. Against them stood the moderate socialists (Marcel Cachin and L.O Frossard), who had only gone over to the communists at the last moment and disagreed with the Comintern on many issues.[6]

In this situation the role of revolutionary syndicalists such as Rosmer, Monatte and others, was viewed as crucial by Moscow. Lenin and Trotsky urged the syndicalists to join the French Communist Party and play an active role in its leadership. Yet, partly because of Zinovieite hostility to the syndicalists, Monatte did not join the party himself until May 1923 and it was not until the following January that he became a member of its Central Committee.[7] Moreover, even though leading syndicalists

4 J. Hinton, *The First Shop Stewards' Movement* (London, 1973), p. 276.

5 R. Wohl, *French Communism in the Making 1914–1924* (Stanford, Calif., 1966), pp. 438–9.

6 F. Borkeneau, *The Communist International* (London, 1938), pp. 200–229.

7 I. Birchill, 'Alfred and Marguerite Rosmer', Paper presented to New Socialist Approaches to History Seminar, London Socialist Historians Group, Institute of Historical Research , University of London, 2 April 2001, pp. 11–13.

were able to integrate serious trade union work into the party's day-to-day activity, they also continued to assist on the 'independence' of the trade unions from party influence and agreed that any revolution in France would have to be realised through the unions and not by the party alone. In a letter to the French Communist Party's congress in September 1922 Trotsky complained:

> Following Tours a considerable number of revolutionary syndicalists joined the party. In and by itself this was a very valuable development. But precisely because there was a total lack of clarity in our party on the question of the interrelations between the party and the trade unions, the syndicalist views, which demand that the party refrain from 'meddling' in the trade union movement, tended to reinforce the utterly false idea that the party and the trade unions constitute two absolutely independent powers whose only bond at best is that of mutual and friendly neutrality. In other words, it was not the revolutionary syndicalists who were remoulded in the party's forge, but, on the contrary, it was they who imprinted upon the party their stamp of anarcho-syndicalism, thereby further increasing the ideological chaos.[8]

The eventual conversion of the CGTU's leadership to communism in 1923 was to mark an important victory for Moscow. By 1925 the Communist-syndicalist Pierre Sémard (secretary of the railroad workers' federation) was willing to call the CGTU's doctrine 'syndical Leninism'. Lenin, he wrote, had not only taught the French syndicalists the role of the unions, he had also shown them 'the indispensable necessity of a doctrinal group with iron discipline, the vanguard of the proletariat – the Communist Party'. And the ties between the party and the CGTU were made public in 1926.[9] Yet other ex-syndicalists were unhappy with the 1923–1924 'Bolshevisation' of the French party. Monatte, Maurice Chambelland and Robert Louzon attributed to the *syndicat* the key role in the revolutionary struggle for the emancipation of the proletariat, with the party having an auxiliary and not directing role.[10] By April 1924, Monatte, Chambelland and Alfred Rosmer collectively resigned from the party's daily newspaper *L'Humanité,* complaining that members of the party who had come from revolutionary syndicalism were treated as 'carriers of the plague'. In November Monatte and Rosmer took the irrevocable step of circulating an open letter to members of the party opposing the adoption of the structure and working methods of the Russian party, and they condemned the party leadership for its attempt to restrict access to Trotsky's writings and speeches. In December Rosmer and Monatte were expelled from the party.[11] In January 1925 Monatte, Chambelland and Louzon launched *La Révolution prolétarienne*, taking for its sub-title, 'revue syndicaliste-communiste'. It returned to the syndicalism of the *Charte d'Amiens*

---

[8] L. Trotsky, 'Letter to the Convention of the French Communist Party', September 1922, *The First Five Years of the Communist International: Vol. 2* (New York, 1972), p. 163.

[9] See M. Adereth, *The French Communist Party: A Critical History (1920–84): From Comintern to the 'Colours of France'* (Manchester, 1984).

[10] J. Jennings, *Syndicalism in France: A Study of Ideas* (Houndmills: 1990), p. 178. Maurice Chambelland and Robert Louzon had been involved with Monatte's re-launched *La Vie ouvriére, with the* former subsequently becoming the leading figure around the small group of militants and theoreticians organised around the newspaper *Ligue syndicaliste* inside the CGTU.

[11] Ibid., pp. 179–180; Wohl, pp. 412–18.

and campaigned for the reconstitution of syndicalist unity, with the merger of the communist-controlled CGTU and the Jouhaux reformist-led CGT. Rosmer, whilst initially playing a role alongside Monatte, eventually left in 1929 to join the ranks of the Trotskyist Left Opposition.[12]

Meanwhile the communist movement that emerged in America in 1919, from the confluence of two general currents in American radicalism, left-wing socialism and IWW-style syndicalism, was hampered by state repression and its own internal factional struggles, the policy of dual unionism and calls to 'boycott' the AFL. But by December 1921, in an attempt to circumnavigate the repression, it successfully resorted to the device of functioning as both an open and legal Workers' Party with a limited programme, as well as an underground Communist Party. It soon adopted the Comintern's policy of working within the 'reactionary' unions, and under the guidance of William Z. Foster the newly-named Trade Union Education League (TUEL) TUEL became the Red International's official American labour body and the organisational base for communists working within the trade unions.[13] The TUEL had neither dues nor membership; instead, militants attempted to win the unions to a radical programme, including: class struggle unionism rather than class collaboration; development of industrial unionism through amalgamation of existing unions; opposition to dual unionism; the shop delegate system of local union organisation; affiliation to RILU; abolition of capitalism and the establishment of a workers' republic; and support for Soviet Russia.

Yet the League's influence, with only about 500 hard-core activists at the movement's height, was minimal, although it allegedly had a newspaper circulation of about 10–15,000 copies.[14] The failure to sink genuine mass roots was partly because of the level of state repression and hostility it suffered from conservative labour leaders, but also because of factional conflicts inside the Communist Party itself, notably between Charles Ruthenberg's group of political Communists based in New York and Foster's ex-syndicalist trade union group of Communists based in Chicago.[15]The Foster faction prided themselves on being proletarian and denounced the other faction as petit-bourgeois and intellectual, while the Ruthenberg dismissed Foster and his colleagues as 'half-educated workers' and 'syndicalists' without coherent communist principles. The widely divergent backgrounds, experiences and interests of the two distinct groups accentuated the party's inherent tensions and laid the foundations for a decade of bitter factional conflict.

---

12 Jennings, p. 211.

13 Foster's Trade Union Educational League, founded in Chicago in November 1920, was the successor to the pre-war Syndicalist League of North America (1912–1914) and the International Trade Union Education League (1915–1917). See J. Zumoff, 'The Syndicalist Roots of American Communism: The IWW and William Z. Foster', Paper presented to seminar on Comparative Labour and Working Class History Seminer, Institute for Historical Research, University of London, 19 January 2001.

14 J.R. Barrett, *William Z. Foster and the Tragedy of American Radicalism* (Chicago, 1999), p. 123.

15 W.Z. Foster, *History of the Communist Party of the United States* (New York, 1952). p. 203.

In a debate with Comintern representatives, Foster argued 'the TUEL ha[d] to be a separate organisation' not subject to the Workers' Party's authority, that 'high politics' should be kept out of the TUEL, and that 'substance and mass strength...be given preference over ideological clarity'. The TUEL programme, he said, had to be 'simplified and concentrated around burning everyday issues in the class struggle'. Foster and his allies were denounced for paying lip-service to the Comintern line while 'following a political policy against the Comintern'.[16] And with Moscow's backing, Ruthenberg took control of the Workers' Party, in 1926 purging its TUEL adherents. Such conflicts were further compounded by the Comintern's subsequent ultra-left 'new line' during the late 1920s, when the party dramatically reverted back to a dual union strategy (of 'red unionism').[17]

In Britain, syndicalism had also been one of the tendencies, along with the various Marxist groupings, that coalesced to form the Communist Party. Indeed the prominent role of a number of central figures from the shop stewards' movement within the leadership of the new British Communist party ensured that some of the positive elements of syndicalism – notably its emphasis on workplace and trade union struggles – were absorbed from the outset. But such syndicalist influence also meant the anti-leadership tradition and avoidance of questions of political action were also carried over with detrimental effect. Thus, the work of the party fractions inside the unions during the early years of the party tended to become submerged in localised and spontaneous strike movements with little attempt to seize the initiative and provide coherent political leadership.

> ... the industrial base of the party in its formative years was purely syndicalist in outlook ... many of the leaders of the party were drawn from this industrial base and ... no attempt was made in the period of the formation of the party to understand the limitations of syndicalism and to draw the lessons of its weaknesses in a period when working-class struggles in all their forms needed to be fought with a political perspective. On the contrary, the party went out of its way to appeal to industrial militants in purely syndicalist terms.[18]

There was a persistent tendency to regard the Shop Stewards' and Workers' Committee Movement and not the party as the essential element in the struggle. At the Third Congress of the Comintern Radek commented: 'In many places the party appears on the scene under the cloak of the Workers' Committees' and any success that is achieved by the propaganda does not bring the masses near to the CP.'[19] Recognition of the need for the subordination of activity in the trade unions to the overall direction of a revolutionary party was only achieved through a considerable

---

[16] Cited in J. Stepan-Norris and M. Zeitlin, *Left-Out: Reds and America's Industrial Unions* (Cambridge, 2003), p. 35.

[17] Barrett, pp. 115–23.

[18] M. Woodhouse, 'Marxism and Stalinism in Britain, 1920–26', in M. Woodhouse and B. Pearce, *Essays on the History of Communism in Britain* (London, 1975), p. 56.

[19] *Communist Review*, December 1921.

struggle against the traditions inherited from past syndicalist methods of work.[20]As J.T. Murphy acknowledged:

> We were of course far from having put into operation all that was required by the [Comintern] resolution to reconstitute the new Communist Party. We had made our political declaration of adherence to its principles, but it is one thing to accept a principle and another to apply it to life ... Naturally it would take time to transform parliamentary socialists, guild socialists, syndicalists, anti-parliamentarians and the like into fully-developed Communists of the standard set by the new Leninist conceptions.[21]

It required behind-the-scenes pressure from the Executive Committee of the Comintern, who strongly criticised the failure of the British Communist Party to depart from previous methods of work and to build a disciplined and centralised party of the Bolshevik type.[22] By 1922 the Shop Stewards' and Workers' Committee Movement was merged within the British Bureau of the RILU with Tom Mann as chairman. And as a result of direct intervention by the Comintern, the industrial work of the party was reorganised in 1924 with the establishment of a National Minority Movement that sought:

> ... not to organise independent revolutionary unions or to split the revolutionary elements away from the existing organisations affiliated to the TUC and through it to the Amsterdam International, but to convert the revolutionary minorities in the various industries, into revolutionary majorities. Hence [it] is not an organisation of unions but only of revolutionary minorities of unions.[23]

Such an industrial strategy, effectively building on the experience of the wartime shop stewards' movement, marked a significant advance in the communist approach to trade union activity in general and the trade union bureaucracy in particular. And the Minority Movement was to achieve a considerable degree of success at national level, notably in getting significant parts of its programme adopted as official policy in the mining, engineering, rail and transport unions and in influencing left-wing union leaders (including miners' leader A.J. Cook) in the run up to the 1926 General Strike. Likewise, the 'Bolshevisation' of the British Communist Party, although implemented in a bureaucratic fashion, marked an important step forward in

---

20 M. Woodhouse, 'Syndicalism, Communism and the Trade Unions in Britain, 1910–1926', originally published in *Marxist*, vol. 4, no. 3, 1966 available at: http://www.whatnextjournal.co.uk/Pages/History/Syndicalism.html, p. 4.

21 J. Murphy, *New Horizons* (London, 1941), pp. 181–2.

22 See J. Klugmann, *History of the Communist Party of Great Britain: Formation and Early Years 1919–1924: Vol. 1* (London, 1968), pp. 75–235; L.J. Macfarlane, *The British Communist Party: Its Origin and Development Until 1929* (London, 1966), pp. 110–32.; Woodhouse, 'Marxism and Stalinism in Britain, 1920–26'; and B. Pearce, 'Early Years of the Communist Party of Great Britain', both in Woodhouse and Pearce, pp. 1–103 and pp. 149–78; Hinton, p. 276.

23 RILU Executive Bureau Report to Delegates to Third RILU Congress, July 1924, *International Labour Movement 1923–24*. See also E.H. Carr, *Socialism in One Country 1924–1926 Vol. 3, Part 1* (London, 1964), pp. 122–23.

breaking the passive, sectarian, syndicalist and propagandist traditions of pre-1920 British revolutionaries. It enabled the party to maximise the influence of its limited membership in the trade unions and led to an enthusiastic revival of party activity.

Nonetheless, the establishment in April 1925 of an Anglo-Russia Trade Union Committee, composed of Russian trade union leaders and members of the TUC General Council (particularly its 'lefts', Purcell, Hicks and Swales) was to have extremely damaging political consequences for the Communist Party and Minority Movement's methods of work in the unions. While the Stalinist bureaucracy that emerged in the internal power struggle that followed Lenin's death in January 1924 hoped a bloc with the left-inclined British union leaders would serve as a deterrent to western military aggression, the Committee granted such leaders a false 'revolutionary' credibility and inhibited the Communist Party from criticising their behaviour and attempting to encourage rank-and-file independence. Ironically of course, such left-wing leaders were to subsequently 'betray' the 1926 General Strike just as readily as their right-wing counterparts.[24]

Direct syndicalist influence was less discernible on the trajectory of the Italian Communist Party, despite the entry of a number of leading USI figures. The party was only founded after the ebb of revolutionary workers' struggles and with fascist violence against working class institutions reaching its peak soon afterwards. Unlike in France, the Italian communists were a definite minority compared with the socialists, and the *Ordino Nuovo* group around Antonio Gramsci was also reduced to a minority within the party's leadership. Control of the party in its first few years fell into the hands of the ultra-left figure of Amadeo Bordiga, who wanted to build a party of the 'pure and the hard'. He urged workers to leave the existing unions, viewed soviets as mere extensions of the party, urged the boycott of parliamentary elections, and refused to collaborate with the Socialist Party, even against the threat of fascism.[25] Mussolini's subsequent March on Rome compounded the new party's difficulties and it was only after Bordiga's removal from the Central Committee and Gramsci's increased role within the leadership that it began to become an effective interventionist body, albeit in very unfavourable objective political circumstances that were compounded by Gramsci's imprisonment.[26]

In Spain, the young militants of the newly-formed Communist Party were self-consciously on the ultra-left of the movement, a manifestation of the 'infantile disorder' that Lenin had condemned within the Comintern. But such ultra-leftism was essentially indigenous in origin, arising in part from the widespread penetration among the urban and rural proletariat of the CNT attitudes that viewed *any* form of parliamentary activity as anathema. However, on trade union activity the Spanish

---

[24] Woodhouse and Pearce; T. Cliff and D. Gluckstein, *Marxism and the Trade Union Struggle: The General Strike 1926* (London, 1986); J. Eaden and D. Renton, *The Communist Party of Great Britain Since 1920* (Houndmills, 2002).

[25] F. Livorsi, *Amadeo Bordiga* (Rome, 1976); A. De Clementi, *Amadeo Bordiga* (Turin, 1971).

[26] J.M. Cammett, *Antonio Gramsci and the Origins of Italian Communism* (Stanford, Calif., 1967); G. Fiori, *Antonio Gramsci: Life of a Revolutionary* (London, 1970); C. Bambery, *A Rebel's Guide to Gramsci* (London, 2006).

Communist Party followed the example of the Comintern and argued that *all* unions, whether affiliated to the UGT or CNT, were worth fighting for influence within.[27] Finally in Ireland, Larkin dismissed the attempt by James Connolly's son, Roddy, to establish a communist party affiliated to the Comintern as 'little wasps'. From the outset the new body encountered endless difficulties, with initial membership not exceeding 100 and dropping to 50 or so activists by 1923 when it was dissolved. Larkin's alternative Irish Worker League, despite links with Moscow, never functioned as a communist party, and retained a syndicalist strategy of pinning its hopes on revolutionary unions, albeit in a very different and completely unfavourable objective context of working class retreat. Frustrated with the lack of communist progress, the Comintern gradually bypassed Larkin, attempting to build an infrastructure of alternative networks and to cultivate support amongst republicans, but Irish communists were to remain scattered and isolated throughout the 1920s.[28]

From Bolshevism to Stalinism

The success of the Bolshevik Revolution had been predicated on the success of similar revolutions elsewhere in Europe. In January 1918 Lenin had written:

> We are far from having completed even the transitional period from capitalism to socialism. We have never cherished the hope that we could finish it without the aid of the international proletariat. We have never had any illusions on that score … The final victory of socialism in a single country is of course impossible.[29]

But while revolutionary upheavals had erupted outside Russia after 1917, these movements had, by the end of 1923, been defeated, notably in Germany. In the wake of such defeats and Russia's economic and political isolation internationally, combined with the devastation of civil war, the gains of the revolution were gradually lost as a distinct bureaucracy around Stalin began to dominate the state. This state (and party) bureaucracy argued the need for, and the possibility of, building 'socialism in one country', thereby effectively ruling out Lenin and Trotsky's previous strategy of attempting to extend the revolution beyond Russia's frontiers. In the process the Comintern was transformed from a body fomenting world revolution to one preoccupied with utilising foreign communist parties as a means of defending Russia from the predatory attacks of imperialist states.

While many historians have assumed Stalinism was the logical and irresistible outcome of the Bolshevik Revolution,[30] Michal Reiman has argued such an interpretation neglects the crucial transformation that occurred with Stalin's growing ascendancy and which culminated in the key turning point of 1927–1929. It was at

[27] G.H. Meaker, *The Revolutionary Left in Spain, 1914–1923* (Stanford, Calif., 1974), pp. 249–62.

[28] E. O'Connor, *Reds and the Green: Ireland, Russia and the Communist Internationals 1919–43* (Dublin, 2004).

[29] Cited in D. Hallas, *The Comintern* (London, 1985), p. 7.

[30] For example see O. Figes, *A People's Tragedy: The Russian Revolution 1891–1924* (Cape, 1996).

this point that Stalinism took final shape as a socio-political system 'diametrically opposed to socialism',[31] resulting from the attempt to solve the problems of Russia's historical backwardness through a process of state-led forced industrialisation, collectivisation and 'Five Year Plans'. Moreover, Tony Cliff has argued these dramatic changes marked the point at which the bureaucracy transformed itself into a conscious state capitalist ruling class that systematically and collectively exploited the working class by embracing the profit motive and the drive for capital accumulation imposed by external pressures of economic and military competition.[32] Those Bolsheviks who resisted such measures, such as Trotsky, were discredited, exiled and killed; peasants were torn from their land, forced into labour camps, and faced torture and death if they resisted; and in the towns, workers were denied the right to strike and trade unions lost any independence from the state. Thus, Stalinism represented a *counter*-revolution in which the remnants of the workers' state that had survived from October 1917 were destroyed and bureaucratic state capitalism was installed in its place.

During the first half of the 1920s the Comintern *had* helped to transform the communist parties into combat and interventionist parties (despite some important ambiguities in relation to the problem of the trade union bureaucracy). Certainly, the early congresses of the Comintern and RILU had represented a huge advance in the development of revolutionary strategy and tactics and marked in many respects the highest point yet been achieved by the revolutionary Marxist movement. But the gradual degeneration of the Russian Revolution and the rise of a Stalinist bureaucracy quickly short-circuited such a positive development. The transformation of the Comintern into an instrument of Russian foreign policy was complimented by the subordination of the communist parties into submissive tools of Moscow with concomitant detrimental implications for their industrial and trade union activities. Thus, what had been a grouping of revolutionary organisations in the early 1920 were slowly neutered through the imposition of tight bureaucratic control from Moscow in the mid-1920s and a lurch towards ultra-leftism in the late 1920s, culminating in a form of reformism by the mid-1930s.[33] Although the exiled Trotsky continued to attempt to mount opposition to Stalinism and the disastrous strategies adopted by the Comintern, the grip of Stalinism over the left internationally was reinforced by the overall retreat that occurred within the workers' movement across Europe, the belief that Moscow was the last hope for socialism in the face of the growing threat of Hitler and fascism, and by Trotsky's own increasing political isolation.

Of course, even during its early 'Leninist' phase, the Communist International, had ultimately been a failure; not only in that it did not produce immediate world revolution, but also in that the national traditions of the communist parties, including that of syndicalism (which had contributed to the development of international communism) proved to be very resistant to the successful union with Bolshevism.

---

[31] M. Reiman, *The Birth of Stalinism: The USSR on the Eve of the: Second Revolution'* (London, 1987), p. 119; 122.

[32] T. Cliff, *Russia: A Marxist Analysis* (London, 1964); P. Binns, T. Cliff and C. Harman, *From Workers' State to State Capitalism* (London, 1987).

[33] Hallas, pp. 105–59.

This was evident in the cleavage between the strategic and tactical decisions of its congresses on the one hand and the actual policies of its national sections on the other. As we have seen, formed in the midst of, or immediately after, a wave of revolutionary workers' struggles, the communist parties tended to be weighed down by their own native traditions, of which syndicalism was an important element. While 'the Bolshevik leaders could help in the teaching of revolutionary strategy and tactics … nothing could replace the actual individual experience of parties in struggle. It was impossible to create revolutionary communist leadership overnight'.[34] The unsuccessful 'grafting of Bolshevism' contributed to the failure of the international revolution and thus to the eventual triumph of Stalinism in Russia and the passive submission of foreign communist parties to Moscow.

Nonetheless, whatever their inherent weaknesses and subsequent distortions via Stalinism, the communist parties that were established, and which drew to some extent on syndicalist ideas of revolutionary unionism, represented success in so far as they were able to attract some of the most advanced shopfloor and trade union militants into their ranks and to have an influence, particularly in the industrial arena, out of proportion to their numerical size. One of the most important legacies bequeathed by the syndicalist tradition to the communist parties that emerged was that they prefigured in many respects the Bolshevik-type revolutionary party approach. As James Cannon, reflecting on the experience of the IWW acknowledged:

> As an organisation of revolutionists, united not simply by the immediate economic interests which bind all workers together into a union, but by doctrine and programme, the IWW was in practice, if not in theory, far ahead of other experiments along this line in its time, even though the IWW called itself a union and others called themselves parties. That was the IWW's greatest contribution to the American labour movement – in the present stage of its development and in those to come. Its unfading claim to grateful remembrance will rest in the last analysis on the pioneering role it played as the first great anticipation of the revolutionary party which the vanguard of the American workers will fashion to organise and lead their emancipating revolution.[35]

Arguably the debates that took place between the syndicalist and communist traditions (notably concerning the relationship between industrial activity and political organisation, the problem of state power, and the relationship between revolutionaries and the working class) have retained their relevance for activists in contemporary social movements, with the efficacy of the revolutionary Marxist critique of syndicalism in no way invalidated by the subsequent emergence, lengthy dominance and eventual demise of the ideology and practice of Stalinism.

---

[34] T. Cliff, *Lenin: Vol. 4: The Bolsheviks and the World Revolution* (London, 1979), p. 53. See also, T. Cliff, *Trotsky: Vol. 2: The Sword of the Revolution: 1917–1923* (London, 1990), pp. 235–6.

[35] Cannon, p. 42.

Bibliography

Newspapers and Periodicals

International

Communist International
Communist Review
International Socialist Review
La Correspondence Internationale

America

Defense News Bulletin
Industrial Solidarity
Industrial Union Bulletin
Industrial Worker
Nation
New Review
One Big Union Monthly
Political Science Quarterly
Solidarity
Sunset
Syndicalist
Voice of the People
Voice of Labour

Britain

Communist
Daily Herald
Hansard
Industrial Syndicalist
International Trade Union Unity
Labour Monthly
Manchester Guardian
Merthyr Pioneer
New Reasoner
Socialist
Solidarity
South Wales Worker
Syndicalist

Syndicalist and Amalgamation News
Times
Worker
Workers' Life

France

L'Ecole émancipée
L'Humanité
La Bataille Syndicaliste
La Voix du peuple
La Lutte de Classe
La Revue socialiste
La Vie Ouvrière
La Voix du Travail
Le Journal du Peuple
Le Libertaire
Le Mouvement socialiste
Le Peuple

Ireland

Eire
Voice of Labour

Italy

Avanti!
Guerra di Classe
Guerra di Classe (Bologna)
L'Internazionale
Ordine Nuovo
Volantá

Spain

España Libre
Lucha Social
Solidaridad Obrera
Solidaridad Obrera (Bilbao)
Tierra y Libertad

Conference Documentation

Congrès national corporatif (IX de la Confédération) et Conférence des Bourses du Travail, tenus á Amiens du 8 au 16 octobre 1906. Compte rendu des travaux (Amiens, 1906).
Confédération Générale du Travail, *XVIII(e) congrès national corporatif XII(e). Compte rendu des travaux* (Le Havre, 1912).
Memoria del Congreso celebrado en Barcelona los días 28, 29, y 30 de junio y 1º de julio de 1918 (Toulouse, 1957).
Memoria del Congreso celebrado en el Teatro de la Comedia de Madrid los días 10 al 18 de diciembre de 1919 (Barcelona: Cosmos, 1932).
Murphy, J.T., *The 'Reds' in Congress: Preliminary Report of the First World War Congress of the Red International of Trade and Industrial Unions* (London: British Bureau of RILU, 1921).
Proceedings of the First Annual Convention of the Industrial Workers of the World (New York: Labor News, 1905).
Résolutions et statuts adoptés au le congrès international des syndicats révolutionnaires – Moscou: 3–19 juillet 1921 (Paris, 1921).
Resolutions and Decisions of the First International Congress of Revolutionary Trade and Industrial Unions, (Chicago: American Labor Union Educational Society, 1921).
Resolutions and Decisions of the Second World Congress of the Red International of Labour Unions, 19 November to 2 December 1922 (London: RILU, 1923).
RILU Executive Bureau Report to Delegates to Third RILU Congress, July 1924, *International Labour Movement 1923–24.*
The First Congress of the Red Trades Union International at Moscow, 1921: A Report of the Proceedings by George Williams, Delegate from the IWW (Chicago: IWW, 1921).
The Third Congress of the Communist International (London, 1922), pp. 141–2.
The IWW Reply to the Red Trade Union International (Moscow) *by the General Executive Board of the Industrial Workers of the World* (Chicago: IWW, n.d [1922]).
Trades Union Congress, *Report* (London, 1912).
XVI Congrès national corporatif (X de la CGT) et 3 Conférence des Bourses du Travail ou Unions des Syndicats, tenus á Marseille du 5 au 12 octobre 1908. Compte rendu sténographique des travaux (Marseille, 1909).

Additional Sources

Abse, T., 'Syndicalism and the Origins of Italian Fascism', *Historical Journal*, 25 (1982), pp. 247–58.
Abse, T., 'Italy', in S. Berger and D. Broughton (eds) *The Force of Labour: The Western European Labour Movement and the Working Class in the Twentieth Century* (Oxford: Berg, 1995), pp. 137–70.
Adereth, M., *The French Communist Party: A Critical History (1920–84): From Comintern to the 'Colours of France'* (Manchester University Press, 1984).

Alexander, R., *The Anarchists in the Spanish Civil War: Vols 1 and 2* (London: Janus, 1999).
Allen, E.J.B., *Revolutionary Unionism* (London: The Industrialist League, 1909).
Allen, K., *The Politics of James Connolly* (London: Pluto Press, 1990).
Amdur, K.E., *Syndicalist Legacy: Trade Unions and Politics in Two French Cities in the Era of World War I* (Urbana: University of Illinois Press, 1986).
'Anarcho-Syndicalism in Britain, 1914–30', *A History of Anarcho-Syndicalism*, Unit 14, www.selfed.org.uk.
Arnot, R.P., *South Wales Miners: A History of the South Wales Miners' Federation, 1898–1914* (London: Allen and Unwin, 1967).
Aron, R., 'Prėface' to B. Lazitch, *Lėnine et la 111e internationale* (Neuchâtel, Paris: Editions de la Baconnière, 1951).
Askwith, G.R., *Industrial Problems and Disputes* (London: Harvester Press, 1974).
Bagwell, P., *The Railwaymen: The History of the National Union of Railwaymen* (London: Allen and Unwin, 1963).
Bagwell, P., 'The New Unionism in Britain: the Railway Industry', in W.J. Mommsen and Husung, H-G. (eds), *The Development of Trade Unionism in Great Britain and Germany, 1880–1914* (London: Allen and Unwin, 1985), pp. 185–200.
Balcells, A., *El arraigo del anarquismo en Cataluña: Textos de 1926–1934* (Madrid: Júcar, 1980).
Bambery, C., *Ireland's Permanent Revolution* (London: Bookmarks, 1986).
Bambery, C., *A Rebel's Guide to Gramsci* (London: Bookmarks, 2006).
Bar, A., *Syndicalism and Revolution in Spain: The Ideology and The Syndical Practice of the CNT in the Period 1915–1919* (New York: Gordon Press, 1981).
Bar, A., 'The CNT: The Glory and Tragedy of Spanish Anarchosyndicalism', in M. van der Linden and W. Thorpe (eds), *Revolutionary Syndicalism: An International Perspective* (Aldershot, Scolar Press, 1990), pp. 119–38.
Barker, C., 'Perspectives', in C. Barker (ed.), *Revolutionary Rehearsals* (London: Bookmarks, 1987), pp. 217–45.
Barnes, D.M., 'The Ideology of the Industrial Workers of the World', PhD, Washington State University, 1962).
Baron, A. (ed.), *Work Engendered: Towards a New History of American Labor* (Ithaca, NY: Cornell University Press, 1991), pp. 1–46.
Barrett, J.R., *William Z. Foster and the Tragedy of American Radicalism* (Chicago: University of Illinois, 1999).
Behan, T., *The Resistible Rise of Benito Mussolini* (London: Bookmarks, 2003).
Bell, T., *Pioneering Days* (London: Lawrence and Wishart, 1941).
Berlanstein, L., *Big Business and Industrial Conflict in Nineteenth Century France: A Social History of the Parisian Gas Company* (Berkeley: University of California Press, 1991).
Berlanstein, L., 'The Distinctiveness of the Nineteenth Century French Labour Movement', *The Journal of Modern History*, 64:4 (December 1992), pp. 660–685.
Bertrand, C., 'Revolutionary Syndicalism in Italy, 1912–1922', PhD thesis, University of Wisconsin (1970).
Bertrand, C.L., 'Italian Revolutionary Syndicalism and the Crisis of Intervention: August–December 1914', *Canadian Journal of History*, 10:3 (1975), pp. 349–67.

Bertrand, C.L., 'Revolutionary Syndicalism in Italy', in M. van der Linden and W. Thorpe (eds), *Revolutionary Syndicalism: An International Perspective* (Aldershot, Scolar Press, 1990), pp. 139–53.

Binns, P., T. Cliff and C. Harman, *From Workers' State to State Capitalism* (London: Bookmarks, 1987).

Birchall, I., 'The "Reluctant Bolsheviks": Victor Serge's and Alfred Rosmer's encounter with Leninism', in C. Barker, A. Johnson and M. Lavalette (eds), *Leadership and Social Movements* (Manchester University Press, 2001), pp. 44–59.

Birchall, I., 'The Success and Failure of the Comintern', in K. Flett and D. Renton (eds), *The Twentieth Century: A Century of Wars and Revolutions?* (London: Rivers Oram Press, 2000), pp. 117–32.

Birchall, I., 'Alfred Rosmer and the RILU', Paper presented to London Socialist Historians Group One Day Conference, Institute of Historical Research, University of London, 6 May 2000.

Birchall, I., 'Alfred and Marguerite Rosmer', Paper presented to New Socialist Approaches to History Seminar, London Socialist Historians Group, Institute of Historical Research, University of London, 2 April 2001.

Bird, S.D., D. Georgakas and D. Shaffer, *Solidarity Forever: An Oral History of the Wobblies* (London: Lawrence and Wishart, 1987).

Bock, H.M., 'Anarchosyndicalism in the German Labour Movement: A Rediscovered Minority Tradition', in M. van der Linden and W. Thorpe (eds), *Revolutionary Syndicalism: An International Perspective* (Aldershot, Scolar Press, 1990), pp. 59–79.

Bookchin, M., *To Remember Spain: The Anarchist and Syndicalist Revolution of 1936* (Edinburgh: AK Press, 1994).

Bookchin, M., *The Spanish Anarchists: The Heroic Years 1868–1936* (Edinburgh: AK Press, 1998).

Bonnell, V.E., *Roots of Rebellion: Workers' Politics and Organization in St. Petersburg and Moscow, 1900–1914* (Berkley: University of California Press, 1988).

Bordogna, L., G.P. Cella and G. Provasi, 'Labor Conflicts in Italy before the Rise of Fascism, 1881–1923: A Quantitative Analysis', in L. Haimson and C. Tilly (eds), *Strikes, Wars and Revolutions in an International Perspective* (Cambridge University Press, 1989), pp. 217–46.

Borghi, A., *Anarchismo e sindacalismo. Conferenza tenuta il 3 aprile 1922 a Roma del Fascio Sindacale d'Azione Diretta* (Rome, n.d.).

Borghi, A., *L'Italia tra due Crispi: cause e conseguenze di una rivoluzione macata* (Paris: Libreria Internazionale, n.d. [1924].

Borghi, A., *Mezzo secolo di anarchia 1898-1945* (Naples: Edizioni scientifiche italiane, 1954).

Borkeneau, F., *The Communist International* (London: Faber and Faber, 1938).

Brenan, G., *The Spanish Labyrinth: An Account of the Social and Political Background of the Spanish Civil War* (Cambridge: Cambridge University Press, 1998).

Brissendon, P.F., *The IWW: The Study of American Syndicalism* (New York: Columbia University, 1919).

Brody, D., *Workers in Industrial America: Essays on the Twentieth Century Struggle* (Oxford University Press, 1981).

Brooks, J.G., *American Syndicalism* (New York, 1913).
Broué, P., *Historie de l'internationale communiste 1919–1943* (Paris: Fayard, 1997).
Broué, P., *The German Revolution 1917–1923* (Chicago: Haymarket Books, 2006).
Brown, G., 'Introduction', in *The Industrial Syndicalist* (Nottingham, Spokesman Books, 1974), pp. 5–29.
Buenacasa, M., *El movimiento obrero español, historia y crítica, 1886–1926* (Paris: Familia y Amigos del Autor [second edition] 1966).
Burgmann, V., *Revolutionary Industrial Unionism: The Industrial Workers of the World in Australia* (Cambridge University Press, 1995).
Cahill, L., *Forgotten Revolution: Limerick Soviet 1919* (Dublin: O'Brien Press, 1990).
Callinicos, A., *The Revolutionary Road to Socialism* (London: Socialist Workers Party, 1983).
Callinicos, A., *Socialists in the Trade Unions* (London: Bookmarks, 1985).
Callinicos, A., 'Marxism and the Crisis in Social History', in J. Rees (ed.), *Essays on Historical Materialism* (London: Bookmarks, 1998), pp. 25–40.
Cammett, J.M., *Antonio Gramsci and the Origins of Italian Communism* (Stanford Calif., Stanford University Press, 1967).
Cannon, J.P., *The IWW: The Great Anticipation* (New York: Pioneer Publishers, 1956).
Cannon, J.P., 'The IWW and Red International of Labor Unions', *James P. Cannon and the Early Years of American Communism: Selected Writings and Speeches 1920–1928* (New York: Prometheus, 1992), p. 186.
Cannon, J.P., *The History of American Trotskyism: 1928–1938* (New York: Pathfinder, 2003).
Cartosio, B., 'Gli emigrati italiani e l'Industrial Workers of the World', in B. Bezza, *Gli italiani fuori d'Italia: gli emirate italiani nei movimenti operai dei paesi d'adozione 1880–1940* (Milan, 1983), pp. 359–97.
Carr, E.H., *The Bolshevik Revolution 1917–1923, Vol. 3* (London: Macmillan, 1966).
Carr, E.H., *Socialism in One Country 1924–1926, Vol. 1* (London: Macmillan, 1964).
Carr, E.H., *Socialism in One Country, 1924–1926, Vol. 3, Part 1* (London: Macmillan, 1964).
Carr, E.H., *Socialism in One Country, 1924–1926, Vol. 3* (Harmondsworth: Penguin, 1972).
Carr, R., *The Civil War in Spain 1936–39* (London: Weidenfield and Nicholson, 1986).
Casanoa, J., 'Terror and Violence: The Dark Face of Spanish Anarchism', *International Labor and Working Class History*, 67 (2005), pp. 79–99.
Chaplain, R., *Wobbly: The Rough and Tumble of an American Radical* (University of Chicago Press, 1948).
Challinor, R., *The Origins of British Bolshevism* (London: Croom Helm, 1977).
Chambelland, C. (ed.), *La Lutte syndicale* (Paris: Maspero, 1976).
Chambelland, C. and J. Maitron (eds), *Syndicalisme Revolutionnaire et Communisme: Les Archives de Pierre Monatte, 1914–24* (Paris: Maspero, 1968).
Charlton, J., *The Chartists: The First National Workers' Movement* (London: Pluto Press, 1997).
Clark, M., *Antonio Gramsci and the Revolution That Failed* (New Haven: Tale University Press, 1977).
Claudin, F., *The Communist Movement* (Markham: Penguin Books, 1975).

Cliff, T., *Russia: A Marxist Analysis* (London: International Socialism, 1964).
Cliff, T., *Lenin, Vol. 1: Building the Party* (London: Pluto Press, 1975).
Cliff, T., *Lenin: Vol. 2: All Power the Soviets* (London: Pluto Press, 1976).
Cliff, T., *Lenin: Vol. 4: The Bolsheviks and the World Revolution* (London: Pluto Press, 1979).
Cliff, T., 'Introduction', *The Mass Strike* (London: Bookmarks, 1987), pp. 5–10.
Cliff, T., *Trotsky: Vol. 2: The Sword of the Revolution 1917–1923* (London: Bookmarks, 1990).
Cliff, T. and D. Gluckstein, *Marxism and Trade Union Struggle: The General Strike 1926* (London: Bookmarks, 1986).
Cole, G.D.H., *The World of Labour: A Discussion of the Present and Future of Trade Unionism* (London: Bell and Sons, 1920).
Cole, G.D.H,. *A Short History of the British Working Class Movement, 1789–1947* (London: Allen and Unwin, 1948).
Cole, G.D.H., *A History of Socialist Thought: The Second International, 1889–1914: Part 1* (London: Macmillan, 1974).
Cole, M.I. (ed.), *Beatrice Webb's Diaries 1912–1924* (London: Longmans, 1952).
Collinet, M., *L'Ouvrier Francais: Essai sur la condition ouvrière 1900–1950* (Paris, Ouvrières, 1951).
Conlin, J., 'A Name That Leads to Confusion', in *Bread and Roses Too: Studies of the Wobblies* (Westport, Connecticut: Greenwood Publishing, 1969), pp. 8–40.
Conlin, J.R., *Bread and Roses Too: Studies of the Wobblies* (Westport, Connecticut: Greenwood Publishing, 1969).
Conlin, J.R. (ed.), *At the Point of Production: The Local History of the IWW* (Westport: Connecticut: Greenwood Press, 1981).
Connolly, J., 'Labour, Nationality and Religion', in O.D. Edwards and B. Ransom (eds), *James Connolly: Selected Political Writings* (New York: Grove Press, 1974), pp. 61–162.
Connolly, J., 'Socialism Made Easy', *Selected Political Writings* ([originally published 1914] New York: Grove Press, 1974), pp. 243–328.
Connolly, J., 'Old Wine in New Bottles' [originally published 30 April 1914], in O.D. Edwards and B. Ransom (eds), *Connolly's Selected Political Writings* (New York: Grove Press, 1974).
Cotterau, A., 'The Distinctiveness of Working Class Cultures in France, 1848–1900', in (eds), I. Katznelson and A. Zolberg, *Working Class Formation: Nineteenth Century Patterns in Western Europe and the United States* (Princeton, N.J., 1986), pp. 111–54.
Cronin, J., 'Neither Exceptional nor Peculiar: Towards the Comparative Study of Labor in Advanced Society', *International Review of Social History*, 38: part 1, (1993), pp. 59–75.
Cross, G.S., *Immigrant Workers in Industrial France: The Making of a New Labouring Class* (Philadelphia, Temple University Press, 1983).
Dangerfield, G., *The Strange Death of Liberal England 1910–1914* (London: Serif, 1997).
Darlington, R., *The Political Trajectory of J.T. Murphy* (Liverpool University Press, 1998).

Darlington, R., 'Revolutionary Syndicalist Opposition to the First World War: A Comparative Reassessment', *Revue Belge de Philologie et d'Histoire*, 84:4 (2006), pp. 983–1003.

Davies, D.K., 'The Influence of Syndicalism and Industrial Unionism on the South Wales Coalfield 1898–1921: A Study in Ideology and Practice, PhD, University of Wales, 1991.

Davies, J.A., 'Socialism and the Working Classes in Italy before 1914', in D. Geary (ed.), in D. Geary (ed.), *Labour and Socialist Movements in Europe Before 1914* (Oxford: Berg, 1989).

Davies, M., *Comrade or Brother?: The Hidden History of the British Labour Movement, 1789–1951* (London: Pluto Press, 1993).

Degras, J. (ed.), *The Communist International, 1919–1943: Documents: Vol. 1* (London: Oxford University Press, 1956).

De Clementi, A., *Amadeo Bordiga* (Turin: Einaudi, 1971).

De Grand, A., *The Italian Left in the Twentieth Century: A History of the Socialist and Communist Parties* (Bloomington: Indiana University Press, 1989).

DeFelice, R., *Sindacalismo rivoluzionario e fiumanesimo nel carteggio DeAmbris –D'Annunzio, 1919–1922* (Brescia: Morcellianna, 1966).

de Llorens, I., *The CNT and the Russian Revolution* (London: Kate Sharpley Library, n.d).

Deutscher, I., *Soviet Trade Unions: Their Place in Soviet Labour Policy* (London: Royal Institute of International Affairs, 1950).

Dolgoff, S. (ed.), *Anarchist Collectives: Workers' Self-Management in Spain 1936–9*, (Montreal: Black Rose Books, 1990).

Draper, H., *The Roots of American Communism* (Chicago: Elephant Paperbacks, 1989 [first published 1957]).

Dreyfus, M., *Histoire de la CGT* (Brussels: Editions Complexe, 1995).

Dubofsky, M., *We Shall Be All: A History of the Industrial Workers of the World* (Chicago Quadrangle Books, 1969).

Dubofsky, M., *Industrialism and the American Worker 1865–1920* (Arlington Heights: AHM Publishing, 1975).

Dubofsky, M., *'Big Bill' Haywood*, (Manchester University Press, 1987).

Dubofsky, M., 'The Rise and Fall of Revolutionary Syndicalism in the United States', in M. van der Linden and W. Thorpe (eds), *Revolutionary Syndicalism: An International Perspective* (Aldershot, Scolar Press, 1990), pp. 203–20.

Dubofsky, M., *Hard Work: The Making of Labor History* (Urbana: University of Illinois Press, 2000).

Durgan, A., 'Revolutionary Anarchism in Spain: the CNT 1911–1937, *International Socialism*, 2:11 (1981), pp. 93–110.

Earlham, C., '"Revolutionary Gymnastics" and the Unemployed: The Limits of the Spanish Anarchist Utopia 1931–37', in K. Flett and D. Renton (eds), *The Twentieth Century: A Century of Wars and Revolutions?* (London: Rivers Oram Press, 2000), pp. 133–55.

Earlham, C., *Class, Culture and Conflict in Barcelona, 1898–1937* (London: Routledge, 2004).

Ebert, J., *The IWW in Theory and Practice* (Chicago, n.d. [1920]).

Ebert, J., *The Trial of a New Society* (Cleveland: IWW Publishing Bureau, 1913).

Eaden, J. and D. Renton, *The Communist Party of Great Britain Since 1920* (Houndmills, Palgrave, 2002).

Edwards, O.D. and B. Ranson (eds), *James Connolly: Selected Political Writings* (London, Jonathan Cape, 1973).

Edwardes, P.K., *Strikes in the United States, 1881–1974* (Oxford: Basil Blackwell, 1981).

Egan, D., 'The Unofficial Reform Committee and the Miners' Next Step', *Llafur*, 2:3 (1978), pp. 64–80.

Egan, D., '"A Cult of Their Own": Syndicalism and the Miners' Next Step', A. Campbell, N. Fishman and D. Howell (eds), *Miners, Unions and Politics: 1910–47* (Aldershot: Scolar Press, 1996), pp. 13–33.

Engels, F., 'The Bakunists at Work: An Account of the Spanish revolt in the Summer of 1873', Marx, Engels, Lenin, *Anarchism and Anarcho-Syndicalism* (New York: International Publishers, 1972), pp. 125–46.

Estey, J.A., *Revolutionary Syndicalism: An Exposition and A Criticism* (London: P.S. King and Son, 1913).

Fedeli, U., 'Breve storia dell'Unione Sindacale Italiana', *Volontà*, 10 (1957), p. 654.

Fickle, J.F., 'Race, Class and Radicalism: The Wobblies in the Southern Lumber Industry, 1900–1916', in J.R. Conlin (ed.), *At the Point of Production: The Local History of the IWW* (Wesport, Conn: Greenwood Press, 1981), pp. 98–113.

Figes, O., *A People's Tragedy: The Russian Revolution 1891–1924* (Cape, 1996).

Fiori, G., *Antonio Gramsci: Life of a Revolutionary* (London: New Left Books, 1970).

Flynn, E.G., *Sabotage: The Conscious Withdrawal of the Workers' Industrial Efficiency* (Cleveland: IWW Publishing Bureau, 1915).

Flynn, E.G., *The Rebel Girl: An Autobiography: My First Life, 1906–1926* (New York: International Publishers, 1994).

Foner, P.S., *History of the Labor Movement in the United States, Vol. 4, The Industrial Workers of the World, 1905–1917* (New York: International Publishers, 1965).

Foner, P.S., *Organised Labor and the Black Worker, 1619–1973* (New York: International, 1978).

Foner, P.S., *Women and the American Labor Movement: From the Trade Unions to the Present* (New York: The Free Press, 1982).

Foner, P.S., *History of the Labor Movement in the United States: Vol 7: Labor and World War 1: 1914–1918* (New York: International Publishers, 1987).

Foner, P.S., *History of the Labor Movement in the United States: Vol. 8: Postwar Struggles 1918–1920* (New York: International Publishers, 1988).

Foot, P., *The Vote: How it was Won and How it was Undermined* (London: Viking, 2005).

Ford, E.C. and W.Z. Foster, *Syndicalism* (Chicago: Charles H. Kerr Publishing Company, 1990 [reprint of 1912 edition]).

Foster, W.Z., *Trade Unionism: The Road to Freedom* (Chicago: International Trade Union Education League, 1916).

Foster, W.Z., *History of the Communist Party of the United States* (New York: International Publishers, 1952).

Friedman, G., *State-Making and Labour Movements: France and the United States, 1876–1914*, (New York: Cornel University Press, 1998).

Friedman, G.C., 'Revolutionary Unions and French Labour: The Rebels Behind the Cause: Or, Why Did Revolutionary Syndicalism Fail?', *French Historical Studies*, 20 (1997), pp. 155–81.

Gabaccia, D.R, 'Worker Internationalism and Italian Labor Migration, 1870–1914', *International Labor and Working Class History*, 45 (1994), pp. 63–79.

Gallacher, W., *Last Memoirs* (London: Lawrence and Wishart, 1966).

Gambs, J.S., *The Decline of the IWW* (New York: Columbia University Press, 1932).

Gammage, R.G., *The History of the Chartist Movement 1837–1854* (London: Merlin Press, 1969).

Garner, J. 'Separated by an "Ideological Chasm": The Spanish National Labour Confederation and Bolshevik Internationalism, 1917–1922', *Contemporary European History*, 15:3 (2006), pp. 293–326.

Geary, D., *European Labour Protest, 1848–1939* (London: Croom Helm, 1981).

Geary, D., *European Labour Politics from 1910 to the Depression* (Houndmills: Macmillan, 1991).

Giovannitti, A., 'Introduction', E. Pouget, *Sabotage* (Chicago: Charles H. Kerr & Company, 1913).

Glatter, P. (ed.), 'The Russian Revolution of 1905: Change through Struggle', *Revolutionary History* [special edition], 9:1 (2006).

Glasgow Labour History Workshop, *The Singer Strike, Clydebank 1911* (Glasgow: Clydebank District Library, 1989).

Gluckstein, D., *The Western Soviets: Workers' Councils versus Parliament, 1915–20* (London: Bookmarks, 1985).

Gonnot, P., *La grève dans l'industrie privée* (Paris: A. Rousseau, 1912).

Goodway, D. (ed.), *For Anarchism: History, Theory and Practice* (London: Routledge, 1989).

Gradilone, A., *Storia del sindacalismo, Vol. 3* (Milan, 1959), p. 109, 196.

Gramsci, A., *Soviets in Italy* (Nottingham: Institute for Workers' Control, 1969).

Gramsci, A., 'The Southern Question', *The Modern Prince and Other Writings* (New York: International, 1957).

Gramsci, A., *Selections from the Prison Notebooks* (London: Lawrence and Wishart, 1971).

Gramsci, A., 'Unions and Councils', *Selections from Political Writings 1910–1920* (London: Lawrence and Wishart, 1977), pp. 98–102.

Gramsci, A., 'Trade Unions and the Dictatorship', *Selections from Political Writings 1910–1920* (London: Lawrence and Wishart, 1977), pp. 103–108.

Gramsci, A., 'Turn and Italy', *Selections from Political Writings 1910–1920* (London: Lawrence and Wishart, 1977), pp. 182–4.

Gramsci, A., 'Syndicalism and the Councils', *Selections from Political Writings 1910–1920* (London: Lawrence and Wishart, 1977), pp. 265–8.

Gramsci, A., 'The Occupation', *Selected Political Writings 1910–1920* (London: Lawrence and Wishart, 1977), pp. 326–9.

Gramsci, A., 'Officialdom', *Selections from Political Writings, 1921–1926* (London: Lawrence and Wishart, 1978), pp. 17–19.

Gramsci, A. and P. Togliatti, 'Workers Democracy', in A. Gramsci, *Selections from Political Writings 1910–1920* (London: Lawrence and Wishart, 1977), pp. 65–8.

Gray, J., *James Larkin and the Belfast Dock Strike of 1907* (Belfast, Blackstaff Press, 1985).

Greaves, C.D., *The Irish Transport and General Workers' Union: The Formative Years, 1909–1923* (Dublin, 1982).

Greaves, C.D., *The Life and Times of James Connolly*, Lawrence and Wishart, 1986).

Griffuelhes, V., *L'Action syndicaliste* (Paris, 1908).

Griffuelhes, V., *Le syndicalisme révolutionnaire* (Paris: Bibliothèque du mouvement socialiste, 4, 1909).

Griffuelhes, V., and L. Jouhaux (eds), *L'Encyclopédie du mouvement syndicaliste* (Paris, 1912).

Guilbert, M., *Les femes et l'organization syndicale avant 1914* (Paris: Editions du CNRS, 1966).

Guerin, D., *Anarchism: From Theory to Practice* (New York: Monthly Review Press, 1971).

Guerin, D. (ed.), *No Gods, No Masters: An Anthology of Anarchism* (Edinburgh: AK Press, 2005).

Halévy, E., *A History of the English People, Vol. 2: 1905–1914* (London: Ernest Benn, 1961).

Hallas, D., *The Comintern* (London: Bookmarks, 1985).

Hanagan, M., *The Logic of Solidarity: Artisans and Industrial Workers in Three French Towns, 1871–1914* (Urbana: University of Illinois, 1980).

Harding, N., *Lenin's Political Thought: Vol. 2: Theory and Practice in the Socialist Revolution* (New York: St Martins Press, 1981).

Hardy, G.H., *Those Stormy Years*, (London: Lawrence and Wishart, 1956).

Harman, C., *The Lost Revolution: Germany 1918 to 1923* (London: Bookmarks, 1982).

Haynes, M., 'The British Working Class in Revolt: 1910–1914', *International Socialism* 2: 22, 1984, pp. 87–116.

Haywood, W.D., *The General Strike* (Chicago: IWW Publicity Bureau, n.d.).

Haywood, W.D., *Bill Haywood's Book: The Autobiography of William D. Haywood* (New York: International Publishers, 1929).

Heywood, A., *Political Ideologies: An Introduction* (Houndmills: Palgrave, 2003).

Heywood, P., 'The Labour Movement in Spain Before 1914', in D. Geary (ed.), *Labour and Socialist Movements in Europe Before 1914* (Oxford: Berg, 1989), pp. 231–65.

Hinton, J., *The First Shop Stewards' Movement* (London: Allen and Unwin, 1973).

Hinton, J., *Labour and Socialism: A History of the British Labour Movement 1867–1974* (Brighton: Wheatsheaf Books, 1983).

Hinton, J. and R. Hyman, *Trade Unions and Revolution: The Industrial Policies of the Early British Communist Party* (London: Pluto Press, 1975).

Hobsbawm, E.J., *The Age of Empire, 1875–1914* (London: Cardinal, 1987).

Hobsbawm, E.J., *Primitive Rebels, Studies in Archaic Forms of Social Movement in the Nineteenth and Twentieth Centuries* (Manchester University Press, 1972).

Hobsbawm, E.J., 'Bolshevism and the Anarchists', in E. Hobsbawm, *Revolutionaries* (London: Abacus, 1993), pp. 57–70.

Holton, B., 'Syndicalism and Labour on Merseyside 1906–14', H.I. Hikens (ed.), *Building the Union: Studies on the Growth of the Workers' Movement: Merseyside 1756–1967* (Liverpool: Toulouse Press, 1973), pp. 121–50.

Holton, B., *British Syndicalism 1900–1914* (London: Pluto Press, 1976).

Holton, B., 'Syndicalist Theories of the State', *Sociological Review*, 28 (1980), pp. 5–21.

Holton, B., 'Revolutionary Syndicalism and the British Labour Movement', in J. Mommsen and H. Husung (eds), *The Development of Trade Unionism in Great Britain and Germany 1880–1914* (London: Allen and Unwin, 1985), pp. 266–82.

Horne, J., 'The State and the Challenge for Labour in France 1917–20', C. Wrigley (ed.), *Challenges of Labour: Central and Western Europe 1917–20* (London: Routledge, 1993), pp. 239–61.

Horrowitz, D.L., *The Italian Labor Movement* (Cambridge, Mass: Harvard University Press, 1963).

Howell, D., *Respectable Rebels: Studies in the Politics of Railway Trade Unionism* (Aldershot: Ashgate, 1999).

Howell, D., 'Taking Syndicalism Seriously', *Socialist History*, 16 (2000), pp. 27–48.

Hoxie, R., *Trade Unionism in the United States* (New York: D. Appleton, 1920).

Hunter, R., *Violence and the Labor Movement* (New York: The Macmillan Company, 1914).

Hyman, R., 'Introduction', in T. Mann, *What a Compulsory 8-Hour Working Day Means to the Workers* (London: Pluto Press, 1972), pp. 3–16.

Hyman, R., 'Foreword', in C.L.G. Goodrich, *Frontier of Control* (London: Pluto Press, 1975 [first printed 1920], pp. vii–xli.

Hyman, R., *The Political Economy of Industrial Relations* (London: Macmillan, 1989), pp. 120–46.

Jefferys, S., 'Review Essay: The Exceptional Centenary of the Confederation generale du travail, 1895–1995', *Historical Studies in Industrial Relations*, 3 (1997), pp. 123–42.

Jenkins, M., *The General Strike of 1842* (London: Lawrence and Wishart, 1980).

Jennings, J., *Syndicalism in France: A Study of Ideas* (Oxford: Macmillan, 1990).

Jennings, J., 'The CGT and the Couriau Affair: Syndicalist Responses to Female Labour in France Before 1914', *European History Quarterly*, 21:3 (1991), pp. 321–37.

Jenson, J. and M. Dubofsky, 'The IWW – An Exchange of Views', *Labor History*, 11:3 (1970), p. 355–72.

Johanningsmeir, E.P., 'William Z. Foster and the Syndicalist League of North America', *Labor History*, 30:3 (1989), pp. 329–53.

Johanningsmeir, E.P., *Forging American Communism: The Life of William Z. Foster* (Princeton University Press, 1994).

Joll, J., *The Anarchists* (London: Methuen, 1964).

Jones, A., 'The French Railway Strikes of January–May 1920: New Syndicalist Ideas and Emergent Communism', *French Historical Studies*, 12, 4 (1982), pp. 508–40.

Judt, T., *The French Labour Movement in the Nineteenth Century, Marxism and the French Left* (Oxford: Oxford University Press, 1986), pp. 24–114.

Julliard, J., *Fernand Pelloutier et les origins du syndicalisme d'action directe* (Paris: Editions du Seuil, 1971).

Katznelson, I. and A. Zolberg, *Working Class Formation: Nineteenth Century Patterns in Western Europe and the United States* (Princeton University Press, 1986).

Kedward, R., *The Anarchists* (London; Macdonald, 1971).

Kelly, J., *Trade Unions and Socialist Politics* (London: Verso, 1988).

Kennedy, D., 'The Decline of the Socialist Party of America 1901–19', *Socialist History*, 9 (1996) pp. 8–22.

Kendall, W., *The Revolutionary Movement in Britain 1900–22* (London: Weidenfield and Nicholson, 1969).

Kendall, W., *The Labour Movement in Europe* (London: Allen Lane, 1975).

Keogh, D., *The Rise of the Irish Working Class: The Dublin Trade Union Movement and the Labour Leadership, 1890–1914* (Belfast: Appletree Press, 1982).

Kessler-Harris, A., *Out to Work: A History of Wage Earning: Women in the United States* (New York: Oxford University Press, 1982).

Keufer, A., *L'Éucation syndicale: Exposé de la méthode organique* (Paris, 1910).

Kimeldorf, H., 'Radical Possibilities? The Rise and Fall of Wobbly Unionism on the Philadelphia Docks', in C. Winslow (ed.), *Waterfront Workers: New Perspectives on Race and Class* (Urbana: University of Illinois Press, 1998).

Kimeldorf, H., *Battling for American Labour: Wobblies, Craft Workers, and the Making of the Union Movement* (Berkeley: University of California Press, 1999).

Kirk, N., *Labour and Society in Britain and the USA: Vol. 2: Challenge and Accommodation, 1850–1939* (Aldershot, Scolar Press, 1994).

Kirkaldy, A.W., *Economics and Syndicalism* (Cambridge: Cambridge University Press, 1914).

Klugmann, J., *History of the Communist Party of Great Britain: Formation and Early Years 1919–1924*, Vol. 1 (London: Lawrence and Wishart, 1968).

Kocka, J., 'Comparative Historical Research: German Examples', *International Review of Social History*, 38: part 3, (1993), pp. 369–79.

Kolko, G., *Main Currents in Modern American History* (London: Harper and Row, 1976).

Kornbluh, J.L. (ed.), *Rebel Voices: An IWW Anthology* (Chicago: Charles Kerr, 1998).

Kornhauser, A., R. Dubin and A.M. Ross (eds), *Industrial Conflict* (New York: McGraw-Hill, 1954).

Kostick, C., *Revolution in Ireland: Popular Militancy 1917 to 1923* (London: Pluto Press, 1996).

Kraditor, A.S., *The Radical Persuasion, 1890–1917: Aspects of the Intellectual History and the Historiography of Three American Radical Organizations* (Baton Rouge: Louisiana State University Press, 1981).

Kriegel, A., *Aux origines du communisme français, 1914–1920: Contribution á l'histoire du mouvement ouvrier français* (Paris: Mouton, 1964).

Kriegel, A. and Jean-Jacques Becker, *1914: La Guerre et le mouvement ouvrier français* (Paris: Armand Colin, 1964).

Labriola, A., *Sindacalismo e reformiso* (Florence, 1905).
Labriola, A., *Storia di dieci anni: 1899–1909* (Milan: Casa Editrice II viandante, 1910).
LaMonte, R.R., 'Industrial Unionism and Syndicalism', *New Review*, 1 May, 1913, p. 527.
Lane, T., 'A Merseysider in Detroit', *History Workshop Journal*, 11 (1981), pp. 138–53.
Larkin, E., *James Larkin: Irish Labour Leader, 1876–1947* (London: New English Library, 1968).
Le Blanc, P., *A Short History of the U.S. Working Class* (New York: Humanity Books, 1999).
Lefranc, G., *Le Mouvement Syndical sous la Troisième République* (Paris: Payot, 1967).
Lenin. V.I., 'Strike Statistics in Russia' *Collected Works, Vol. 16* (London: Lawrence and Wishart, 1963) pp. 395–421.
Lenin, V.I., *On Trade Unions* (Moscow: Progress, 1970).
Lenin, V.I., 'The Three Sources and Three Component Parts of Marxism', *Selected Words, Vol. 1* (Moscow: Progress, 1970), pp. 66–70.
Lenin, V.I., 'The War and Russian Social Democracy', *Selected Works: Vol. 1* (Moscow: Progress, 1970), pp. 650–57.
Lenin, V.I., 'What is to be Done?', *Selected Works*: *Vol. 1* (Moscow: Progress, 1970), pp. 122–270.
Lenin, V.I., 'The State and Revolution', *Selected Works: Vol. 2* (Moscow: Progress, 1970), pp. 287–375.
Lenin, V.I., 'Marxism and Insurrection: A Letter to the Central Committee of the R.S.D.L.P. (B), *Selected Works: Vol. 2* (Moscow: Progress, 1970), pp. 380–84.
Lenin, V.I., '"Left-wing" Communism: An Infantile Disorder', *Selected Works*, Vol. 3 (Moscow: Progress Publishers, 1971), pp. 291–370.
Lenin, V.I., 'Theses on the Fundamental Tasks of the Second Congress of the Communist International', *Collected Works: Vol. 31* (Moscow, Progress, 1977), pp. 184–202.
Levine, L., *The Labor Movement in France: A Study in Revolutionary Syndicalism* (London: King, 1912).
Levine, L., 'The Development of Syndicalism in America', *Political Science Quarterly*, 28 (September 1913), pp. 451–79.
Levy, C., 'Italian Anarchism, 1870–1926', in D. Goodway (ed.), *For Anarchism: History, Theory and Practice* (London: Routledge, 1989).
Levy, C., 'Currents of Italian Syndicalism before 1926', *International Review of Social History*, 45 (2000), pp. 209–50.
Lichtheim, G., *A Short History of Socialism* (Glasgow: Fontana, 1970).
Lindemann, A.S., *A History of European Socialism* (New Haven, NY, 1983).
Livorsi, F., *Amadeo Bordiga* (Rome: Riuniti, 1976).
Lovell, J., *Stevedores and Dockers* (London: Macmillan, 1969).
Lozovsky, A., *Marx and the Trade Unions* (London: Martin Lawrence, 1935).
Lukács, G., *Lenin* (London: Pluto Press, 1970).

Lukács, G., *History and Class Consciousness: Studies in Marxist Dialectics* (London: Merlin, 1971).

Lukács, G., 'The Crisis of Syndicalism', Kommunismus, vol. 1, no. 40 [1920], *Political Writings, 1919–1929: The Question of Parliamentarism and other Essays* (London: New York Books, 1972), pp. 81–6.

Luxemburg, R., 'Social Reform or Revolution', *Selected Political Writings* (New York: Monthly Review Press, 1971[originally 1908], pp. 52–134.

Luxemburg, R., *The Mass Strike, the Political Party and the Trade Unions* ([first published 1906] London: Bookmarks, 1986).

MacDonald, R., *Syndicalism: A Critical Examination* (London: Constable, 1912).

Maitron, J., *Le Mouvement anarchiste en France: De 1914 á nos jours: Vol. 2* (Paris: F. Maspéro, 1975).

Macfarlane, L.J., *The British Communist Party: Its Origin and Development Until 1929* (London: Macgibbon and Kee, 1966).

Macintyre, S., *A Proletarian Science: Marxism in Britain 1917–1933* (London: Lawrence and Wishart, 1986).

Magraw, R., *France 1814–1915: The Bourgeois Century* (Oxford: Fontana, 1983).

Magraw, R., 'Socialism, Syndicalism and French Labour Before 1914', in D. Geary (ed.), *Labour and Socialist Movements in Europe before 1914* (Oxford: Berg, 1989).

Magraw, R., *A History of the French Working Class, Vol. 1: The Age of Artisan Revolution* (Oxford: Blackwell, 1992).

Magraw, R., *A History of the French Working Class, Vol. 2: Workers and the Bourgeois Republic* (Oxford: Blackwell, 1992).

Magraw, R., 'Paris 1917–20: Labour Protest and Popular Politics', and J. Horne, 'The State and the Challenge of Labour in France, 1917–20', in C. Wrigley (ed.), *Challenges of Labour: Central and Western Europe, 1917–1920* (London: Routledge, 1993), pp. 125–48.

Malatesta, E., 'Syndicalism: An Anarchist Critique', in G. Woodcock (ed.), *The Anarchist Reader* (Glasgow, 1977), p. 223.

Mann, T., *Russia in 1921* (London: n.p, n.d).

Martin, B., *The Agony of Modernisation: Labour and Industrialisation in Spain* (Ithaca, NY, 1990).

Martin, R., *Communism and the British Trade Unions: A Study of the National Minority Movement* (Oxford University Press, 1969).

Marx, K., *The Civil War in France* (Moscow: Progress, 1970).

Marx, K., *The First International and After* (Harmondsworth: Penguin, 1974).

Marx, K., F. Engels and V.I. Lenin, *Anarchism and Anarcho-Syndicalism* (New York: International Publishers, 1972).

Marx, K., and F. Engels, 'Critique of the Gotha Programme', *Selected Works* (Moscow: Progress, 1970), pp. 311–31.

Marx, K., and F. Engels, *The Communist Manifesto* (Harmondsworth: Penguin, 1972).

McFarlane, L.J., *The British Communist Party: Its Origin and Development until 1929* (London: Macgibbon and Kee, 1966).

McGirr, L., 'Black and White Longshoremen in the IWW: A History of the Philadelphia Marine Transport Workers Industrial Union Local 8', *Labor History*, 36 (1995), pp. 377–402.

Mcllroy, J. and A. Campbell, 'New Directions in International Communist Historiography', *Labour History Review*, 68:1 (2003), pp. 3–7.

Meaker, G.H., *The Revolutionary Left in Spain, 1914–1923* (Stanford University Press, 1974).

Meltzer, A., *First Flight: The Origins of Anarcho-Syndicalism in Britain* (Berkeley, CA: Kate Sharpley Library, 2004).

Michels, R., *Political Parties: A Sociological Study of the Oligarchical Tendencies of Modern Democracy* (New York: Collier Books, 1962 [first published 1915]).

Milner, S., *Dilemmas of Internationalism, French Syndicalism and the International Labour Movement, 1900–1914* (New York: Berg, 1991).

Miller, D., *Anarchism* (London: Dent, 1984).

Mitchell, B., 'French Syndicalism: An Experiment in Practical Anarchism', in M. van der Linden and W. Thorpe (eds), *Revolutionary Syndicalism: An International Perspective* (Aldershot, Scolar Press, 1990), pp. 25–43.

Mitchell, B., *The Practical Revolutionaries: A New Interpretation of the French Anarchsyndicalists* (New York: Greenwood Press, 1987).

Monatte, P., *Anarcho-syndicalisme et syndicalisme révolutionnaire*, http://en.internationalism.org/ir/120_cgt.html.

Monjo, A., *Militants. Participació i Democràcia a la CNT als Anys Trenta* (Barcelona, 2003).

Molyneux, J., *Marxism and the Party* (London: Pluto Press, 1978).

Molyneux, J., 'The Birth of Bolshevism', *Socialist Worker*, 4 April 1987.

Monreal, A., *El pensamiento político de Joaquín Maurín* (Barcelona: Ediciones 62, 1984).

Montgomery, D., 'The "New Unionism" and the Transformation of Workers' Consciousness in America 1909–1922', *Journal of Social History*, 7:4 (1974), pp. 509–29.

Montgomery, D., *Workers' Control in America* (Cambridge University Press, 1979).

Montgomery, D., 'New Tendencies in Union Struggles and Strategies in Europe and the United States, 1916–1922', in J.E. Cronin and C. Sirianni (eds) *Work, Community and Power: The Exercise of Labor in Europe and America, 1900–1925*, (Philadelphia: Temple University Press, 1983), pp. 88–116.

Montgomery, D., 'What More to Be Done?', *Labor History*, 40:3 (1999), pp. 356–61.

Morrow, F., *Revolution and Counter-Revolution in Spain* (New York: Pathfinder Press, 1974).

Moss, B., *The Origins of the French Labor Movement: The Socialism of Skilled Workers 1830–1914* (Berkeley: University of California Press, 1976).

Moss, B., 'Socialism and the Republic in France', *Socialist History*, 18, (2000) pp. 32–49.

Muller, D.H., 'Syndicalism and Localism in the German Trade Union Movement', in W. J. Mommsen and H-G. Husung, *The Development of Trade Unionism in Great Britain and Germany, 1880–1914* (London: Allen and Unwin, 1985), pp. 239–49.

Murphy, J.T., *The Workers' Committee: An Outline of its Principles and* Structure (Sheffield Workers' Committee, 1917 [republished London: Pluto Press, 1972]).

Murphy, J.T., *Compromise or Independence? An Examination of the Whitley Report with a Plea for the Rejection of the Proposals for Joint Standing Industrial Councils* (Sheffield: Sheffield Workers' Committee, 1918).

Murphy, J.T., *The Trade Unions: Organisation and Action* (Oxford, 1919).

Murphy, J.T., *The 'Reds' in Congress: Preliminary Report of the First World War Congress of the Red International of Trade and Industrial Unions* (London, 1921).

Murphy, J.T., *New Horizons* (London: John Lane/The Bodley Head, 1941).

Murphy, J.T., *Preparing for Power* (London: Pluto Press, 1972 [originally published 1934]).

Newsinger, J., 'Jim Larkin, Syndicalism and the 1913 Dublin Lock-Out', *International Socialism*, 2:25 (1984), pp. 3–36.

Newsinger, J., '"A Lamp to Guide Your Feet": Jim Larkin, the Irish Workers, and the Dublin Working Class', *European History Quarterly*, 20:1 (1990), pp. 63–99.

Newsinger, J., 'Irish Labour in a Time of Revolution', *Socialist History*, 22 (2002), pp. 1–31.

Newsinger, J., *Rebel City: Larkin, Connolly and the Dublin Labour Movement* (London: Merlin Press, 2004).

Newsinger, J., 'Review Article: Recent Controversies in the History of British Communism', *Journal of Contemporary History*, 4:3 (2006), pp. 557–72.

Nomura. T., 'Who Were the Wobblies? The Defendents of the Chicago IWW Trial of 1919: Collective Biographies', *Journal of the Aichi Prefectual University* (1985), pp. 135–150.

Norman, D., *Terrible Beauty: Constance Markievicz* (Dublin: Poolbeg, 1987).

Novak, G., D. Frankel and F, Fedlman, *The First Three Internationals: Their History and Lessons* (New York: Pathfinder, 1974).

O'Connor, E., *Syndicalism in Ireland* (Cork University Press, 1988).

O'Connor, E., *A Labour History of Ireland, 1824–1960* (Dublin: Gill and Macmillan, 1992).

O'Connor, E., *James Larkin* (Cork University Press, 2002).

O'Connor, E., *Reds and the Green: Ireland, Russia and the Communist Internationals 1919–43* (University College Dublin Press, 2004).

O'Connor, E., 'What Caused the 1913 Lockout? Industrial Relations in Ireland, 1907–13', *Historical Studies in Industrial Relations*, 19 (2005), pp. 101–21.

Olivetti, A.O.,'I sindicalisti e la élite', originally published 1 July 1909, *Cinque anni di sindicalismo e di lotta proletaria in Italia* (Naples: Società Editrice Partenopea, 1914).

Olssen, E., *The Red Feds: Revolutionary Industrial Unionism and the New Zealand Federation of Labour 1908–1913* (Auckland: Oxford University Press, 1988).

Pagés, P., *Andreu Nin: Su evolución política 1911–37* (Bilbao: Zero, 1975).

Palme Dutt, R., *The Internationale* (London: Lawrence and Wishart, 1964).

Paturd, E. and E. Pouget, *How We Shall Bring about the Revolution: Syndicalism and the Co-Operative Commonwealth* [first published 1909] (London: Pluto Press, 1990).

Pearce, B., 'Early Years of the Communist Party of Great Britain', M. Woodhouse and B. Pearce, *Essays on the History of Communism in Britain* (London: New Park Publications, 1975), pp.149–78.

Peirats, J., *Anarchists in the Spanish Revolution* (London: Freedom Press, 1990).

Pelling, H., 'The Labour Unrest 1911–1914', *Popular Politics and Society in Late Victorian Britain* (London: Macmillan, 1968).

Pelloutier, F., *Historie des bourses du travail* (Paris, 1902).

Perlman, S., *A Theory of the Labor Movement* (New York: Macmillan, 1928).

Peterson, L., 'The One Big Union in International Perspective: Revolutionary Industrial Unionism 1900–1925', in J.E. Cronin and C. Sirianni (eds), *Work, Community and Power: The Experience of Labour in Europe and America 1900–1925* (Philadelphia: Temple University Press, 1983), pp. 49–87.

Peterson, L., 'Revolutionary Socialism and Industrial Unrest in the Era of the Winnipeg General Strike: The Origins of Communist Labour Unionism in Europe and North America', *Labour/Le Travail*, 13 (1984), pp. 115–31.

Pollitt, H., *Serving My Time* (London: Lawrence and Wishart, 1940).

Postgate, R.W., *The Builders' History* (London: The National Federation of Building Trade Operatives, 1923).

Pouget, E., *Le parti du travail* (Paris: la guerre sociale, 1905).

Pouget, E., *L'Action directe* (Paris: Bibliothéque syndicaliste, 1907).

Pouget, E., *Les bases du syndicalisme* (Paris: Bibliothéque syndicaliste, 1906).

Pouget. E., *Le Sabotage* (Paris: La guerre sociale, s.a. Bibliothéque syndicaliste, 4, 1910).

Pouget, E., 'What is the Trade Union', in D. Guerin (ed.), *No Gods, No Masters: An Anthology of Anarchism* (Edinburgh, 2005), pp. 432–3.

Preston, W., 'Shall This Be All? U.S. Historians Versus William D. Haywood *et al.*', *Labor History*, 11: 3 (1971), pp. 435–53.

Pribicevic, B., *The Shop Stewards' Movement and Workers' Control* (Oxford: Blackwell, 1959).

Price, R., 'Contextualising British Syndicalism c.1907–c.1920', *Labour History Review*, 63:3 (1998), pp. 261–76.

Reid, D., 'Guillaume Verdier et le Stndicalisme rèvolutionnaire aux usines de Decazeville 1917–1920', *Annales du Midi*, 166 (April–June 1984).

Reiman, M., *The Birth of Stalinism: The USSR on the Eve of the: Second Revolution'* (London: I.B. Tauris and Co. Ltd, 1987).

Renshaw, P., *The Wobblies: The Story of Syndicalism in the United States* (London: Eyre and Spottiswoode, 1967).

Richards, V. (ed.), *Errico Malatesta: His Life and Ideas* (London: Freedom Press, 1977).

Riddell, J. (ed.) *Lenin's Struggle for a Revolutionary International: Documents, 1907–1916, The Preparatory Years* (New York: Monad Press, 1984).

Riddell, J. (ed.), *Workers of the World and Oppressed Peoples, Unite! Proceedings and Documents of the Second Congress 1920* (New York: Pathfinder, 1991).

Ridley, F.F., *Revolutionary Syndicalism in France: The Direct Action of Its Time* (Cambridge University Press, 1970).

Riguzzi, B., *Sindacalismo e riformismo nel Parmense* (Bari: De Donato, 1974).

Riottat, Y., *Joaquín Mauŕin, De l'anarcho-syndicalisme au communisme 1919–1936* (Paris: L'Harmattan, 1997).

Roberts, D.D., *The Syndicalist Tradition and Italian Fascism* (Manchester: Manchester University Press, 1979).

Roberts, D.D., 'How Not to Think About Fascism and Ideology, Intellectual Antecedents and Historical Meaning', *Journal of Contemporary History*, 35:2 (2000), pp. 185–211.

Rocker, R., 'The Methods of Anarcho-Syndicalism', *Anarcho-Syndicalism* (London: Phoenix Press, 1987), pp. 63–73.

Rosmer, A., 'Il y a quarante ans', *La Révolution prolétarienne*, January 1951, pp. 1–3.

Rosmer, A., *Lenin's Moscow* (London: Pluto Press, 1971).

Rosmer, A., 'La Liquidation du "Putschisme"', *La Rèvolution prolètarienne*, no. 14, pp. 1–4, 1926, in *Revolutionary History*, 7:4 (2000), pp. 109–16.

Rowbotham, S., *Hidden From History: 300 Years of Women's Oppression and the Fight Against It* (London: Pluto Press, 1973).

Second Congress of the Communist International: Minutes of the Proceedings: Vols. 1 and 2 (London: New Park, 1977).

Schecter, D., *Radical Theories: Paths Beyond Marxism and Social Democracy* (Manchester University Press, 1994), p. 36.

Schofield, A., 'Rebel Girls and Union Maids: The Woman Question in the Journals of the AFL and IWW, 1905–1920', *Feminist Studies*, 9 (Summer 1983), pp. 335–58.

Screpanti, E., 'Long Cycles and Recurring Proletarian Insurgencies', *Review,* 7:2 (1984), pp. 509–48.

Screpanti, E., 'Long Cycles in Strike Activity: An Empirical Investigation', *British Journal of Industrial Relations*, 25:1 (1987), pp. 99–124.

Scumpter, J.A., cited in R. Wohl, *French Communism in the Making, 1914–1924* (Stanford, Calif., 1966), p. 27.

Shalev, M., and W. Korpi, 'Working Class Mobilisation and American Exceptionalism', *Economic and Industrial Democracy*, 1 (1980), pp. 31–61.

Sellars, N.A,. *Oil, Wheat and Wobblies: The Industrial Workers of the World in Oklahoma, 1905–1930* (Norman: University of Oklahoma Press, 1998).

Shor, F., '"Virile Syndicalism" in Comparative Perspective: A Gender Analysis of the IWW in the United States and Australia', *International Labor and Working Class History*, 56 (1999), pp. 65–77.

Shorter, E. and C. Tilly, *Strikes in France 1830–1968* (Cambridge University Press, 1974).

Smith, A., 'Spain', in S. Berger and D. Broughton (eds) *The Force of Labour: The Western European Labour Movement and the Working Class in the Twentieth Century* (Oxford: Berg, 1995), pp. 171–209.

Smith, A., 'Anarchism, the General Strike and the Barcelona Labour Movement, 1899–1914, *European History Quarterly*, 27:1 (1997), pp. 5–40.

Smith, A., 'Spain', in S. Berger and D. Broughton (eds), *The Force of Labour: European Labour Movements and the European Working Class in the Twentieth Century* (Oxford: Berg, 1995), pp. 171–209.

Smith, J., 'Labour Tradition in Glasgow and Liverpool', *History Workshop Journal*, 17 (1984), pp. 32–56.

Snowden, P., *Socialism and Syndicalism* (London: Collins, c1913).

Solano, E.G., *El Sindicalismo en la teoría y en la práctica* (Barcelona, 1919).

Sorel, G., *Reflections on Violence* (New York: B.W. Huebsch, 1912, third edition [first published 1908]).

Spero, S.D. and A.L. Harris, *The Black Worker: The Negro and the Labor Movement* (New York: Columbia University Press, 1931)

Spriano, P., *The Occupation of the Factories: Italy 1920* (London: Pluto Press, 1975).

Stearns, P.N., *Revolutionary Syndicalism and French Labor: A Cause without Rebels* (New Brunswick: Rutgers University Press, 1971).

Stepan-Norris, J. and M. Zeitlin, *Left-Out: Reds and America's Industrial Unions* (Cambridge University Press, 2003).

St. John, V., *The IWW: Its History, Structure and Method* (Chicago: IWW Publishing Bureau, n.d. [revised edition 1917]).

Surace, S.J., *Ideology, Economic Change and the Working Classes: The Case of Italy* (Berkeley: University of California, 1966).

Sykes, T.R., 'Revolutionary Syndicalism in the Italian Labor Movement: The Agrarian Strikes of 1907–8 in the Province of Parma', *International Review of Social History*, 21 (1976), pp. 186–211.

Taplin, E., *Near to Revolution: The Liverpool General Transport Strike of 1911* (Liverpool: Bluecoat Press, 1994).

Tax, M., *The Rising of the Women* (New York: Monthly Review Press, 1980), pp. 125–63.

Taylor, P., 'Syndicalism', *Socialist Worker Review*, 77 (1985), p. 24.

The Miners' Next Step: Being a Suggested Scheme for the Re-Organization of the Federation, issued by the Unofficial Reform Committee (Tonypandy: Robert Davies and Co, 1912 [reprinted London: Pluto Press, 1973]).

Thomas, P., *Karl Marx and the Anarchists* (London: Routledge, 1980).

Thompson, E.P., 'Homage to Tom Maguire', A. Briggs and J. Saville (eds), *Essays in Labour History 1886–1923* (London: Macmillan, 1967), pp. 276–316.

Thorpe, A., 'Comintern "Control" of the Communist Party of Great Britain, 1920–43', *English Historical Review*, 113: 452 (1998), pp. 637–62.

Thorpe, W., *'The Workers Themselves': Revolutionary Syndicalism and International Labour, 1913–1923* (Dordrecht: Kluwer Academic Publishers, 1989).

Thorpe, W., 'Towards a Syndicalist International: The 1913 London Congress', *International Review of Social History*, 23 (1978), pp. 33–78.

Thorpe, W., 'Syndicalist Internationalism and Moscow, 1919–1922: The Breach' *Canadian Journal of History*, 14:1 (1979), pp. 199–234.

Thorpe, W., 'The European Syndicalists and War, 1914–18', *Contemporary European History*, 10: part 1 (2001), pp. 1–24.

Thorpe, W., 'Syndicalist Internationalism Before World War II', in M. van der Linden and W. Thorpe (eds), *Revolutionary Syndicalism: An International Perspective* (Aldershot: Scolar Press), pp. 237–60.

Tilly, C., 'Introduction' in L.H. Haimson and C. Tilly (eds), *Strikes, Wars and Revolutions in an International Perspective* (Stanford. California: Cambridge University Press, 1989).

Tinghino, J.J., *Edmoundo Rossoni: From Revolutionary Syndicalism to Fascism* (New York: Peter Lang, 1991).

Tosstorff, R., '"Moscow" or "Amsterdam"? The Red International of Labour Unions, 1920/21–1937', Thesis, Johannes Gutenberg University, Mainz, Germany, 1999.

Tosstorff, R., 'Moscow Versus Amsterdam: Reflections on the History of the Profintern', *Labour History Review*, 68:1 (2003), pp. 79–97.

Tosstorff, R. *Profintern: Die Rote Gewerkschaftsinterntionale, 1920–1937* (Paderborn: Schoeningh, 2004).

Trotsky, L., *Marxism and the Trade Unions* (London: New Park, 1972).

Trotsky, L., 'Communism and Syndicalism: On the Trade Union Question' [May 1923], *Marxism and the Trade Unions* (London: New Park, 1972), pp. 19–29.

Trotsky, L., 'The Anarcho-syndicalist Prejudices Again!' [May 1923] *Marxism and the Trade Unions* (London: New Park, 1972), pp. 30–34.

Trotsky, L., *The First Five Years of the Communist International*, vol. 1 (New Park: Pathfinder, 1972).

Trotsky, L., 'Speech at a General Party Membership Meeting of the Moscow Organization, July 1921', *The First Five Years of the Communist International: Vol. 2* (New York: Mondad Press, 1972), p. 1–43.

Trotsky, L., 'Letter to the Convention of the French Communist Party', September 1922, *The First Five Years of the Communist International: Vol. 2* (New York: Pathfinder, 1972), p. 162–80.

Trotsky, L., 'On the Coming Congress of the Comintern', *The First Fives Years of the Communist International: Vol 1* (New York, 1972), p. 93.

Trotsky, L., *1905* (Harmondsworth, Penguin, 1973).

Trotsky, L., 'The Lesson of Spain', *The Spanish Revolution 1931–9* (New York: Pathfinder Press, 1973), pp. 306–26.

Tuñón de Lara, M., *El movimiento obrero en la historia de España: Vol. 1.* (Madrid: Taurus, 1977).

Vandervort, B., *Victor Griffuelhes and French Syndicalism, 1895–1922* (Louisiana State University Press, 1996).

van der Linden, M. 'Second Thoughts on Revolutionary Syndicalism', *Labour History Review*, 63:2, (1998), pp. 182–96.

van der Linden, M., *Transnational Labour History: Explorations* (London: Ashgate, 2003).

van der Linden, M. and W. Thorpe, 'The Rise and Fall of Revolutionary Syndicalism (1890–1940)', in M. van der Linden and W. Thorpe (eds), *Revolutionary Syndicalism: An International Perspective* (Aldershot, Scolar Press, 1990), pp. 1–24.

van der Walt, L., '"The Industrial Union is the Embryo of the Socialist Commonwealth", The International Socialist League and Revolutionary Syndicalism in South Africa, 1915–1919', *Comparative Studies of South Asia, Africa and the Middle East*, 15:1 (1999), pp. 5–30.

Watson, B., *Bread and Roses: Mills, Migrants and the Struggle for the American Dream* (New York: Penguin, 2005).

Webb, S. and B. Webb, 'What Syndicalism Means: An Examination of the Origin and Motives of the Movement with an Analysis of its Proposals for the Control of Industry', *The Crusade*, August 1912.

Webb, S., and B. Webb, *What Syndicalism Means: An Examination of the Origin and Motives of the Movement with an Analysis of its Proposals for the Control of Industry* (London, 1912).

Webb, S., and B. Webb, *History of Trade Unionism 1666–1920* (London: Longman, 1919).

Webb, S., and B. Webb, *Industrial Democracy* (London: Longman, 1920).

White, J., *Tom Mann* (Manchester University Press, 1991).

White, J., 'Syndicalism in a Mature Industrial Setting: The Case of Britain', in M. van der Linden and W. Thorpe (eds), *Revolutionary Syndicalism: An International Perspective* (Aldershot, Scolar Press, 1990), pp. 101–18.

Wilentz, R.S., 'Against Exceptionalism: Class Consciousness and the American Labor Movement', *International Labor and Working Class History*, 26 (1984), pp. 1–24.

Williams, G.A., *Proletarian Order: Antonio Gramsci, Factory Councils and the Origins of Italian Communism in Italy, 1911–1921* (London: Pluto Press, 1975).

Wohl, R., *French Communism in the Making, 1914–1924* (Stanford University Press, 1966).

Woodcock, G. (ed.), *The Anarchist Reader* (London: Fontana, 1977).

Woodcock, G., *Anarchism: A History of Libertarian Ideas and Movements*, (Harmondsworth: Penguin, 1979).

Woodhouse, M., 'Syndicalism, Communism and the Trade Unions in Britain, 1910–1926', *Marxist*, vol. 4, no. 3 (1966) available at: http://www.whatnextjournal.co.uk/Pages/History/Syndicalism.html.

Woodhouse, M.G., 'Rank and File Movements amongst the Miners of South Wales 1910–26', D.Phil thesis, University of Oxford, 1970.

Woodhouse, M., 'Marxism and Stalinism in Britain', in M. Woodhouse and B. Pearce, *Essays on the History of Communism in Britain* (London: New Park Publications, 1975), pp. 1–103.

Woodhouse, M., and B. Pearce, *Essays on the History of Communism in Britain* (London 1975).

Wolfe, B., *Strange Communists I Have Known* (London: Allen and Unwin, 1996).

Yeates, P., *Lockout: Dublin 1913* (Dublin: Gill and Macmillan, 2001).

Yvetot, G., *L'ABC syndicaliste* (Paris: la guerre sociale, 1908).

Zieger, R.H., Book Review of 'Bread and Roses Too: Studies of the Wobblies', *Labor History*, 11:4 (1970), pp. 564–69.

Zumoff, J., 'The Syndicalist Roots of American Communism: The Industrial Workers of the World and William Z. Foster', Paper presented to seminar on Comparative Labour and Working Class History, Institute for Historical Research, University of London, 19 January 2001.

Index